Mental Images and
Their Transformations

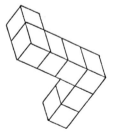

Mental Images
and Their
Transformations

Roger N. Shepard
Lynn A. Cooper

With chapters coauthored by

J. E. Farrell
C. Feng
R. J. Glushko
S. A. Judd
J. Metzler
P. Podgorny
C. Robins

A Bradford Book

THE MIT PRESS
CAMBRIDGE, MASSACHUSETTS
LONDON, ENGLAND

This book was set in IBM Century type
by Horne Associates, Inc., Hanover, N.H.
and printed and bound
in the United States of America.

Library of Congress Cataloging in Publication Data

Shepard, Roger N.
    Mental Images and their transformations.

    "A Bradford book."
    1. Imagery (Psychology)   2. Thought and thinking.
I. Cooper, Lynn A.   II. Title.   [DNLM: 1. Imagination.
BF 367 S547m]
BF367.S55   153.3'2   81-14276
ISBN 0-262-19200-4   AACR2

For our parents, with admiration and affection:

O. Cutler Shepard
Grace N. Shepard

James H. Cooper
Barbara G. Cooper

Contents

(continued)

Acknowledgments

The work assembled in this volume arose in large part out of an uncommonly productive and mutually rewarding collaboration between its two authors. Even so, it could never have been brought to its present state of fruition without the essential contributions provided, in its early stages, by Jacqueline Metzler and, in its later stages, by the following other co-workers who, along with Metzler, each shared in the original authorship of one or another of the papers reprinted here: Joyce Farrell, Christine Feng, Robert Glushko, Sherryl Judd, Peter Podgorny, and Clive Robins. Still other of our associates who deserve special thanks include Emily Bassman, Jih-Jie Chang, James Cunningham, and Joseph Klun, for particular contributions noted elsewhere in this volume, and Teresa Putnam for her effective and always cheerful assistance in preparing the final manuscript.

The research reported here was supported by research grants from the National Science Foundation, including grants GS-2283, GB-31971X, BNS75-02806, and BNS80-05517 to Roger Shepard and BNS 75-15773 to Lynn Cooper, and by National Institute of Mental Health Small Grant MH 25722-01 to Lynn Cooper. Additional support was provided by a predoctoral National Science Foundation fellowship awarded to Lynn Cooper; and by fellowships awarded to Roger Shepard by the John Simon Guggenheim Foundation and the Center for Advanced Study in the Behavioral Sciences. Initial planning of the volume itself was facilitated by a sabbatical award to Roger Shepard by the James McKeen Cattell Fund and by the hospitality shown him during that year (1979–80) by the Department of Psychology, University College London.

Mental Images and
Their Transformations

1 | Introduction

Students of the human mind have long noted its ability to mimic, internally, the possible motions and transformations of objects in the external world. In the middle of the eighteenth century, the British empiricist David Hume wrote that to "join incongruous shapes and appearances costs the imagination no more trouble than to conceive the most natural and familiar objects," and that "this creative power of the mind amounts to no more than the faculty of compounding, transposing, augmenting, or diminishing the material afforded us by the senses and experience" (Hume, 1748, Section II, pp. 15-16). Similarly, in the middle of the following century the German empiricist, physicist, and sensory physiologist Hermann von Helmholtz observed that "memory images of purely sensory impressions . . . may be used as elements of thought combinations without it being necessary, or even possible, to describe these in words," and, further, that "equipped with the awareness of the physical form of an object, we can clearly imagine all of the perspective images which we may expect upon viewing from this or that side, and we are immediately disturbed when such an image does not correspond to our expectations" (Helmholtz, 1894; translated in Warren & Warren, 1968, pp. 252-254).

Representation of Spatial Transformations in Biological Adaptation

The evolution of a mental faculty for the simulation of spatial transformations would seem inexplicable if it had no purpose other than an idle, ephemeral, and epiphenomenal play of sensory shadows for one's purely private delectation. In fact, however, situations of practical moment or even urgency do arise in which one can

1

avoid unnecessary effort, excessive delay, or unacceptable risk by mentally trying out a proposed rearrangement—of, for example, heavy furniture, plumbing connections, surgical· implements, or broken bones—before undertaking the rearrangement in physical reality. Notice, here, that in order to serve its purpose, such a preliminary mental modeling must preserve the essential structural relations inherent in the corresponding external objects. If, in imagining a massive desk moved into a certain alcove, we allowed arbitrary topological deformations, our successful completion of the mental move would provide no valid indication that the alcove would accommodate the desk when it was then moved physically and, hence, rigidly.

The need to anticipate the consequences of structure-preserving transformations, though most obvious in the species that has advanced furthest in the use of tools and the construction of shelters and other artifacts, does not appear to be exclusively human. The possible utility of mental rotation for the canine species is suggested by the following behavior that one of us witnessed on the part of a German shepherd (Alsatian). In pursuit of a long stick hurled over a fence, the dog passed through a narrow opening where one of the vertical boards was missing from the fence and, seizing the stick, plunged back toward that same narrow opening—with the long stick now clamped in its teeth. Just as catastrophe appeared certain, the dog stopped short, paused for a (thoughtful?) moment and, rotating its head and, thus, the stick through 90 degrees, proceeded through the opening without mishap (Shepard, 1981).

There are, in fact, compelling ecological reasons for some internalization of the constraints governing the rigid transformations of objects in space. Throughout evolutionary history, rigid structure has been a prominent aspect of the surrounding world and of many of the most significant objects that populate that world. On the largest scale, there is the global frame with respect to which we and members of various other species have been shown to orient and to plan our movements and migrations—including the fixed terrain of ground, horizon, distant mountains, and the like (Gibson, 1950, 1966), the constellations in the celestial sphere (Emlen, 1975; Sauer, 1958), the more local canopy of branches and leaves (Hölldobler, 1980) or other surrounding landmarks (Maier, 1929; Thorpe, 1950). On a smaller scale, there are the movable sticks, stones, and tools that many organisms and, preeminently, humans retrieve, assemble, rearrange, fasten together, and use for a variety of purposes.

Moreover, the most significant of the nonrigid objects in our environment—namely, other animals and, especially, other members of our own species—are generally composed of articulated parts (head, trunk, segments of limbs, fingers, and so on) that are constrained by an underlying skeletal framework to move with respect to each other by essentially rigid rotations about hinged joints. Indeed, even the most flimsy, limp, liquid, insubstantial, and evanescent objects tend, in the absence of external disturbance, to preserve their three-dimensional shapes over significant periods of time and, hence, to yield perspective transformations approximating those of rigid objects as we move around them in space. This is true, alike, of a crumpled piece of paper, a pile of laundry, a hanging drape, the surface of a pond, a cumulus cloud, or a curling wisp of smoke in a closed room.

Biological evolution would seem to have embarked on an uncharacteristically profligate course if the very most enduring and pervasive facts about our world—such as that it is three-dimensional, locally Euclidean, isotropic (except for the unique upright direction conferred by the earth's gravitational field), and populated with objects that therefore have just six degrees of freedom of rigid motion—had not been in any way incorporated into our genetically transmittable perceptual wisdom. Without such incorporation, this wisdom, so crucial for survival in such a world, would have to be learned, laboriously and at appreciable risk, by each and every newborn individual *de novo*.

Curiously, though, the internal constraints implied by the ability to preserve structure while mentally simulating transformations in space have until recently hardly been acknowledged, let alone submitted to systematic investigation. In part, this may be because these constraints originally evolved in the service of the concrete perceptual discrimination of positions and motions of objects when those were physically given. As a result of eons of selective tuning to their external counterparts, these internal constraints may have achieved such efficiency and automaticity in the perceptual system that they are now relatively inaccessible to conscious introspection. Any resulting "creative power" of this system is therefore taken for granted; and even a thinker of Hume's critical acumen could say that it "amounts to no more" than a faculty for such operations as assembly, disassembly, translation, and rotation—failing (more than Kant, 1781) to see that such a "faculty," like any other mechanism, can make a contribution only by virtue of some definite inner constraints of its own.

We have been forced to acknowledge, of course, that a significant portion of our more peripherally oriented neural circuitry is pre-wired in the species in such a way that it does not have to be acquired anew by each individual member. There is, for example, the well known neurophysiological and neuroanalomical evidence that mechanisms for the visual detection of lines, edges, and their junctions are already present at birth (see, e.g., Hubel & Wiesel, 1963, 1968). And this evidence is corroborated by the following pair of contrasting behavioral observations: (a) The visual system can adapt to a simple global transformation, such as an inversion of the whole field induced by a prism (Kohler, 1962; Stratton, 1897)—a transformation that preserves local features such as lines and edges in the retinal projection. (b) But the same system is utterly defeated by a more drastic and chaotic transformation, such as a permutation of the elements of the field imposed by a scrambled set of optic fibers—a transformation that (although still one-to-one) disrupts all local structure.

However, in the case of the higher-order structural constraints that correspond to the invariants of rigid transformations in the external three-dimensional world, but that no longer correspond so simply and directly to local features of the retinal projection, physiological evidence for inborn circuitry is still largely lacking. Nevertheless, behavioral and psychophysical results still implicate a deep neurological entrenchment of such spatial wisdom. We experience a two-dimensional projection of a rotating structure as rigid (Wallach & O'Connell, 1953)—but only if the structure is rigidly rotating in the three-dimensional space in which we have evolved, not if the structure is rigidly rotating in a different, four-dimensional space (cf. Green, 1961; Noll, 1965; Shepard, 1981). Moreover, in the three-dimensional case the discrimination of motion that is rigid from motion that is nonrigid appears to be well developed by early infancy (Gibson, Owsley, & Johnston, 1978; Spelke & Born, 1980).

The dependence of imagined spatial transformations on internalized structure-preserving constraints of the underlying perceptual apparatus is further suggested by the highly orderly way in which the brain automatically interpolates an appearance of a rigid motion between two alternately presented static views of the same three-dimensional object—as in the illusion of "apparent" visual rotation considered in Part III of this volume. And the brain evidently is capable of extrapolation as well as interpolation—as in the reported case in which an observer moving through total darkness may, following a momentary flash of illumination, experience a residual afterimage of a nearby object undergoing appropriate perspective changes with the observer's continuing advance (Gregory, Wallace, & Campbell, 1959).

Spontaneous, hallucinatory imagery and dreams have also been reported to obey such transformational constraints. As just one example, Sir John Herschel, Helmholtz's contemporary and the eminent British astronomer, chemist, and co-inventor of photography, described a remarkable incident in which, while fully awake and passing by the place where he had recently witnessed the demolition of a structure familiar to him since childhood, he was astonished "to see it as if still standing . . . projected against the dull sky." "I walked on," he said "keeping my eyes directed to it, and the perspective of the form and disposition of the parts appeared to change with the change in the point of view as they would have done if real" (Herschel, 1867, p. 405).

Representation of Spatial Transformations in Creative Thought

These last observations suggest that even if the constraints governing the spatial transformations of objects in the three-dimensional world were first internalized solely as an aid to the perceptual interpretation of external events while those events were actually taking place, the representational machinery embodying these constraints would subsequently have become to some extent autonomous. Except on those occasions when external events become so rapid, captivating, or threatening as to preempt the full resources of the interpretive machinery, that machinery might now be at least partially susceptible to actuation from within. Perhaps it is in this way that even in the absence of corresponding external events, we are able to anticipate their concrete outcomes. (Consider, in this connection, what internal resources made it possible to comprehend, in the story of the German shepherd's retrieval of the stick, just what the problem was that confronted the dog as it approached the fence, or just how the problem could be solved by a 90-degree rotation of the head.)

In sufficiently quiescent circumstances, machinery that has already evolved internal analogs of the constraints governing external transformations might even be allowed the luxury of essentially recreational play—as in dreams, or as when the modern sculptor James Surls, while lying on a couch and listening to music, mentally planned his next project. Surls himself reported that "he manipulated the image around in his mind. He saw it tumbling and rolling, took an arm off, put an arm on . . ." (Samuels & Samuels, 1975, p. 261). Indeed, it is tempting to press this line of reasoning one step further and suppose that once the machinery for the simulation of spatial operations had attained a critical degree of computational power and autonomy, it could, by analogical extension, provide aid in the solution of abstract intellectual problems far removed from the concrete perceptual exigencies of everyday life—including, possibly, some of the most profound and far-reaching achievements of the human mind.

The theory of relativity, in particular, is said to have had its inception when the young Albert Einstein performed his epochal *Gedanken* experiment of imagining himself traveling along with a wave of light at 186,000 miles per second. For it was in this way that he first confronted the paradox that had long lain unnoticed at the very foundations of Newtonian mechanics and Maxwellian electromagnetics alike (Einstein, 1949; Holton, 1972)—a paradox that could only be resolved by a total restructuring of our concepts of space and time. Einstein himself said explicitly that he "very rarely" thought in words (Wertheimer, 1945, p. 184), and that his particular ability did not lie in mathematical calculation either, but in "visualizing . . . effects, consequences, and possibilities" (Holton, 1972, p. 110). In a statement reminiscent of Helmholtz's already quoted remarks, he further indicated that for him this "visualizing" consisted primarily of "more or less clear images which can be 'voluntarily' reproduced and combined" (Einstein, in Hadamard, 1945, appendix 2).

James D. Watson's (1968) account of how he and Francis Crick deciphered the double-helical structure of DNA contains still more specific references to the mental performance of spatial transformations, particularly rigid rotations—as when he had the sudden, crucial realization that under an appropriate rotation in space (see Watson, 1968, p. 116), "an adenine-thymine pair . . . was identical in shape to a guanine-cytosine pair" (p. 123), and when he then came into the laboratory to find Crick "flipping the cardboard base pairs about an imaginary line" (p. 128).

No matter how abstract or removed from concrete, everyday concerns such discoveries may be, however, the often spontaneous, unbidden visual-spatial character of their emergence points, once again, to the unconscious, automatic, and deeply hidden perceptual roots from which they arose. The conjoint inventions of the self-starting, reversible induction motor and the now generally adopted polyphase system of electrical distribution, which together contributed so much to the consummation of the industrial revolution, provide a striking illustration. For these two interlocking conceptions burst suddenly, simultaneously, and without warning upon the Hungarian-born inventor Nicola Tesla in the form of an almost hallucinatory vision of the rotating magnetic field that would be induced by a circle of electromagnets, each energized by the same alternating current but successively shifted in phase (Tesla, 1956, p. A-198; see Hunt & Draper, 1964, p. 34).

An autonomous perceptual component is suggested, too, by Watson's remark that on a night when he and Crick were on the verge of cracking the genetic code, he lay in bed for over two hours with, as he put it, "pairs of adenine residues whirling in front of my closed eyes" (Watson, 1968, p. 118). The significance of an isolated subjective report of this kind might be doubted. But notice its similarity to the claim made much earlier by the German Chemist Kekulé that it was spontaneous imagery, during idle reveries, of atoms joining and rejoining to form chainlike molecules "whirling in a giddy dance" (see Findlay, 1948, p. 42) that later culminated in his celebrated dream in which such a writhing chain suddenly curled around until, like a snake swallowing its tail, it formed a closed ring. At that moment, Kekulé later said, he awoke "as if struck by lightning" (see Mackenzie, 1965, p. 135), realizing that he at last had the solution to the long-vexing puzzle of the molecular structure of benzine—a discovery that was crucial to the modern development of organic chemistry.

The notions that we have expressed as to the possible source of visual-spatial insights suggest why such insights are not infrequently reported to have arisen through dreams, twilight states, or reveries. For, the most effective, autonomous play of the underlying spatial system might well tend to occur to the extent that that system is, at the same time, (a) aroused and active and yet (b) liberated from the preemptive demands of sensory input and, perhaps, from the distractive machinations of the more discrete, sequential, and linguistic apparatuses of logic and syntax.

In any case, the very line of chronometric studies of the transformations of mental images assembled in this volume had its origin in a state of hyponopompic suspension between sleep and wakening, in the early morning of November 16, 1968. Just before 6:00 A.M. on that morning and in the absence of any noticed precursors, one of us experienced a spontaneous kinetic image of three-dimensional structures majestically turning in space. Within moments and before full emergence from sleep, the basic design of the first of the chronometric experiments on "mental rotation of three dimensional objects," as it later appeared in the journal *Science* (Shepard & Metzler, 1971), took essentially complete—although as yet completely unverbalized—shape (see Shepard, 1978b, p. 183).

Importance of Rotational Transformations

Although we consider the internal representation of a variety of transformations in this book, including (especially in Part II) the translation, folding, or joining together of rigid objects or parts, our primary focus is in fact on the representation of simple rigid rotations. There are several reasons for a particular interest in rotations. First, as our brief review of anecdotal accounts by scientists and inventors indicates, mental transformations of this particular type seem to have played a central role in a number of major creative achievements. Second, rotations constitute a very significant subclass of the possible motions of objects in space: (a) Of the six degrees of freedom of rigid motion, three are rotational and three are translational. (b) Any rigid motion of three-dimensional space into itself can in fact be decomposed into a rotation together with a translation along the axis of rotation—that is, a "screw displacement" (Coxeter, 1961, pp. 101, 321). (c) And in the special case of the two-dimensional plane, any rigid motion can be regarded simply as a rotation (with the limiting case of a translation obtained as the center of rotation moves off to infinity). Third, purely linear translation in three-dimensional space induces a rotational component in the observer's perspective view of an object. (In looking at a stationary building, the passenger in a passing train sees first one side, then the front, and then the other side of the building). And, fourth, even in the restricted case of rigid transformations in the two-dimensional frontal plane (and hence equivalently, on the retina), rotations, more than translations, present a special challenge to the interpretative machinery because readily extractable visual features like the vertical, horizontal, or oblique orientations of component lines remain invariant under translation but not under rotation.

Figure 1.1 Mach's (1886) example of pairs of irregular shapes that are more readily seen to be identical when presented in the same orientation (A) than when presented in two different orientations (B).

As early as 1886, Einstein's influential predecessor Ernst Mach demonstrated this last point in the context of the perception of visual form. He noted that when two identical shapes are separated only by a translational displacement (Figure 1.1A), their identity of form is immediately apparent, but that when the two shapes differ by a rotation as well (Figure 1.1B), their identity of form is "recognizable" only by turning the figure around or by an *intellectual* act (Mach, 1959, p. 107). Indeed, the recognition of the identity of a single object sometimes depends on such an additional "intellectual act." To illustrate with two examples adapted from Rock (1973), depending on whether people mentally perform a 45-degree clockwise or counterclockwise rotation, they can recognize the outline shape in Figure 1.2A as the profile of a man in a chef's hat or as a cartoon of a dog, and they can recognize the one in Figure 1.2B as a profile of Uncle Sam or as an outline map of the United States.

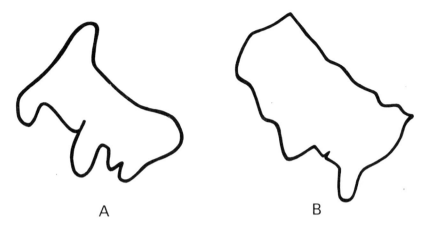

A   B

Figure 1.2 Rock's (1973) examples of ambiguous shapes, which tend to lead to quite different interpretations under 45 degree clockwise or 45 degree counterclockwise rotations.

Experimental Approach

How can things as intangible as mental images and their mental transformations be made the subject of a precise, objective, and, in short, scientific study? Having no external access to mental representations or their transformations, we cannot directly detect even the occurrence of such inner events—let alone record and measure them. Instead, we have to content ourselves with the measurement of externally observable events—namely, test stimuli that can be presented at precisely controlled times and in quantitatively specified positions, orientations, or other variations; and overt responses like key presses or vocalizations that can be electrically recorded and timed.

Of course, neither the observable inputs nor the observable outputs are themselves the mental events of interest. And even if we were able to record patterns of neural activity that intervened in the brain between these inputs and outputs, we could establish that such neural patterns had something to do with the representational events of interest only by correlating them with those already observable inputs and outputs. So, in adopting an objective, experimental approach, we have no choice but to proceed from the outside in, and to develop any theory about the inner processes of mental representation and transformation by inference from the external observables. Nevertheless, we claim that the temporal properties of the responses, when considered in conjunction with the spatial properties of test stimuli, are capable of placing significant constraints on the functional form of the intervening representational processes.

We have argued that the automaticity and efficiency of the perceptual mechanism underlying our ability to imagine spatial transformations may account for the failure of empiricist thinkers to appreciate the power and specificity of the internal constraints that must be embodied in that mechanism. Consideration of an experimental approach to the study of mental transformations by means of the quantitative specification of test stimuli and the timing of overt responses enables us to elaborate this argument by means of two additional points.

The first of these concerns timing. It is tautological that the mind cannot think at a rate exceeding the rate of its own most efficient operations. Moreover, a limit on the speed of such operations is fixed by the finite velocity of neural conduction—which was first measured, in fact, by Helmholtz (see Boring, 1950, p. 41). Indeed, there is reason to suppose that the limiting rate of flow of informational codes in the brain may entail constraints that are in some ways analogous to the constraints connected, in the theory of relativity, with the fact that the propagation of causal disturbances in physical space cannot exceed the velocity of light (viz., the constraints of the Lorentz transformations—see Caelli, Hoffman, & Lindman, 1978). On introspection, then, the mind's most efficient and automatic operations appear to the mind itself to be virtually instantaneous as well as effortless. Little wonder that philosophers like Hume, who based their conclusions on the subjective observation of their own mental processes rather than on the use of more objective and faster-operating physical instruments to clock such processes in others, could speak as if a more complex or extensive mental transformation "costs the imagination no more trouble" (Hume, 1748, Vol. 2, p. 16) than a simpler or less extensive one.

It was not until 1969, following the successful application of refined chronometric techniques to processes of mental comparison by such experimental psychologists as Sternberg (1966), Moyer & Landauer (1967), and Posner & Mitchell (1967; see also Posner, 1969) that we actually began our attempt to time mental processes corresponding specifically to spatial transformations. As the ensuing chapters attest, the result has been the discovery that the patterns of latencies of overt responses mediated by such covert mental operations bear a remarkably consistent and orderly relation to the complexities and extents of the spatial transformations corresponding to those internal operations.

The second additional point concerns the use of precisely controlled test stimuli. Here it is tautological that the mind cannot reach, by thought alone, a more accurate result than that to which it is guided by its own inner constraints. But in the case of spatial transformations, we believe that there exists a whole hierarchy of such inner constraints, ranging from the strongest, which ensure conservation of the unique rigid structure of the transformed object as a whole, to the weakest, which ensure conservation of no more than the primitive figure-on-ground identity of the object as a single but otherwise undifferentiated blob. Moreover, there are theoretical reasons (Shepard, 1981) and supporting evidence (Chapter 15, herein) for believing that the time required to complete a transformation increases with the stringency of the constraints that are imposed. In the absence of internal access to the underlying transformational machinery, the failure to provide an external check on the accuracy of the result must leave us in doubt about the degree to which a mental transformation corresponds to any particular transformation in physical space.

In speaking of joining "incongruous shapes and appearances," Hume (1748) evidently was not concerned with the demonstrable maintenance of any particular structural constraints. It may be for this reason, too, that the processes of "compounding, transposing, augmenting, or diminishing," of which he spoke, seemed to him to be so uniformly easy and, presumably, fast. By contrast, in the experiments described in this volume, we implicitly encouraged participants to maintain the rigid structure of an object during any mental transformation by explicitly assessing their speed and accuracy in discriminating whether a test stimulus, actually presented in the transformed position or orientation, was or was not structurally identical to the original, untransformed object. Under these more demanding conditions, the mental operations are not always so uniformly fast or easy, but (as we already noted) their times reveal a particularly clear dependence on the magnitudes of the rigid spatial transformations to which we can, with greater confidence, now say they correspond.

The presentation of external stimuli in this work might at first seem inimical to the goal of studying purely imagined transformations. After all, such transformations are, by definition, ones that are performed in the absence of external counterparts. However, we do not present the transformations as such, but only static stimuli that can be regarded as corresponding to two points along the path of some connecting transformational trajectory. Indeed, in several of the experiments no stimulus related to the object to be transformed is physically displayed during the entire period available for the performance of the mental transformation. In any case, the times, upon which everything else rests in this line of work, can be measured only if there is some externally available reference event that can be used to start the clock, and in our experiments the most appropriate event for this purpose is always the onset or offset of the visual display of a suitably chosen stimulus.

Theoretical Issues

Our entire program of research is predicated on the notion that there are different levels of description of internal processes and that significant theoretical statements about such processes can be framed at a level of abstraction that does not entail any commitment to a particular mechanization of these processes within the neurophysiological substrate. When we do make reference to the underlying neural processes, it is not to say anything about what those processes are; it is only to say such things as that the process underlying one type of performance, say an imaginal one (whatever its neurophysiological details), must have much in common with the process underlying another, related type of performance, say a corresponding perceptual one (cf., Place, 1956; Shepard, 1975, 1981; Shepard & Chipman, 1970; Shepard & Podgorny, 1978; Smart, 1959; and, in a slightly different connection, Neisser, 1976).

As is suggested by the title of this volume, we regard the principal theoretical issues as dividing naturally into two types: (a) those that concern the nature of the internal representations (or "mental images") that are internally transformed; and (b) those that concern the nature of the internal transformations that are performed on those representations. As this formulation suggests, however, we also regard these two issues as closely interdependent. We cannot determine precisely what transformation is internally modeled (e.g., whether a rigid or nonrigid one) without determining what structural properties in the representation of the object are preserved during the transformation. And crucial evidence concerning precisely what properties of the external object are preserved in its internal representation (e.g., those inherent in the three-dimensional structure of the object itself or those confined to the momentary two-dimensional projection of that object on the retina) can be gleaned from comparisons between different kinds of transformations (e.g., those in which structural invariants in the external object are or are not preserved in its retinal projection).

The most fundamental issues, with regard both to the internal representation of objects and to the internal representation of their transformations, concern the type and degree of correspondence or isomorphism between the representational processes and their external referents. Indeed, the single most basic distinction that we draw in this connection is between *analog* representational processes, in which the relational structure of the external events is essentially preserved in the corresponding relational structure of the internal representations, and *nonanalog* (e.g., categorical, symbolically recoded, or logical) representational processes, in which it is not.

To illustrate this distinction with regard to the representations of the objects themselves, perceptual or memorial images of colors are analog representations in that the psychological relations between such representations have a close and continuous correspondence to the physical relations between the colors actually presented, for example, by combining three primary colors in different proportions (e.g., on a spinning color-mixing wheel). As the proportions of the primaries are made more alike or different in two mixtures, the two resulting colors appear more similar or dissimilar, respectively; and by gradually shifting the relative contributions of any two such mixtures (of, say, pink and orange) to one resulting mixture, one can generate a correspondingly gradual shift in the internal representation (from pink, through a graded series of increasingly orangish pinks, to orange). By contrast, color names are inherently discrete and categorical. Between any two words like "pink" and "orange" there is no graded series of color names that are correspondingly intermediate with respect, say, to phonological or orthographic shape.

The distinction applies in much the same way to mental transformations. We classify an internal process as the analog of a particular external transformation if and only if the intermediate stages of the internal process have a demonstrable one-to-one relation to intermediate stages of the corresponding external process—if that external process were to take place. Thus a mental transformation of an object is said to be an analog rotation if it can be shown that the individual who is carrying out the transformation is internally representing that object in successively further rotated orientations in the very specific, objective sense that during the process, that individual is capable of a faster and more accurate discriminative response to appropriate physical test stimuli in correspondingly more and more rotated orientations. By contrast, the computation of the new coordinates for a rotated system of points by means of a matrix multiplication would not be classified as an analog process because the intermediate stages of that row-into-column calculation have no one-to-one relation to intermediate orientations and do not, at intermediate times, place the machine that is performing the computation in any special states of readiness for the actual presentation of such intermediate orientations.

In accordance with our earlier caveat, we make no claim concerning the neural mechanism underlying an analog process. In particular, although it is perhaps conceivable that something of the sort will eventually be found to be the case, we do not in any way imply that during a mental rotation, there is anything (such as a pattern of neural firing, electric field, or whatever) that is literally rotating within the physical brain. (Certainly, we would not want to suppose that when one is imagining the color green, there is anything literally green going on inside one's head!) The isomorphism that we do claim is a more abstract, "second-order" one (Shepard, 1975; Shepard & Chipman, 1970)—namely, that the brain is passing through an ordered series of states that (whatever their neurophysiological nature) have much in common with the perceptual states that would occur if the appropriate physical object were presented in successively more rotated orientations in the external world.

Our work is motivated by the realization that we are faced with significant and empirically testable issues even though they neither predict nor presuppose any particular neurophysiological facts. Principally, these concern the extent to which the processes by which objects are internally represented and transformed are analogical in the sense defined and therefore can meaningfully be characterized as processes of mental modeling or simulation.

Organization of This Volume

The ensuing chapters include what we believe to be the most complete and definitive of our previously published studies of mental transformations on representations of objects in space. The overall organization is roughly chronological except for a few minor departures—required, in most cases, to group the studies into three major topical sections: Part I, which is confined to mental rotation; Part II, which extends consideration to other and more complex transformations and sequences of transformations; and Part III, which returns to rotational transformations but in the context of the quite different paradigm of the perceptual illusion of "apparent motion." The concluding chapter in each of these three parts is a newly written "epilogue" that discusses some subsequent developments and issues related to the papers included in that part.

Particularly in the case of the longer papers, some of the less central material has been deleted in the interest of brevity and pertinence. Otherwise, the papers are reprinted with their original titles and are essentially verbatim, except for occasional minor editorial changes and the addition of initial abstracts, where there originally were none, for the sake of uniformity. Which of us originally authored each paper, and in collaboration with which (if any) of our coworkers, is indicated on the title page of each corresponding chapter.[1] All references, notes, and an extensive index are assembled at the back of the book.

I | Mental Rotation

Introduction to Part I

We have already remarked that the idea for the chronometric study of mental rotation was conceived on November 16, 1968. For what historical interest it may serve, in Chapter 2 we have reproduced for the first time in published form the brief written description of the proposed initial experiment as, two days after its conception, Shepard circulated it among some of the students in experimental cognitive psychology at Stanford—including a newly arrived graduate student named Jacqueline Metzler. The major part of the most extensive published report of the results that were obtained when that initial experiment was subsequently carried out (the report by Metzler and Shepard, 1974) is included as the following Chapter 3.

Within about a year of its sudden onset, the experimental investigation of mental rotation attained its full momentum when Cooper, having arrived from the University of Michigan as another new graduate student in the summer of 1969, joined in the barely started enterprise. The focus of the ensuing studies (reproduced in Chapters 4 through 7) shifted from the initial two-stimulus paradigm, in which Shepard and Metzler (1971) had measured the time that subjects required to determine whether two differently oriented objects were the same or different in intrinsic shape, to a one-stimulus paradigm, in which Cooper, Shepard, and co-workers (including Klun and Podgorny) measured both (a) the time that subjects took to discriminate whether a single rotated object was the same as an object in a previously learned "upright" orientation, and (b) the time that those subjects took to prepare for such a discrimination when the test orientation was indicated in advance. The culmination of this series of studies of mental rotation is reached in Chapters

6 and 7, which we regard as providing the most conclusive evidence currently available for the analog character of the representations of the objects and for the analog character of the representations of their transformations, respectively. The experiment by Cooper and Podgorny (1976) reported in Chapter 6 also furnished the first evidence for the striking qualitative individual differences between holistic and analytic processes of visual comparison that have continued to emerge in subsequent work by Cooper and her co-workers (Cooper, 1976b, 1980, 1982; Cunningham, Cooper, and Reaves, 1980).

Finally, in the Epilogue to Part I (Chapter 8), we briefly review more recent findings that throw further light on mental rotation, and we offer a response to criticisms that have been raised by Pylyshyn and others against some of the interpretations of our findings.

2 | On Turning Something Over in One's Mind

Preliminary Proposal for Some Experiments

Originally authored by Roger N. Shepard

This previously unpublished note, originally circulated at Stanford as a typed memorandum of this title, dated November 18, 1968,[1] contains the earliest description of the type of experiment on "mental rotation" that was subsequently carried out and first published, over two years later, by Shepard and Metzler (1971). For a full account of what happened in the experiment itself, see the following Chapter 3.

Basic Experimental Procedure

On each trial the subject is presented with two line drawings, each of which portrays a three-dimensional object in space. The subject's task is to determine, as rapidly as possible, whether the two objects are the same (except for a rotation in space) or are different (i.e., cannot be rotated into congruence with each other). The principal dependent variable to be recorded is the latency of the response.

Basic Idea Behind the Experiment

If, as introspectively seems to be so in my own case, the subject determines whether the two depicted objects are the same by performing a "mental rotation" in order to bring the two objects into congruence, then the time required to reach a decision might be linearly related to the angle of rotation between the spatial orientations of the two objects. Conversely, if an approximately linear relation is found, this would be indicative that such a mental rotation is in some sense performed. By contrast, if a rotationally invariant description is mentally generated for each of the two figures separately, the time required for decision would presumably be independent of angular difference in orientation. The results, thus, would bear on the question of the status of mental images and on the question of the reality of imagined spatial transformations.

Details of Equipment and Procedure

The subject would sit looking into a two-field tachistoscope in readiness to operate either a left- or a right-hand switch. Each new trial would either be signaled by a preceding warning tone or else would be initiated by the subject (e.g., by depressing a foot pedal). After a brief, fixed delay, the blank field of the tachistoscope would then be replaced by the pair of line drawings to be judged on that trial. The subject would be instructed to operate the right-hand switch as soon as the depicted objects are determined to be the same in three-dimensional shape, and to operate the left-hand switch as soon as those objects are determined to be different (i.e., not congruent under any rotation).

Proposed Stimuli

For stimuli, I propose to use perspective line drawings portraying a fixed number of cubes fastened face-to-face to make a three-dimensional structure that cannot be transformed into itself by any reflection. I further propose that when the two structures are different (i.e., cannot be rotated into congruence), they differ only by a reflection. This would make it maximally difficult for the subject to use a verbal or other non-rotational strategy to determine whether the two objects are the same or different. Two illustrative pairs are shown in Figure 2.1.

Many different structures should be used in order to prevent the subject from devising a special strategy that would short-circuit the process for a particular structure. Since, moreover, many different orientations must be presented, the figures would best be generated by means of computer graphics (e.g., by the Stromberg-Carlson 4020 microfilm recorder at the Bell Telephone Laboratories, together with a rotation program of the type devised there by Ruth Weiss or by Mike Noll). Of course, in view of the fact that the non-identical alternative is always the mirror image of the identical alternative, it would be essential to prevent perceptual reversals of the objects in depth. Accordingly, it would be preferable to use perspective rather than parallel projections of the three-dimensional objects and to ensure that lines and edges on the side away from the viewer are not portrayed.

Some Variables to be Explored

There are three degrees of freedom of rotation of a three-dimensional object in space. For if we define an axis through the object,

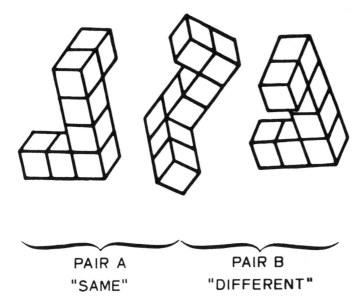

PAIR A   PAIR B

"SAME"   "DIFFERENT"

Figure 2.1 Perspective view of three-dimensional objects differing only
by a rotation (Pair A) and by a reflection as well as a rotation (Pair B).

then the specification of the orientation of the axis is like the specification of a point on the surface of a sphere and thus requires two
degrees of freedom (e.g., latitude and longitude). There then remains
one further degree of freedom, corresponding to the angle of rotation
about that axis. The principal independent variable—when the two
objects are in fact the same—is, of course, the degree of difference
in orientation of the two objects. However, there are several dis-
tinguishable ways in which the orientation can be different:

a. Rotation in the two-dimensional plane of the line drawing
   (leaving the intrinsic shape of the two-dimensional drawing itself
   unchanged).
b. Rotation about a horizontal or vertical axis parallel to the two-
   dimensional plane of the line drawing (and thus resulting in a
   perspective deformation of that drawing).
c. Rotation about a natural axis through the three-dimensional
   object; i.e., an axis that is orthogonal to one face of the cubes
   (and generally resulting, again, in a perspective deformation of
   the two-dimensional drawing).
d. Rotation about an arbitrary axis—i.e., an axis that is not aligned
   either with the global coordinate framework natural to the space
   surrounding the subject (as it was in a or b, above) or with the
   local coordinate framework natural to the object (as it was in c).

These evidently exhaust the possibilities, since the appropriate fixed-point theorem of topology implied that for any general rotation of a sphere, there must be a fixed point on the surface, hence a fixed axis of that rotation. Accordingly, in all cases we can simply use the angle of rotation about the fixed axis as a measure of physical difference in orientation. Still, we should expect that rotations around certain, preferred axes may lead to shorter reaction times, and it would be of psychological interest to compare reaction times for these different types of axes.

It might also be desirable to obtain judgments of the similarities of the two figures as two-dimensional patterns. If we were to obtain such judgments of similarity without regard to orientation in the two-dimensional plane, angular difference should have little or no effect in the case of rotations of Type a, above—but a marked effect in the case of rotations of Types b or c.

Finally, if suitable equipment were available for stereoscopic display, it would be interesting to compare such a three-dimensional presentation with the two-dimensional perspective projection proposed here.

Suggested Preliminary Experiment

For a first, exploratory experiment, we might do the following: Construct, say, ten different three-dimensional objects each composed of seven cubes fastened face-to-face as already described, with each such object constructed so that it cannot be transformed into itself by any reflection (or rotation short of 360 degrees). For the "different" pairs, construct ten more such objects each of which is the mirror image of one of the ten objects just mentioned (obtained by reflecting that object through some plane in three-dimensional space). Then, for each of the ten original objects, generate two series of perspective pictures—one in which the object rotates in small steps in the plane of the picture (and so remains unchanged in terms of the intrinsic structure of the two-dimensional picture), and a second in which the object rotates in small steps in three-dimensional space about, say, an axis orthogonal to the line of regard (and so results in perspective deformations of the two-dimensional picture).

Two sequences of test pairs would then be constructed. One, involving rotations within the picture plane, would consist of a series of pairs in which, for each pair, one of the ten shapes is selected at random in one of its possible orientations and is paired with that shape or its mirror-image shape in the same or in one of the different orientations within the picture plane. The other, involving rotations in depth, would be constructed in the same way, but from the series of objects rotated about an orthogonal axis. If rotations about only one axis are required in any one series, the subject should become adept at making the required kind of rotation. (Only the angular extent—not the axis—of the rotation would be uncertain prior to the presentation of each pair.)

Final Query

Consider the case in which a subject learns to identify a particular one of these three-dimensional objects regardless of its orientation. Is it more useful to account for such a performance in terms of feature analyzers or in terms of a mental transformation with respect to a canonical "deep" representation of the object? (Or can these two kinds of accounts be shown to be equivalent?)

November 18, 1968

Postcript (1981)

The added Figure 2.2 shows one of the two (mirror-image) sets of perspective views that I proceeded to have generated by the computer-driven Stromberg-Carlson microfilm recorder at the Bell Telephone Laboratories, with the generous programming aid of my former collaborator there, Jih-Jie Chang. These views (and their mirror-image counterparts) were then used in the first experiments on mental rotation of three-dimensional objects, described in the following chapter. In those experiments, however, the line drawings were presented against a white rather than a black background. It was only for heightened contrast in the particular display shown in Figure 2.2, which appeared as the cover photograph of the issue of *Science* containing the first published report of this experiment (Shepard & Metzler, 1971), that the projections of the objects were mounted on a black background.

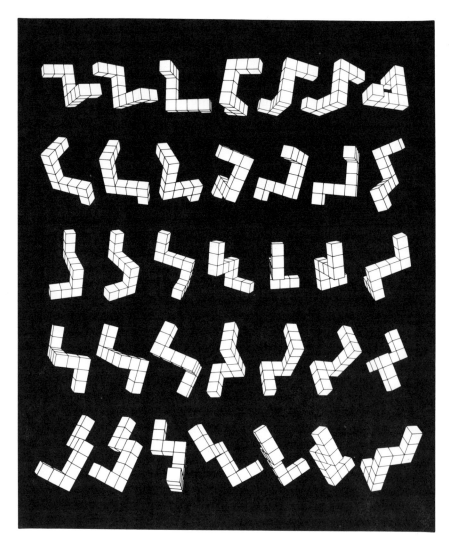

Figure 2.2 Half of the set of computer-generated perspective views used in the subsequent experiments. (Reproduced from the cover of the February 19, 1971 issue of *Science.*)

3 | Transformational Studies of the Internal Representation of Three-Dimensional Objects

Originally authored by Jacqueline Metzler and Roger N. Shepard

We begin by presenting a full account of the first chronometric experiment on mental rotation of three-dimensional objects, which was only partially covered in the first published report (Shepard & Metzler, 1971). The time subjects required to determine that two perspective views were of intrinsically identical, rather than enantiomorphic (mirror-image), three-dimensional shapes (a) increased linearly with the angular difference between their portrayed orientations in three-dimensional space, and (b) was essentially independent of whether this angular difference corresponded to a simple (rigid) transformation of the retinal projection, or to a complex (nonrigid or even topologically discontinuous) transformation of the retinal projection. We then report the similar results that were obtained in a second experiment in which the ends of the two portrayed objects were color coded to reduce the time subjects might require to determine which ends correspond before undertaking a mental rotation; and review the principal findings of some related experiments that were subsequently carried out as a part of Metzler's (1973) doctoral dissertation. Finally, we discuss the implications of all of these results for the analog nature of the internal representation of three-dimensional objects and of their transformations in space.

In 1969 we initiated the first experiment in a continuing series designed to measure the times that human subjects require to respond discriminatively to spatially transformed visual objects. Our primary focus here will be on those experiments that have used objects of one particular kind, namely, abstract three-dimensional structures (composed of cubes attached face-to-face), as well as transformations on such objects of one particular kind, namely, single rigid rotations about some fixed axis in three-dimensional space.

Reprinted by permission from Chapter 6 of the volume *Theories in cognitive psychology: The Loyola Symposium*, edited by R. Solso and published by Lawrence Erlbaum Associates, 1974.[1]

General Nature of the Experiments

Basic paradigm. The experiments we wish to consider here have the following features in common. The subject is presented, on each trial, with a pair of perspective drawings of three-dimensional objects and is instructed to determine as rapidly as possible whether the two portrayed objects have the same three-dimensional shape (even though they may be portrayed in very different orientations), or whether they have inherently different three-dimensional shapes (and so could not be brought into mutual congruence by any rigid motion). In the first two experiments to be described here, the two perspective views are displayed simultaneously and the reaction-time clock starts with the presentation of the pair. In some more recent experiments (Metzler, 1973) that we shall also describe, however, the two views are displayed sequentially and the clock starts with the presentation of the second member of the pair. In either case, the clock is stopped as soon as the subject actuates either a right-hand switch or a left-hand switch (one of which is used to register the decision "same shape," the other of which is used to register the decision "different shape").

The objects portrayed in the two perspective drawings are always abstract three-dimensional shapes consisting of cubical blocks attached face-to-face to form a rigid, asymmetrical arm-like structure with two free ends and two or three right-angled bends. On a random half of the presentations the two objects are identical in three-dimensional shape, though generally displayed in different orientations. On these trials the subject should actuate the switch indicating that, despite possible differences in orientation, the objects are of the same three-dimensional shape. On the other half of the presentations the two objects differ by a reflection through some plane in three-dimensional space as well, possibly, as by a rotation. Since all objects are inherently asymmetric, such objects can not be brought into congruence with each other by any rigid rotation and, hence, the subject should actuate the other switch indicating that the two objects are different in three-dimensional shape. The choice of objects that are mirror-images of each other for the "different" pairs was intended to ensure that the decision as to whether the two objects were the same or different was made only on the basis of global shape and not on the basis of any local features.

Factors investigated. The objective of these experiments has been to determine how the time required to make the decision as to whether the two perspective views portray objects of the same three-dimensional shape depends upon such factors as the following:

1. Whether the two objects are in fact the same or different in three-dimensional shape.

2. The angle of rotation that would have to be performed in three-dimensional space in order to bring the two objects into congruence if they are the same in three-dimensional shape (or into partial congruence if they are not).

3. Whether the axis of this rotation is or is not known by the subject in advance of the presentation.

4. Whether this axis is or is not a natural axis of the three-dimensional object itself.

5. Whether this axis is vertical, horizontal, or inclined with respect to the external frame of reference.

6. Whether this axis coincides with the line of sight (in which case the difference in orientation corresponds to a simple rigid rotation of the two-dimensional perspective drawing itself) or is orthogonal to the line of sight (in which case the difference in orientation corresponds to a much more complex nonrigid deformation of the perspective drawing).

7. Whether, for a given angular difference, such a nonrigid deformation of the perspective view would or would not pass through certain topological discontinuities or singularities in which parts of the object become completely fore-shortened, disappear, or emerge into view.

8. Whether, for a given axis of rotation, the particular (clockwise or counter-clockwise) direction in which the subject has been set to imagine the rotation is, for a given pair of objects, the short or the long way around the 360° circle (i.e., whether it is less than or greater than 180°).

9. Whether both perspective views are perceptually available during the entire decision process, or whether the first view is available only in memory while the subject is preparing for the presentation of the second.

10. Whether the subject must determine which end of the second object corresponds to a particular end of the first object, or whether this correspondence has been explicitly indicated (by color coding).

11. The over-all complexity of the three-dimensional object (as measured in terms of the number of cubical blocks or the number of right-angled bends in the resulting arm-like structure).

12. Individual differences among subjects.

Major Theoretical Issues

Analog nature of mental transformations. The major theoretical issues to which this program of experimental research has been directed were initially advanced by Shepard (e.g., see Shepard, 1975). A particularly central one, here, concerns the nature of the internal process by means of which the subject determines whether two differently oriented objects are or are not the same in intrinsic shape. Specifically, the question arises as to whether the internal process is in any sense an analog process, i. e., a *mental* process that corresponds in some way to a *physical* process of actual rotation of the one object into congruence with the other. Moreover, if there is a sense in which this internal process is indeed a mental analog of an external physical rotation, it becomes important to formulate, in as clear a way as possible, just what this sense may be.

There are two connected implications of the claim that the decision is reached by means of a mental analog of a physical rotation: One is that, whatever the nature of the neurophysiological process that goes on when the subject is comparing two differently oriented objects, that process has something important in common with the internal process that would go on if the subject were actually to perceive the one external object physically rotating into congruence with the other. The other implication is that, in the course of such a process, the internal representation passes through a certain trajectory of intermediate states each of which has a one-to-one correspondence to an intermediate stage of an external physical rotation of the object. And here, again, the one-to-one correspondence between an intermediate internal representation and an intermediate external orientation of the object is not necessarily one of structural resemblance, but only the casual, dispositional one of being especially prepared for the appearance of that external object in just that orientation at just that time (cf., Cooper & Shepard, 1973b, Experiment II—reprinted in Chapter 4).

These two implications are closely related in that the reason that a subject is especially prepared for a particular object at a particular orientation is presumably that the neural activity, whatever its nature, has at that moment much in common with the neural activity that would be caused by the external presentation of that physical object in that specific orientation. However, neither of these implications requires either that the internal representation of the object structurally resemble the external object or that the internal representation of its rotation structurally resemble its physical rotation. Either or both of these more concrete kinds of structural isomorphism may to some extent hold, but it is not necessary that either hold in order to speak of such a thing as mental rotation or to characterize it as a process that, though more or less abstract, is nevertheless basically an analog type of process.

To speak of it as an analog type of process is, at the most fundamental level then, to contrast it with any other type of process (such as a feature search, symbol manipulation, verbal analysis, or or other "digital computation") in which the intermediate stages of the process have no sort of one-to-one correspondence to intermediate situations in the external world. In the strictest sense, a fully analog representation of a continuous process (such as a physical rotation) should itself be a continuous process. Hence the distinction between analog and digital computation is often drawn in terms of continuous versus discrete processes. We do not wish to take a stand here on the neurophysiological question of whether the internal simulation of external physical processes by the brain is, at the finest level of analysis, basically discrete or continuous. For the present, we prefer to formulate the hypothesis that mental rotation is an analog process in a somewhat weaker or more general way that does not entail strict continuity. We are willing to concede that sufficiently small differences in orientation may be handled in discrete jumps. The most essential and general implication of classifying the process of comparing two differently oriented objects as an analog process is that, if the two orientations are sufficiently different, *then* the comparison can be made only by passing through some other internal states that correspond to intermediate orientations of the external object.

Internal representation of three-dimensional objects. Among those mental operations that may be performed in an analog manner, mental rotation has been singled out as an example that seems particularly interesting in connection with the problem of the internal representation of three-dimensional objects. Notice that for most rigid spatial transformations, such as translation or dilation (uniform expansion or contraction), there is a very simple, direct relationship between the change in the three-dimensional object and the resulting change in a two-dimensional perspective projection of the object—such as the retinal projection. The same is also true of rotation in the special case in which the rotation is about one particular axis—namely, the line of sight (or, in other words, the axis through the point of projection). In all of these cases a rigid transformation of the external three-dimensional object induces an essentially rigid transformation of the two-dimensional projection.

In the case of a rotation about any axis other than the line of sight, however, the relationship between the change in the object and the change in its planar projection becomes much less direct. The three-dimensional object itself is still rigid under rotation, but its two-dimensional projection is subjected to a very complex nonrigid deformation in which not only the metric but even the topological structure is often altered. (Portions of the projection not only shrink and deform relative to other portions, they even disappear completely and then reappear on the other side of the object.)

Clearly then, the way in which subjects deal with rotations in depth should provide information that bears on questions of how three-dimensional objects are internally represented. Of particular interest in this regard is the question of whether the internal representation is more akin to the two-dimensional projection of the object, which deforms in complex ways under rotation but which is at least directly available at the sensory surface, or whether it is more akin to the three-dimensional object itself, which is structurally invariant under rotation but has somehow to be indirectly constructed on the basis of the retinal projection. The answer to this question should be attainable through an examination of those pairs of perspective views that correspond to objects that differ by the same angle of rotation in three-dimensional space but that differ in different ways or to different extents in terms of their two-dimensional representations (particularly as indicated in items 6 and 7, listed earlier).

EXPERIMENT I

Method

Subjects. Eight adult males served as experimental subjects. Of these, six were graduate students at Stanford University and two (including one of the present authors, RNS) were faculty members. All subjects had 20:20 vision or vision corrected to 20:20. In addition, all were found able to complete 90% of the items—with less than 10% errors on the completed items—on both of two timed paper-and-pencil pretests of mental manipulation of objects in space (viz., Thurstone's Card Rotation Test and Cube Comparison Test, as modified and supplied by the Educational Testing Service). Two of the eight subjects were left handed.

Generation of the individual stimuli. The stimuli used for the experiment itself were perspective line drawings of relatively abstract and unfamiliar three-dimensional objects as viewed in space. Each such object consisted of ten cubical blocks attached face-to-face to form a connected string of cubes with three right-angled bends and two free ends (see Figure 3.1). The locations and relative directions of the three bends were chosen (*a*) so that each object was inherently asymmetric, i.e., so that it could not be transformed into itself by any reflection or rotation (short of 360°) in three-dimensional space; and (*b*) so that each object was inherently distinct from every other, i.e., so that it could not be transformed into any of the other objects by any rigid rotation in three-dimensional space. Altogether ten distinct objects were selected for use in the experiment. These ten form two groups of five each such that (*a*) within either group of five no object can be transformed into any other by any rotation *or* reflection, while (*b*) for each object in either group there is a corresponding object in the other group that is identical to it except for a reflection through a plane in three-dimensional space. Such mirror-image pairs or "isomers" were used to construct the "different" pairs in the "same-different" tests (thus preventing discrimination on the basis of merely local features).

For each of these 10 structurally distinct objects, 18 perspective views were generated corresponding to 18 equally-spaced 20° steps of rotation of the object about a vertical axis through the object in three-dimensional space. Since each object was oriented more or less at random prior to rotation, the axis of rotation in this experiment never corresponded to a natural axis of the object itself. These 10 X 18 or 180 perspective views were generated at the Bell Telephone Laboratories especially for this research by Jih-Jie Chang in accordance with specifications outlined by one of the present authors (RNS). The generation was achieved by means of special computer graphic facilities at the Bell Laboratories (including, particularly, the Stromberg-Carlson 4020 microfilm recorder) and an associated program for three-dimensional spatial transformation on two-dimensional perspective projections developed there by A. M. Noll (e.g., see Noll, 1965). The possibility of perceptual reversal was eliminated by preparing an ink tracing of each of the perspective views to be used in the experiment on a blank sheet of paper, omitting all lines that would be invisible if the object were opaque.

In order to facilitate subsequent construction of the stimulus pairs actually to be presented to the subjects, an ink circle of fixed size was drawn around each of these revised perspective drawings, and a small tic mark was added on the outside edge of the top of the circle, to indicate the top of the vertical axis for the rotations in depth. Each of the resulting individual perspective line drawings with its enclosing circle was then photographically reduced and a number of copies were printed by a photo-offset process. The reduction was chosen so that, in the final printed copies, the circle was eight cm. in diameter while the enclosed perspective drawing of the object averaged between four and five cm. in maximum linear extent. Changes in orientation corresponding to rotations within the two-dimensional plane of the picture itself were achieved simply by rotating the picture itself so that the tic mark was at the desired position about the circle.

Construction of the depth pairs. We found that it was possible to select a fixed pattern of seven of the 18 views of each object without encountering any of the orientations that had objectionable singularities (regions in which a part of the object coincides with the line of sight) or hidden parts. Moreover, these seven were so spaced in orientation that they could be used to construct two pairs of views at each of the equally-spaced angular separations, in 20° steps, from 0° to 180° in such a way that (a) the two pairs at any one angular difference generally came from widely separated orientations and (b) all views appeared approximately the same number of times. (The seven acceptable views selected, in accordance with this scheme for five of the ten objects—viz., those that can not be brought into congruence with each other by any rotation or reflection—can be seen in the earlier Figure 2.2 (p. 24) and on the cover of the issue of *Science* in which the Shepard-Metzler (1971) paper appeared. The corresponding views of the other five objects differ simply by a reflection of the three-dimensional objects through the picture plane.)[2]

A set of 400 distinct depth pairs was prepared. Of these, 200 were "same" pairs consisting of 20 pairs for each of the 10 distinct objects. The remaining 200 were "different" pairs which were constructed in the same way except that for one of the two views, a view of the three-dimensional mirror image of the object (corresponding to its reflection through the picture plane) was substituted for one of the two pictures—with the consequence that the two objects could no longer be rotated into congruence. The two perspective pictures constituting each pair were mounted side-by-side on the face of a 5 × 8 in. card so that the tic mark remained at the top center of each circle, and so that in the case of the "same" pairs, a clockwise rotation (as seen from the top of the vertical axis) would bring the object portrayed on the left into congruence with the object on the right through the minimum angle (i.e., the short way around the 360° circle).

Construction of the picture-plane pairs. A set of 400 distinct pairs of perspective views was prepared, also, for rotations within the picture plane. Again, these consisted of 200 "same" pairs (in which, in this case, a rotation of one of the two-dimensional pictures itself would bring it into congruence with the other picture) and 200 "different" pairs (in which, as before, a picture of the inherently different three-dimensional mirror image of the object was substituted for one of the two pictures). Of the seven different perspective views prepared of each of the ten objects for the construction of the depth pairs, one particular view was selected to construct all the picture-plane pairs for that object. The views selected for five of the ten objects are shown in Figure 3.5. The views selected for the other five objects (required for the construction of the "different" pairs) differ from these only by a reflection through the picture plane and, as illustrated in Figure 3.8, project a similarly shaped outline in that two-dimensional plane.

Although the problem of singularities and hidden parts does not arise with rotations in the picture plane, in order to achieve optimum correspondence between the picture-plane and depth conditions, the pairs of orientations for the picture-plane condition were constructed on the basis of the pattern of seven orientational positions as has already been set forth for the depth condition. By aligning the tic mark at the top of each picture with the appropriate mark at each 20° interval around the circles on the 5 × 8 in. stimulus cards, we ensured that the two pictures making up each picture-plane pair differed by the appropriate angle in the two-dimensional plane. As before, the pairs were all prepared so that, for the "same" pairs, a clockwise rotation of the left-hand picture would bring it into congruence with the right-hand picture via the smallest rotation (where, this time, the rotation is about the line of sight).

Conditions. Each subject was successively tested under each of three conditions: "depth," "picture-plane," and "mixed." The *depth condition* consisted in the presentation, in a random order, of just the 400 ("same" and "different") depth pairs. Similarly, the *picture-plane condition* consisted in the random presentation of just the 400 ("same" and "different") picture-plane pairs. The *mixed condition* was a randomly sequenced composite of all the depth and picture-plane pairs and, therefore, consisted of 800 presentations. On any one trial of any of these three conditions, the rotation was either about the vertical axis (depth pairs) or about the line of sight (picture-plane pairs), but never by a combination about both of these two axes at once. The distinguishing aspect of the mixed condition was that the axis of rotation remained unpredictable from trial to trial.

Of the six possible permutations of these three conditions, the two orders in which the mixed condition was in the middle position were omitted. The eight subjects were then assigned to the remaining four possible orders as follows: On the basis of their scores on the paper-and-pencil pretests, the highest- and lowest-scoring subjects were paired, the next-highest and next-lowest were paired, and so on, until all eight subjects were assigned to four pairs. Then each of these pairs was assigned, at random, to one of the four orders of presentation of the three conditions. At the beginning of each condition, the subject was told the nature of that condition (viz., that the rotation would be around a vertical axis, in depth; that the rotation would be in the plane of the picture; or that the rotation would switch at random between these two axes). The nature of the rotations included in that condition was further clarified for the subject by the preliminary practice or warm-up trials mentioned below.

Apparatus. The subject sat in a dimly illuminated room, looking into a simple mirror tachistoscope with a 5 × 8 in. half-silvered window at the front and a slot for a horizontally oriented 5 × 8 in.

stimulus card at the back. On each trial the experimenter inserted the card with the stimulus pair selected for that trial and then closed a switch that exposed the stimulus pair to the subject's view by turning on a set of lights inside the otherwise darkened box. Simultaneously, the closing of that same switch also started a reaction-time clock calibrated in 1/100ths of a second. At the viewing distance (about 60 cm.), the perspective drawing of each object subtended a visual angle of some four to five degrees. In front of the slot for the stimulus cards was a permanently fixed black mask with two circular apertures 7.6 cm. in diameter positioned so that each of the two perspective views would appear in the center of one of the apertures, but so that the circle and tic marks used for positioning the perspective views on the card would not be visible. Figure 3.1 shows how a typical picture-plane "same" pair (A), a depth "same" pair (B), and a "different" pair (C) would appear when exposed to view in the tachistoscope.

As soon as possible, the subject responded to the exposed stimulus pair by pulling one of two spring-loaded levers. The right-hand lever was always used to signal "same" and the left-hand lever "different." Although large deflections were possible, the first slight deflection of either lever toward the subject actuated a microswitch that simultaneously stopped the reaction-time clock and turned off the lights inside the tachistoscope. Each lever also turned on one of two external signal lights that provided both the subject and the experimenter with feedback as to which response had been made "same" or "different."

Procedure. Each subject participated for a total of eight to nine hours in about as many sessions, completing on the average 200 trials per session for a total of 1600 trials. Prior to the first session the subject was verbally instructed as to the nature of the task and was given 40 practice trials. In addition, each subject was informed as to which of the three experimental conditions would be first, and of the two subsequent changes in conditions when they occurred. Before each session the subject also received ten warm-up trials representative of the type of rotation (i.e., depth, picture plane, or mixed) to follow. (The stimulus pairs presented during the practice and warm-up trials were drawn from extra pairs that would not reappear during the recorded experimental trials.)

The beginning of each trial was signaled by a warning tone followed, approximately one half second later, by the visual presentation of the pair of perspective drawings selected for that trial. The subject's instructions were to pull the appropriate lever as quickly as possible to indicate whether the two drawings represented objects of the same or different three-dimensional shape, while keeping errors to a minimum.

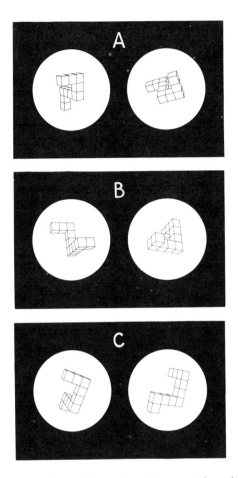

Figure 3.1 Illustrative pairs of perspective views, including a pair differing by an 80 degree rotation in the
picture plane (A), a pair differing by an 80 degree rotation
in depth (B), and a pair differing by a reflection as well as a
rotation (C).

Results

Reaction time as a function of angular difference. The principal
independent variable of interest is the angular difference between the
portrayed orientations of the two three-dimensional objects— whether
around the vertical axis, in depth, or around the line of sight, in the
picture plane. Figure 3.2 presents the group mean reaction times,
computed for "same" responses only, at each 20° interval of rotation
from 0° to 180°. The data are displayed separately for the two kinds of
pairs, depth and picture-plane, but have been combined over the pure
and mixed conditions.

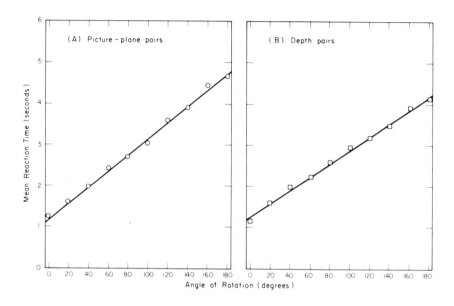

Figure 3.2 Mean time to determine that two objects have the same three-dimensional shape as a function of the angular difference in their portrayed orientations, plotted separately for pairs differing by a rotation in depth (squares) and by a rotation in the picture plane (circles).

In the cases of both depth and picture-plane pairs, reaction time increases according to a remarkable linear function of angular difference in portrayed orientation, ranging from about one second at 0° (i.e., for pairs of identical perspective views) to between four and five seconds at 180°. Since the angle through which the "different" three-dimensional shapes must be rotated to achieve congruence is not strictly defined, functions like those plotted for the "same" pairs cannot be readily constructed for the "different" pairs (cf., however, the section on "recent experimental findings"). Still, the *over-all* mean reaction time for "different" pairs was about 3.8 seconds, nearly a second longer than the over-all mean for the "same" pairs.

Error rates. Generally the error rates, though correlated positively with reaction times, were quite low. Over all, nearly 97% of the 12,800 recorded responses of the eight subjects were correct, with error rates ranging for 0.5% to 5.7% for individual subjects. In the ensuing graphical plots of mean reaction times, and in the reported statistical analyses, reaction times associated with incorrect responses have been excluded. However such incorrect reaction times exhibit a pattern resembling that presented for the correct responses.

Results for individual subjects. The mean reaction times for each subject, plotted separately for "same" pairs differing either by a rotation in depth or by a rotation in the picture plane, are shown in Figure 3.3. The order in which the three experimental conditions were presented to each subject is indicated in the lower right-hand corner of the corresponding graph. The mean reaction times for individual subjects increased from a value of one second at 0° to values ranging from four to six seconds at 180° of rotation, depending upon the particular individual. Note that, despite such variations in slope, the functions for each subject are also remarkably linear. Polynomial regression lines were computed separately for each subject and for the group data for each type of rotation. In all 18 cases, the data were found to have a highly significant linear component ($p < .001$) when tested against deviations from linearity. No significant quadratic or high-order effects were found ($p > .05$, in all cases).

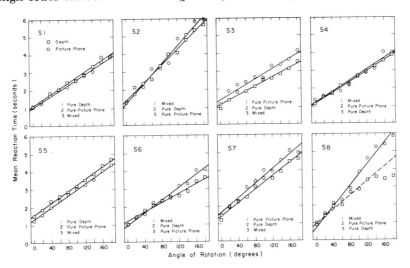

Figure 3.3 Mean reaction time as a function of angular difference, plotted separately for depth and picture-plane pairs for each of the eight individual subjects.

The one suggestion of a departure from linearity (and from equivalence of slope for the depth and picture-plane pairs) may be seen in the last two points for the depth pairs in the case of the last subject, S8. Although the statistical analysis did not indicate that this seeming departure from linearity was reliable, it is at least suggestive that this one subject spontaneously reported the use of a different strategy just in the case of depth pairs differing by about 180° that permitted him to determine sameness or difference without actually carrying out the mental rotation. This strategy was based upon certain surface features of the two-dimensional perspective pictures and resembled a strategy that led to bimodality in the distribution of "different" reaction times for depth pairs differing by 180° in a third experiment (see section on "recent experimental findings"). On the basis of this conjecture, anyway, the last two points (for 160° and 180°) were ignored in fitting the dashed line to the data for the depth pairs for S8.

Results for depth, picture-plane, and mixed conditions. Another important finding is the relative lack of dependence of reaction time upon the kind of rotation ("depth" versus "picture plane") required to bring the two objects into alignment. As can be seen in Figure 3.2, both functions are very similar to each other with respect to intercept and slope; the mean response time for a given angular difference is just as large when this difference consists simply in the rigid rotation of one of the pictures itself within its own two-dimensional plane as when it corresponds to the two-dimensionally much more complex rotation of one of the objects about its vertical axis, in depth. In fact if there is any difference, reaction times at the larger angular separations appear to be somewhat shorter for rotation in depth than for rotation in the picture plane. However, this difference is of doubtful significance; for, when subjects are individually considered (Figure 3.3), the relative position of the two functions appears to be directly dependent upon the order of administration of the "pure" depth and picture-plane conditions, with but one exception. As might be expected on the assumption that there would be some general improvement with practice, the "pure" condition that was presented first yields the function having the slightly higher mean intercept and/or steeper slope.

Group mean reaction times for the "pure" blocks of trials (in which subjects knew the axis of the required rotation prior to each block) and the "mixed" blocks (in which the axis of rotation was unpredictable from trial to trial) are presented in Figure 3.4. The two functions are again remarkably linear. They also have nearly the same intercepts. Not surprisingly, then, when the two perspective pictures are identical and no rotation is required, knowledge of the axis rotation for that block of trials has little effect. When, however, the axis of rotation is not known in advance, reaction times do tend to be longer for pairs of objects differing by an appreciable angle. Even at the larger angular differences, however, reaction times were no more than 20 percent greater for pairs on which the axis of rotation was unpredictable than for pairs on which the axis of rotation was known.

Results for individual three-dimensional objects. Reaction-time functions were also plotted for each of the five structurally different types of three-dimensional objects used in this experiment. These

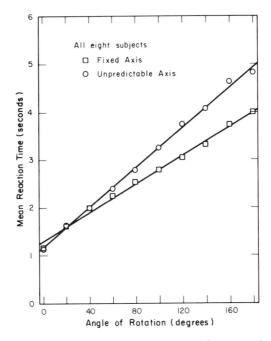

Figure 3.4 Mean reaction time as a function of angular difference, plotted separately for the "pure" conditions, in which the axis of rotation was fixed throughout any one block of trials, and for the "mixed" condition, in which the axis of rotation varied unpredictably from trial to trial.

functions, as presented here in Figure 3.5, are averaged over all eight subjects, over both axes of rotation, and also over the two objects that differ from each other simply by a reflection in each case. Thus the picture exhibited in the upper left corner of each of the five plots is an illustration of one of the two "isomeric" objects upon which the data in that plot were based. However, as in all previous figures, the reaction times plotted here are for the "same" pairs only.

Note that the function for Object C has the steepest slope and that the reaction times are particularly long for large rotations in the picture plane. This is consistent with the subjects' reports that, owing to the approximately symmetric relationship between the two ends of this one object, it was sometimes more difficult to determine which end of one of the two views corresponded to which end of the other view in the presented pair—and that this was especially so when the rotation was in the picture plane (cf., the following Experiment II). Despite such differences in slope, however, the reaction-time functions retain their consistent linearity even when the data are broken down in this way. The small residual departures

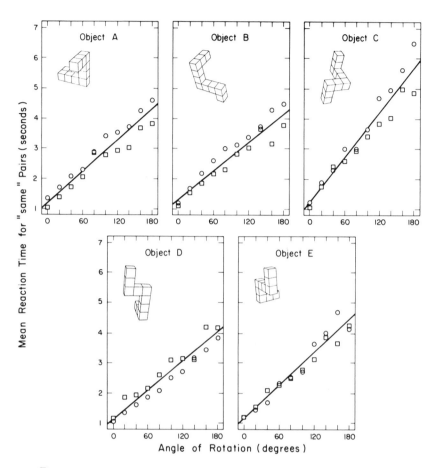

Figure 3.5 Mean reaction time as a function of angular difference, plotted separately for depth pairs (squares) and picture-plane pairs (circles) for each of the five basically different types of objects. (The data in each panel are averaged over both the object portrayed within that panel and its reflected version.)

from the fitted linear functions do, however, appear to be somewhat larger and, possibly, more systematic (in local structure) than the deviations from linearity in the plots for the individual subjects. The fact that these small step-like perturbations are more evident in the data for the depth pairs (plotted as small squares) suggests that they may be a reflection of purely surface features that appear and disappear in the two-dimensional projection of the object as it rotates. The possible influence of a particular kind of "surface feature" will be examined more systematically in the immediately following section.

Effect of intervening singularities in the two-dimensional projections. For each object there were two pairs of views differing by a depth rotation of 40° and two pairs differing by a depth rotation of 60°. For each of these two angular differences, moreover, such a rotation would carry the two-dimensional projection through what we have called a singularity in the case of one pair but would encounter no such singularity in the case of the other pair.

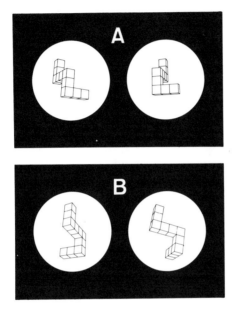

Figure 3.6 Illustrative pairs in which the two objects differ by a 40 degree rotation in depth with (A) and without (B) crossing a topological discontinuity or "singularity" in the two-dimensional projection.

The difference between these two cases is illustrated, for a rotational difference of 40°, in Figure 3.6. Note that even though the same object is portrayed in both pairs and even though the angle of rotation is exactly the same for both pairs, the topological structure of the two-dimensional projections is preserved only in the lower pair (B). In the case of the upper pair (A), the rotation, if carried out, would pass through a singular orientation in which certain surfaces of the object coincide with the line of sight. At that point in the rotation certain of these surfaces, visible only in the left-hand picture, disappear from view while other of these surfaces, visible only in the right-hand picture, emerge into view. In the case of the lower pair (B), by contrast, exactly the same surfaces of the object remain in view in both pictures and throughout the intervening rotation.

In order to obtain evidence concerning the relative effect on reaction time of a 20° difference in extent of rotation of the three-dimensional object itself versus a topological discontinuity in the surface features of the two-dimensional projection of that object, we undertook a two-by-two analysis of the reaction times for the pairs differing by 40° or by 60° according to whether they did or did not involve an intervening singularity or "crossing." The relevant data, averaged over all subjects and all objects, are summarized

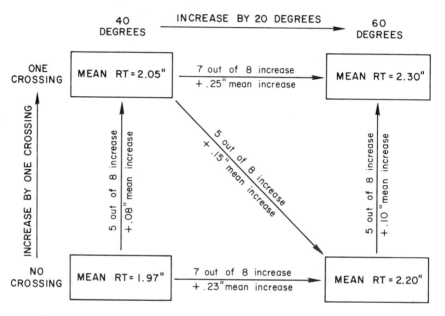

Figure 3.7 Effects on reaction time of crossing one singularity in the two-dimensional projection versus a 20 degree increase in angle of rotation in three-dimensional space.

in Figure 3.7. Note that there was a consistent increase of about 240 msec when the angle of rotation increased by only 20° whether or not the rotation crossed a singularity. Moreover, seven out of the eight subjects showed such an increase. The addition of one crossing of a singularity, however, produced an increase of no more than 90 msec. regardless of the extent of the rotation. And, this time, only five out of the eight subjects showed a change in this direction. Indeed, when the two factors, of rotation of the three-dimensional object and discontinuity of the two-dimensional projection, are pitted against each other (as indicated by the diagonal arrow) there was a mean increase in reaction time (of 150 msec) as predicted by the 20° increase in angle of rotation rather than a mean decrease as might be expected from the elimination of the crossing.

These indications were supported by a three-way analysis of variance of the reaction times: angle × crossings × subjects. This analysis revealed the increase in mean reaction times as a function of angle of rotation to be significant ($F = 21.32$, $df = 1, 7$, $p < .005$). However, the effect of the number of crossings on reaction times was found to be nonsignificant ($F = 0.89$, $df = 1, 7$, $p > .10$) as was the interaction between angle of rotation and the number of crossings ($F = 0.03$, $df = 1, 7$, $p > .10$). Of course there may well be a real effect of passing through a singularity even though this test is not powerful enough to establish its existence. Indications are, however, that if such an effect exists it is in all probability quite small. On the basis of the slope of the over-all mean reaction time function for "same" depth pairs (about 17.5 msec per degree), the mean increase in reaction time produced by the addition of one crossing (viz., about 90 msec) is equivalent to the increase produced by a rotation in depth of only about five degrees.

Conclusions

The linearity of the reaction time functions. The first of two findings of Experiment I that we regard as especially significant is that the time required to determine that two perspective pictures portray objects of the same three-dimensional shape increases according to a strikingly linear function of the angular difference in the portrayed orientations of the two objects. Indeed this linearity is consistently found even in those subsets of the data that were obtained just (*a*) for those pairs of objects differing by a rotation in depth, or by a rotation in the picture plane (Figure 3.2), (*b*) for the conditions in which the axis of rotation was held constant or was unpredictable (Figure 3.4), (*c*) for each of the eight subjects individually (Figure 3.3), and (*d*) for each of the five differently shaped isomeric pairs of three-dimensional objects (Figure 3.5).

This linearity provides strong evidence for an additive process in which the time required to go from one orientation, A, to another orientation, C, is the sum of the time required to go from A to an intermediate orientation, B, and the time required to go from that intermediate orientation, B, to C. It is consistent with the more specific proposal that the subject makes the determination of sameness of shape by carrying out some sort of internal analog of an external rotation of the one object into congruence with the other, and, further, can perform this analog process at no faster than some limiting rate. If so, this limiting rate is given by the reciprocal of the slope (again about 17.5 msec per degree) of the reaction-time function. For these subjects and these objects, then, it averages on the order of 55 to 60 degrees per second.

The relative unimportance of surface features of the two-dimensional pictures. The second finding of Experiment I that seems to have important implications is that the reaction time depends almost entirely on the angle of the orientational difference between the two portrayed objects in three-dimensional space. The degree of similarity between the two perspective pictures, taken as two-dimensional patterns, seems to have little or no independent effect. Thus, reaction times for depth pairs differing by the same angle in three-dimensional space were not significantly longer for pairs in which the two-dimensional pictures were topologically very different than for pairs in which the pictures were topologically equivalent. (By contrast, only a 20° increase in difference in three-dimensional orientation led to a highly significant increase in reaction time.) Indeed, the small (and statistically nonsignificant) mean increase in reaction time that was observed as the result of the addition of one crossing of a singularity in the two-dimensional picture was equivalent to that produced by a rotation of no more than about five degrees in three-dimensional space (Figures 3.6 and 3.7).

A further indication of the unimportance of the surface features of the two-dimensional perspective views is that the two isomeric versions of each object nearly always led to the response "different" —even when they were oriented in such a way as to project very similarly shaped two-dimensional patterns (as shown in Figure 3.8).

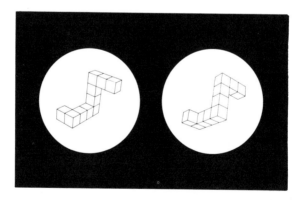

Figure 3.8 Objects differing only by a reflection through the picture plane. (Notice the similarity in outlines of their two-dimensional projections.)

The most striking evidence that the surface features of the two-dimensional pictures are unimportant is to be found in the fact that the slope of the reaction-time function was just as great for pairs differing by a simple rigid rotation of one of the pictures within its own picture plane as for pairs differing by the much more complex transformation of one of the two-dimensional pictures that is induced by a rotation of the three-dimensional object in depth (Figures 3.2 and 3.3).

These results seem to be consistent with the notion that (with the possible exception of certain very special cases, such as that suggested in connection with the lower-right subject in Figure 3.3) subjects were performing their mental operations upon internal representations that were more analogous to the three-dimensional objects portrayed in the two-dimensional pictures than to the two-dimensional pictures actually presented. The subjects themselves indicated that they interpreted the two-dimensional drawings as objects in three-dimensional space, and, having done so, could as easily imagine the objects rotated about whichever axis was required.

EXPERIMENT II[3]

Subjects in Experiment I reported that they sometimes experienced difficulty in determining which end of one object corresponded to which end of the other object. Not surprisingly, this difficulty seemed most noticeable in the case of certain objects (particularly Object C, Figure 3.5) for which the two ends resembled each other most closely—in terms of the number of blocks in each terminal arm and the relationship of each outer bend to the intervening middle bend. In addition, this difficulty seemed especially troublesome in the case of pairs differing by a rotation in the picture plane, presumably because rotations in depth were always about a vertical axis and, so, (in the pure depth condition, anyway) subjects could infer that the uppermost end of one object must correspond to the uppermost end of the other.

These considerations suggest that the slopes of the linear reaction-time functions plotted for Experiment I may reflect two different components of the reaction times; namely, (a) a search time needed to discover which end of one object corresponds to a given end of the other and (b) a rotation time needed to bring the corresponding ends into congruence, once they have been discovered. Indeed it seems probable that the greater slope of the reaction-time function obtained under the mixed condition (Figure 3.4) was in large part a consequence of the increase in search time that resulted when the axis of rotation was not known in advance of each trial.

If it is true that the search component is a larger portion of the reaction time for responses to the picture-plane pairs than for responses to the depth pairs, then the nearly equivalent slopes of the depth and picture-plane functions (Figure 3.2) may have been fortuitous. Possibly, if the search component could be eliminated, rotations in the picture plane would turn out to be considerably

faster than rotations in depth after all. Experiment II was undertaken, primarily, for the specific purpose of evaluating this possibility and, secondarily, for the more general purpose of estimating
the extent to which the slopes of all the reaction-time functions
obtained in Experiment I reflect such a process of search—as opposed
to a process of mental rotation. The principal change from Experiment I was to minimize the need to search for corresponding ends by
the simple device of attaching same-colored dots to the corresponding ends of the two objects in each stimulus pair.

Method

Subjects. Eight Stanford students, none of whom had participated
in the earlier Experiment I, served as subjects.

Stimuli. The same perspective line drawings of three-dimensional
objects used in Experiment I were again used here, with the exception of the two isomeric versions of Objects A and C (cf., Figure 3.5)
which were eliminated because they had seemed to lead to the most
confusion and need for prerotational search in that experiment.
However, on the perspective drawing of each object a circular red dot
was now attached beside the cube at one end of the object and a circular blue dot was attached beside the cube at the other end. These
color codes were attached so that, in each pair, the two corresponding ends of the two objects were always assigned the same color.

Procedure. Each subject participated in one practice session and
three test sessions of 160 trials each. The 160 pairs presented during
practice trials were blocked according to whether the rotation was
in depth or in the picture plane. During the three test sessions,
however, pairs of objects differing by either of the two types of rotation were randomly presented and, so, the axis of rotation remained
unpredictable, as in the "mixed" condition in Experiment I. In other
respects, the procedure and apparatus were as described in
Experiment I.

Results

Over-all reaction-time results. The group results for the test
sessions are shown in Figure 3.9. Once again, reaction times are for
correct responses only, are averaged over all eight subjects, and
are plotted as a function of the angular difference in portrayed
orientation, from 0° (i.e., for pairs of identical perspective views)
to 180°. Although they were obtained from the same "mixed"
condition, the means are plotted separately for the pairs differing
by a rotation in depth (again, always about a vertical axis) and for
pairs differing by a rotation simply in the picture plane. In both
cases the plotted data are for the "same" pairs only since the minimum

angle through which one object in the pair would have to be rotated
in order to achieve congruence simply is not defined for objects of
inherently different shape. As before, though, the over-all mean
reaction time for the "different" pairs (about 4.6 seconds) was
longer than the over-all mean reaction time for the "same" pairs
(about 4.1 seconds).

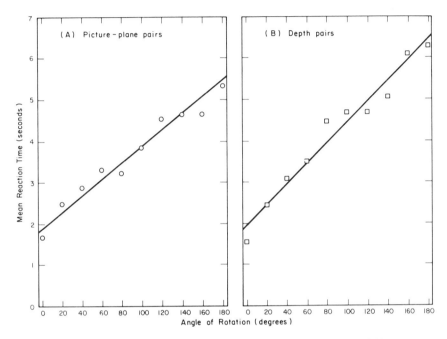

Figure 3.9 Mean reaction time as a function of angular difference,
plotted separately for depth and picture-plane pairs (from the principal,
"mixed" condition) in Experiment II.

The means shown here are somewhat more variable than those
obtained in Experiment I owing, probably, to the smaller amount of
data upon which they are based, to the correspondingly smaller total
amount of practice that each subject acquired during the experiment
and, possibly, to differences in the populations from which the
subjects in Experiments I and II were sampled. Perhaps because of
the last two of these circumstances, the over-all mean reaction times
in this experiment tended also to between a half and a full second
longer than those in the corresponding "mixed" condition in
Experiment I.

Nevertheless, the results provide further confirmation of the
principal findings of the earlier experiment. The linear increase in
reaction time with angular difference is again clearly evident for both

depth and picture-plane pairs, ranging from about 1.6 seconds at 0° to between 5.5 and 6.5 seconds at 180°. Polynomial regression lines computed for each type of pair separately were found in both cases to have a significant linear component ($p < .01$) when tested against deviations from linearity, whereas no quadratic or higher-order effects approached statistical significance ($p > .10$ in all cases). Moreover, the functions obtained for the two contrasting types of rotation (depth and picture-plane) are again very similar to each other with respect to intercept and slope. Indeed, the introduction of the color coding of corresponding ends of the objects seems, if anything, to have brought the two functions into even closer agreement with each other.

Error rates. As in Experiment I, the error rates were quite low, ranging from 1.3% to 6.8% for individual subjects with an over-all mean of 3.8%.

Results for individual subjects. Mean reaction time plots, corresponding to that shown in Figure 3.9 for the whole group, are shown separately for each of the eight subjects in Figure 3.10. The data for the individual subjects, like the data for the whole group, are appre-

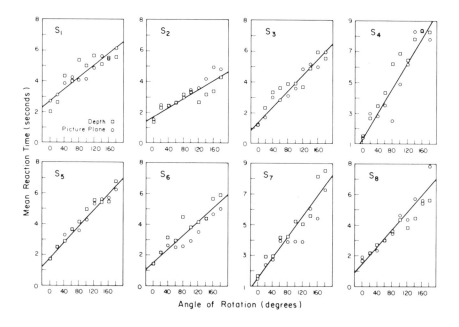

Figure 3.10 Mean reaction time as a function of angular difference, plotted separately for depth and picture-plane pairs (from the "mixed" condition) for each of the eight individual subjects in Experiment II.

ciably more variable than they were for the larger Experiment I. Moreover, the slopes and intercepts vary considerably from subject to subject, so that the best-fitting functions increase from values ranging between 1.3 and 2.8 seconds at 0° to values ranging from about 4.5 to 8.7 seconds at 180°. Nevertheless the over-all linearity and the coincidence of the functions for the depth and picture-plane pairs holds up well for each individual separately. Indeed, despite the considerable between-subject variation, this within-subject coincidence is so close that it did not appear feasible to display the fitted functions for the two types of rotation separately in each panel of Figure 3.10.

Results for pure versus mixed conditions. In Experiment I the reaction-time function was found to be steeper in slope for the condition in which the depth and picture-plane pairs were randomly intermixed rather than blocked by axis of rotation (Figure 3.4). If, as we suggested, this difference in slope reflected a difference in the time required to search for corresponding ends of the two objects, the difference between such pure and mixed conditions might be considerably reduced when, as here, the need for search has been minimized by the addition of color coding. Unfortunately, the results of this second experiment do not lend themselves to a clear-cut test of this notion because the pure condition was given only for the purpose of preliminary training and, so, consisted of trials that (*a*) were substantially fewer in number and (*b*) were always presented *before* the mixed condition (rather than according to a counter-balanced order). Nevertheless the results for these preliminary, pure trials were reasonably orderly and, so, are displayed here, in Figure 3.11.

As before, these points are based on correct responses only, which ranged from 24, the maximum possible, down to only 17 correct responses per point. The appreciable variability of the points is presumably a consequence of these small sample sizes. Even so, the functions are again quite linear for both the picture-plane and the depth conditions. Moreover, although the intercepts are about 200 msec. higher than in the mixed condition which followed, the slopes are indistinguishable from those found for that mixed condition (cf., Figure 3.9). Again, the confounding of conditions with order of presentation precludes the drawing of any definite conclusions. Still, the virtual identity of the slopes for the pure and mixed conditions is at least consistent with the notion that the difference in slope found in Experiment I was, as we conjectured, a reflection of the additional time required for prerotational search when the axis of rotation was not known in advance.

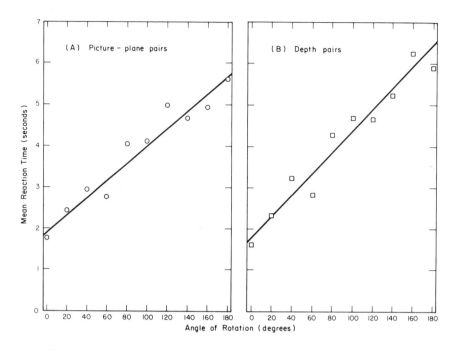

Figure 3.11 Mean reaction time as a function of angular difference, plotted separately for depth and picture-plane pairs from the corresponding pure conditions administered at the beginning of Experiment II.

Conclusions

Corroboration of the conclusions of Experiment I. With an entirely new set of subjects, Experiment II has succeeded in replicating the two principal findings of Experiment I; viz., that reaction time (*a*) increases linearly with angular difference in orientation and (*b*) is relatively independent of whether this angular difference corresponds to a rotation in the picture plane or in depth. These further results thus contribute additional support for the conclusions already advanced; namely, that subjects arrive at their judgments of sameness or difference in this task (*a*) by carrying out an internal process that is a kind of analog representation of an external rotation and (*b*) by performing this process upon an internal representation that is more akin to the three-dimensional object portrayed in the perspective picture than to that two-dimensional picture itself.

Search versus mental rotation components of reaction time. The introduction of color coding in order to minimize the need to search for corresponding ends of the two objects in each pair has eliminated the former slight superiority of the depth pairs over the picture-plane pairs. This provides some objective evidence in support of the subjective impression that a larger portion of the reaction times in Experiment I was taken up with such a search process in the case of the picture-plane pairs than in the case of the depth pairs. However, this change in procedure has reduced the reaction times to the picture-plane pairs only to the level of the reaction times to the depth pairs—not to an appreciably lower level. Evidently, then, the approximate equivalence of depth and picture-plane rotations in Experiment I was not in fact fortuitous. Even more compellingly than before, then, it appears that the internal representations upon which the subjects were performing their mental operations were more analogous to objects in isotropic three-dimensional space than to their perspective projections in the special two-dimensional picture plane.

Any direct quantitative comparison between the two experiments is subject to some uncertainty owing, principally, to differences between the populations from which the two sets of subjects were sampled. Still, the fact that the reaction times in Experiment II, despite the addition of the color coding, were not appreciably shorter (and, in fact, averaged between a half to a full second longer) than in Experiment I tends to support the notion that, if the decision process can be divided into a process of searching for corresponding parts followed by a process of mentally bringing those corresponding parts into mutual congruence, then the search component was relatively small even in Experiment I. Such, anyway, are the grounds for taking, as we have, the reciprocal of the empirically obtained slope of the reaction-time function as an estimate of the limiting rate of "mental rotation."

SUBSEQUENT EXPERIMENTAL FINDINGS

To conclude our presentation of experimental results, we turn now to three new findings that have emerged from two further experiments on mental rotation of three-dimensional objects that one of us has recently completed (Metzler, 1973). These three new findings are concerned with how reaction time depends upon angular difference in orientation in the following three types of cases: (a) those in which the two objects are isomeric rather than identical, and so can be rotated only into partial congruence rather than into complete congruence; (b) those in which the direction in which subjects have been set to carry out a mental rotation corresponds to the long way around the 360° circle; and (c) those in which the presentation of the second perspective view is delayed until the required mental rotation of the first could already be completed. Although the presentation of these new findings will necessarily be quite brief here, we shall argue that these findings bear in important

ways upon alternative theories of how subjects determine sameness
or difference of three-dimensional shapes.

The stimuli again were perspective views of differently oriented
three-dimensional arm-like structures formed of cubes attached
face-to-face. This time, however, a somewhat simplified set of objects
was used: There were only seven (rather than ten) cubes in each
object, only two (rather than three) right angled bends, and only two
(rather than ten) structurally distinct objects. In the case of the
depth pairs, moreover, the rotation was always about the natural
axis of the object; that is, about the axis of the central and longest
straight row of cubical blocks. In order to avoid undesirable singularity, this axis was always slightly inclined with respect to the picture
plane, rather than contained within it (as in the case of the strictly
vertical axes of depth rotation in the earlier experiments). And,

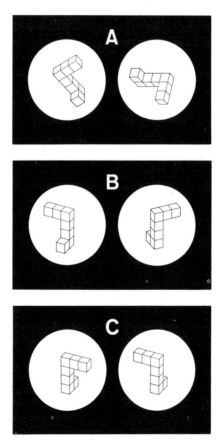

Figure 3.12 Illustrative pairs in which two simplified objects differ by a
135 degree rotation in the picture plane (A), by a 135 degree rotation in
depth (B), and by a reflection (C). (In the case of the depth pair (B), notice
that the axis of rotation is the natural axis of the object.)

finally, different depth conditions were devised in which the orientation of the projection onto the picture plane of the axis of depth rotation, in addition to being vertical (as in the earlier experiments), was sometimes either horizontal or inclined 45° to the left or to the right. Examples of the pairs of perspective views used in these experiments are exhibited in Figure 3.12. The depth pair (B) illustrates a rotation about an axis that (in the picture plane) is vertical, and the "different" pair (C) shows the two structurally distinct objects to which these further experiments were confined.

Reaction Times for "Different" Pairs

Rationale. The first of the more recent experiments carried out by Metzler (1973) was similar in basic procedure to our original experiment. For present purposes, the most important differences were (*a*) the just-described changes in the manner of construction of the pairs of perspective views and (*b*) certain deliberate manipulations designed to induce subjects to rotate the long way around on some trials. We shall return to the consequences of the second difference in the following section. In this section we shall confine our attention to one consequence of the first difference; specifically, the consequence that (owing to the altered manner of construction of the stimuli) it became for the first time convenient to look at the reaction-time function for "different" pairs.

As we have already noted, the angle through which differently shaped three-dimensional objects must be rotated to achieve congruence can not be defined. However, according to the theory of mental rotation, a subject can determine whether or not two objects are the same only by attempting to rotate one into congruence with the other. What we assume, then, is that the subject carries out a mental rotation in order to bring one part of one object into congruence with the corresponding part of the other object and *then* checks whether the other part(s) of the objects have been brought into congruence as well by this mental operation. In fact, in a questionnaire administered at the end of the experiment, all eight subjects reported that they generally attempted to bring the longer (and, except in the case of the horizontally oriented axis, uppermost) two-block arm of one object into alignment with the corresponding longer (and uppermost) two-block arm of the other object. If, after achieving this partial alignment, they determined that the shorter, one-block arms at the other (and usually lower) end of the two objects were brought thereby into coincidence as well, they could then respond "same." If, on the other hand, they discovered that, as a result of the mental transformation, the one-block arms of the two objects now pointed in opposite directions in three-dimensional space, they could infer that the opposite response, "different," was required. If this account is correct, when reaction time is plotted against the angle of rotation required to bring the two longer arms into congruence, a linearly increasing function should be obtained for the "different" pairs just as for the "same" pairs.

Results. The results of this experiment are exhibited in Figure 3.13 for both the "same" pairs (A) and for "different" pairs (B). The plot for the "same" pairs is exactly analogous to those shown earlier (in Figures 3.2 and 3.9). The data are averaged over all eight subjects and plotted separately for depth pairs and picture-plane pairs (though, this time, the depth rotations were about natural axes of the objects, and the plotted times have been averaged over the cases in which these axes were vertical, horizontal, or inclined). Note that, despite the changes in the objects and their axes of rotation, reaction time again increases linearly with angular difference in the orientations of the two identical objects in these "same" pairs. The fact that the slope of the fitted reaction-time function is steeper in the case of the picture-plane pairs supports the notion that mental rotation is easier when the rotation is about a natural axis of the objects (as it was only in the case of the depth pairs). The further fact that the slopes

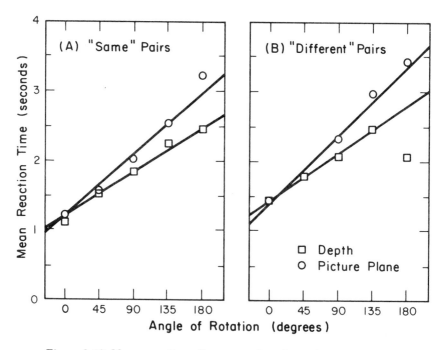

Figure 3.13 Mean reaction time as a function of angle of rotation needed to achieve congruence, in the case of "same" pairs (A), or to achieve partial congruence, in the case of "different" pairs (B). (In both cases the data are plotted separately for depth and picture-plane pairs.)

in both cases are somewhat less than in Experiments I and II suggests that mental rotation may be faster with structurally simpler objects (i.e., in this case, objects with fewer blocks and bends).

The principal new result however is that, when the reaction times for the "different" pairs are plotted against the rotation needed to achieve *partial* congruence (in the manner described above), reaction-time functions are obtained that are generally very similar to those obtained for the "same" pairs. (Compare the B and A halves of Figure 3.13.) The only discrepant point (which was not included in fitting the straight line) is the one for 180° depth pairs. The unexpectedly short mean reaction time for this one particular case was evident in the individual data for seven of the eight subjects. The reaction times for these subjects at this angular difference in orientation are bimodally distributed, with the upper mode at the reaction time predicted for 180° by the best-fitting linear function through the modes of the distributions from 0° to 135°, while the lower mode is slightly longer than the modal response time to 0° pairs which differ only by a reflection.

We conjecture that on those trials in which reaction time is closely approximated the predicted value for 180° rotations of different objects, subjects were using the strategy generally employed—namely, rotating so as to bring the longer arms of the two objects into congruence, and only then assessing the relative position of the shorter arms. However, on those trials in which the modal response time approached the reaction time to pairs of objects differing by a reflection only, it seemed likely that subjects realized that the shorter arms of the two objects were already similarly oriented and so, upon discovering that the upper arms pointed in different directions, arrived at their judgment of "different" without having to carry out a rotation. Additional support for this reasoning may be found in the fact that a number of the subjects explicitly reported in a post-experimental interview that they did often use a different, nonrotational strategy in the special case of just these pairs (viz., those differing by a 180° rotation in depth as well as by a reflection). Some described it as a strategy of noting that while the bottom arms of the two objects pointed in the same direction, the top arms pointed in opposite directions.

Although the way in which the "different" pairs were generated in the earlier experiments makes it difficult to determine the angle through which the subjects may have rotated the objects into partial congruence, informal checks on the reaction times to certain "different" pairs in which this angle seemed especially well defined suggest that results similar to those shown in Figure 3.13 B could also be found in the earlier data. Over all, though, reaction times to "different" pairs were nearly a full second longer than reaction times to "same" pairs in the earlier experiment rather than only 200 to 300 msec. longer as indicated for the more recent results plotted in Figure 3.13. In any case, the new results for "different" pairs, presented in section B of the figure, provide additional evidence largely consistent with the theory of mental rotation.

Reaction Times for Pairs Differing by More Than 180°

Rationale. Like the corresponding earlier figures, Figure 3.13 included reaction times for pairs differing by rotations only up to 180°. However, an important new feature of that same experiment was the presentation of certain other pairs under conditions designed so that, if the subjects were carrying out a mental rotation, they might go the long way around the circle. Specifically, trials were blocked by direction of rotation in such a way that, for all except a few pairs presented in the last half of a block, a particular (e.g., clockwise) rotation would carry the object on the left into the orientation of the object on the right by the shortest rotation (i.e., the rotation of no more than 180°). Then, on a few randomly inserted trials toward the end, the direction of shortest rotation was unexpectedly reversed so that, if the subjects were continuing to rotate in the same direction as before, they would end up going the long way around. In order to minimize the likelihood of their discovering that they were going the long way around on these special trials, these pairs were confined to just the next step beyond 180° which, in view of the 45° increments used in this experiment, was 225° (as opposed to 135°, if they happened to reverse direction of rotation on that trial).

These special trials could provide crucial information concerning the nature of the internal process by means of which the subjects determined sameness or difference of the two objects on each trial. For, according to the theory of mental rotation, the internal process is in a sense a simulation of an external process of rotation and, as such, has a definite trajectory and a definite direction along that trajectory. Thus, to the extent that subjects always go the long way around on these special trials, their reaction times should be even greater than at 180° and, indeed, should coincide with the linear extrapolation to 225° of the reaction-time function already obtained for angular departures from 0° to 180°. Or, to the extent that subjects sometimes go the long way around and sometimes reverse direction to take advantage of the 135° short-cut, their reaction times should be bimodally distributed with an upper mode corresponding to the linear extrapolation to 225° and a lower mode corresponding to the reaction time previously found for 135°. In contrast to this, a nonrotational theory (e.g., of feature-by-feature comparison) would seem to predict no such directional effect. The controlling variable would then be simply the absolute difference between the two pictures and, hence, the reaction time should be the same for what we have called 135° and 225° and, in both cases, should be shorter than for 180°.

Results. If the data are combined for depth and picture-plane pairs, the group mean reaction time to these special "same" pairs (which differed, the long way around, by rotations of 225°) was 2.79 sec—very close to the 2.84 group mean reaction time to "same" pairs differing by 180°. Hence, it was not as long as predicted by extrapolation of the linear functions shown in Figure 3.13. Indeed, in the case of the depth pairs, the mean reaction time for these special 225° pairs fell below the extrapolated value for five out of the eight subjects. As we have noted, however, some of the subjects may sometimes have reversed their direction for these pairs in order to go the short way around. If so, the distribution of reaction times would become bimodal with the consequence that the mean would no longer be an appropriate index of central tendency and, certainly, would not be representative of either of the two modes. Accordingly, we turn now to an examination of the distributions themselves.

In order to obtain the most stable representation of the 225° distribution, the reaction-time data were pooled from all eight subjects. Since the intercepts and, particularly, the slopes of the best-fitting reaction-time functions varied considerably from subject to subject, the data from each subject (and, indeed, for each axis of rotation used by each subject) were first linearly transformed in such a way that the linear function that then best fit the data for that subject (and for that axis of rotation) exactly coincided with the linear function that best fit the over-all group data. This normalization was performed solely on the basis of the reaction-time data for angular differences from 0° to 180° and, hence, was not biased in any way by the to-be-examined data for the special 225° pairs.

The reaction-time distributions obtained by thus combining the individually normalized distributions for each subject (and axis of rotation) are presented in Figure 3.14. Notice that the combined distributions for angles from 0° through 180° are all sharply peaked, unimodal distributions and, further, that the modal reaction times increase according to a very linear function (in close agreement with the linear increase of the means already noted Figure 3.13 A). The straight line in Figure 3.14 represents the linear function that best fits the modal points (from 0° to 180°). It has an intercept of 1.25 seconds and a slope of about 8.3 msec per degree. (This modal function is slightly lower than the corresponding mean function

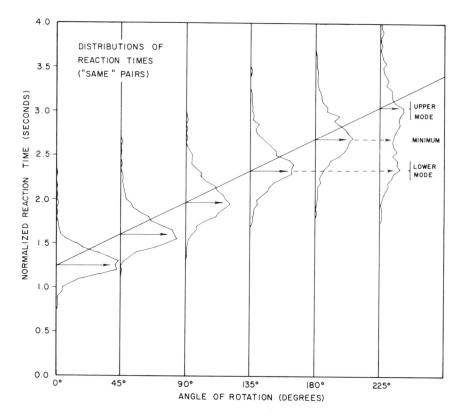

Figure 3.14 Distributions of reaction time for "same" pairs at various angles of rotation. (See text for explanation of normalization of reaction times and of bimodality at 225 degrees.)

owing to the tendency of the distributions to be somewhat skewed toward the longer reaction times.)

More important, notice that the distribution for the special pairs at 225°, which did not enter in any way to the normalization of each subject's time scale, exhibits an appreciable bimodality. And, in excellent agreement with the hypothesis that on each trial a subject either rotated the long or the short way around, the two modes correspond closely to the forward and backward extrapolations of the linear function to 225° and to 135°, respectively. Indeed, whereas the mean of the distribution was close to that found for 180° (as noted above), this mean was not at all representative of the individual reaction times and, in fact, falls close to the minimum separating the two modes. (Although the individual subjects differed considerably in their tendency to go the long or the short way around, all but one of the eight subjects had more reaction times either within the time interval centered at the linearly predicted value for 225° or for the 135° than within the same-sized intervening interval centered at the value for 180°.)

Reaction Times Following Delayed Presentations of the Second Stimulus

Rationale. In the experiments described so far, the two perspective drawings were viewed simultaneously by the subject during the entire decision process on each trial. According to the theory of mental rotation, however, it might be possible to delay the presentation of the second stimulus without affecting the over-all reaction time (from the onset of the first stimulus to the execution of the response)—provided that the subject knows both the axis and direction of the required rotation in advance. This is because the subject can then begin the mental rotation of the first stimulus as soon as it appears and, as long as the second stimulus is presented before the rotation reaches the angle of that stimulus, the subject will be able to proceed to that orientation and to make the required match-mis-match comparison just as rapidly as if the second stimulus had been present all along.

In fact, if the delay of the second stimulus is made equal to the rotation time previously estimated for that angular difference when the two stimuli were presented simultaneously, the rotation would be essentially completed upon the onset of the second stimulus. Since the subject would then be in a postiion to make a direct template-like match of an already rotated internal representation against the externally presented second stimulus, the reaction time, when measured from the onset of that second stimulus, should now become uniformly short and relatively independent of that angular difference. This prediction is in apparent contrast to predictions from alternative, nonrotational theories which would seem to require the physical presence of the second stimulus in order for the decision process (e.g., of feature-by-feature comparison of the two pictures) to get under way.

Accordingly, in a further experiment using six of the eight subjects from the experiment just described, Metzler (1973) revised the procedure so that, following an instruction as to the axis of rotation, each trial had the following sequential structure: First one of the two perspective views was presented until the subject actuated a foot switch to signal a state of readiness to maintain an adequate mental image of its shape. Thereupon that first perspective view vanished, to be immediately replaced by a uniformly colored field that, according to a predetermined random sequence, was either red or blue. The subject had previously been trained to imagine a clockwise or counterclockwise rotation of the object (about the already specified axis) depending upon this color. Then, after a delay that was predetermined but unknown to the subject, the second perspective view appeared in place of the colored field. As before, the subject was then to actuate a right- or a left-hand switch as rapidly as possible to indicate whether the second object was the same as or different from the first.

For each subject and for each axis and angle of rotation, the delay was chosen to be identical to the mean rotation time estimated for that subject, axis, and angle from the preceding experiment (in which the views were presented simultaneously). This rotation time was estimated simply by subtracting (for that subject and axis of rotation) the previously measured reaction time for $0°$ from the previously measured reaction time for the angular difference on the given trial. However, one angular difference that was included ($270°$) exceeded any of the angular differences in the previous experiment and, so, had to be determined by linear extrapolation. The subject's reaction time was measured from the onset of the second stimulus.

The prediction of the theory of mental rotation in this situation would seem to depend upon the variability of a subject's rate of mental rotation. To the extent that a subject's rate of rotation (for a given axis) is constant and independent of the presence or absence of the corresponding external stimulus, the reaction time to the onset of the appropriately delayed second stimulus should, as we noted, be constant (i.e., independent of the angle of rotation) and short (i.e., close to the intercept of the reaction-time function for simultaneous presentation).

To the extent that a subject's rate of rotation varies from one trial or situation to the next, however, the mean time used to determine the delay on a particular trial will tend to lead to an overshoot or an undershoot, depending upon whether the subject was rotating faster or slower than average on that trial. In such cases, a further, corrective rotation would presumably have to be carried out following the presentation of the second stimulus. Since the average undershoot or overshoot will tend to be larger for larger angular differences in orientation, the reaction-time function would be expected to increase monotonically, rather than remain strictly horizontal, for subjects who had more variable rotation times as estimated from the previous experiment. For this reason, it is desirable to examine the reaction-time data separately for the two subgroups of subjects whose estimated rotation times were, respectively, least and most variable in the preceding experiment.

Results. The results, which are displayed in Figure 3.15 for the "same" pairs, are in gratifying agreement with expectations based on the theory of mental rotation. The six subjects are divided, here, into the four whose reaction times in the previous experiment were relatively stable (S s 1, 3, 4, 5, included on the left), and the two remaining subjects whose reaction times had been appreciably more variable and, in addition, whose error rates had been markedly greater in that experiment (S s 2 and 6, included on the right). Note that, for the four subjects whose rotation rates were estimated to be relatively constant, reaction times to the second stimulus were uniformly short (generally varying only between one second and about one-and-a-half seconds), whereas, for the two more variable subjects, reaction times increased monotonically with the angle of rotation (from a little over one second to somewhat over two full seconds at 270°). Even for these two more variable subjects, however, the slope has been considerably reduced by the introduction of a delay in the presentation of the second stimulus. The product-moment correlation between the variances for individual subjects in the preceding experiment and the slopes of the reaction-time functions for these same subjects in this experiment was .82 ($p < .05$).

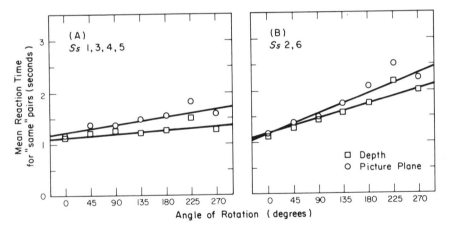

Figure 3.15 Mean reaction time, measured from the onset of the delayed member of each "same" pair, plotted as a function of angle of rotation, separately, for the four subjects with relatively small variability in rotation time (A) and for the two subjects with much greater variability (B) as estimated in a previous experiment.

The functions fitted, separately, to the data for the depth and picture-plane pairs indicate that the dependence of reaction time on angle of rotation is again quite linear and, as noted, nearly horizontal for the four most consistent subjects. The only noticeable departure of the points from the fitted linear functions is the consistently upward displacement of all four points at 225°. Even this discrepancy is interpretable however (and, for this reason, these points were not taken into account in finding the best-fitting straight line), for, as we subsequently discovered, subjects sometimes went the short (135°) way around for the 225° pairs in the preceding experiment. The consequence was that the distribution of reaction times was bimodal (Figure 3.14) and the mean reaction time was spuriously reduced. Thus the delay of the second stimulus was in effect based on an average of rotation times for 225° and 135° and, generally, too short for the 225° rotation required here. Presumably, then, on most trials subjects had to continue their rotation after the somewhat premature presentation of the second stimulus and, so, yielded the longer reaction times found at 225°. The results for the "different" pairs, which are not shown here, are entirely consistent with this explanation and show, in addition, an upward discrepancy at 180° due to the similar phenomenon of bimodality for the depth pairs at that angle already mentioned in connection with Figure 3.13. (See Metzler, 1973.)

Effects of Certain Other Factors

Same versus different objects. A few of the "factors investigated" which we listed in the introduction have not yet been evaluated in the light of the experimental results because, although they are of some interest in their own right, they do not bear in any crucial way upon the issues with which we are most centrally concerned. The factor that distinguished "same" pairs from "different" pairs, for example, does not tell us much about the structure of internal representations of three-dimensional objects or their transformations. Nevertheless, it does seem to be relevant for a more general concern with the over-all organization of the internal cognitive processes of which mental rotation may be one component.

The consistent result has been that the over-all mean time required to determine that two views are of objects of different three-dimensional shapes is longer than the mean time required to determine that they are the same. The recent findings, shown in Figure 3.13, suggest the further conclusion that this difference is independent of angle of rotation. That is, the reaction-time functions for the "different" pairs are higher than the corresponding functions for the "same" pairs primarily by virtue of their intercepts—their slopes are virtually identical. This same finding has uniformly emerged from studies that our colleagues and we have completed on the rotation of two-dimensional objects as well (see Cooper & Shepard, 1973b—partly reproduced in the following Chapter 4). The interpretation we favor is that subjects first test for a direct match between their (rotated) internal representation and the external stimulus. Whenever they detect a mismatch, then, they require an additional fixed amount of time to switch to the other response (cf., Clark & Chase, 1972; Trabasso, Rollins, & Shaughnessy, 1971).

Inclination of (natural) axis of rotation. We have already indicated the theoretical significance of the finding that rotations about an axis orthogonal to the line of sight, despite the greater complexity of the resulting transformation of the two-dimensional picture, require no longer than rotations about the line of sight itself. With respect just to the case in which the axis is nearly orthogonal to the line of sight, the recent experiments by Metzler (1973) provide new information concerning whether the projection of that axis onto the picture plane is oriented vertically, horizontally, or at 45° (with respect to true vertical as defined by the gravitational field). Although the slopes of the reaction-time functions were found to be very similar for all three of these cases, an apparently consistent tendency toward a smaller slope was noted in the case of rotations about the axis that projected vertically (with over-all reaction-time slopes of 6.9, 7.4, and 8.2 msec per degree for the vertical, inclined, and horizontal orientations, respectively). This is consonant with indications, e.g., from experiments by Shepard & Feng (see Shepard, 1975) and by Taylor (1972), that a slightly shorter time may be needed to imagine reflections of two-dimensional objects about the vertical than about the horizontal axis. It may also be related to the generally greater salience of bilateral symmetry when the axis of the symmetry has a vertical orientation (Zusne, 1970). (For some theories as to why the vertical axis might have a unique status see, e.g., Corballis and Beale, 1970; Sutherland, 1969, Uttley, 1956.)

Complexity of objects and naturalness of rotational axis. Despite the small differences just noted among the variously inclined axes of rotation in depth, we regard it as more significant that the reaction-time slopes for all of these depth rotations were quite similar to each other and uniformly quite a bit less than the slope for rotations about the line of sight. Since the slopes of the reaction-time functions in the earlier experiments were approximately equal for rotations in depth and in the picture plane, we tentatively attribute the present shorter reaction times for rotations in depth to the new circumstance that, for the depth pairs only, the axis of rotation coincided with the natural axis of the object itself.

Another new feature of these more recent experiments is, of course, that the objects themselves were simpler (in terms of number of component cubes and number of right-angle bends). A comparison of the reaction times for these simple objects with the reaction times for the more complex objects employed in the preceding experiments is complicated in the case of depth rotations, however, by the confounding of complexity with the just-discussed factor of naturalness of rotational axis. In the case of picture-plane rotations, on the other hand, the axis of rotation (viz., the line of sight) did not coincide with a natural axis of the object in any of the experiments. Nevertheless, for the picture-plane "same" pairs the slopes were about 20 and 26 msec per degree in Experiments I and II, respectively, but only about 8.3 msec per degree in the subsequent experiment with simpler objects. Correspondingly, the estimated rate of mental rotation in the picture-plane was well over twice as great for the objects consisting of three fewer cubes and one less bend.

THEORETICAL DISCUSSION [4]

Consideration of Some Alternative, Nonrational Theories

Comparison of rotationally invariant structural codes. For purposes of contrast, consider the following alternative model: First, by means of visual feature detectors or sensory analyzers of the sorts envisaged by Hubel and Wiesel (1962, 1968), Selfridge (1959), Sutherland (1969), and others, the subject detects the presence and interrelationships of the basic components of one of the two-dimensional perspective drawings—particularly, the variously oriented straight lines, the several types of vertices by which they are connected and, presumably, something of the structural realationships among these components *within the two-dimensional pattern.* Then, on the basis of some higher-level processing of these extracted features and their interrelationships, an internal representation, code, or verbal description is generated for each picture separately that captures the intrinsic structure of the three-dimensional object in a form that is independent of the particular orientation in which that object happens to be displayed. Finally, the two rotationally invariant codes that have been thus independently derived are directly compared with each other, and the subject responds "same" or "different" according to whether there is or is not an exact, part-for-part match between these two separately generated codes. However, because in this model the two pictures are analyzed independently, there could not on the average be any dependence of over-all reaction time upon the *relative* orientations of the two objects. As it stands, then, this model predicts that, when mean reaction time is plotted as a function of angular departure, the resulting function should be horizontal rather than monotonically increasing to a value that is four to five times as great at 180° as at 0°. Moreover, this model predicts that subjects should have no difficulty in learning to recognize each of the two isomeric versions of one of the objects absolutely—without reference to the other version. For, a subject who derives some sort of a rotationally invariant structural description for one version should have no difficulty in learning to associate one arbitrary name with that version and another arbitrary name with its mirror image. Even after 1600 trials of our first experiment, however, subjects still reported that they could not identify any of the objects absolutely but could only determine whether two pictures were of identical objects or of mirror images by comparing them with each other. (And, of course, they claimed that in order to make this comparison they generally had first to perform a mental rotation.)

This is not at all to say that subjects could not be trained to adopt a nonrotational strategy of the sort just considered. In fact perhaps the strongest argument for the claim that most subjects do not spontaneously do so (and that subjects in our experiments, in particular, did not do so) is that, when subjects *are* induced to adopt such an alternative strategy, they apparently generate very different reaction-time functions. This is suggested, anyway, by the preliminary results (for only three subjects) from an experiment carried out at Stanford by Arthur Thomas. In that experiment subjects were trained to encode each stimulus in the way we have been considering and to judge sameness or difference in terms of a match or mismatch of the generated codes. As a result, their reaction-time functions became very nearly flat. Indeed, for one subject, the reaction time at 180° was only about 150 msec. longer than at 0°, rather than some three to four full seconds longer as in our own experiments.

Perhaps significantly, even these subjects, who had been trained to adopt a "nonrotational" strategy, reported the extensive occurrence, during the encoding phase, of visual imagery and, particularly, of visual and/or kinesthetic representation of transformations in space. Hence, although neither of the two codes generated in this way nor the subsequent comparison between them are visual or spatial in character, the process of deriving the two codes from the two visually presented pictures seems to depend upon mental analogs of motions in three dimensional space including, apparently, a sequence of rotations. Despite the apparent feasibility of a very different strategy of verbal analysis, therefore, it remains doubtful whether it is possible for human subjects to discriminate between isomeric three-dimensional shapes, when these are presented in different orientations, without some recourse to analog operations including mental rotations.

Direct feature-by-feature comparison. We have argued that any explanation based upon the notion that rotationally invariant representations extracted from each of the two pictures separately are then compared with each other can be rejected because it fails to explain the fact that reaction time continues to increase monotonically as far as 180°. However, a related possibility remains—i.e., that the subject compares the two presented pictures feature by feature and, without either generating a rotationally invariant code or carrying out any sort of mental rotation of either object as a whole, is able to determine whether or not all of the corresponding features of the two objects achieve a suitable match. The monotonic increase in reaction time would then be explained by the claim that the comparison of corresponding features becomes more difficult and hence more protracted as the angular difference in portrayed orientation of the two objects increases.

Theories of this type, too, encounter several difficulties. First, although they provide a basis for explaining the monotonic increase in reaction time with orientational discrepancy, they do not seem to offer a comparable basis for explaining why this increase should be so precisely linear. Nor do such theories provide a ready account for the equivalence of the slopes of the reaction-time functions for the picture-plane and depth pairs. For, in order to explain the dependence of reaction time upon angular difference, we must suppose that the features that are being compared are the features of the two-dimensional drawings, which differ more and more with angular departure, and not the features of the three-dimensional objects, which are the same regardless of orientation. But, if the comparison is between features of the two-dimensional pictures, one would expect that the comparison would take appreciably less time when these features differ by a simple rigid rotation in the picture plane than by the two-dimensionally much more complex, nonrigid deformation induced by a rotation of the object in depth. And, for similar reasons, if the features of the two-dimensional pictures are what are being compared one would expect that (relative to a fixed angle of rotation in three-dimensional space) the effect of intervening discontinuities in those features would be considerably more pronounced than was found (see Figure 3.7).

Further objections to such nonrotational theories are raised by two more recent experimental findings reported by Metzler (1973) and, briefly, in the preceding experimental section. One of these is the finding that, beyond 180°, reaction time is bimodally distributed with the upper mode corresponding to the linear extrapolation of the reaction-time function to angles larger than 180° and the lower mode corresponding to the linear extrapolation of that function *backward* to a point the same distance from 180°. (Figure 3.14). In view of the fact that the reaction-time distributions up to 180° are sharply-peaked unimodal distributions, the particular bimodality found at 225° strongly suggests the following conclusion:

Contrary to theories of feature-by-feature comparison, it is not the difference between the two pictures as such that determines reaction time. Rather, as required by a theory of mental rotation, it is the particular path or trajectory that the subject takes in passing from one picture to the other—specifically, whether by mentally rotating the long or the short way around the 360° circle.

The second additional finding that appears to pose a problem for theories of feature-by-feature comparison is this: When the presentation of the second picture is delayed until the subject should have reached that orientation by a process of mental rotation, the response to that second picture is made with a reaction time that, for most subjects, is uniformly short and independent of that orientation (Figure 3.15). Indeed, this is true even for rotations beyond 180°. This, too, fits nicely with the notion that the subject starts with one picture and then mentally passes over a certain trajectory toward the second picture and, further, that comparison between the internally transforming representation and the second picture need not be made until the transformational process is completed at the end of the trajectory. This is in contrast to any theory of feature-by-feature comparison that requires that, even after the appearance of the second picture, the comparison process will take longer when the second picture is more different from the first.

We can not of course rule out the possibility that some elaboration of a theory of feature-by-feature comparison or some perhaps quite different, nonrotational theory will be shown capable of accounting for all of our empirical findings. For the present, however, the theory of mental rotation seems to us to provide the account of our findings that is at once the simplest, the most complete, and the most consonant with the introspective reports of the subjects themselves.

Analog Representation of External Objects and Their Transformations

Mental rotation as an analog process. What we wish to argue is the following: In order to prepare for the presentation of a rotated object, subjects are able to imagine that object in the rotated orientation and, so, are able to respond to it with considerable speed and accuracy when it then appears (Figure 3.15). But, if the angle of rotation is at all large, subjects can only prepare for the appearance of the object in the rotated orientation by first passing through other states of preparation corresponding to an ordered sequence of intermediate orientations (see, also, Cooper & Shepard, 1973b, Experiment II—in the following Chapter 4).

It is as if the only way the subject can represent the three-dimensional object is by means of some sort of internal model that is, at some suitably abstract level, structurally isomorphic to that object (cf., Attneave, 1974b). Consequently, any intermediate stage of processing must also preserve this internal model, or the structural information about that object will no longer be available for comparison with the second stimulus. But, according to this reasoning, the structural information can be preserved only through small adjustments in the representation. Thus, in order to prepare for a large rotational displacement, there is no choice but to carry out a sequence of these small adjustments, each of which preserves the essential structure, until the desired orientation is finally achieved.

Some subjects reported that they imagined the upper L-shaped part of one object rotated into congruence with the corresponding L-shaped part of the other object and then returned to carry out this same mental rotation on the lower part to see whether it was thereby brought into congruence with the corresponding lower part of the other object. Possibly other subjects may, without necessarily realizing it, have been rotating each object piece by piece rather than as a unit. Thanks to our colleague Dr. Norman Mackworth, we were able to use the eye camera that he developed (Mackworth, 1967) to videotape the patterns of fixations of both an experienced and an inexperienced subject while each was making "same"-"different" judgments for some pairs selected from our first experiment. Preliminary examination of these recordings indicates that, for both subjects, fixation shifted back and forth between the two perspective views during the course of the mental rotation, and the number of such shifts tended to be smaller in the case of the more experienced and faster subject. However the results of the experiment in which the presentation of the second stimulus was delayed indicate strongly that, in that experiment anyway, the objects were rotated in a unitary manner rather than piecemeal. Still, the possibility that eye movements provide useful indications of the fine-grain structure of the inner process seems to warrant further exploration.[5]

In summary, the theory of mental rotation seems to furnish the only presently available account for the principal findings of the experiments reported here: namely, (a) that the time required to complete the process increases linearly with the angle of rotation, (b) that it is bimodally distributed for angles beyond 180°—in correspondence with the subject's choice of going the short or the long way around the 360° circle, and (c) that the process can be completed in advance of the presentation of the second stimulus—provided that the subject already knows the axis and direction of the required rotation.

Representation of three-dimensional objects. But what exactly is the nature of the "internal model" that is transformed in this way?

Although we can not yet say anything specific about the representation of three-dimensional objects at the neurophysiological level, our results do seem to place some significant formal or abstract constraints on the nature of the representation. Perhaps the most important of these is that the internal representation embodies important structural features of the three-dimensional object that are not manifest in the two-dimensional projection of that object on the surface of the retina, while the features peculiar to this two-dimensional projection appear to have little influence on the internal process.

This conclusion is supported by the finding that, for a given angle of rotation of the object in three-dimensional space, the reaction time is relatively independent of whether the two-dimensional projection undergoes (a) a simple, rigid rotation in its own plane, (b) a more complex, nonrigid deformation that nevertheless preserves topological structure, or (c) a still more complex, discontinuous transformation that alters even topological structure. It is also consonant with the postexperimental introspective reports of the subjects who generally claimed the following: (a) They interpreted the perspective drawings as rigid three-dimensional objects and, in an important sense, "saw" the angles corresponding to the corners of the cubes as right angles even though these angles varied widely from 90° in the two-dimensional picture plane. (b) They imagined the rotations as carried out in isotropic three-dimensional space and, in most cases, were completely unaware that the rotations differed with respect to the conservation of rigid or of topological structure in the resulting two-dimensional projection.

This is not, however, to say that the internal representation is structurally isomorphic to the three-dimensional object in itself, or that it has no unique relationship to the two-dimensional perspective view. For the three-dimensional structure of each object is inherent in that object and not in any way affected by rigid rotation. So, if the internal representations of two presented objects each encoded the intrinsic and rotationally invariant structure of its own object as such, these two representations could be compared for a match or mismatch, directly. No mental rotation would then be necessary, and reaction time would be independent of angular separation. Contrary to our experience, it would then also be easy to learn to recognize a particular object in itself, without regard to its presented orientation and without regard to any other object.

Clearly, then, the internal representation of an external object captures its three-dimensional structure—not as that structure exists in the object absolutely—but only as it appears *relative* to a particular angle of regard. Thus the internal representation shares properties with both the three-dimensional object and its two-dimensional perspective projection, without being wholly isomorphic to either. It resembles the perspective view in its incorporation of information (not contained in the object itself) concerning the relation of the object to the viewer. And it resembles the object, in that cognitive operations upon the representation are more simply related to properties specifiable in three-dimensional space than to properties peculiar to the particular two-dimensional projection. What the representation really represents, then, is the appearance, from a particular point of view, of the object in depth.

But what do we mean by "the appearance of the object in depth" —particularly in view of introspective indications that the internal representation may often be rather schematic and not purely visual? It is tempting to suppose that the internal representation is a relatively abstract scheme that, although partially isomorphic to the spatial structure of the external object, is not exclusively tied to any one modality. In part the representation resembles a "program" or "subroutine" that can be variously executed to cause the hand to reach out appropriately in depth to grasp the object (cf., Festinger, Ono, Burnham, & Bamber, 1967; Shepard, 1975) as well as to generate a set of two-dimensional features for the purposes of rapid test against a retinal projection. The results of spatial transformations appear to be anticipated by means of a succession of small parametric adjustments that progressively alter the properties of the representation corresponding to the particular point of view, while leaving invariant the properties corresponding to the object's inherent structure.

Implications concerning cognitive processes generally. In the context of the general subject of human cognitive processes, the problem of a particular, apparently nonverbal process such as mental rotation of three-dimensional objects may seem rather special. However, the possibility should be considered that the long-standing preoccupation of psychologists with exclusively verbal processes in learning, memory, problem solving, and the control of behavior generally may be a reflection more of the relative accessibility of verbal processes than of the preeminent role that verbal processes play in human thought.

Nonverbal mediating representations including mental images and mental transformations on such images are much more difficult to externalize. Moreover, because such mediators differ in kind (not just in degree) from overt responses, they can not, as some have proposed for subvocal speech, be theoretically treated simply as previously learned overt responses; that is, as responses that have merely retreated inward where their now covert occurrences are still governed by the original, externally reinforced habits. It is hardly surprising that, during its long submission to the strictures of extreme behaviorism, psychology found little room for even the term "mental image." However, with the increasing awareness of how much has been systematically ignored and with the consequent search for new techniques for the experimental study of inner processes, work on the structure and function of mental imagery has increased dramatically.

By definition, any "imaginable" physical operation can be tried out in a purely mental way before taking the time, making the effort, or running the risk of carrying it out in physical reality. Possibly a significant part of the planning and internal guidance of individual behavior depends upon such nonverbal, analogical thinking. This possibility is suggested, anyway, by the appreciable improvement in complex perceptual-motor skills that have been found to follow purely mental practice (Rawlings, Rawlings, Chen, & Yilk, 1972; Richardson, 1969).

Among those external operations that can be simulated internally, rigid transformations on objects in three-dimensional space would seem to be of fundamental importance. The analog operation that we are specifically considering here, viz., "mental rotation," seems to play a central role in tasks ranging from the relatively mundane and concrete one of planning the arrangement of furniture in a room, to the relatively more intellectual and abstract ones of solving problems in geometry, engineering design, or stereochemistry.

4 | Chronometric Studies of the Rotation of Mental Images

Originally authored by Lynn A. Cooper and Roger N. Shepard

The experimental paradigm introduced in this chapter differs from that used in the original experiment on mental rotation (described in the preceding Chapter 3). Instead of determining how the time that subjects need to compare two simultaneously presented objects depends on the angular difference between their two orientations, we determine how the time that subjects take either to prepare for or to respond to a single object (alphanumeric character) depends on its angular departure from the orientation in which that object is expected —whether its conventionally defined upright orientation or some other, prespecified orientation. The findings indicate (a) that discrimination between standard and reflected versions of a rotated character requires a compensating mental rotation, (b) that subjects who are given advanced information as to the orientation of a prespecified test stimulus can carry out the required mental rotation before that stimulus is actually presented, and (c) that during such a preparatory process, the orientation in which the test stimulus would (if presented) be most rapidly discriminated, is actually rotating with respect to external space.

Accumulating evidence indicates that to be more prepared for a stimulus is to have, in advance, a more appropriate internal representation of that stimulus. In a particularly relevant line of work, Posner and his associates have developed successful paradigms for determining the form of the internal representation remaining from a previously presented stimulus by measuring the time subjects take to respond discriminatively to an ensuing, related stimulus (e.g., Posner, Boies, Eichelman, & Taylor, 1969). They have shown that when subjects are instructed to indicate whether the second of two successively presented letters has the same name as the first, their response "same" is approximately 80 to 100 msec faster

Reprinted by permission from Chapter 3 of the volume *Visual information processing,* edited by W. G. Chase and published by Academic Press, 1973.[1]

when the two letters are physically identical ("R" and "R") than when they are identical only in name ("R" and "r"). The notion here is that a subject whose internal representation in short-term memory is of the most appropriate form (e.g., a "visual code" of the same internal structure as the ensuing visual stimulus) can respond very rapidly by matching this internal representation against that ensuing stimulus by some relatively direct, template-like process. When, however, the memory representation is of a less appropriate form (e.g., a visual code of a different structure—lower as opposed to upper case—or an auditory-articulatory code of the name of that letter), additional time is needed to access the name of the ensuing stimulus and then to test for a match between the two derived (but case-invariant) names.

Additional evidence that a visual representation mediates physical-identity matching lies in the disappearance of the superiority of the physical-identity match when the interval between the two letters reaches about two seconds. Presumably the visual representation of the first letter has faded during intervals of this length. Posner et al. (1969) also report that when subjects are motivated to attend specifically to the visual aspects of the first stimulus (i.e., when subjects always know what the case—upper or lower—of the second stimulus will be), then the speed of the physical-identity match, relative to the name-identity-only match, is maintained over longer interstimulus intervals. Finally, Posner and his associates have presented evidence that visual codes can be generated in the absence of an external visual stimulus. If subjects are given the name of the first letter in auditory form only, some 750 msec prior to the onset of the second stimulus, and if the case of this second letter is known in advance, then reaction times are as fast as those obtained for visual-visual matches of physical identity. The approximately .75-sec lead time that seems to be required for this is, presumably, the time it takes a subject to construct an internal visual representation of the named letter.

Mental Transformations

Reaction-time experiments of the sort reported by Posner and his associates appear to furnish rather strong evidence concerning the nature of particular internal representations—specifically whether they are principally visual or verbal in form. However, the question still remains whether these particular internal representations or "codes" are what we ordinarily refer to as mental images. The implied contrast, here, is with the possibility that the "visual code" postulated by Posner consists (as he himself has suggested) solely in the priming of certain relevant feature detectors in the sensory receptor system. The resulting state of heightened readiness of the receptor system for certain specific patterns could account for the demonstrated reduction in reaction times to just those patterns. However, this selective priming of lower-order feature detectors would not in itself constitute what we ordinarily refer to as a mental image, for, by hypothesis, the state of readiness would not have any cognitive consequences for the subject in the absence of the subsequent presentation of a related external stimulus. (Consider, for example, that one's perceptual system is more tuned to register the appearance of a familiar than an unfamiliar word without one's in any sense having a prior mental image of the more familiar word.) Presumably, to have a mental image, then, is to activate an internal representation that—in addition to preparing one for a specific external stimulus —can be used as a basis for further information processing even if the relevant stimulus is never actually presented. Such further information processing could include, for example, the generation of a verbal description of the mental image.[2]

The experiments that we wish to describe here follow Posner in the use of the selective reduction of reaction times to an ensuing visual stimulus for purposes of demonstrating a structural correspondence between (a) the internal representation with which the subject attempts to prepare for an upcoming stimulus and (b) the external stimulus itself. In addition, we introduce the new requirement that, in order to be fully prepared for the anticipated stimulus, the subject must first perform a transformation on the internal representation —specifically, a transformation that corresponds to a rigid rotation of the stimulus in space. This addition serves two purposes. First, by demonstrating that the subject can perform such a transformation on an internal representation, we establish that this representation is accessible to that subject for further cognitive processing. The representation then satisfies the important condition just set forth for its classification as a mental image. Second, by requiring a transformation that corresponds specifically to a spatial rotation, we provide further support for the claim that the representation or "image" is primarily visual or at least spatial in form.

Evidence that these internal representations are spatial in nature comes, also, from the postexperimental introspective reports. Our subjects typically claim that in preparing for the anticipated presentation of a rotated stimulus, they did in fact (a) form a mental picture of the anticipated stimulus and then (b) carry out a mental rotation of that picture into its anticipated orientation. Their tendency to generate such a verbal report is consistent with the supposition that the internal representation was accessible to introspection— as we should require of a mental image.

Of course, the verbalization of introspections need not be confined to reporting merely the existence and principal modality of a mental image. Reports dependent upon specific structural features of internal representations are of greater evidential value. To illustrate, in an experiment by Shepard and Feng (see Shepard, 1975) times were measured for subjects to report the identity of the letter that results when a specified spatial transformation is applied to a letter that is designated only by name. The subjects could readily report, for example, that the letter "N" turns into the letter "Z" when rotated 90°. Evidently, the internal representation they were manipulating had a definite internal structure that was analogous to the structure of the corresponding physical letter and that was internally available for further processing—including spatial transformation, visual analysis, and verbal report. Moreover, reaction times were consistently longer for more extensive transformations (e.g., longer for 180° than for 90° rotations), providing additional support for the notion that the images and operations were of a basically spatial character.

In the experiments that we shall be describing, mental transformations and the selective reduction of reaction times are used, jointly, to establish that the internal representations and mental operations upon these representations are to some degree analogous or structurally isomorphic to corresponding objects and spatial transformations in the external world. In all of these experiments, each transformation consists simply of single rigid rotation of a visual object about a fixed axis. In order to make the discrimination more demanding, hence to force subjects to carry out a mental rotation, we adopted the technique (introduced by Shepard and Metzler, 1971) of requiring the subject to discriminate between a stimulus and its mirror image—not merely between one stimulus and an entirely different stimulus.

EXPERIMENT I. DETERMINATION OF THE TIMES REQUIRED TO PREPARE FOR AND RESPOND TO A ROTATED STIMULUS

In the experiment we report now, we controlled the time during which advance information about orientation was available to the subject prior to the presentation of the rotated test stimulus itself. If subjects do indeed carry out some sort of mental rotation in the process of preparing for a tilted stimulus, this process should require more time for its completion, since the orientation indicated in the advance information departs by larger angles from the standard upright orientation. Moreover, failure to complete this process of preparation prior to the onset of the ensuing stimulus should result in an increase in the reaction time to that stimulus, since in this case some further mental rotation will have to be carried out *after* the onset of the tilted stimulus itself. Thus by determining how reaction time depends both upon the angle of the tilted stimulus and upon the duration of the advance information as to that angle, we hoped (a) to obtain somewhat more direct evidence that the generation and rotation of a mental image is in fact a part of the process of preparation for a rotated stimulus, and (b) to determine something about the time required to carry out this preparatory mental rotation.

Method

Subjects. Eight subjects—seven Stanford students and one of the authors (RNS)—were run under all experimental conditions. The first four subjects were run in the complete factorial design, which required about seven hours of participation from each subject. The second four were run in a half-replicate design and served for three to four hours each. (Although five male and three female subjects were included, no consistent differences were observed in the performances of the two sexes.)

Stimuli. The stimuli were all asymmetrical alphanumeric characters, specifically the three upper-case letters (R, J, G) and the three arabic numerals (2, 5, 7) exhibited in Figure 4.1. Each of these

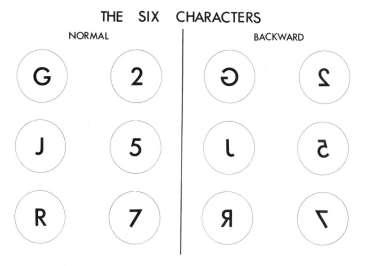

THE SIX CHARACTERS

Figure 4.1 Normal and backward versions of the six alphanumeric characters used as test stimuli in Experiment I.

six characters appeared in each of six equally spaced orientations around the circle (in 60° steps starting from the standard upright position, 0°) as illustrated for the letter "R" in Figure 4.2. Since subjects were familiarized with both the set of six characters and the set of six orientations, and since each occurred the same number of times in the test stimuli, the informational uncertainties concerning identity and orientation were equivalent in the absence of advance information. The subjects' task was simply to discriminate the normal versions of the characters (left-hand panels in the figures) from the reflected or backward versions of those same characters (right-hand panels) regardless of their orientations within the picture plane (Figure 4.2).

THE SIX ORIENTATIONS

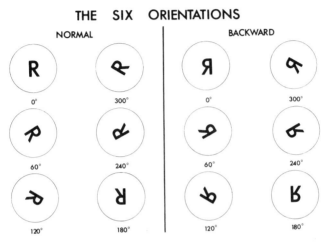

Figure 4.2 Normal and backward versions of one of the six characters, illustrating the six orientations in which it might appear as a test stimulus.

Following Shepard and Metzler (1971), we hoped that by requiring subjects to discriminate between mirror images of the same objects, we would prevent them from responding merely on the basis of some simple distinctive feature (such as the presence of an enclosed region in the case of the letter "R"), and thereby force them to carry out a "mental rotation" in order to compare a tilted character with the normal upright representation preserved in long-term memory. Notice, for example, that any one of the characters displayed in Figure 4.2 can almost immediately be identified as *some* version of the letter "R." In the cases in which that character is markedly tipped, however, it seems to take some additional time to determine whether that letter is normal or backward. Typically, subjects report that they do in fact imagine a markedly tilted character rotated back into its upright orientation to determine whether it is normal or backward, but that this is unnecessary for merely determining its identity. Indeed we suggest that subjects may have to identify a character before they can determine which is the top of the character and thereby know how the character must be rotated to bring it into its upright orientation.

The advance information cues, when presented, appeared centered within the same circular aperture as the subsequently ensuing test stimulus. The identity cue was displayed in the form of an outline drawing of the normal, upright version of the upcoming test stimulus, and the orientation cue appeared as an arrow passing through the center of the circular field and pointing in the direction at which the top of the test stimulus would appear. Figure 4.3, which shows the sequence of visual displays that would appear within the circular aperture on an illustrative trial, provides a more concrete idea of the appearance of the identity and orientation cues.

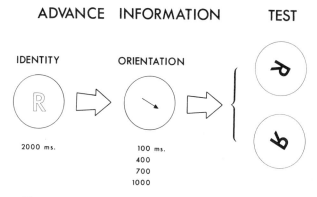

Figure 4.3 Sequence of visual displays appearing within the circular aperture on a trial of type B, in which *both* identity and orientation information were presented in advance of the test stimulus (illustrated here at 120 degrees).

The alphanumeric characters, which appeared both as test stimuli and as advanced information cues, subtended a visual angle of about 1½°. The visual angle of the circular aperture within which these characters appeared was 4°, and the luminance levels of the two or three fields that succeeded one another within this aperture (depending upon the condition) were all approximately 20 foot-Lamberts.

Structure of individual trials. The subject sat in a dimly illuminated room with head pressed against the shaped rubber light shield surrounding the viewing window of the tachistoscope. This permitted binocular viewing of all stimuli, but prevented physical rotation of the head. Following a warning signal at the beginning of each trial, the subject fixated the circular field where the test stimulus and the advance information cues (if any) were about to appear, with left and right thumbs positioned on the two response buttons located on a hand-held box. The subject always used the preferred thumb (i.e., the right thumb except in the case of our one left-handed subject) to register a decision that the test stimulus was normal, and the nonpreferred thumb to signal that the stimulus was backward. The two cases, normal and backward, occurred equally often according to a random sequence. The test stimulus always remained on until after the subject's response.

Each subject ran in eight different conditions of type and duration of advance information. Of central concern are the four variable time conditions (labeled "B" in Figures 4.3 and 4.4) in which *both* identity and orientation information were supplied. On these trials, the identity cue was displayed for 2000 msec, immediately followed by the orientation cue, which persisted for 100, 400, 700, or 1000 msec (depending upon which of the four conditions of type B was in effect). The orientation cue was then immediately replaced by the actual test stimulus. As indicated in Figure 4.3, even after having been provided with advance information about both the identity and orientation of the ensuing test stimulus, the subject still had to await the actual presentation of that stimulus in order to determine whether it was the normal or the backward version of that character at that orientation.

Figure 4.4 schematically illustrates the other four conditions, along with the conditions of type B (described above), for the case in which the test stimulus was to appear at 120°. The remaining four conditions were as follows: N, in which *no* advance information was provided (but only a 2000 msec blank warning and adaptation field); I, in which only *identity* information was supplied; O, in which only *orientation* information was furnished; and finally C, in which the identity and orientation information were presented in a *combined* form followed by a 1000 msec blank field before the onset of the test stimulus. The purpose of interposing the blank field in this last condition, C, was to ensure that the response to the test stimulus was based upon comparison with a representation in memory and not upon a purely sensory discrimination of continuity or change in the outline of the external visual display (for normal or backward test stimuli, respectively). For all conditions illustrated in Figure 4.4 the large unfilled arrows signify *immediate* replacement, upon the offset of one visual display, of the display shown just to its right (always within the same circular aperture).

Conditions I and C provided two reference points with which to compare the four variable time conditions B. At one extreme, when the duration of the orientation information is made very short (as in the B-condition with only 100 msec), we should expect that the subjects' reaction times to the test stimuli would approximate

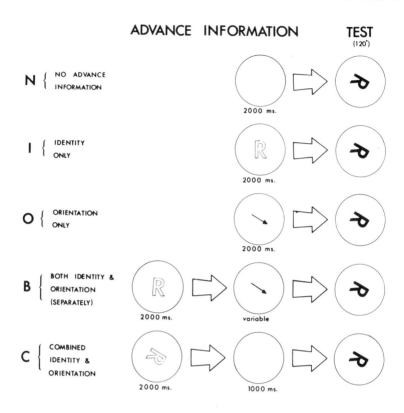

Figure 4.4 Schematic illustration of the five basically different types
of conditions, N, I, O, B, and C. (Since type B subsumes four conditions,
with different durations of orientation information specified in Figure 4.3,
the total number of distinct conditions is eight.)

their reaction times to those same test stimuli when no advance information as to orientation has been provided (as in the I-condition). At
the other extreme, when the duration of the orientation information
is made sufficiently long (as in the B-condition with 1000 msec),
subjects may have time to generate an appropriate mental template
of the normal version of that character and to rotate it into the
designated orientation. If so, their reaction times to the ensuing
test stimulus should approximate those obtained when such a rotated
template is supplied visually (as in the C-condition), hence does
not have to be subjected to any mental rotation before comparison.

Overall experimental design. Individual trials were blocked by
condition, with 12 trials to a block. At the beginning of each such
block the subject was given explicit instructions concerning the
nature and duration of the advance information to be provided
on all trials within that block, and was then given practice trials

of that type until ready to proceed with the actual trials of the block. The order of trials within blocks was randomized subject to the constraint that each of the six orientations occurred twice within each block. Hence, although the subject knew whether there would be advance information and how long it would last, until that advance information (if any) was actually presented on a given trial, the subject did not know which of the six characters would come up next or in which of the six orientations it would appear.

The complete factorial design (used for the first four subjects) required the completion of 576 trials per subject in order to obtain one observation for each cell of the design. Each of these subjects was run for six one-hour sessions consisting of eight blocks (one for each of the eight different conditions) of 12 trials each. The order of conditions was counterbalanced over sessions. Prior to these six sessions, each subject was given an initial practice session to ensure familiarity with the stimuli, the experimental procedure, and the various conditions of advance information.

After all data had been collected from the first four subjects, we found that the mean reaction times in which we were interested were virtually unchanged when we recomputed them on the basis of only half of the observations selected from the entire factorial design by means of a "checkerboard" half-replicate design. Accordingly, the remaining four subjects were run only on the trials specified by this half-replicate design. After the initial practice session, therefore, each of these subjects completed only three one-hour sessions of 96 trials each, yielding a total of 288 observations per subject.

Subjects were instructed, for all conditions, to indicate whether the test stimulus was normal or backward (regardless of its orientation in the picture plane) as rapidly as they could, without making errors, by pressing the appropriate button on the response box. Although error rates for the different conditions and orientations were positively correlated with mean reaction times, error rates averaged over all conditions were uniformly quite low, ranging from 3.6 to 8.7 percent for individual subjects. Nevertheless, throughout the experiment all trials on which errors were made were later repeated until an errorless reaction time had been obtained from each subject for each combination of character, orientation, version (normal or backward), and condition called for by the factorial design (or its half-replicate variant).

Reaction-time Results

The effect of orientation of the test stimulus. First we consider the condition, N, in which the subject was given no advance information concerning the identity or orientation of the upcoming test stimulus. The mean reaction times for this condition (averaged over all correct responses to either the normal or the backward version of the test stimulus) are plotted as the uppermost curve in Figure 4.5. The independent variable, here, is the orientation of the test stimulus as specified in degrees of clockwise rotation from the standard upright orientation of the character. (In this and subsequent plots of this type, all points are independent except the points at 360° which merely duplicate the points at 0°.)

In the absence of any advance information concerning the upcoming stimulus, reaction time increases very markedly as the orientation of that stimulus departs from its standard upright orientation. Indeed, as we move from 0° to 180° there is a roughly twofold increase in mean reaction time, from between 500 and 600 msec at the upright orientation to nearly 1100 msec at the completely inverted orientation. From the symmetry of the curve we see that the increase in reaction time resulting from a given angle of tilt is the same for both clockwise and counterclockwise rotations. This increase is not strictly linear, however, but concave upward, with the sharpest increase occurring as we approach the completely inverted orientation of 180° from 60° away on either side (i.e., from the orientations of either 120° or 240°).

The reliability of the shape of this curve is indicated by its highly symmetric form as well as by the highly similar shapes of the two reaction-time curves plotted in Figure 4.5 just below the curve for condition N—namely, the curves for the conditions I and O, in which the subjects were given either identity information or orientation information only.

Despite the nonlinearity of these functions, we take the very marked increase in reaction time with departure of the test stimulus from its standard upright orientation to be supportive of the notion that the subject carries out some sort of a mental rotation. In particular, we suggest (a) that, in order to compare a markedly tilted character with the representation of the normal version of that character in long-term memory, the subject must first imagine the tilted character rotated into its upright orientation, and (b) that the greater this tilt, the longer it will take to complete the corrective rotation. Reasons for the nonlinearity of the increase in reaction time that are consistent with this notion of mental rotation will be presented in the theoretical discussion.

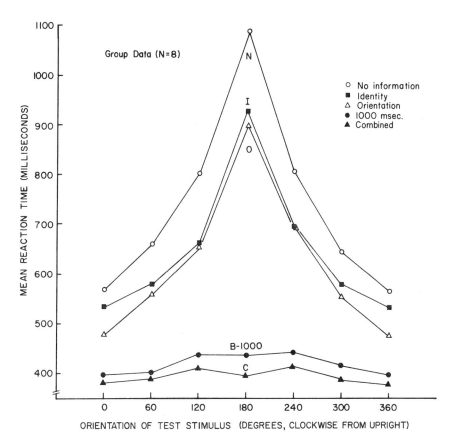

Figure 4.5 Mean reaction time as a function of orientation of the test stimulus for those conditions in which advance information, if presented at all, persisted for the maximum duration.

The effect of advance information as to identity and/or orientation. We turn, now, to a comparison among all five conditions in which the subjects were given adequate time to take full advantage of whatever advance information (if any) was provided; namely, conditions N, I, O, C, and the one B-condition in which the orientation cue persisted for the full 1000 msec. The five different curves plotted in Figure 4.5 exhibit the dependence of reaction time on orientation of the test stimulus for these five conditions.

These results show that the reaction-time curves for the two conditions (I and O) with advance information as to identity or orientation only—though somewhat lower than the corresponding curve for the condition (N) with no advance information—are nevertheless relatively close to it in height and, particularly, in overall shape. Moreover, and of central importance, they establish that the reaction-time curve for the condition (B), in which both identity and orientation information were separately presented, is dramatically lower than the other three curves and virtually flat.

Another aspect of the present results, not shown in Figure 4.5, is that the response used to signal that the test stimulus was the normal version of that character was consistently faster than the response used to signal that it was the backward version of that character—by a difference that was essentially constant over all conditions and orientations and that ranged from roughly 10 to 150 msec, depending on the particular subject. On the basis of other experiments in which the functions of the two hands have been systematically interchanged, it appears that the factor of overriding importance is the subject's choice of what to test for first (in this case, normalness or backwardness), rather than the particular hand that is then set to register a positive outcome of that test (cf. Clark & Chase, 1972; Trabasso, Rollins, & Shaughnessy, 1971).

The present results indicate three further things: First, relative to the condition in which no advance information is provided (N), the conditions in which either identity or orientation information is supplied (I or O) tend to produce reaction times that are shorter by a constant amount (roughly 100 msec), regardless of the orientation of the test stimulus. Second, the curve for the condition with both kinds of advance information presented separately (B) achieves a close approximation to a completely flat function. And third, by comparison with the new condition in which complete advance information was presented in combined form (C), we can now conclude that the internal representation that the subject constructs on the basis of separate information about identity and orientation (in condition B) is just about as efficient a mental template as a memory image of the rotated character itself (in condition C).

The effect of varying the duration of the orientation information. We turn now to a consideration of the remaining three B-conditions. In these conditions the duration of the advance information as to orientation was reduced (from the full 1000 msec) to values of only 700, 400, or 100 msec. The mean reaction times for these conditions (again averaged over all correct responses to both normal and backward stimuli) are plotted as a function of the orientation of the test stimulus in Figure 4.6. For purposes of comparison we also include the limiting reference or control conditions I and C already shown in Figure 4.5. As before these group curves are highly reliable and representative of the curves for individual subjects.

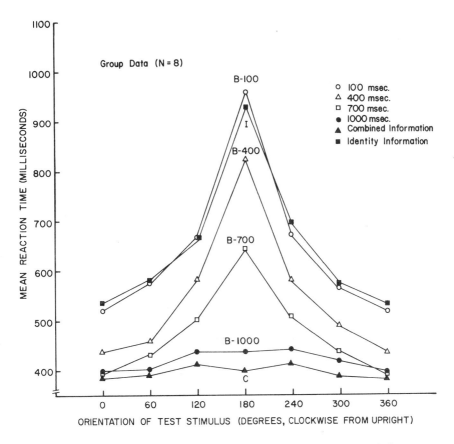

Figure 4.6 Mean reaction time as a function of orientation of the test stimulus for those conditions in which identity information was provided.

Comparisons among these curves enable us, for the first time, to make some quantitative inferences concerning the time that it takes to prepare for a stimulus that is about to appear in some rotated orientation. From the flatness of the function for the 1000-msec. B-condition, we know that this process of preparation can generally be completed within one second. However, when the duration of the orientation cue is reduced to 700 msec, a pronounced peak in the reaction-time function emerges at 180°, indicating that on the average the discriminative response to the ensuing test stimulus takes over 200 msec longer whenever that test stimulus appears in an inverted position. When the duration of the orientation cue is further shortened to 400 msec, the reaction times increase by another 200 msec at 180°, and also by some 80 msec at 60° on either side of 180°. Finally, when this duration is cut down to only 100 msec, the reaction times are essentially identical, at all orientations, to the reaction times when only identity information is provided (Condition I).

Following the experiment, the subjects themselves offered explanations for their reaction times under these B-conditions. Their explanations ran along the following lines: When the duration of the orientation cue was reduced below a second (e.g., to 700 msec), they were often unable to rotate their mental image of the anticipated stimulus around to 180° before that stimulus actually came on, although they usually were able to complete rotations of only 60° or even 120°. When the duration was further reduced (e.g., to 400 msec.), they were almost never able to get to 180° before the onset of the test stimulus and, now, often failed even to reach 120°. Finally, they reported that a duration of only 100 msec. was generally of no use at all, for by the time they were able to interpret the orientation cue, they had discovered that the test stimulus itself had already appeared.

Results for individual subjects. When we turn from the average reaction times for the group of eight subjects as a whole (Figures 4.5 and 4.6) to the corresponding reaction times for individual subjects, we immediately discover that there were stable and very substantial differences among subjects in their mean reaction times. However, these differences were very pronounced only for those conditions that tended to produce long reaction times; they all but disappeared for the conditions (B-1000 and C) in which complete advance information was furnished. Thus for the most difficult case in which no advance information preceded a completely inverted test stimulus (condition N at 180°), the mean reaction times varied over a more than twofold range, from just under 700 msec for the fastest subject to just over 1700 msec for the slowest. At the same time, though, the reaction times for the 1000-msec. B-condition (averaged over all orientations) ranged only from about 350 msec to a little under 500 msec for these same two subjects.

It appears that the average rate of mental rotation (which can be very roughly estimated as 180° divided by the difference between the reaction time at 0° and 180° under the N condition) varied from something like 800° per second for the fastest subject to something like 164° per second for the slowest. However, when subjects are already prepared with an appropriately oriented image of the upcoming stimulus (as in conditions B-1000 and C), these very different individual rates of mental rotation are not involved.

Consequently, in these conditions most subjects respond with approximately equal rapidity—within some 350 to 500 msec.[3]

If now we plot entire sets of reaction-time curves corresponding to those already displayed for the group of eight subjects as a whole (in Figures 4.5 and 4.6), we find that despite these enormous individual differences in average reaction time, the shapes and relational pattern of the curves are strikingly constant from subject to subject. Athough we have examined these curves for all eight subjects individually, it appears impractical to present them all here. Instead, we present complete sets of curves for just two representative subjects—namely, the one with the shortest and the one with the longest overall average reaction time. The patterns exhibited by these two appear to us to be typical of the patterns exhibited by the other, intermediate subjects.

The individual curves for these two extreme subjects are all displayed in Figure 4.7. The plots on the left, which correspond to earlier Figure 4.5, are for the conditions in which the advance information (if any) persisted for its maximum duration. The plots on the right, which correspond to the earlier Figure 4.6, are for all conditions in which identity information was provided (including those in which the advance information as to orientation was reduced in duration). The two upper plots are for the subject whose responses were, on the average, the quickest. The two lower plots are for the subject whose responses were, on the average, the slowest. Because the longest mean reaction times for this second subject were over twice as long as the longest mean reaction times for the first subject, the vertical scales in the two lower plots have been linearly compressed with respect to the vertical scales in the upper plots. Note, particularly, the extreme flatness of the curve produced by the faster subject under the B-1000 condition.

Various statistical analyses confirmed (a) that all eight subjects showed significant effects of duration, orientation, and interaction between duration and orientation, but (b) that there was no significant difference between the shapes of the flat reaction-time functions for conditions B-1000 and C or between the shapes of the peaked reaction-time functions for conditions N, I, and O.[4]

Distributions of reaction times under different conditions. So far we have been concerned with just the *means* of the distributions of reaction times for different conditions and orientations (whether for individual subjects or for the whole group). An examination of the entire distributions can provide additional information relevant to notions about what kinds of processes are going on within individual subjects. Although we have surveyed the computer-plotted distri-

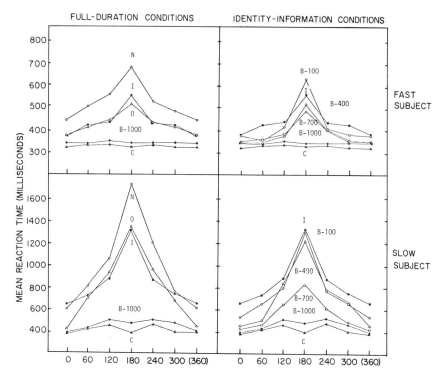

FULL-DURATION CONDITIONS   IDENTITY-INFORMATION CONDITIONS

Figure 4.7 Mean reaction time as a function of orientation of the test stimulus for two individual subjects—the fastest subject (upper panels) and the slowest subject (lower panels). Left-hand panels correspond to the group functions displayed in Figure 4.5, and right-hand panels correspond to the group functions displayed in Figure 4.6.

butions for all eight subjects, under all eight conditions, at each of the six orientations, it is impractical to display all 384 of these individual distributions here.

Comparisons among the distributions obtained from different subjects indicated, however, that the eight subjects could be divided into a group of five subjects with relatively long reaction times and a group of three subjects with relatively short reaction times. Moreover, distributions plotted for either group as a whole then turned out to be reasonably representative of all subjects within that group. Among all 48 combinations of condition and orientation, the most informative cases appeared to be (a) those in which the test stimulus came on, essentially without advance information as to orientation, at each of the four degrees of departure from upright, 0°, 60°, 120°, and 180° (whether in the clockwise or counterclockwise direction); and (b) those in which the test stimulus came on at 180°, but following periods in which advance information as to this orientation had been presented for 100, 400, 700, or 1000 msec.

Distributions of the first sort are displayed in Figure 4.8. In order to obtain relatively stable shapes, each curve is based upon the pooled data for the two essentially equivalent conditions I and B-100 and for all (three or five) subjects within the indicated group (fast or slow). The distributions for the three "fast" subjects (shown by solid lines) are relatively compact and symmetrical. The distributions for the five "slow" subjects (shown by dashed lines) tend to be somewhat broader (particularly at 120°). For both groups of subjects, the distributions shift to the right and become broader as the test stimulus departs more and more from upright. This rightward shift is considerably more marked for the five slower subjects. Perhaps what most characterizes these slower subjects, then, is a slower speed of mental rotation.

The second set of distributions of interest includes those for reaction time to a completely inverted test stimulus following various durations of advance information as to the 180° orientation. These distributions are displayed in Figure 4.9, for the three fast subjects, and in Figure 4.10, for the five slow subjects. Again, these pooled distributions, though slightly broader, appeared to be quite representative of the distributions for individual subjects from each group. At the top of these figures we see that when the orientation information was available for a full second (B-1000), the reaction-time distribution was quite compact, sharply peaked and, indeed, very similar in shape to that obtained under Condition C (in which the preparatory image had already been rotated for the subject). At the bottom we see that when the orientation information was available for only a tenth of that time (B-100), the distribution was shifted markedly to the right, spread out, and similar in shape to that obtained under Condition I (in which there was no orientation information). As in earlier Figure 4.8, this shift to the right was much greater for the slower subjects— which we should expect if their longer reaction times were due primarily to a slower rate of mental rotation (in this case, of the preparatory image rather than of the test stimulus itself).

Here, however, the intermediate cases (B-400 and, for the five slow subjects, B-700 too) yield distributions that are more spread out than the distributions even for the extreme case B-100. We could explain this by supposing that the rate of preparatory rotation is somewhat variable from trial to trial, depending in part upon the particular character to be rotated. (In fact, most subjects reported

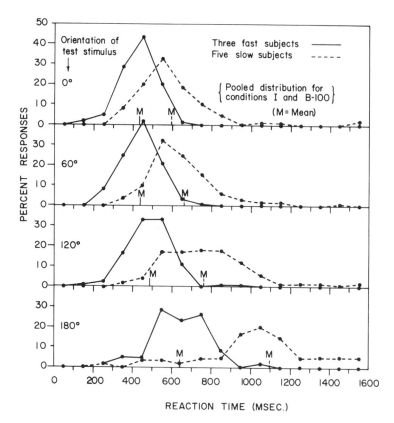

Figure 4.8 Distributions of reaction times to test stimuli presented at
0 degrees, 60 degrees, 120 degrees, and 180 degrees angular departures
from the upright orientation. Distributions are pooled over conditions in
which, effectively, no orientation information was provided (Conditions I
and B-100). Separate distributions are plotted for the three fast subjects
(solid lines) and the five slow subjects (dashed lines).

that some characters, e.g., R and 2, were generally easier than others,
e.g., 7 and J.) Under the extreme conditions we should expect
that on virtually all trials, the subjects either would be fully prepared
(Condition B-1000) or would not be at all prepared (Condition
B-100) for the inverted test stimulus. Consequently, their reaction
times would be consistently short or long, respectively. Under the
intermediate conditions, however, we should expect that on some
proportion of the trials the subjects would be prepared and on some
proportion they would not. When they were prepared, they would
be able to respond rapidly (perhaps as rapidly as under Condition
B-1000). When they were not prepared, though, their reaction times
would be longer and more variable. In the latter case they might

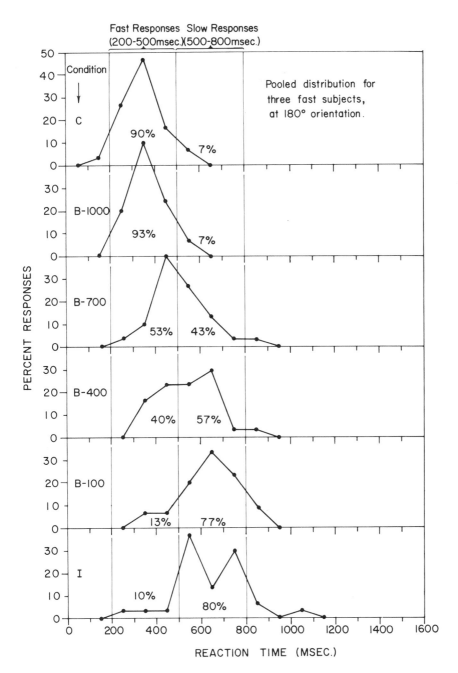

Figure 4.9 Distributions of reaction times to test stimuli presented at 180 degrees for the three fast subjects. Separate distributions are plotted for each condition in which identity information was provided.

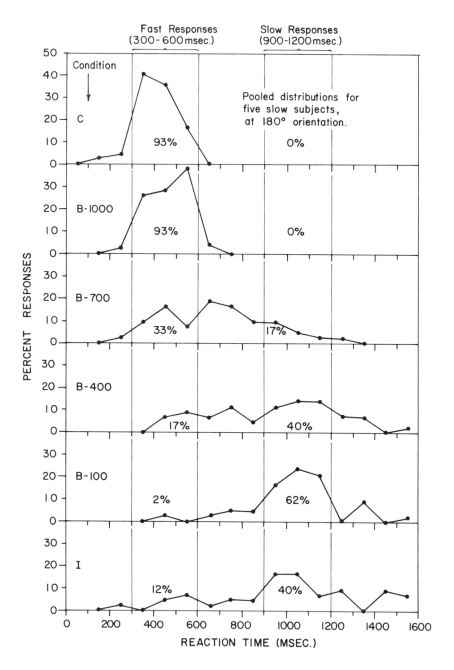

Figure 4.10 Distributions of reaction times to test stimuli presented at 180 degrees for the five slow subjects. Separate distributions are plotted for each condition in which identity information was provided.

drop their preparatory rotation and start all over with the test stimulus itself, in which case their reaction times would be comparable to their times under Condition B-100. Alternatively, they might continue their preparatory rotation into congruence with the test stimulus, in which case their reaction times could fall anywhere between their times for B-100 and for B-1000, depending on how far along they were with their preparatory rotation before the onset of the test stimulus.

It appears from Figure 4.9 that a fast subject typically responds in 200 to 500 msec when prepared for the inverted test stimulus and in 500 to 800 msec otherwise; and from Figure 4.10 that a slow subject usually responds in 300 to 600 msec when prepared and in 900 to 1200 msec when initiating rotation upon the presentation of the test stimulus itself. These two cases, labeled "fast responses" and "slow responses," are indicated in Figures 4.9 and 4.10 by the two vertical bands drawn there. Numbers have also been included to indicate, for each distribution, the percentage of its total area that falls within each of these two vertical bands. These numbers thus provide a very rough estimate of the percentage of trials of each type for which the subject was prepared for the inverted test stimulus either fully or not at all. For the five slow subjects, for example, we see that the estimate of the percentage of trials on which the subjects were fully prepared systematically declines from 93 when they had a full exposure to advance information as to orientation (in both Conditions C and B-1000), to only about 10 or less when they had little or no chance to take advantage of that advance information (in Conditions B-100 and I, respectively). The intermediate responses, which were made in 600 to 900 msec (e.g., in Condition B-700), may represent trials in which a subject, though not fully prepared at the onset of the test stimulus, was nevertheless able to continue the preparatory rotation until congruence was achieved. This would explain the reduction in overall processing time, as measured from the onset of the test stimulus.

Discussion

The nonlinear effect of orientation of the test stimulus. In the experiment by Shepard and Metzler (1971), the time subjects required to determine that two perspective pictures were of the same three-dimensional object increased in a remarkably linear manner with the angular difference in their portrayed orientations. This, together with the subjects' introspective reports, was taken to support the notion that they made each comparison by imagining one object rotated into congruence with the other and that this "mental rotation" could successfully be carried out no faster than about 60° per second in that task. If we wish to invoke a similar notion of mental rotation to account for the marked increase in reaction time to rotated alphanumeric characters, we need to explain why the increase in reaction time (shown in Figures 4.5 and 4.6) consistently departs from linearity.

At least four explanations appear consistent with the data. First, the representation or "template" for the normal, upright character in long-term memory may be so broadly tuned that this discrimination can often be made for characters tilted by 60° or even more without any need for mental rotation. Second, it may be that the rate at which an object can be mentally rotated increases with the familiarity of that object, and that letters and numbers are less familiar when viewed in more or less inverted orientations. Third, when the character was completely upside down, instead of imagining it rotated into its upright orientation within its own picture plane, subjects may sometimes have imagined it flipped rightside up about its horizontal axis. Then they either would imagine it flipped about its vertical axis (which is necessary to restore its original parity—normal or backward) or else would remember to reverse their response to the uprighted character (using the left thumb to indicate "normal" and the right thumb to indicate "backward"). An experiment by Shepard and Feng (see Shepard, 1975) has shown that it does take longer to imagine a letter flipped first about a horizontal and then a vertical axis than to imagine that same letter rotated 180° in the picture plane—even though the two ways of transforming the image result in the same final state. And fourth, the operations of determining the identity and/or the orientation of the test stimulus (which presumably must be completed before the rotation can even be started) may themselves increase nonlinearly, at least to some small extent, as the test stimulus departs from upright.

It is possible that any or all of the above explanations are to some degree correct for at least some subjects. Moreover, all four are specifically designed for the case of stimuli, such as alphanumeric characters, that have a well-defined standard or upright orientation. Hence, the fact that the reaction-time functions obtained by Shepard and Metzler were perfectly linear is compatible with these explanations (the three-dimensional nonsense shapes presented in that study had no uniquely established conventional or preferred orientation). We conclude, therefore, that the finding of a consistently nonlinear relation between reaction time and orientation of the test stimulus here does not weigh against the hypotheses that subjects typically used mental rotation to determine whether an inverted test stimulus was normal or backward.[5]

The nonadditive effects of advance information as to identity and orientation. A very central finding is that of a virtually flat reaction-time function under the 1000-msec B-condition (in which complete advance information is given, separately, for both identity and orientation). This finding offers substantial support for the notion that in preparing for the presentation of a tilted stimulus, the subject carries out a purely mental rotation of something that might be called a mental image of the anticipated stimulus. Further support comes from the subjects themselves who, after completing the experiment, typically claimed that in this B-condition—just as much as in the C-condition (in which the appropriate visual image was supplied to the subject already rotated)—they were ready with what seemed, introspectively, to be the same sort of mental image. Regardless of whether the orientation of this internal representation had been achieved by external, physical rotation (Condition C) or by purely internal, mental rotation (Condition B-1000), these subjects were equally ready to use this "rotated" internal representation as a template against which they could rapidly match the visually presented test stimulus when it then appeared in that same orientation.

What needs to be noted, however, is that such a mental rotation evidently cannot be carried out on the basis of just the orientation information alone. For, the curve for Condition O—far from being completely flat—has the same steep slope as the curves for the N, I, and 100-msec B-conditions, in which subjects were not given (or were not able to utilize) any orientation information.

This might seem surprising. To the extent that the subject has already been given information as to the orientation of a stimulus, it is natural to suppose that the redundant reappearance of the same information in the actual test stimulus should then have little effect. And this is, in fact, what has happened in the 1000-msec B-condition. There, as a result of having provided advance access to the orientation variable, that variable no longer had any effect on the latency of the subsequent response to the stimulus itself. Why is it, then, that advance access to the orientation variable did not in any way diminish the effectiveness of that same variable when it reemerged in the test stimulus in condition O?

The answer seems to be that, under the conditions of this experiment, subjects can only rotate the mental representation of a specific, concrete object or character. They evidently are not able to rotate a general, abstract frame of reference—at least when their head orientation is fixed with respect to gravitational upright (cf. Attneave & Olson, 1967; Rock & Heimer, 1957). In our experiment, when subjects were informed of both the character (e.g., the letter "R") and its orientation (e.g., at "4 o'clock"), they were able to imagine that character rotated into that orientation in advance of its actual presentation. When, however, they were informed only that the character would appear in, say, the 4 o'clock position without being told *which* character would appear in that position, they could only wait until the actual presentation of the character itself and then had to imagine it rotated into the upright orientation in order to determine whether it was normal or backward.

A consequence is that the effects of identity information and orientation information, though possibly quite additive when the stimulus appears in its upright orientation, become increasingly nonadditive as the orientation departs from upright. As is evident in Figure 4.5, each kind of information alone results in a roughly 100-msec drop in the reaction-time function as a whole, without having any appreciable effect on the shape of the function. When both kinds of information are provided, however, the reaction-time function becomes so much lower and flatter that there is a drop of at least 600 msec at 180°.

We are not saying that the advance presentation of orientation information alone has no effect on subsequent reaction time—only that it has no effect on the way in which reaction time depends upon the orientation of the ensuing test stimulus. The advance presentation of either identity or orientation information alone does have an effect—indeed, approximately the *same* effect—as is evident from the 100-msec decrease at all orientations. This is especially striking at 0° where the test stimulus appears in the standard upright position for all conditions. Consider, in particular, Conditions I and C at the 0° point. In both cases the subject sees essentially the same thing; namely, an upright outline of the appropriate character followed by the upright presentation of that same character (or its mirror image). Yet from Figure 4.5 we see that at 0°, mean reaction time was over 100 msec longer under Condition I than under Condition C; and this difference is statistically reliable.[4]

We think that the explanation for this difference does not lie in any difference in the physical displays under the two conditions. (That a one-second blank field is interposed between the advance information and the test stimulus in Condition C could only account for a longer, not a shorter, reaction time under that condition.) The explanation lies, rather, in the different interpretations that the subject has been instructed to place on the same advance information cue in the two types of trials. Under Condition C the appearance of an upright outline of the letter "R," for example, informs the subject both that the test stimulus will be the letter "R" and that it will appear in the upright orientation. Under Condition I, however, the appearance of that very same cue informs the subject only that the test stimulus will be the letter "R"; it provides no basis for assuming anything about the orientation in which it will appear.

How, then, does advance information about either identity or orientation alone have its effect upon reaction time? We argue that the only effect of presenting advance information either about identity or about orientation alone is to cut down, by a constant amount of about 100 msec., the time that it would otherwise take to determine the identity or orientation of the test stimulus itself. When, however, both kinds of advance information are furnished, the subject is able to proceed with an entirely different preparatory process of rotating a mental image of the indicated character into the indicated orientation and, thus, becomes able to respond with uniform rapidity to the ensuing test stimulus. (See Appendix, pp. 120-1).

The relationship between prestimulus and poststimulus rotation. The present experiment, unlike previously reported experiments on mental rotation, permits us to estimate not only the time required to respond to a rotated stimulus but also the time required to *prepare* for a rotated stimulus. We assume that both times include the time needed to carry out the rotation of a mental image. However, there are differences between the two cases.

When (as in Condition I) the rotation is started only after the onset of the test stimulus, we assume that the mental image of the test stimulus is rotated from the tipped orientation in which it has been presented back into the standard upright orientation in which it can be compared with the normal representation in long-term memory. When (as in Condition B-1000) the rotation is completed prior to the onset of the test stimulus, we assume that the mental image of the normal version of the designated character is rotated from the standard upright orientation in which its outline has appeared as the identity cue into the tipped orientation in which it is about to appear as the actual test stimulus. Moreover, the character that is being mentally rotated is continuously present as a visual stimulus in the first case, but is present, if at all, only as a memory representation in the second. The question naturally arises as to whether the mental images in these two cases (which require rotation in opposite directions and in the presence of different degrees of external support) are nevertheless rotated at similar rates.

Now, whenever some portion of the required mental rotation has been carried out in preparation for the upcoming test stimulus, the subsequent reaction time should depend less strongly upon the orientation of that test stimulus. Condition B-1000 furnishes the extreme example. Here the entire rotation is completed in advance and so results in a virtually flat reaction-time function. In the case of Condition B-400, however, the reaction-time function—though lower than the functions for Conditions I and B-100—does not differ from either of them in shape (Figure 4.6). (An analysis of variance for Conditions I and B-400, in particular, showed that the condition-by-orientation interaction was nonsignificant.

Essentially the same picture emerges from the reaction-time distributions plotted in Figures 4.9 and 4.10. Although the proportion of "fast" responses does increase as we move from Condition I to Condition B-400 (particularly for the three "fast" subjects), the modal peak of the 180° distribution shifts no more than 100 msec for either the "fast" or the "slow" subjects. A full 700-msec duration of the orientation cue is necessary for the reaction-time function to flatten appreciably (Figure 4.6) and for the modal peak of the reaction-time distribution to shift markedly to the left (Figures 4.9 and 4.10). Apparently orientation information must be supplied for a 400-msec period before there is a significant reduction in the amount of post-stimulus rotation on most trials.

By analogy with the time apparently required to determine orientation on the basis of the test stimulus itself, we might have expected that the time required to determine orientation on the basis of the advance cue would also take about 100 msec. However, if 100 msec sufficed to extract this information from the inclined arrow in a fully usable form, then the curve for Condition B-100 should have been displaced downward by some 100 msec from the curve for Condition I (in which the orientation information had to be determined *after* the presentation of the test stimulus). But there is no difference between the heights of the reaction-time curves for I and B-100, whereas the curve for Condition B-400 *is* displaced downward from both of these by about 100 msec. Accordingly, we tentatively arrive at the unexpected conclusion that close to 400 msec may be needed to complete the processing of the orientation cue. In addition to the time needed merely to determine the orientation of the tipped arrow, this time may include times needed to convert this information into a form applicable to an ensuing alphanumeric character and, possibly, to overcome any backward masking of the arrrow or disruption of its interpretation caused by the sudden onset of the test stimulus.

As a rough approximation, we suggest that following the onset of the orientation cue, (a) a period of about 400 msec is usually required before the preparatory rotation is effectively started and (b) a period approaching 1000 msec is needed to ensure that nearly all of the subjects have completed a rotation of 180°. By subtraction we conclude that the time required to complete a 180° preparatory rotation for one of these stimuli is 600 msec—or less, in view of the variability in the more directly estimated poststimulus rotation times (Figure 4.8). For if 600 msec suffices to ensure completion of a 180° rotation on almost *all* trials, then the time required to complete the preparatory rotation on an *average* trial is less than 600 msec.—perhaps closer to 400 or 500 msec. This estimate agrees well with the estimated time required to rotate 180° *after* the presentation of the test stimulus, since the differences between the mean reaction times for 0° and 180° under all of the four conditions, N, I, O, and B-100 (Figures 4.5 and 4.6), range between roughly 400 and 500 msec.

Separate consideration of the "fast" and "slow" subjects permits a further comparison of the prestimulus and poststimulus rotations. Notice in Figure 4.8 that as we move from 0° to 180°, the mean reaction time under conditions of poststimulus rotation (I and B-100) shifts about 200 msec for the three fast subjects and about 500 msec for the five slow subjects. Then notice in Figures 4.9 and 4.10 that as we move from Condition B-400 to the condition of prestimulus rotation, B-1000, the peak of the reaction-time distribution for a stimulus at 180° correspondingly shifts about 300 msec for the three fast subjects and about 500 msec for the five slow subjects. Again there is reasonably good agreement between the prestimulus and poststimulus cases (except, possibly, for the 100-msec discrepancy for the smaller group of three fast subjects).

We have been focusing here on those conditions in which a preparatory rotation either could be completed before stimulus onset (B-1000) or else, in most cases, could not even be started (I, B-100, and B-400). We turn now to a consideration of the relation between prestimulus and poststimulus rotation in the intermediate condition, B-700, in which the preparatory rotation is usually initiated but not completed prior to the onset of the test stimulus. Again it is best to discuss the groups of fast and slow subjects separately.

In the case of the group of five slow subjects, the reaction-time distribution for Condition B-700 (Figure 4.10) is widely spread out and contains the suggestion of three components—with modal peaks centered, respectively, in the 300-600 msec fast range, in the 600-900 msec intermediate range, and in the 900-1200 msec slow range (as these three ranges are depicted by vertical bands in the figure). We could interpret the (33%) fast responses as resulting from trials in which subjects were able to complete the 180° rotation before stimulus onset, and the (17%) slow responses as resulting from trials in which subjects abandoned their incomplete preparatory rotation and started over with a (reverse) rotation of the test stimulus itself. If so, it is most natural to attribute the remaining intermediate responses to trials in which the subject continued a preparatory rotation (which had been started but not completed before stimulus onset) until it was completed *after* stimulus onset.

The quantitative values of the means and relevant modal points of the reaction-time distributions are in satisfactory agreement with this account in the case of the larger group of five "slow" subjects. Notice, again, that as we move from Condition B-400 to B-700 to B-1000 in Figure 4.10, the modal point (and indeed the overall mean) shifts left by roughly 300 msec, each time, from the middle of the band of slow responses to the middle of the band of intermediate reponses to the middle of the band of fast responses. In other words, each additional 300 msec of time allowed for preparatory rotation cuts about 300 msec off the time that the subject then requires to complete that rotation after the presentation of the actual stimulus.

This trade-off between pre- and poststimulus rotation time does not emerge so clearly in the case of the smaller group of three "fast" subjects. In Figure 4.9, the leftward shift of the mode of the reaction-time distribution from Condition B-400 (or B-100) to B-700 is closer to 200 msec than to 300 msec, and the full 300-msec shift is not achieved until condition B-1000 when, according to our analysis, the subjects have had at least 600 msec in which to complete their preparatory rotation. If the three fast subjects were faster simply by virtue of faster mental rotation (as their poststimulus reaction-time distributions suggest in Figure 4.8), we should expect that they would nearly always be ready for the test stimulus in Condition B-700. The distribution for B-700 would then be essentially identical to that for B-1000, rather than displaced 100 msec to the right— as it is in Figure 4.9. (Possibly there is a connection between this 100-msec discrepancy and the other 100-msec discrepancy, noted earlier, for these same three subjects.)

Indeed, several of the differences between the results for these two internally homogeneous groups of subjects suggest that the "fast" subjects may have used a different method in addition to their postulated greater rate of mental rotation. These differences include (a) the two 100-msec. discrepancies that, as we just noted, occurred only for the group of fast subjects, (b) the more compact reaction-time distributions obtained from this group (Figures 4.8 and 4.9), and (c) the greater tendency of the individual reaction-time functions obtained for this group to bend sharply at about 60° on either side of 180° (as is illustrated for one of these subjects at the top of Figure 4.7). Because of the small number of subjects in the "fast" group, we do not feel prepared at this time to make a definite claim concerning their method of processing.

Despite some uncertainty about these three subjects, we believe that the data from all eight subjects support our general conclusion that subjects carried out mental rotations both to respond to a rotated stimulus in the absence of advance information as to its orientation, and to prepare for a rotated stimulus on the basis of such advance information. Moreover, we believe that the data from the majority of the subjects agree quite well with our more specific conclusion that subjects carried out such prestimulus and post-stimulus rotations at essentially the same rates.

EXPERIMENT II. DEMONSTRATION OF A CORRESPONDENCE BETWEEN AN IMAGINED AND AN ACTUAL ROTATION

Our purpose in undertaking this second experiment was to obtain evidence bearing upon two notions that have been implicit throughout our discussion of Experiment I but that could not be directly substantiated on the basis of that experiment. One notion concerns the nonlinearity of the obtained relationship between reaction time and orientation of test stimulus. Although the original evidence for a process of mental rotation was largely based upon the finding of a strongly linear relationship (Shepard & Metzler, 1971), we have been arguing that the relationship found in the present Experiment I (as well as in some pilot experiments by Shepard and Klun[6])—despite a consistent and marked nonlinearity—is also the result of an underlying process of mental rotation. The other notion concerns the sense in which this mental process is one specifically of rotation. Since the term "rotation" is ordinarily defined only in relation to an external physical process, our use of this term in connection with an internal mental process implies that there is some sort of one-to-one correspondence or isomorphism between mental and physical processes of rotation.

It is possible that an internal process quite different from rotation—such as visual search, feature detection, verbal analysis, or some other digital computation—might enable a subject to determine that two objects (or images) are identical except for orientation. Such a process might even become more difficult and protracted as the two objects differ more widely in orientation. In order for an internal process to qualify as the kind of analog process that we would call a mental rotation, however, intermediate stages of the process must have a one-to-one correspondence to intermediate stages of an actual physical rotation of the one object into congruence with the other in the external world. Central to the concept of an analog process, then, is the idea of the path or trajectory of the process. If the internal process is one of rotation, not only should the starting point and end point of such a process correspond to the two objects compared, but also any intermediate point on this trajectory should correspond to an external object in an intermediate orientation—even though such an external object may not be physically present.

But what does it mean to say that at a given point in time an internal process has a one-to-one correspondence to a particular external object that is not physically present? It does not necessarily mean that there is any concrete structural resemblance or first-order isomorphism between the pattern of activity in the subject's physical brain at that moment and the corresponding external object (if it were present). Nor does it mean that there has been anything actually rotating within the subject's physical brain. It means only that there is a one-to-one relation between the internal representation and the corresponding external object in the specific sense that the subject is especially disposed to respond to that particular object in that particular orientation at that particular moment—if it were actually to be presented (Shepard, 1975).

To be "turning something over in one's mind," then, is to be passing through an ordered series of dispositional states. On the basis of introspective evidence and other considerations presented earlier, we are inclined to refer to these states as successive mental images of a rotating object. Although there are reasons to suppose that there may be some degree of abstract "first-order" isomorphism between such an internal process and a corresponding external rotation of the imagined object (Shepard, 1975) all we require in order to speak of "mental rotation" is that the internal process produces the necessary series of dispositional states. This may be achieved by means of a second-order isomorphism (Shepard & Chipman, 1970) according to which the internal process—whatever its neurophysiological nature—has an important part in common with the internal process that goes on when one is actually *perceiving* such an external rotation.

In this second experiment we have subjects imagine an alphanumeric character rotating at a certain (externally paced) rate within a blank circular field. At a random point during this purely mental process, we display a normal or backward version of the imagined character—either in the orientation that the subjects should be imagining at that moment in their rotation or in some other orientation chosen at random. If the subjects are actually carrying out a mental rotation, the speed with which they can discriminate whether this probe stimulus is normal or backward should be greatest when the probe appears in the orientation momentarily assumed by their mental image, for only then will they be able to make an immediate match between their internally rotating image or template and the externally presented test probe. Results of this sort should enable us to say that something is indeed rotating during this process—namely, the orientation at which the subjects are most prepared for the external presentation of the corresponding physical stimulus.

With regard, next, to the matter of nonlinearity, all four of the alternative explanations that we offered for the concave upward shape of the reaction-time functions were based on two observations. The first was that the alphanumeric characters (unlike the stimuli used by Shepard and Metzler) have a uniquely defined and well-learned upright orientation. The second was that the hypothesized rotation was always between the orientation of the presented test stimulus and this unique upright—not (as in the experiment by Shepard and Metzler) between the two orientations within all possible pairs. If any or all of the four explanations that we offered for the obtained nonlinearity are correct, we should be able to counterbalance the asymmetrical effects of the unique upright orientation and thus be able to obtain a more nearly linear function. We merely need to ensure that any mental rotations that the subject must perform *after* the onset of the test probe have starting and stopping points that are *both* evenly distributed around the 360° circle.

The theoretically critical point therefore resides not in the linearity itself but in the indication that it can give us that the underlying process is composed of parts (corresponding to rotations through smaller angles) that are necessarily performed in sequential order and for which, consequently, the performance times are additive. Thus no matter what the effective rotation times may be between particular adjacent points separated by 60° around the circle, if the time required to go from any one point to any other nonadjacent point is an additive combination of the component times to go between the intervening adjacent points, then the average time to go between the points in all pairs separated by n 60° steps should increase linearly with n. To show that the time to rotate from A to C is an additive combination of the times to rotate from A to B and from B to C is to furnish another kind of evidence that the process of rotating from A to C passes through a point, B, corresponding to an intermediate orientation. A finding of linearity would thus support further our claim that the process of mental rotation is an analog process.

In order to provide for a test of this predicted linearity, we depart from the previous procedure in which the presentation of the test stimulus was always in strict agreement with any advance information as to identity or orientation. This time the test stimulus does not always appear in the orientation for which the subject is preparing at the given moment. On half of the trials it appears in each of the five other evenly spaced orientations with equal probability. In this way we are for the first time able to determine the relationship of reaction time to departure of the test probe—not only from upright but also from the orientation in which that probe was expected. On the basis of our previous results, we might anticipate that any nonlinearity will be confined to the former relationship.

If our explanations as to the source of this nonlinearity are correct, we should expect the latter relationship to approximate the linearity found by Shepard and Metzler (1971).

Method

Subjects. Eight subjects were individually run through the complete experimental design, requiring four hours of participation from each. Of these subjects, two were female and two others (including RNS) had previously participated in Experiment I. (The results for the two females and for the two experienced subjects were all typical of those for the remaining four experimentally naive male students.)

Stimuli. This time we used only two from the set of six asymmetric alphanumeric characters employed in Experiment I—the upper-case "R" and the numeral "2." As before, each of these characters could appear as a normal or backward test stimulus in any of the six orientations, spaced in equal 60° steps around the circle. And again the subjects were instructed to determine, as rapidly as possible, whether each such test stimulus had appeared in its normal or in its backward version, regardless of its orientation within the two-dimensional test field (see Figures 4.1 and 4.2). The tachistoscopic apparatus, the visual angles of the stimuli, and the right- and left-hand pushbutton responses were all the same as described for Experiment I.

Structure of individual trials. All trials in this experiment were analogous to trials of type B in Experiment I in that cues as to both identity and orientation were available in advance of the onset of every test stimulus. There were, however, three important changes from the procedure used in Experiment I. (a) The advance cues were presented in auditory rather than in visual form. (b) While the cue as to the identity again agreed with the identity of the ensuing test stimulus on all trials, the cue as to the orientation this time agreed with the orientation of the test stimulus on half of the trials only. (c) The cue as to orientation, rather than being fixed in a single, random orientation on each trial, indicated an orientation that was progressively moving in a clockwise direction throughout the course of any one trial.

During each trial, the subject sat fixating the blank circular field in the tachistoscope. To start a new trial, the experimenter orally announced which of the two characters, "R" or "2" (with which the subject had previously been visually familiarized), was scheduled to appear as the test stimulus on that trial. Then the experimenter started playing a magnetic tape on which the verbal commands "up," "tip," "tip," "down," "tip," "tip" had previously been recorded at a controlled rate of one command per half second. On the basis of prior instructions and practice trials, the subject was to imagine the normal version of the announced character starting in its upright orientation and rotating clockwise at a rate of 60° per half second, in synchrony with the auditory commands. (Thus the initial command "up" notified the subject to begin rotating the internally generated mental image from its initial upright orientation and, three commands later, the word "down" indicated that this image should now be rotated around into its 180° orientation.) To assist the subject to keep pace with the auditory commands, there were six small tick marks visible around the border of the circular field at 60° steps (starting at the center of the top).

Quickly following a randomly preselected one of these verbal commands, the probe stimulus appeared in one of the six equally spaced orientations within the circular field. Thereupon the subject was to actuate the right- or left-hand switch as rapidly as possible to indicate whether the visual probe was the normal or backward version of the character, respectively. (As in Experiment I, however, this response assignment was reversed for the one left-handed subject.) The auditory commands terminated with the onset of the visual test stimulus, but the test stimulus remained on until after the subject made a response. The interval from the onset of the visual probe to the actuation of one of the two response buttons was recorded as the reaction time.

Overall experimental design. One half of the trials, determined according to a random sequence, were "probe-expected" trials in which the probe stimulus was presented in the orientation designated by the current auditory command. The other half of the trials were "probe-unexpected" trials in which the probe appeared, with equal probability, in any one of the five other possible orientations. (As a consequence, at each orientation there were five times more probe-expected observations than probe-unexpected observations.) Within both the probe-expected and probe-unexpected trials, one half of the probe stimuli were presented in their normal and one half in their backward versions, again according to a random sequence. This entire set of observations was collected for both test characters ("R" and "2"), yielding a total of 240 experimental trials per subject (following an initial set of 48 practice trials). Order of trials was randomized anew for each subject, and there was no blocking of trials by any experimental factor. Trials on which errors were made were retaken, if possible within the same session, and error rates were low (ranging from 10% to 2% for individual subjects).

Reaction-time Results

The effect of absolute orientation of an expected test stimulus. "Probe-expected" trials, in which the visual probe appeared in the orientation corresponding to the current auditory command, could be considered analogous to trials of Type B-1000 in Experiment I. For if the subjects were in fact rotating a mental image of the designated character in time with the auditory commands, they should be able to make a direct match of their current mental image against the visual probe when it suddenly appears. Thus they should be able to determine with great rapidity whether that probe is normal or backward—whatever the currently designated orientation happens to be. Just as in the earlier Condition B-1000, the function relating reaction time to absolute orientation of the test stimulus should be relatively flat (cf. the earlier Figures 4.5 and 4.6).

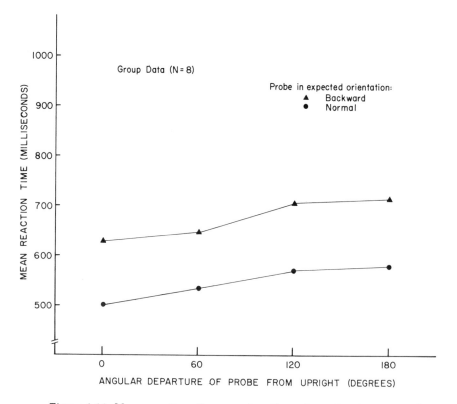

Figure 4.11 Mean reaction time as a function of angular departure of the probe stimulus from the upright orientation for those trials on which the probe stimulus appeared in the expected orientation. Separate curves are plotted for reaction times to "normal" and "backward" test stimuli.

Mean reaction times for those trials in the present experiment in which the probe stimulus appeared in the expected orientation are plotted in Figure 4.11 as a function of the angular departure of the (expected) probe from its standard upright orientation. These times are averaged over correct responses to both test characters for all eight subjects. However, they are plotted separately for trials in which the probe was normal or backward, as indicated in the figure.

In agreement with Experiment I, the responses to the backward probes were consistently longer than the responses to the normal probes—by an amount that was independent of departure from upright (and also independent of departure from expected orientation—as we shall soon see). In the present experiment, this difference in reaction time was on the order of 100 to 150 msec. The average difference is therefore some 50 msec longer than the average difference between reaction times to normal and backward stimuli in Experiment I. We shall argue that this is the result of an additional operation that must be carried out in the present experiment. Since the test stimulus was always presented in the orientation indicated by any advance orientation cue in Experiment I, a mismatch with an already rotated preparatory image automatically ensured that the stimulus was backward. In the present case, however, the subject must make a further determination as to whether the mismatch was the result of the probe's being presented in its backward version *or* in an unexpected orientation.

For simplicity of presentation in this and the following figures, we have averaged the reaction times for the symmetrically related orientations of 60° and 300° and of 120° and 240°. Thus the independent variable is now departure from upright in either direction, rather than absolute orientation in a specifically clockwise direction. As a consequence, the points plotted for 60° and 120° are based upon twice as many observations as the points plotted for 0° and 180°. However, if these reaction-time functions are "unfolded," so that all six orientations of the test stimulus are plotted separately, the functions become symmetrical about 180°—as in the earlier Figures 4.5 and 4.6.

The results displayed in Figure 4.11 are in good agreement with our expectations. The slight humping up near 180° in the previously obtained reaction-time functions for Conditions C and B-1000 reappears here as the small but consistent rise in reaction time from 0° to 180°. As we suggested before, subjects may simply require a little more time to compare two images when those images are both in a less familiar orientation. In any case, the average increase from 0° to 180° is only about 80 to 90 msec. If we contrast this with the 400 to 500 msec increase in reaction time at 180° found (in the previous conditions N or I) when no orientation information was provided, we see that the effect of the absolute orientation of an expected test stimulus is again very small.

That subjects in the present experiment were able to classify a test stimulus as normal (as opposed to backward) in only 500 to 600 msec, as long as the orientation of that stimulus coincided with the rotating orientation expected, supports our claim that they arrived at their classification by matching the presented probe against a "rotating" mental image. As further support, however, we also need to show that subjects required appreciably more time whenever the probe appeared in an unexpected orientation.

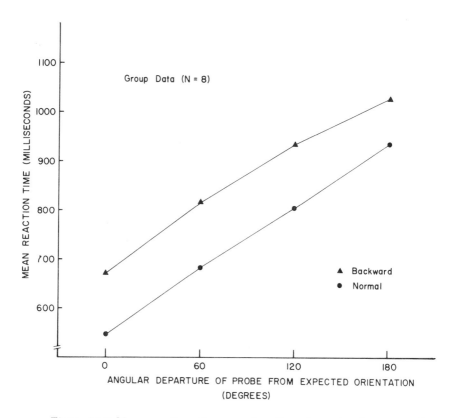

Figure 4.12 Mean reaction time as a function of angular departure of the probe stimulus from the expected orientation. Separate curves are plotted for reaction times to "normal" and "backward" test stimuli.

The effect of angular departure from expected orientation. In this experiment we can observe for the first time what happens when the test stimulus is presented in an orientation that departs from what the subject has been led to expect. Figure 4.12 illustrates the main result. Mean reaction time is plotted as a function of the angular difference between the orientation of the visual probe and the orientation that the subject should have been expecting at that point in the sequence of auditory commands. As in the preceding figure, separate curves are presented for trials in which the probe was normal or backward and, again, responses to probes of the latter type were some 100 to 150 msec slower. Also as before, the reaction times have been averaged over corresponding clockwise and counterclockwise departures at both 60° and 120° over both test characters and over all eight subjects. In addition, for this figure the reaction times have also been averaged over all angular departures of the probe from upright.

As predicted, when the probe appeared in some orientation other than the (rotating) orientation expected, reaction time increased markedly with the difference between the expected and the actually presented orientations. Indeed the overall increase, from 0° to 180°, is close to 400 msec. This increase is some five times greater than the 80 to 90 msec increase shown in the preceding Figure 4.11. At the same time, it is comparable to the 400 to 500 msec increase observed in Experiment I for departure from the orientation naturally expected when there was no advance information about orientation—namely, the standard upright orientation.

However, although the functions exhibited in Figure 4.12 thus agree with the functions displayed (in Figures 4.5 and 4.6) for the earlier conditions N, I, O, and B-100 with respect to overall slope, they differ markedly from those earlier functions with respect to shape. For whereas the earlier functions were uniformly concave upward, the functions shown in Figure 4.12 are both strikingly linear. But the linearity of these new functions is just what we have predicted on the basis of two assumptions. The first is that when the orientation of the probe fails to agree with the imagined orientation, the subject must undertake an additional poststimulus rotation in order to achieve a match between that probe and the internal representation of the corresponding normal character. The second assumption is that when the starting and ending points of the required poststimulus rotations are evenly distributed around the circle, the biasing effects of the special upright orientation should cancel out in such a way as to reveal the linear and, hence, the underlying sequential-additive nature of mental rotation.

The joint effects of departures from expected and upright orientations. We have argued that any nonlinearity in the present data should emerge when reaction time is plotted against departure from upright (as in Experiment I) rather than against departure from expected orientation (as in the preceding Figure 4.12). Evidence supporting this argument is illustrated in Figure 4.13. Here the dependence of reaction time upon angular departure of the probe from upright is separately plotted for each value of angular departure of the probe from its expected orientation. The plotted means are averaged over subjects, characters, and, this time, both "normal" and "backward" responses as well. The lowest curve (for 0°) is thus the average of the two curves displayed earlier in Figure 4.11. Again, the flatness of this bottommost function shows that when the probe appears in the expected orientation, the absolute angle of this orientation has relatively little effect on reaction time. In this case we cannot expect to find any nonlinearity.

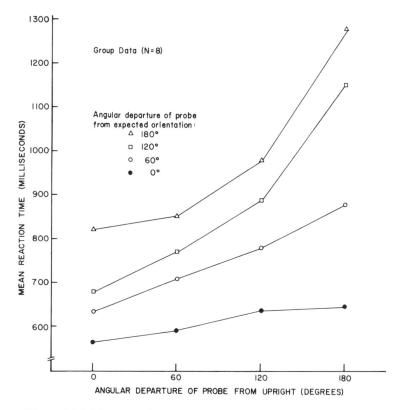

Figure 4.13 Mean reaction time as a function of angular departure of the probe stimulus from the upright orientation, plotted separately for each of the four angular departures of the probe stimulus from the expected orientation. (Reaction times to "normal" and "backward" test stimuli are averaged together.)

As the visual probe departs more and more from its expected orientation, however, three changes take place in the average data. The function relating reaction time to departure from upright (a) rises in overall height, (b) increases in positive slope, and (c) becomes increasingly concave upward. The first change—the increasing height of successive functions in Figure 4.13—is just the effect illustrated in Figure 4.12. As we saw there, this increase is essentially linear with departure from expected orientation. The second and third changes—the increasing steepness and curvature of the successive functions—are to some extent analogous to the changes in the family of curves for the B-conditions in Experiment I (Figure 4.6). In both cases the relation of reaction time to departure from upright becomes stronger and more nonlinear as the advance information as to orientation is decreased in effectiveness—whether by a reduction in duration (Figure 4.6) or in accuracy (Figure 4.13).

The analogy between the family of curves in the present Figure 4.13 and the B-family curves in the earlier Figure 4.6 should be advanced with caution in view of the smaller number of observations contributing to each of the points in the three upper "probe-unexpected" curves of Figure 4.13 (particularly at 0° and 180°). Moreover, an additional consideration, which does not arise in connection with Experiment I, may come into play in the present experiment. Consider trials represented by the leftmost datum point of the highest curve in Figure 4.13. These are trials on which the subject has presumably rotated a mental image of the designated character into its upside-down position but on which the test probe unexpectedly appears in its upright position. Some subjects reported that when this happened, they identified the upright test probe as normal or backward without rotation—presumably by comparing it against the normal upright representation in long-term memory, rather than by continuing to rotate their short-term image (which was then at 180°) all the way back to 0° for comparison with the upright probe. We would expect subjects who operated in this way to yield relatively short reaction times to probes that unexpectedly appear near 0°. Such relatively rapid reaction times may contribute considerably to the slopes of the upper curves in Figure 4.13.

Perhaps the most striking comparison illustrated in Figure 4.13 is between the rightmost point of the lowest curve and the leftmost point of the highest curve. This comparison reveals that on the average subjects responded nearly 200 msec faster to an expected test stimulus at 180° than to an unexpected test stimulus in the standard upright orientation. As a consequence of the relatively small number of observations contributing to the upper point, the numerical value of this difference is somewhat unreliable; however, the direction of this difference is the same for all eight subjects. This comparison therefore furnishes strong evidence that the internal representation that the subjects were "mentally rotating" in time with the auditory commands was more available for matching against the externally presented test stimulus than was the permanent representation of the normal upright character that the subjects presumably retain in long-term memory.

Analysis of variance indicated that the effects of angular departure of the probe from upright, angular departure of the probe from the expected orientation, and the interaction between these two were all statistically reliable. [7]

Results for individual subjects. In Figure 4.14 we follow our earlier convention of presenting the curves for the two subjects that were most extreme with respect to overall reaction time. The two panels on the left correspond to the earlier Figure 4.11, while the two panels on the right correspond to the earlier Figure 4.12. There is a considerable difference in overall height of the curves obtained for the "fast" subject (top panels) and the "slow" subject (bottom panels). (Note, incidentally, that the vertical scales for the "slow" subject have been linearly compressed with respect to the vertical scales for the "fast" subject.) Nevertheless both subjects yielded functions that were essentially flat when the probe appeared in the expected orientation and increased monotonically and approximately linearly with departure of the probe from its expected orientation.

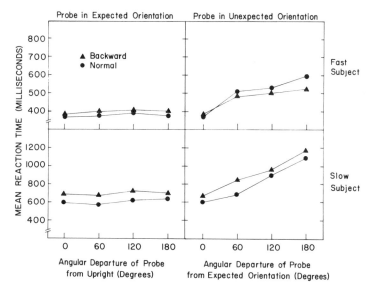

Figure 4.14 Mean reaction-time functions for two individual subjects—the fastest subject (upper panels) and the slowest subject (lower panels). Left-hand panels correspond to the group functions displayed in Figure 4.11, and right-hand panels correspond to the group functions displayed in Figure 4.12.

Curves for all of the other subjects were similar in shape to these curves (and for some of the subjects the curves corresponding to those plotted on the right in Figure 4.14 were even more linear).

Discussion

The introspective reports that the subjects gave us following their participation in Experiment II are consonant with our interpretations of their reaction times. The subjects claimed that they were indeed able to imagine the normal version of the designated character rotating clockwise in time with the auditory commands. The subjects also indicated that they used this rotating mental image as a sort of template against which to compare the test stimulus when it suddenly appeared within the circular field. If a match was achieved, they immediately executed the readied (e.g., right-hand) response. If not, they then had to determine whether the mismatch resulted from the fact that the stimulus had been presented in its backward version or in an unexpected orientation.

If the subjects determined that the visual probe was backward (perhaps by performing an additional mental operation of reflection), they then switched control to the other hand before executing their response. The average additional time for a mismatch response in Experiment II was some 50 msec longer than in Experiment I. This difference may be the time required for the additional operation (possibly of reflection) that was required only in Experiment II (in which, for the first time, the probe could differ from what was expected by a reflection *or* a rotation).

Concerning trials on which the visual probe differed from the subject's internal representation by a rotation, subjects reported two different strategies: When the probe departed markedly from upright, they tended to carry out a further (poststimulus) rotation in order to bring their rotating mental image into congruence with the external probe and then proceeded as described above for the case in which no such further rotation was necessary. When the probe was close to upright while their mental image was far from upright, they tended to abandon their rotating mental image and to determine whether the probe was normal or backward directly—after imagining the probe itself rotated back to upright, if necessary.

With respect to the reaction-time results, we regard as especially significant (a) that reaction times were short and relatively independent of orientation whenever the probe appeared in the (rotating) orientation expected and (b) that these times increased as the probe departed from this expected orientation—even when this very departure brought the probe closer to its standard upright orientation.

This conclusively demonstrates that during the alleged process of mental rotation, something was indeed rotating—namely, the orientation in the external world at which the subject was most prepared for the presentation of the test stimulus. It also demonstrates that this process of mental rotation was an analog process, at least to the extent that it went through intermediate states that had a one-to-one relation to intermediate orientations in the external world. As the lowest curve in Figure 4.11 shows, the subjects required an average of only 500 to 600 msec to perceive the probe, to match it against the "mentally rotating" internal representation, and to make a correct response. This suggests that the representation was in a form that was particularly suitable for comparison with the visual stimulus. Although for several subjects there undoubtedly were kinesthetic concomitants, it is tempting to refer to this "rotating" internal representation as a visual image.

CONCLUSIONS

Empirical Findings

The stimuli used in both experiments were two-dimensional visual patterns (certain upper-case letters and numerals) that (a) are highly familiar, (b) are characteristically seen in a well-learned and uniquely defined upright orientation, and (c) are not symmetrical about any axis. On each trial one such stimulus or its mirror image was presented in some orientation within its two-dimensional plane. The subjects were instructed to actuate a right-hand or left-hand switch, as rapidly as possible after the onset of the stimulus, to indicate whether that stimulus was presented in its normal or backward version, respectively—regardless of its orientation within the picture plane. The principal findings concerning the measured reaction times can be summarized as follows:

1. Throughout, reaction times were consistently shorter to the normal stimuli than to their mirror images. The difference averaged about 100 msec or somewhat less and was independent of orientation and several other experimental variables (Experiment I, and Figures 4.11, 4.12). This difference varied somewhat from subject to subject, however, and it averaged some 50 msec longer when the stimulus could depart from what was expected by a rotation as well as by a reflection (Figures 4.11, 4.12).

2. When the stimulus appeared in an orientation for which the subject was not specifically prepared, reaction time increased monotonically with the departure of the stimulus from the natural upright orientation (Experiment I, Conditions N and I), or from the rotated orientation that the subject had been set to expect

(Experiment II). For the maximum possible departure of 180°, the average increase in reaction time was on the order of 400 to 500 msec (but, again, varied from subject to subject).

3. When the subject was not set to expect the stimulus in a particular (rotated) orientation, the increase in reaction time with departure from upright consistently conformed to a concave upward function (Figure 4.5, Conditions N and I).

4. When the subject was set to expect a particular stimulus in a particular orientation, the increase in reaction time with departure from that expected orientation (when averaged over all such orientations) conformed to a remarkably linear function (Figure 4.12)—reminiscent of the functions reported by Shepard and Metzler (1971) for rotated three-dimensional objects.

5. When the subject was given advance information only about the identity of the stimulus or only about its orientation, reaction time was reduced by a constant amount of about 100 msec in either case, regardless of the (nonconflicting) orientation of the ensuing stimulus (Figure 4.5, Conditions I and O versus Condition N).

6. When the subject was given valid advance information about both identity and orientation, reaction time to an upright stimulus was reduced by the sum of the reductions attributable to the two kinds of advance information provided separately—i.e., by a total of some 200 msec (Figures 4.5 and 4.6, Condition B-1000 at 0° or Condition B-400, as compared with Condition N).

7. When the subject was thus set for a specific stimulus in *any* specific orientation, reaction time to such a stimulus was consistently short (about 500 msec) and remarkably independent of the angle of that expected orientation (Figure 4.5, Condition B-1000, and Figures 4.11 and 4.14). Consequently, when the expected orientation was other than upright, the reduction in reaction time resulting from the two kinds of advance information exceeded the sum of the reductions attributable to either kind alone. (For a stimulus at 180° from upright, the reduction averaged about 600 msec rather than the 200 msec prescribed by simple additivity.)

8. When a particular stimulus was expected in a particular rotated orientation, the reaction time to such a (rotated) stimulus was consistently shorter than the reaction time to that stimulus presented in the standard upright orientation—in which it was then no longer expected (Figure 4.13, second, third, and fourth points on the lowest curve versus the corresponding leftmost points on the second, third, and fourth curves, above).

9. The time required to be fully prepared for presentation of a particular stimulus at a particular orientation increased as the (validly) indicated orientation departed from the standard upright orientation.

For an orientation of 0°, minimum reaction times (of about 500 msec) were achieved if the orientation information had been available 400 msec prior to stimulus onset. But for an orientation of 180°, reaction times approaching this minimum (500 msec) level were not achieved until the orientation information had persisted for about 1000 msec (Figure 4.6, Conditions B-400 and B-1000).

10. Except, possibly, in the case of a few "fast" subjects, there was an approximate trade-off between preparation time and reaction time such that each additional 300 msec of orientation information (beyond the 400 msec needed for optimum performance at 0°) reduced the subsequent reaction time to a stimulus at 180° by another 300 msec (Figures 4.6, Conditions B-400, B-700, and B-1000 at 180°; and Figure 4.10).

11. Reaction times to an expected stimulus had approximately the same short (500 msec) values whether the advance information was presented (a) in the form of a visual outline of the stimulus already rotated to the orientation in which it was to appear (Figure 4.5, Condition C), (b) in the form of a visual outline of that stimulus in its upright orientation followed by a rotated arrow to indicate the orientation in which it was to appear (Figure 4.5, Condition B-1000), or (c) in a purely auditory form (Figure 4.11).

12. Subjects were able to maintain an optimal level of readiness for the appearance of a visual stimulus in an orientation that was rotating clockwise (in accordance with concurrent auditory cues) at a rate of 120° per second (Figure 4.11). (Higher rates may also be feasible for some subjects but have not yet been tried.)

Theoretical Interpretations

Nowhere in the preceding list of "empirical findings" did we speak of any such things as a mental image or a mental rotation. Our intention in preparing that list was to confine ourselves to objective and, we hope, reproducible patterns evident in the "hard data" of the recorded reaction times. We even avoided any mention of the subjects' postexperimental introspective reports. The list was thus put forward as a set of facts standing in need of a theory. It may be that someone will be able to formulate a theory that satisfyingly accounts for this particular set of facts without invoking any such concepts as mental imagery or mental rotation. Until this happens, however, we are inclined to favor a theory (a) that *has* now been formulated (at least in outline) and (b) that *is* consonant with the subjects' own introspective reports that they did indeed rotate mental images. Accordingly, the theoretical interpretations that we have been proposing to account for the empirical findings can be summarized as follows:

1. Subjects determine whether a familiar asymmetrical stimulus has been presented in its normal or in its backward (mirror-image) version by comparing the stimulus against an internal representation or mental image. Unless instructed otherwise (or unless presented in advance with the other version to be used as a model), subjects use the internal representation of the normal version for this purpose. (See Findings 1, 2, and 7, listed above.)

2. If the stimulus fails to match the image, subjects perform an additional operation (requiring 100 msec or somewhat less) in order to switch control to the alternative response (Finding 1). If there is the possibility (as in Experiment II) that the mismatch may result from a rotation rather than just from a reflection, subjects may perform still another operation (requiring perhaps 50 msec more) in order to verify that the mismatch was the result specifically of a reflection (Finding 1).

3. If the stimulus appears in its familiar upright orientation for subjects who are not specifically expecting it in that orientation, the internal representation used for comparison against the stimulus is the permanent representation of the normal upright version of that stimulus in long-term memory (Findings, 2, 6, 8).

4. If the stimulus appears in some other orientation that departs markedly from any orientation that the subject may have been specifically expecting, a mental image of the presented stimulus is mentally rotated from the orientation in which the stimulus appeared back into its standard upright orientation for comparison with the upright representation in long-term memory (Findings 2, 8).

5. Before subjects can compare a stimulus against an internal representation or can begin to rotate a mental image of it into a particular orientation, they must know both the identity and the orientation of that stimulus. Either or both of these two pieces of information that they do not have in advance must be independently extracted from the stimulus itself at the cost of about 100 msec for each piece—hence of about 200 msec for both (Findings 5, 6).

6. If information about both the identity and the orientation of the ensuing stimulus is provided sufficiently in advance, a mental image of the normal version of the designated stimulus is formed in its standard upright orientation (from the identity cue, in Experiment I, or from long-term memory, in Experiment II) and is mentally rotated into the designated orientation for rapid comparison with the stimulus when it appears (Findings 4, 7, 8, 10, 11).

7. If the stimulus appears in a (rotated) orientation different from the orientation of the preparatory mental image, the preparatory

image is then rotated into the orientation of the stimulus for purposes of comparison. This is true whether the difference in orientation arises because the preparatory rotation has not been completed (Findings 9, 10) or because the orientation of the stimulus is different from what the subject has been set to expect (Findings 2, 4). In the former case, however, the preparatory rotation will not even be started unless the advance orientation information (when presented in the form of a rotated arrow) has been available for some 400 msec (Findings 9, 10). When the duration of the orientation cue is too short, preparatory rotation is abandoned and an image of the stimulus itself is rotated back into upright, as described in Point 4, above.

8. Although the rate of mental rotation depends upon the individual subject (and, perhaps, upon the complexity and familiarity of the stimulus), on the average subjects can rotate a mental image of an alphanumeric character through 180° in some 500 msec (Findings 2, 9, 12). Moreover the rate is about the same whether the rotation is carried out in the presence of the external stimulus, after it has appeared (Finding 2) or in the absence of that stimulus, in preparation for it (Finding 9).

9. Subjects are able to carry out only the mental rotation of an internal representation of a particular concrete object, not a general abstract frame of reference. Thus even though subjects are given adequate advance information about the orientation of an upcoming stimulus, they are unable to perform any preparatory rotation unless they are also given advance information about the identity of that stimulus (Findings 5, 7).

10. In the case of stimuli (such as alphanumeric characters) that have characteristically been seen in (or close to) one particular orientation, that familiar upright orientation plays a special role in processes of rotation and/or matching. Such processes are relatively slow when the mental image being rotated or matched is in an unfamiliar orientation, and especially so when the image is close to 180° from upright (Finding 3).

11. Mental rotation is an analog process with a serial structure bearing a one-to-one relationship to the corresponding physical rotation. The time required (mentally) to rotate from an orientation A to an orientation C is just the sum of the times required to rotate from A to some intermediate orientation B, and to rotate from B to C (Finding 4). Moreover, in mentally rotating an object between any two widely separated orientations, A and C, the internal process passes through the mental image corresponding to that same object in some intermediate orientation, B (Finding 12). Consequently, the orientation at which the subject is most prepared for

the appearance of that object at each moment is actually rotating with respect to the external world (Findings 7, 8, 12).

12. Even though the mental image may be internally generated in the absence of the corresponding visual stimulus (Finding 11), it nevertheless possesses an internal structure that is at least abstractly isomorphic to the structure of that external visual stimulus, since the image can be transformed in a way that corresponds specifically to a rigid rotation of the external stimulus (Finding 12); and, even after such a transformation, the image can be matched against the subsequent presentation of the rotated visual stimulus with essentially the same speed and precision as if it were a straight memory image remaining from an immediately preceding presentation of the identical rotated stimulus (Findings 7, 11).

Final Remarks

We are not claiming that the many familiar objects that we all encounter in various positions in our every-day lives have to be mentally rotated into some canonical orientation before they can be recognized. In the case of most objects and symbols with which we have to deal, there are sufficiently numerous, redundant, or orientationally invariant distinctive features that we may well achieve recognition directly—without need of a preliminary mental transformation. However, we *are* claiming that a demonstration that human subjects are capable of mentally rotating spatially structured objects is of considerable importance, even if a sharp demonstration requires special circumstances.

If rotation is mentally performed in an analogical manner, then the imagining, understanding, and planning of many other kinds of operations in the physical world may also be accomplished in an analogical manner. Hence, the mere demonstration that humans solve some problems (however contrived) by means of a basically analog process has important implications for the nature of the human mind. At the very least, it raises a question about the advisability of formulating theories of human behavior solely in terms of discrete processes of verbal mediation of symbol manipulation—as has been characteristic in experimental psychology and in computer simulation, respectively. Moreover, the fact that internal representations can be operated upon by such analog processes tells us something important about the nature of those representations. Clearly, such an internal representation cannot adequately be regarded either as an undifferentiated neural event (such as the activation of a particular neuron or population of mutually interchangeable neurons) at the physiological level, or simply as an unanalyzable symbol at the information-processing level. Instead, such a representation must have an internal structure that is itself to some extent analogically related to the structure of its corresponding external object. For during the process of rotation, the parts and the relationships among the parts must be transformed in very constrained ways in order to enable the kind of rapid, template-like match against an ensuing visual stimulus that we have demonstrated here.

Appendix: A Tentative Information-Processing Model

Figure 4.15 schematically portrays our first approximation to what may take place when a subject without advance information attempts to determine whether an alphanumeric character presented in some arbitrary orientation is normal or backward, as in a trial of type N in Experiment I. Following the onset of the blank field, the subject fixates that circular field and readies the hand used to signal that the ensuing character is normal (Box 1). Then, upon the appearance of the test character in that field, the subject determines the identity of the character (Box 2) and its orientation (Box 3). Evidently, each of these operations takes about a tenth of a second: advance presentation of either piece of information alone lowers the entire reaction-time function by about 100 msec (Conditions I and O), and advance presentation of both pieces of information lowers the reaction time for an upright test character by about 200 msec (Condition B). Possibly the times to determine identity and orientation increase slightly with departure from upright (e.g., see Kolers & Perkins, 1969). However, our results provide no indication of this. Moreover, in a subsidiary experiment, one of us (LAC) found that the mean reaction time for orally reporting the identity of each of the six characters (about 550 msec) was virtually the same for all six orientations. In any case, once the identity and the orientation of the presented character have been established, the subject imagines the character rotated into its upright orientation—requiring roughly 100, 250, or 500 additional msecs for stimuli tipped by 60, 120, or 180 degrees, respectively (Box 4). The mentally righted image of the presented character is then compared with the representation of that character in long-term memory (Box 5). If there is a match, the response that has previously been readied is immediately initiated (Box 7); otherwise, control is first switched to the other hand (Box 6)—consuming (for a typical subject) another tenth of a second.

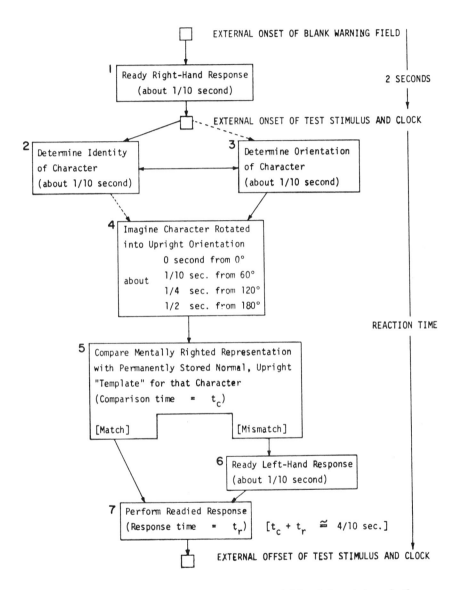

Figure 4.15 An information-processing model for determining whether a rotated alphanumeric character is normal or backward.

5 | Mental Rotation of Random Two-Dimensional Shapes

Originally authored by Lynn A. Cooper

Two experiments are reported in which subjects were required to determine whether a random, angular form, presented at any of a number of picture-plane orientations, was a "standard" or "reflected" version. Average time required to make this determination increased linearly with the angular departure of the form from a previously learned orientation. The slope and intercept of the reaction-time function were virtually constant, regardless of the perceptual complexity of the test form and the orientation selected for initial learning.

When subjects were informed in advance as to the identity and the orientation of the upcoming test form and, further, were permitted to indicate when they were prepared for its external presentation, reaction time for determining the version of the form was constant for all test-form orientations. However, the time needed to prepare for the test-form presentation increased linearly with the angular departure of the form from the learned orientation.

It is argued that the processes both of preparing for and of responding to a disoriented test form consist of the mental rotation of an image, and that both sorts of mental rotation (pre-stimulus and post-stimulus) are carried out at essentially the same constant rate.

During recent years, the investigation of imagery has increased; but it has continued to focus mainly on questions of the degree of functional significance of mental imagery (e.g., Bower, 1972; Paivio, 1971). With the exception of evidence concerning the modality or the coded form of internal representations—deriving primarily from selective interference (Brooks, 1968; Segal, 1971; Segal & Fusella, 1970; Segal & Gordon, 1969) and selective reduction of reaction times in matching tasks (Posner, 1969; Posner, Boies, Eichelman, & Taylor, 1969)—little indication of the nature or internal structure of mental images has been provided.

Through chronometric techniques for investigating transforma-

Reprinted by permission from *Cognitive Psychology*, 1975, 7, 20–43 (copyright © 1975 Academic Press, Inc.).[1]

tions of internal representations, however, we are now obtaining new evidence concerning the structural properties of mental images (Chapters 3 & 4, here; Shepard, 1975). Still, several issues remain unclarified. The first problem concerns the relationship between pre-stimulus or preparatory mental rotation and poststimulus rotation (i.e., rotation of a transformed test stimulus in the absence of prepa-ration). Cooper and Shepard (1973b) proposed that both processes involve the rotation of a mental image, hence should be carried out in the same manner and at the same rate. The evidence for this pro-posal was not conclusive, for in the Cooper-Shepard experiments a direct measure of the time required to complete the preparatory mental rotations was not obtained. Experiment II reported here was designed to explore further the process of preparing for a rotated test stimulus and its relationship to poststimulus mental rotation by providing direct estimates of the time needed to carry out both in-ternal processes.

A second unresolved matter concerns the nonlinearity of the reaction-time functions obtained in the experiments with alphanu-meric stimuli. Cooper and Shepard (1973b) have suggested several possible explanations for the nonlinear effect of test-stimulus orien-tation on reaction time, all of which are consonant with the notion that a mental rotation is carried out in order to determine the version of a tilted test character. Experiment I reported here was designed to evaluate an explanation which attributes the nonlinearity to two relat-ed conjectures concerning familiarity. First, alphanumeric characters, which are generally encountered in or close to the conventional up-right position, may seem less familiar when viewed at markedly tipped orientations (cf., Egeth & Blecker, 1971). Second, the rate at which an object can be mentally rotated may increase with the familiarity of that object. Under this account, rotation rate should be slowest for a test stimulus close to an unfamiliar orientation and should accelerate as the stimulus approaches a familiar or learned position.

A final unexplored issue concerns the relationship between rate of mental rotation and complexity of the internal representation undergoing the mental transformation. Rotation rates estimated by Cooper and Shepard for alphanumeric characters were some six times faster than the 60°/sec rate estimated by Shepard and Metzler for complex perspective drawings. The possibility that rotation rate de-creases wtih increasing complexity of the test form being rotated was evaluated in both experiments reported here by employing stimuli which differ on a well-defined measure of perceptual complexity. The implications of the complexity manipulation for the nature of the internal processes and representations underlying these tasks will be discussed in connection with the experiments.

EXPERIMENT I

Method

Subjects. Eight subjects, all students and staff at Stanford University, were paid for their participation in six one-hour experimental sessions. Six of the subjects were male, two were female, and one male was left-handed. Three of the subjects had participated in pilot work for this experiment (cf., Cooper, 1973).

Stimuli. The stimuli were the eight random shapes illustrated in Figure 5.1. These angular forms were generated by Attneave and Arnoult's (1956) Method I for the construction of random nonsense shapes. The particular forms used as stimuli were selected from a set of shapes which Vanderplas and Garvin (1959) reported to be low in verbal association value.

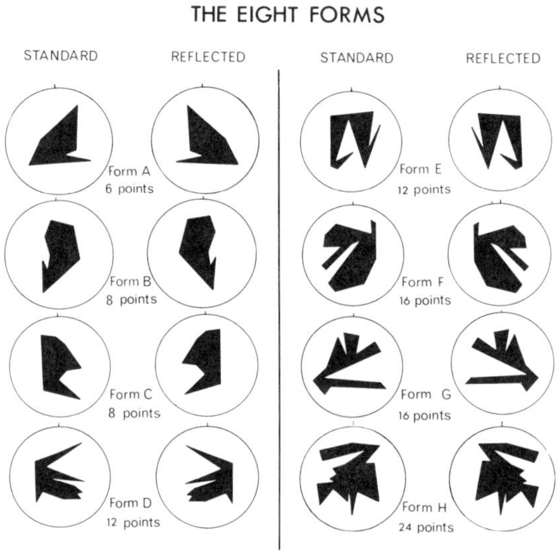

THE EIGHT FORMS

Figure 5.1 The eight random forms used in Experiment I, displayed in both standard and reflected versions.

Studies of rated complexity of forms generated by this method indicate that judged perceptual complexity depends strongly upon the number of points which determine inflections on the perimeter of the form (Attneave, 1957; Attneave & Arnoult, 1956; Vanderplas & Garvin, 1959). Attneave (1957) found a linear relationship between the logarithm of the number of points and judged complexity and also reported that the number of points (usually identical to the number of angles in the contour) accounts for 80 percent of the variance of the ratings.

The eight forms depicted in Figure 5.1 represent five levels of rated complexity—6, 8, 12, 16, and 24 points. Thus the stimulus set included one form of the lowest and highest complexity values (forms A and H), and two forms of each of the intermediate levels of complexity (forms B, C, D, E, F, and G).

Different subjects learned to discriminate "standard" versions of the forms from "reflected" or mirror-image versions at different previously determined training orientations. The training positions were six equally-spaced orientations about a circle in the picture plane. For standard versions of all forms, the six training orientations consisted of angular departures of 60° steps of clockwise rotation from the orientation depicted in Figure 5.1 (including, of course, the depicted orientation itself). In order to preserve the mirror-image relationship between standard and reflected forms, the six corresponding training orientations for reflected versions consisted of the orientation illustrated in Figure 5.1 plus angular departures of 60° steps of *counterclockwise* rotation from this orientation.

Training orientation was varied over subject. Three subjects had participated in pilot work in which a subset of the forms had been presented in the orientation illustrated in Figure 5.1. Hence, all three were assigned to this orientation for initial training. The other subjects were assigned randomly to the five remaining orientations.

The forms were presented in an Iconix three-field tachistoscope and appeared centered within an illuminated circular field with a black surround. The forms themselves subtended a visual angle of about 2°, and the circular aperture in which they appeared subtended an angle of 4°. Luminance of all fields of the tachistoscope was about 20 ft-L.

Procedure. During the first experimental session, subjects learned to discriminate standard from reflected forms at the appropriate training orientation only. Each subject was permitted to study a visual display containing drawings of the eight forms, in both standard and reflected versions in the training position only, for about ten minutes. Individual forms were then presented tachistoscopically (in the training orientation only), and the subject was required to determine as quickly as possible whether each form presented was a standard or a reflected version.

"Standard" responses were signaled by pushing a right-hand button, and "reflected" responses were signaled by pushing a left-hand button. This response assignment was reversed for the one left-handed subject; thus, the preferred hand was always used to signal "standard." A two-second gray warning field preceded the presentation of the test form, and the subject's button-pressing response terminated the visual display. For each subject, each of the eight forms was presented in both standard and reflected versions ten times, for a toal of 160 training trials.

Sessions two through six were test sessions. At the beginning of each such session, the subject was familiarized with the forms by means of a small set of training trials consisting of two presentations of both standard and reflected versions of each of the eight forms at the trained orientation. Subjects were required to discriminate standard from reflected versions, and reaction times were recorded.

During the remainder of each session, the same eight forms were presented, but each form could appear in any of six possible orientations about the circle. The six orientations were equally spaced and consisted of the trained orientation plus 60°, 120°, 180°, 240°, and 300° angular departures of clockwise rotation from the trained orientation. Regardless of the orientation at which each test form appeared, subjects always had to determine as quickly as possible whether the form was a standard or a reflected version. As in the training session, choice responses were registered by pushing a right- or left-hand button.

On each of the five test days (in addition to the initial relearning trials) each subject saw each of the eight forms in both standard and reflected versions *twice* at the trained orientation, *twice* at the orientation departing 180° from the trained orientation, and *once* at each of the four other orientations. These unequal probabilities of appearance were designed to yield an equal number of observations at each angular departure, collapsed over clockwise and counterclockwise directions, from the trained orientation. Thus each test session consisted of 32 retraining trials and 128 test trials. The order of test trials was randomized anew for each session within each subject.

Trials on which errors were made were retaken within the same session in order to obtain a complete set of error-free data for each subject. Session two, the first of the five test sessions, was considered a practice day. The data from this session were not included in the analysis. Consequently, the complete set of test-session data consists of 512 errorless reaction times for each of the eight subjects.

Results

Figure 5.2 illustrates mean reaction time (averaged over subjects, forms, and sessions) for correctly determining the version of rotated test forms. Although error reaction times are not included in the mean reaction times in Figure 5.2, error rates are plotted as a function of angular departure from the trained orientation and standard versus reflected versions. Since individual subjects learned the forms in different positions, the 0° orientation does not correspond to any unique position of the forms. In addition, clockwise and counter-clockwise departures from the trained orientation have been averaged in Figure 5.2 and in all of the figures which follow. However, if the reaction-time function is "unfolded" about the 180° point, the shape is remarkably symmetrical (cf., Cooper, 1973).

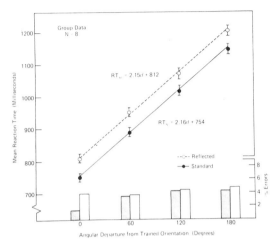

Figure 5.2 Mean reaction time as a function of angular departure of the test form from the trained orientation for the group data from Experiment I. "Standard" and "reflected" reaction time functions are plotted separately, and equations for the best-fitting straight lines are shown. Vertical bars about each mean reaction time represent one standard error of the mean. Error rates are plotted as a function of orientation and version, with solid bars and open bars representing errors on standard and reflected test stimuli, respectively.

The most striking features of the data presented in Figure 5.2 are the linearity of the increase in reaction time with angular departure of the test stimulus from the trained orientation and the parallelism between the functions for "standard" and "reflected" responses. The greater speed of the "standard" response and the parallelism of the two functions has also emerged in previous studies using alphanumeric stimuli (Cooper & Shepard, 1973b).

In Figure 5.3, group reaction-time functions, averaged over "standard" and "reflected" responses, are plotted separately for each of the eight forms. The striking linearity depicted in Figure 5.2 is also apparent when each form is considered separately. The equations for least-square linear fits, shown for each form in Figure 5.3, indicate that the complexity of the test form, measured by the number of points, does not produce systematic differences in intercept or slope. This suggestion is confirmed by the fact that correlations between (a) rank order of complexity of the forms and rank order of the corresponding intercepts, and (b) rank order of the complexity of

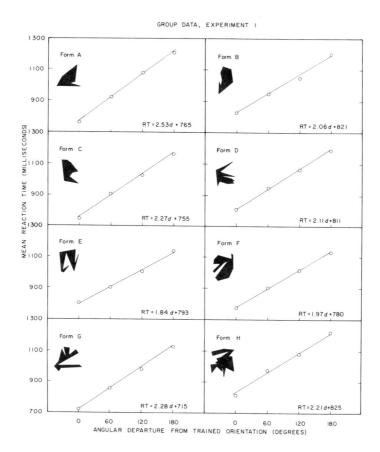

Figure 5.3 Mean reaction time as a function of angular departure of the test form from the trained orientation, plotted separately for each of the eight forms used in Experiment I. Equations for the best-fitting straight lines are shown.

the forms and rank order of the associated slopes, were nonsignificant (for complexity and intercept, r_s = +.24; for complexity and slope, r_s = –.26, with N = 8 for both correlations).

The left-hand panel of Table 5.1 presents the slope estimate and its standard error for the data of each subject (over forms) and for the group data. In addition, a subset of the data for individual subjects is plotted in Figure 5.6 in connection with Experiment II. For a complete presentation of the data for individual subjects, see Cooper (1973).

In a five-way analysis of variance with subjects and forms treated as random factors, the main effects of subjects, sessions, orientations, and versions were all highly significant, but the main effect of forms did not approach statistical significance. [2]

Table 5.1

Slope Estimates and Standard Errors, Collapsed over Forms,
Sessions, and Versions, for Individual Subjects and for the
Group Data from Experiments I and II[a]

	Experiment I		Experiment II	
Subject	Slope	Standard Error of Slope	Slope	Standard Error of Slope
1 (JC)	1.54	.12	2.15	.12
2 (IF)	1.82	.07	1.82	.04
3 (CH)	2.55	.17	1.99	.06
4 (DK)	2.54	.06	3.10	.07
5 (JK)	3.04	.11	4.23	.13
6 (SR)	2.55	.04	3.75	.25
7 (GL)	1.18	.05	1.77	.05
8 (LC)	2.07	.08	2.85	.12
Group	2.16	.06	2.71	.08

[a] Estimates for Experiment I are based on all eight forms; estimates for Experiment II are based on only four forms.

Polynomial regressions were computed on the mean reaction times for each form within each subject, and for the group data. In all the analyses, no quadratic or higher-order effects were significant. Root mean square deviations (RMSD's) were computed from the residual variance not attributable to linearity. RMSD's for individual subjects ranged from 23 to 5 msec, for individual forms from 18 to 6 msec, and for the group data the RMSD was 8 msec. None of the RMSD's indicated statistically significant departures from linearity.

Although all error trials were retaken, errors were recorded and the computed error rates were quite low, ranging from 1.2% to 7.9% for individual subjects, with an average rate of 3.6% (cf. Figure 5.2).

Discussion

The linearity of the reaction-time functions illustrated in Figures 5.2 and 5.3 has implications for (a) the nature of the internal processes involved in determining the version of a rotated form, and (b) the "familiarity" explanation for the nonlinearity obtained with alphanumeric stimuli (cf. Cooper & Shepard, 1973a, 1973b). With respect to the internal processes underlying the standard-reflected discrimination, these data support the following claims: (a) An internal representation of the visual test form is first mentally rotated from its externally presented orientation into the trained orientation.[3] (b) The mentally transformed image of the test form is then compared to the memory representation of the standard version of that form in the learned position. The overall difference between "standard" and "reflected" reaction times suggests that a match between the transformed representation of the test form and the standard version of that form is generally tested for first. If this match fails, then extra time is evidently needed to switch to the non-preferred "reflected" response. This initial comparison of the transformed internal representation with a memory image of the *standard* version is consistent with the "congruence" principles discussed by Clark and Chase (1972) and Trabasso, Rollins, and Shaughnessy (1971). (c) For these random two-dimensional forms and these particular subjects, this process of mental rotation is carried out at an average constant rate of 460°/sec.

The linear reaction-time functions obtained not only for the group data but also for each individual subject (cf. Figure 5.6), indicate that relatively long-term memory representations of these forms were established in whatever orientation they were presented during initial training. It is noteworthy that after a mere 160 exposures to the random forms at the trained orientation, subjects apparently continued to use a memory representation of each form in the trained orientation as a "mental template" for comparison with the transformed images of the test forms during the 640 subsequent trials.

If subjects either developed "mental templates" for standard and reflected versions at all orientations or learned to recognize these versions on the basis of distinctive features unique to each orientation, then we should expect the reaction-time function to become flat during the later test sessions. However, although practice effects are evident in that the average slope decreases monotonically over test sessions, the reaction-time function is linear for all sessions, and even for the final session the slope is considerable: 1.79 compared with 2.57 for the first test session. Thus we can tentatively conclude that while practice *does* affect the slope of the reaction-time function, nonetheless the same basic internal process of mental rotation was used during the entire sequence of test trials.

Perhaps the most significant outcome of the present experiment is the lack of relationship between complexity of the random forms and rate of mental rotation, as measured by the slope of the reaction-time functions (cf. Figure 5.3). The six-fold difference between rotation rate for the complex perspective drawings studied by Shepard and Metzler (1971) and rotation rate for the alphanumeric characters studied by Cooper and Shepard (1973a, 1973b) constituted cogent *a priori* evidence for expecting reaction time to depend upon variations in complexity within the set of stimuli studied here.

One possible explanation for the failure of complexity variations in the random forms to produce systematic reaction-time differences relates to the nature of the subjects' internal representations or mental images of the forms. Note that in the present experiment, complexity was confounded with redundancy of useable cues for making the standard-reflected determination. Thus, subjects could have achieved the correct response by imagining only a few distinctive features of the test form, regardless of its actual perceptual complexity, rotated into the trained orientation. A related possibility is that the internal representation of the visual test form was highly schematic in comparison with the rich detail of the form itself.

If either a schematic representation or an image of one or more salient features was sufficient for comparing the transformed internal representation with a memory representation of the appropriate test form, then complexity variations in the external stimulus objects were not necessarily incorporated in the internal representations of those objects. Consequently, stimulus complexity would not be expected to produce reaction-time differences. Thus the data from this experiment do not legislate conclusively on the issue of complexity in that they fail to provide an indication of the degree of specificity and completeness of the transformed internal representation. Further experiments, currently in progress, are addressed specifically to this question.

Finally, the reaction-time functions obtained in the present experiment suggest that the "familiarity" explanation for the nonlinearity obtained with alphanumeric characters is incorrect. If subjects in the present experiment learned the random forms at the trained orientation, then we should expect that the forms would become most familiar in this position and progressively less familiar when shown at larger and larger angular departures from the trained orientation. Thus if speed of rotation is positively related to familiarity, then reaction time should increase monotonically but nonlinearly with angular departure from the familiar orientation.

While the predicted nonlinearity is not evident in Figures 5.2 and 5.3, these data do not conclusively infirm the familiarity interpretation for alphanumeric stimuli. First, alphanumeric characters are much more overlearned in the unique upright orientation than were these random forms in the arbitrarily chosen training orientations. Consequently, any familiarity effect in the case of the random shapes may be relatively weak. Moreover, since the forms were presented in only one training orientation (unlike alphanumeric characters, which are frequently encountered in orientations departing somewhat from the upright), the spread of any familiarity effect resulting from pretraining may have extended only to orientations departing by less than 60°. Thus the present experiment may not have been sensitive enough to reveal appreciable effects of familiarity. However, the linear reaction-time data do lead us to regard this explanation with much less enthusiasm.

EXPERIMENT II

Cooper and Shepard (1973b) have proposed that both the time required to *respond* to an externally presented test character and the time required to *prepare* for the external onset of such a test character reflect the amount of time needed to carry out the rotation of a mental image. Although these two sorts of mental rotation (post-stimulus and prestimulus) differ in several respects, it was argued that both methods of image transformation should be carried out in essentially the same manner and at essentially the same rate.

In the present experiment, the rate of preparatory mental rotation is measured directly. This is accomplished by providing the subjects with advance information concerning the identity and orientation of an upcoming test form and, further, by requiring them to indicate when they are prepared for the external onset of that test form. In order to consider this reaction time a direct measure of the time needed to prepare for the test stimulus, it must also be established that a subject is, in fact, fully prepared. This is accomplished by presenting the actual test form immediately following the "preparation" response and by requiring a second, discriminative response to the test form.

By comparing the shapes and the slopes of (a) the function relating prepraration reaction time to anticipated test-form orientation, and (b) the function relating choice reaction time to angular departure of the test form from a trained orientation (cf., Experiment I above), it should be possible to assess the relationship between the nature and rate of both pre-stimulus and post-stimulus mental rotation.

Method

Subjects. The same eight subjects who had previously participated in Experiment I also participated in the present experiment.

Stimuli. The stimuli were the random forms used in Experiment I. In order to reduce the length of the experiment, each subject was tested with only four of the eight original forms. The stimulus set for each individual subject consisted of the four forms which (in the data from Experiment I for that subject) had yielded the largest F-values for linear components and had accounted for less than 25% of that subject's errors. Although only four forms were used per subject, the eight forms used in Experiment I were represented approximately equally across subjects.

In addition to the test stimuli, advance-information cues were presented visually. Identity information consisted of an outline drawing of the standard version of the upcoming test form in the trained orientation. Orientation information consisted of a black arrow, passing through the center of a circular field and pointing to the orientation at which the top of the test form would appear. The specifications of the apparatus and the stimuli were identical to those in Experiment I.

Procedure. The experiment consisted of four one-hour sessions per subject. During the first half of the initial session, the subject was refamiliarized with the four random forms which were to be used throughout the experiment by means of tachistoscopic presentation of individual forms in the trained orientation only. The subject was required to indicate *vocally* whether each test form was a standard or a reflected version. "Standard" responses were signaled by saying "S," and "reflected" responses were signaled by saying "R." This voice response activated a noise-operated relay and stopped the reaction-time clock. After completing a block of 32 retraining trials (four presentations of both standard and reflected versions of each of the four forms), the remainder of the session consisted of practice for the test trials in subsequent sessions.

During the test trials, the subject was required to discriminate standard from reflected test forms presented at any of the six orientations used in Experiment I. Prior to the onset of the test form, the subject was given advance information concerning both its identity and orientation. Figure 5.4 schematically illustrates the structure of the test trials and the appearance of the advance information. At the beginning of each trial, the subject was instructed to prepare for the upcoming test form by rotating an image of the pre-indicated form in either a clockwise or a counterclockwise direction. Thus the orientation cue shown in Figure 5.4 could indicate either a 60° clockwise rotation or a 300° counterclockwise rotation, depending upon the prior instruction.

Identity information was always presented for a fixed duration of 3000 msec and was immediately replaced by an arrow, indicating the position at which the top of the test form would appear. The duration of the orientation cue was controlled by the subject. When fully prepared for the presentation of the test form at the indicated orientation, the subject pushed a right-hand button (a left-hand button for the one left-handed subject).

The button-pressing response (henceforth called the "preparation" response) stopped a timer which displayed the total duration of the orientation cue. Immediately following the preparation response, the test form designated in advance appeared in the orientation designated in advance. The subject was required to determine the version of the test form as quickly as possible by saying "S" for a standard form and "R" for a reflected form. This vocal response stopped a second clock which displayed the total duration of the test stimulus and terminated the visual display. Thus two reaction times, the button-pressing preparation reaction time and the vocal discriminative reaction time, were recorded on each test trial.

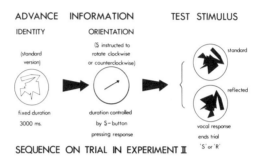

Figure 5.4 Schematic illustration of the sequence of visual displays and required responses on a trial in Experiment II.

Following the initial training and practice session, each subject complete three one-hour test sessions. Within each test session, trials were blocked by direction of rotation such that on half of the trials, clockwise rotations were specified and on the other half of the trials, counterclockwise rotations were specified. The order of clockwise and counterclockwise trial blocks was balanced over sessions. Within each clockwise or counterclockwise block, each of the four forms was presented in both standard and reflected versions at each of the six orientations, for a total of 48 trials per block and 96 trials per test session. Thus each of the eight subjects completed 288 test trials (half clockwise, half counterclockwise), and 576 reaction times (half preparation, half discriminative) were obtained for each subject. As in Experiment I, all error trials were retaken.

Results

The principal results for the group data are illustrated in Figure 5.5. The plotted points in the uppermost function, which represent group data from Experiment I, were computed by averaging within each subject over the four forms subsequently used in Experiment II, and then averaging over all eight subjects. Thus the data from Experiments I and II reflect reaction times to the same set of forms within each subject and are perfectly comparable.

The function labeled "RT_1" represents mean preparation time in

Experiment II, averaged over clockwise and counterclockwise rotations. The function labeled "RT$_2$" represents mean discriminative reaction time, averaged over "standard" and "reflected" responses. Though not shown in Figure 5.5, "standard" responses were about 20 msec faster than "reflected" responses for all test-stimulus orientations. Error reaction times are not included in the plotted points; however, error rates are plotted as a function of orientation and version.

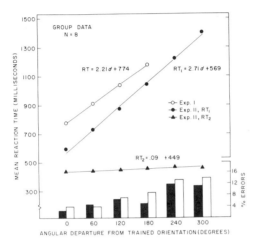

Figure 5.5 Mean reaction time as a function of angular departure of the test form from the trained orientation. The uppermost function illustrates a subset of the group data from Experiment I. The other two functions illustrate group data for both preparation and discriminative reaction times from Experiment II. Equations for the best-fitting straight lines are shown. Error rates are plotted as a function of orientation and version, with solid open bars representing errors on standard and reflected test stimuli, respectively.

The average time required to prepare for an upcoming rotated test form (RT$_1$) is a remarkably linear function of the angular departure of the test form from the trained orientation. Furthermore, we can see for the first time that this linear function extends beyond a 180° departure from the trained orientation all the way to 300° (of clockwise or counterclockwise departure, depending upon prior instructions). The average time needed to make the discriminative (verbal) response (RT$_2$) is virtually constant for all angular departures from the trained orientation. This choice reaction time does increase slightly with orientation; however, the range of mean RT$_2$ is only 26 msec, compared with the 800-msec range for RT$_1$.

This flat RT$_2$ function demonstrates that subjects were indeed prepared for the onset of the test form when they so indicated. If subjects were not prepared for the onset of the test form when they made the preparation response, then we should expect discriminative reaction time to increase with angular departure of the test form from the trained orientation and to reach a maximum value at the 180° departure. Such a relationship is virtually absent in the RT_2 function in Figure 5.5. Note, also, that the zero-intercept of the RT_2 function is some 325 msec lower than the post-stimulus reaction-time function from Experiment I.

The rates of prestimulus (preparatory) and post-stimulus mental rotation can be estimated directly from the slopes of the reaction-time functions in Figure 5.5. Average rate of post-stimulus rotation for the set of data from Experiment I is about 450°/sec, and average rate of prestimulus rotation for the same subjects and the same random forms, estimated from the slope of the RT_1 function, is about 370°/sec. For the group data, post-stimulus rotation appears to be somewhat faster than preparatory rotation; however, this relationship between rotation rates is evident for only six of the individual subjects. For two of the subjects, prestimulus rotation is faster than post-stimulus rotation.

For the group data, the mean difference between the slopes of the Experiment I reaction-time function and the preparation reaction-time function failed to achieve traditional levels of statistical significance ($t(7) = 2.20$; $.05 < p < .07$).[4] For five of the eight subjects, similar t-tests revealed that the functions were not significantly different in slope, and for the three other subjects the difference was marginally significant ($p < .05$).

Reaction-time functions corresponding to the group functions shown in Figure 5.5 are plotted for each of the individual subjects in Figure 5.6. (In the figure the scale for RT_2 has been displaced downward by 200 msec for JK and SR.) Although the eight subjects differ considerably in overall reaction time (particularly in rotation rate), the data for each of the subjects capture the principal features of the group data. In addition, each subject shows cross-experiment consistency. That is, there is a significant positive correlation, among the individual subjects, between rank order of the slopes of the post-stimulus reaction-time functions and rank order of the slopes of the preparation reaction-time functions ($r_s = .74$, $N = 8$, $p < .05$). On the other hand, a similar Spearman rank order correlation between slopes of the RT_1 functions and slopes of the RT_2 functions is nonsignificant ($r_s = .36$, $N = 8$, $p > .05$). The right-hand panel of Table 5.1 (p. 124) presents additional data for individual subjects, and Cooper (1973) provides complete data for each of the eight subjects.

In a five-way analysis of variance of the group preparation times (RT_1), the only main effects to reach statistical significance were subjects and orientations (for both, $p < .001$). With regard to the effect

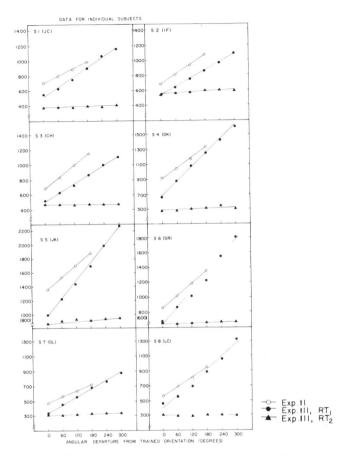

Figure 5.6 Mean reaction time as a function of angular departure of the test form from the trained orientation, plotted separately for each of the eight individual subjects. The functions for each subject correspond to the group functions illustrated in Figure 5.5.

of practice on the slope of the RT_1 function, the sessions × orientations interaction proved nonsignificant, even when just the linear component of the orientation factor, was used in the analysis of variance ($p > .10$).

In the analysis of variance on the RT_2 data, the main effects of subjects, standard-vs-reflected versions, and orientations were statistically significant. (The significance of the main effect of orientation for the group data is due, primarily, to the data of one of the eight subjects.)[5]

Polynomial regressions for both RT_1 and RT_2 functions were computed for the group data, for individual subjects, and for forms within subjects. For RT_1 all these regressions revealed a highly significant linear trend ($p < .001$), and no quadratic or higher-order effects were significant ($p > .05$). For RT_2, several of the regressions yielded marginally significant linear components ($p < .05$).

Error rates were somewhat higher than in Experiment I. For individual subjects, error rates ranged from 1% to 13.3%, with an average of 7.9% (cf. Figure 5.5).

DISCUSSION

The linearity of the RT_1 function supports the notion that subjects prepare for an upcoming, rotated test form by imagining the standard version of the form indicated by the identity cue rotated into the orientation designated in advance. The internally generated and prerotated mental image can then be compared directly with the ensuing test form. If the two representations match, the subject can respond "standard" immediately. If the two representations are incongruent, extra time is needed to respond "reflected."

The flatness and overall lowness of the RT_2 function indicates that subjects are fully prepared for the onset of the test form when they execute the preparation response. This flatness further indicates that comparisons between the transformed preparatory image and the visually presented test form can be made equally rapidly at any angular departure from the trained position *for which the subject is prepared.* Thus we can conclude that to be prepared for the onset of an external stimulus is to have, in advance, an appropriate internal representation of that external stimulus.

The extension of the linear preparation-time function beyond 180° has theoretical significance. One might suppose that the process of preparing for a rotated stimulus consists merely in the selective priming of feature detectors appropriate to the upcoming stimulus in the designated orientation, and, further, that it is more difficult (and hence takes more time) to activate detectors at greater angular departures from a familiar orientation. If this account were correct, then we should expect the RT_1 function to peak at 180° and to be symmetrical about the inverted position. This symmetrical shape would result from the differential difficulty of priming feature detectors at 0°, 60°, 120°, and 180° angular departures from the trained orientation. Instructions for clockwise or counterclockwise "rotations" should not affect the RT_1 function, for, presumably, the process of activating feature detectors at a certain orientation does not have a directional component.

Such a feature-priming theory has in itself no mechanism to account for the sensitivity of the RT_1 function to direction-of-rotation instructions. A process of mental rotation, however, predicts exactly the relationship illustrated in Figure 5.5. The extension of the RT_1 function out to a 300° angular departure provides strong support for the claim that subjects carry out a mental analog of an external physical rotation in preparing for an upcoming test stimulus. For, the linear increase in preparation time up to and, particularly, beyond 180° indicates that the mental process is passing through a trajectory in a specific direction, and that the time required to complete the process is a function of the length of the trajectory rather than the physical departure of the end point (in either direction) from the trained position.

Like Experiment I, the present experiment is not sensitive enough to specify the degree of structural correspondence between the preparatory image and its perceptual counterpart. However, the flatness of the RT_2 function and the reasonably low error rates indicate that the preparatory image must have embodied a sufficient degree of the spatial structure of the corresponding external stimulus to be used for rapid and accurate matching against that stimulus when it physically appeared.

The primary objective of the present experiment was to examine the relationship between prestimulus and post-stimulus mental rotation. While both processes consist of the transformation of a mental image, they differ with respect to the degree of external support. In the case of preparatory rotation, the transformed representation is an internally maintained image of a visual object which is no longer externally present. In the case of post-stimulus rotation, the internal representation is extracted from a visual stimulus which remains externally present during the entirety of the subsequent rotational process.

For the group data and for six of the individual subjects, the estimated rate of preparatory rotation was somewhat slower than the rate of post-stimulus rotation. Nevertheless, the difference, even when present, was generally quite small for both the group data (cf. Figure 5.5) and for the individual subjects (cf. Figure 5.6). Indeed, the group data and over half of the subjects showed no statistically significant differences between prestimulus and post-stimulus rotation rates. These results thus provide more direct confirmation of the earlier, indirectly derived suggestion of Cooper and Shepard (1973b) that the external (but nonrotating) presence of the object that is being mentally rotated has little effect on the rate of that mental rotation.

The data plotted in Figure 5.5 reveal a difference of 325 msec between the intercept of the post-stimulus rotation reaction time function (Experiment I) and the intercept of the discriminative function (Experiment II). This may seem surprising at first, for in both cases the test stimulus—a form presented in the trained orientation—and the required response—determination of the version of the upright form—are identical. However, this intercept difference may relate to an information-processing model which proposes that before post-stimulus rotation can be initiated, subjects must first determine the identity and the orientation of the tilted test stimulus (cf. Cooper & Shepard, 1973b).

In the present experiment, subjects were provided with advance information as to *both* the identity and the orientation of the upcoming test form prior to the choice response. However, in Experiment I *neither* sort of information was provided in advance. It is tempting to suppose that the 325-msec difference between the intercept in these two situations reflects the time needed to determine the identity and the orientation of the test form when given no advance information (Experiment I).

SUMMARY AND CONCLUDING REMARKS

In this final section the central findings from the experiments reported above are reviewed, and general implications of these findings are discussed.

(a) RT for determining whether a rotated test form is standard or reflected in version increases linearly with the angular departure of that form from a previously trained orientation (Experiment I). This linearity provides evidence that subjects mentally rotate an internal representation of the test form into the trained orientation in order to determine whether the presented version is standard or reflected.

(b) "Standard" responses are faster than "reflected" responses for all test-stimulus orientations (Experiments I and II). This constant RT difference suggests that subjects initially compare the mentally transformed representation of the test form with a memory image of the *standard* version of that form at the trained orientation.

(c) The intercepts and slopes of the RT functions for each of the eight random forms are approximately equal (Experiment I). This unexpected finding suggests that regardless of the perceptual complexity of the test form, mental rotation is carried out at a constant rate of some 460°/sec (for these particular subjects).

(d) When subjects are given advance information concerning the identity and the orientation of an upcoming test form, the time required to prepare for the onset of that test form is a linearly increasing function of the angular departure of the predesignated orientation from the previously learned position (Experiment II). Furthermore, this linear function extends from 0° to 300° of clockwise or counterclockwise departure, depending upon which direction was specified in advance. This finding indicates that subjects prepare for the up-coming test form by mentally rotating an image of that form, in the specified direction, into the predesignated orientation even though that orientation sometimes indicates a preparatory rotation of more than 180°.

(e) Following a preparatory mental rotation, reaction time for determining whether a visually presented test form is a standard or a reflected version is rapid and constant, regardless of the orienta-tion of the test form (Experiment II). The flat reaction-time func-tion demonstrates that subjects are prepared for the test-form onset, in the sense of having an appropriate internal representation prerotated into the designated position when they so indicate.

(f) The slope of the post-stimulus reaction-time function (Ex-periment I) is somewhat smaller than the slope of the prestimulus reaction-time function (Experiment II); however, they do not dif-fer significantly. This similarity in slope indicates that both sorts of mental rotation are carried out at comparable rates.

In the experiments reported above, discussions of the processes involved in preparing for and responding to disoriented test stimuli have made reference to the "rotation of a mental image." The central assumption has been that the internal processes and repre-sentations underlying performance in these tasks are structurally analogous to the external operations and objects to which they correspond. Recently, a fundamentally different view of the nature of these mental operations and representations has emerged (see Pylyshyn, 1973). These alternative accounts claim that the internal representations and processes involved in tasks such as those studied here bear no structural resemblance to their corresponding external objects and operations.

An example of one such model for the representations and pro-cesses underlying "mental rotation" tasks has recently been pro-posed by Levin (1973). In this model, visual objects are represented propositionally in the form of networks, and orientation is repre-sented in the network in the form of a reference point and position predicates which relate the orientation of subparts of the represen-tation to the reference point. Rotation is accomplished by succes-sively changing these orientation predicates. This model (and other models of the same variety) makes a clear and interesting predic-tion: The amount of time required "to rotate mentally" an in-ternal representation of a visual object should increase not only with the amount of disorientation of the object, but also with its visual complexity.

The results of Experiment I above indicate that rotation rate does *not* depend upon complexity for random forms within the range of six to twenty-four points. Unfortunately, this experiment does not rule out the possibility that the internal representations of the test forms were reduced or highly schematic in nature. One way to test between these alternatives is to require subjects to distinguish between standard versions of random forms and test probes which differ from the standard in fairly subtle aspects (rather than merely reflection). Such research might provide an indication of the degree of structural detail embodied in a transformed internal representation, as well as resolve the question of the relationship between complexity and rotation rate.

6 | Mental Transformations and Visual Comparison Processes

Originally authored by Lynn A. Cooper and Peter Podgorny

Subjects were required to discriminate previously learned "standard" versions of angular shapes from randomly perturbed "distractor" versions that varied in similarity to the standard. Advance information concerning the identity and the orientation of the test form was provided. Subjects were instructed to prepare for the presentation of the test form by mentally rotating an internal representation of the designated standard form (identity cue) into the designated orientation. The time needed to prepare for the presentation of the test form increased linearly with the angular departure of the indicated orientation from a previously learned position. This finding suggests that, in accordance with instructions, subjects performed a mental rotation in preparing for the upcoming test shape. Rate of preparation was not affected by the complexity of the standard form presented as the identity cue. Discriminative reaction time was not affected by either test-form complexity or angular departure of the test form from the learned orientation. In addition, striking individual differences in the pattern of discriminative reaction times were found. The implications of these results for (a) the nature of the processes and representations underlying the mental rotation task and (b) the nature of visual comparison processes are discussed.

A question of current interest concerns the internal representation and processing of visual information. A general technique for investigating this question involves measuring the time required to compare and/or mentally manipulate internally generated representations of visual objects. In a series of experiments, Shepard and his colleagues (Cooper, 1975; Cooper & Shepard, 1973; Metzler & Shepard, 1974; Shepard, 1975; Shepard & Metzler, 1971) have used this chronometric method in tasks that require subjects to compare the shape of visual objects that differ in orientation. In all of these studies, the time needed to determine whether two visual objects

Reprinted by permission from the *Journal of Experimental Psychology: Human Perception and Performance*, 1976, *2*, 503-514.[1]

were the same in shape or mirror images increased linearly with the angular difference in their orientations. The above investigators have interpreted these linear reaction-time functions as indicating that subjects performed the tasks by "mentally rotating" an internal representation of one object into congruence with the other and then comparing the two representations for a match or a mismatch in shape.

The internal processes and representations underlying the rotation task have been conceptualized as "analog" in nature (Cooper & Shepard, 1973; Metzler & Shepard, 1974; Shepard, 1975). More specifically, this notion implies that during a mental rotation, the internal representation passes through a trajectory of intermediate states, each of which has a one-to-one correspondence to the intermediate spatial locations in the external rotation of an object. In addition, the internal representation undergoing the rotation is viewed as preserving some degree of the spatial structure of its corresponding external object.

In contrast, several investigators have recently challenged the notion that, under some circumstances, visual information is processed and represented in a basically analog fashion (e.g., Baylor, 1971; Palmer, 1975; Pylyshyn, 1973). Rather, they have suggested that abstract, propositional data structures provide a more satisfactory format for the representation of visual information. A specific representation of this sort, which uses network structures like those used in recent models of semantic memory (see Norman & Rumelhart, 1975), could be applied to the mental rotation task (see Levin, 1973). Features and relations among features of visual objects could be represented by nodes and links between nodes in the network. Orientation could be represented in the network by means of a reference point and position predicates that relate the orientation of subparts of the representation to the reference point. Rotation could be accomplished by successively changing these orientation predicates and accumulating a running count of the number of such replacements.

How could a simple propositional model of this sort be distinguished from an analog explanation of the rotation task? Both forms of representation predict that reaction time will increase with the angular difference between the two visual objects. Note, however, that the simple propositional model makes an additional prediction that is not necessarily made by the analog representation: "The time required to "rotate mentally" an internal representation of a visual object should increase with the complexity of the visual object, or with the number of orientation-sensitive nodes in its representation.

This is a consequence of that fact that as the complexity of the representation increases, more time will be required to replace successively the relative position predicates, thereby accomplishing the rotation. *Indeed, this dependence of rotation rate on form complexity must be predicted by all models which assume that the internal representation of a visual object is rotated piece-by-piece or feature-by-feature.*

It is suggestive, therefore, that in an earlier experiment (Cooper, 1975, Experiment I; reprinted here in the preceding Chapter 5) the slope of the reaction-time function, which presumably reflects the rate of mental rotation, was not systematically related to test-form complexity.

Unfortunately, this experiment does not adequately demonstrate that rate of mental rotation is unaffected by form complexity. It is possible that the failure to find a complexity effect resulted from the fact that the required discrimination was always between a random shape and its mirror image. That is, a standard form can be distinguished from its reflected version on the basis of only a small set of the features available in the entire structure of the form. If subjects were mentally rotating and then using for memory comparison only a few features or a reduced representation of the test form, then complexity variations in the forms themselves were not necessarily incorporated in the internal representations of those forms. Thus, the Cooper (1975) experiment does not conclusively address the issue of complexity in that it provides no indication of whether the full spatial structure of the test forms was preserved in their corresponding internal representations.

The present experiment was designed to explore more incisively possible effects of stimulus complexity on the rate of mental transformation. An experimental situation was constructed in which subjects would be unable to achieve the required discrimination by using a reduced representation of the stimulus. This was accomplished by requiring subjects to distinguish not only between standard and reflected versions of random shapes, but also between standard shapes and distractors that varied systematically in their similarity to the standards. If the rate of mental rotation were unaffected by stimulus complexity in this situation, one simple class of propositional models for the rotation task would be discredited.

In addition, a two-reaction-time procedure was used in order to permit separate assessment of the effects of the independent variables on both the time required to perform a mental transformation and the time required to compare a transformed internal representation with an external test stimulus (cf. Cooper, 1975).

146   CHAPTER 6

Method

Subjects. The six subjects, all students and staff at Stanford University, were paid for their participation in five 1-hr. sessions. Five of the subjects were male, one subject was female, and one of the male subjects was left-handed. This group of subjects consisted of all of the original participants in a set of earlier, related experiments (Cooper, 1975) who were still residing in the Stanford area. Only experienced subjects were used in order to enable a precise quantitative comparison between the results of the earlier Cooper (1975) experiments and the results of the present experiment.

Stimuli. The stimulus set was based upon the eight random, angular shapes used by Cooper (1975). These original or "standard" shapes were generated by Attneave and Arnoult's (1956) Method I for the construction of random nonsense forms. The shapes varied in the number of angles or points determining inflections on the perimeter, a measure highly correlated with ratings of perceptual complexity of such forms (Attneave, 1957). The standard shapes included in the stimulus set of the present experiment consisted of one form from each of the five levels of complexity (6, 8, 12, 16, and 24 points) studied by Cooper (1975). These five standards are depicted in the leftmost column of Figure 6.1.

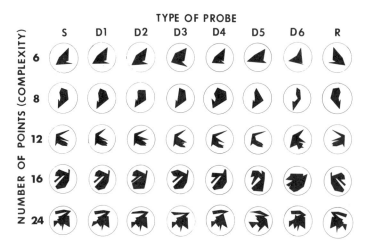

Figure 6.1 The complete set of alternative test forms. (Standard shapes at each of the five levels of complexity are shown in the leftmost column, and reflected versions are shown in the rightmost column. Perturbations of the standard shapes, varying in rated similarity to the standards, are shown in the middle six columns.)

In order to obtain a set of distractors that differed from the standards and that varied in similarity to the standards, a computer program was written that randomly perturbed the coordinates of the points of the standard shapes. For each of the five standards, approximately 40 *different* perturbations were generated that varied in both the number of points perturbed and the extent of each point's perturbation. In constructing a perturbation of any given standard shape, a specified number of points of the standard (from 1 to n, where n = the total number of points in the shape) were randomly selected to be perturbed. Each of the coordinates of these selected points was then randomly changed by an amount between specified upper and lower boundaries. The values of the boundaries varied depending upon the extent of perturbation desired. Perturbations that resulted in new intersections of contours were eliminated, yielding from 22 to 26 usable perturbations for each standard shape.

In general, increasing both the number of points perturbed and the extent of each perturbation produced forms of greater dissimilarity to the original standard shape. However, since certain angles of the standard shapes seemed more perceptually salient than others, there was no guarantee that random perturbations of an equal number of points and of equal extent would result in forms of equal perceptual similarity to the standard. Thus, the final selection of those perturbations to be included in the stimulus set was based upon ratings of the perceptual similarity of each perturbation to the standard shape from which it derived. Eight subjects, none of whom subsequently participated in the major experiment reported here, rated the similarity of each perturbation to its standard on a 1 (highly similar) to 7 (highly dissimilar) scale. Subjects were encouraged to use the entire 1 to 7 scale and to maintain a constant criterion for the use of each rating category for all standard shapes.

Rated similarity of each perturbation to its standard was averaged across subjects. From these average ratings, six perturbations of each standard were selected as *different* probes for the final stimulus set. These perturbations were selected in the following manner: (a) For each standard, the average similarity ratings associated with its perturbations were grouped into six categories, corresponding to the intervals between the seven similarity scale values. That is, all perturbations with average ratings between 1 and 2 were placed in one category, all perturbations with average ratings between 2 and 3 were placed in a second category, and so on, for the remaining four categories. (b) Within each category defined above, that perturbation whose average similarity rating had the lowest variance over raters was selected for use in the final stimulus set.

The complete set of stimuli is illustrated in Figure 6.1. The five standards are shown in the leftmost column, and the perturbations resulting from the selection procedure described above are shown in

the middle six columns. The column labeled "D1" contains perturbations rated highly similar to the standards (between scale values of
1 and 2). Column "D2" contains perturbations with average similarity ratings between values of 2 and 3, and so forth, with column
"D6" containing perturbations with average similarity ratings between values of 6 and 7. Thus, rated similarity to the standard decreases monotonically from a D1 to a D6 perturbation. In addition,
the procedure used to select the perturbations in Figure 6.1 was designed to ensure that the six steps of decreasing similarity (from D1
to D6) were roughly equal in magnitude both within a given standard shape and across standards at the different complexity levels.
The final type of *different* test probe, depicted in the rightmost
column, consisted of mirror-image or reflected versions of the standard forms.

Prior to presenting these test stimuli, advance information cues
were displayed. Identity information consisted of an outline drawing
of one of the five standard forms, presented in the originally trained
orientation. (In the previous Cooper, 1975, experiments, the subjects
participating in the current study had learned to distinguish standard
from reflected versions of these random forms at one of six orientations. For any given subject, the orientation learned originally was
preserved as the "trained" orientation, and hence the orientation of
the identity cue, in the present experiment.) Orientation information
consisted of a black arrow, passing through the center of a circular
field, and pointing to the orientation at which the top of the test
form would appear. The orientation cue, and hence the test form,
could be presented at any one of six equally spaced orientations
around a circle in the two-dimensional picture plane. The six possible
orientations consisted of 60° steps of clockwise rotation from the 0°
position.

The stimuli were presented in an Iconix three-field tachistoscope
and appeared centered within an illuminated circular field with a
black surround. Luminance of the circular field was about 68.5
cd/m^2, and it subtended a visual angle of 4°. Both the test forms and
the advance information cues subtended an angle of about 2°.

Procedure. The procedure was similar to that used in Experiment
II of Cooper (1975). On each experimental trial, subjects were presented with both identity information and orientation information
prior to the onset of the test form. Identity information was always
displayed first for a fixed duration of 3,000 msec. Immediately upon
the offset of the identity cue, the black arrow constituting the orientation cue was presented. The duration of the orientation cue was
controlled by the subject. Subjects were instructed to use the advance information to prepare for the upcoming test form by mentally

rotating a memory representation of the standard form—indicated by the identity cue—into the position designated by the orientation cue. Subjects were instructed always to perform these preparatory rotations in a clockwise direction, regardless of the angular departure of the orientation cue from the trained position.

When the subject had completed the preparatory mental rotation and, hence, felt fully prepared for the presentation of the test form, he or she indicated this readiness by pushing a right-hand button (a left-hand button for the one left-handed subject). This button pressing or "preparation" response stopped a timer that displayed the total duration of the orientation cue. Immediately upon actuation of the preparation response, the test form appeared in the orientation designated in advance. The subject was required to distinguish as rapidly as possible between test forms the same as or different in any respect from the previously presented standard shape by saying "S" or "D," respectively. This vocal response activated a noise-operated relay and stopped a second clock, displaying the total duration of the test stimulus and terminating the visual display. Thus, two reaction times were recorded on each trial: (a) the button-pressing preparation reaction time and (b) the vocal *same-different* choice reaction time.

General experimental design. Prior to the experimental sessions, each subject participated in two types of practice trials. In the first practice block, the subject was required to distinguish between standard shapes and distractors (D1–D6 perturbations and reflected versions) that were presented only in the trained orientation. The subject responded "S" or "D" as rapidly as possible, and feedback was given concerning the correct response. The second block of practice trials consisted of a randomly selected set of 30 of the experimental trials. By the end of both blocks of practice, the subject had viewed each of the seven possible *different* probes for each standard shape at least once.

During the actual experimental trials, test forms from each of the five levels of complexity were presented 14 times at each of the six orientations. On half of these trials the test form was the same as the standard shape, and on the other half of the trials the test form was different. Each of the seven types of *different* probes appeared equally often. Thus, each of the six subjects completed 420 test trials, and 840 reaction times (half preparation, half discriminative) were obtained for each subject. Subjects were informed that the probability of *same* and *different* trials was equal, and they were instructed for both speed and accuracy. Feedback concerning response accuracy was given after every trial.

The experimental trials required five 1-hr. sessions of participation for each subject. Each session began with a series of 10 practice trials. At the end of each session, error trials were retaken, randomly interspersed with filler trials, in order to obtain a complete set of error-free data for each subject.

Results and Discussion

Group data. The principal results for the group data are illustrated in Figure 6.2. The plotted points in Figure 6.2, as well in all subsequent figures, and the data on which all statistical analyses were performed are based on correct reaction times.

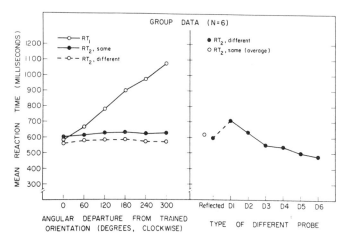

Figure 6.2 Reaction-time results for the group data. (In the left-hand panel, mean preparation time, RT_1, and mean *same* and *different* discriminative reaction times, RT_2, are plotted as a function of angular departure of the test form from the trained orientation. In the right-hand panel, mean *same* reaction time is shown, and mean *different* reaction time is plotted as a function of type of different probe.)

In the left-hand panel, both preparation time (RT_1) and discriminative reaction time (RT_2, plotted separately for *same* and *different* responses) are shown as a function of angular departure of the test stimulus from the trained orientation. Mean preparation time and mean *same* RT_2 are averaged over subjects, complexity of test form, and replications; whereas mean *different* RT_2 is averaged over subjects, test-form complexity, and type of *different* probe. In the right-hand panel, *different* RT_2—averaged over subjects, test-form complexity, and angular departure from the trained orientation—is plotted as a function of type of *different* probe. Mean *same* RT_2 is also shown. As can be seen from the right-hand panel of Figure 6.2, *different* reaction time decreases monotonically with increasing dissimilarity of the standard shape to the test probe (from the

highly similar D1 perturbations to the highly dissimilar D6 perturbations). Mean reaction time to reflected test probes and mean *same*
reaction time are of intermediate speed.

Error rates for the group data, shown in the leftmost column of
Table 6.1, correspond well to the reaction time data in the right-hand
panel of Figure 6.2. Percentage of errors to perturbed *different*
probes decreases as the probes become less similar to the standards,
and error rates for both reflected probes and *same* test forms fall between the error rates for D1 and D6 perturbations.

Table 6.1
Error Rates to Same *Test Forms,* Different *Test Forms,*
and the Seven Types of Different *Probes, for the*
Group Data and for the Two Types of Subjects

Type of test probe	Group data	Type I (fast) subjects	Type II (slow) subjects
Same	6.81%	6.04%	7.18%
Different	11.95%	13.93%	10.92%
D1	33.58%	34.78%	32.96%
D2	18.18%	17.81%	18.37%
D3	7.22%	14.29%	3.22%
D4	1.64%	3.23%	.00%
D5	.83%	1.64%	.00%
D6	.00%	.00%	.00%
Reflected	11.33%	14.29%	9.77%

Note. For group data, $N = 6$; for Type I subjects, $N = 2$; for Type II subjects, $N = 4$.

Consider, now, the reaction time data shown in the left-hand panel
of Figure 6.2. Average time to prepare for an upcoming, rotated test
form (RT_1, Figure 6.2) is a strikingly linear function of the angular
departure of the test form from the trained orientation. A polynomial regression computed for the RT_1 function revealed a highly significant linear component, $F(1, 4) = 1,379.43$, $p < .001$, and no
significant quadratic or higher-order effects. In contrast, average times
to make both *same* and *different* responses (RT_2, Figure 6.2) are virtually constant for all angular departures from the trained orientation.

The linearity of the preparation-time function and flatness of the
discriminative reaction time function suggest that subjects prepared
for the presentation of the test form by mentally rotating a representation of the standard shape into the orientation indicated in advance.
The mentally transformed representation could then be rapidly
matched against the ensuing test form. The flatness of the RT_2

functions indicates that subjects were prepared for the onset of the test form when they so indicated. Hence, all of the time required for rotational processing is reflected in the RT_1 function, while the RT_2 functions represent only the time needed to compare a transformed internal representation with the test form and the time needed to execute the discriminative response.

Note, in addition, that the linear RT_1 function extends beyond the maximum physical angular departure of 180° out to 300° of clockwise angular departure from the trained orientation. This extension provides further evidence that the process of preparation consists of a mental rotation. That is, it indicates that the internal preparation process is passing through a trajectory in a specific direction, and that the time required to complete the process is a function of the length of the trajectory, rather than the physical departure of the end point from the trained position (cf. Cooper, 1975).

A three-way analysis of variance on the RT_1 data showed that the main effects attributable to subjects' angular departures from trained orientations, and all two-way interactions with subjects, were highly significant. *However, neither the main effect of the factor form complexity nor the interaction between form complexity and angular departure from trained orientation achieved statistical significance (for both, $F < 1$).* The failure to find effects of complexity on reaction time is also evident upon examination of the slopes of the RT_1 functions for each of the five standard shapes. The values of the slopes for the five standard shapes, from the smallest number of points to greatest number of points, are 1.74, 1.59, 1.62, 1.75, and 1.64. A correlation between rank order of complexity of the forms and rank order of the corresponding slopes was nonsignificant ($r_s = +.20$, with $n = 5$).

This absence of a complexity effect speaks directly to the issue motivating the present experiment, namely, the nature of the processes and representation underlying the rotation task. However, before we can definitively conclude that the rate of preparatory mental rotation is unaffected by stimulus complexity, several alternative possibilities must be examined.

In line with the above objections to the Cooper (1975) experiment, it may be that subjects in the present experiment were unable to generate and to mentally manipulate internal representations with a complex spatial structure and, rather, prepared for the test form by rotating reduced or partial representations of the standard shape. This account is consistent with the lack of effect of complexity on the slope of the RT_1 function. However, this account does predict that discriminative reaction time and error rates should vary with form complexity. Specifically, RT_2 should be longer and error rates higher for more complex forms. This prediction follows from the fact that internal representations of the more complex forms would be more highly reduced than representations of the simpler forms. Consequently, comparisons of the internal representations of the more complex forms with the visual test probes should be more difficult and, hence, more time consuming and less accurate.

There is no evidence from the present experiment of a systematic relationship between form complexity and either RT_2 or error rates. Analyses of variance performed separately on the *same* and *different* RT_2 data showed that for neither response did the main effect of form complexity achieve statistical significance ($p > .10$ in both cases). In addition, group error rates are shown in the leftmost column of Table 6.2. As with the reaction time data, there does not appear to be any systematic relationship between form complexity and percentage of errors. This suggestion is confirmed by the nonsignificant correlation between rank order of form complexity and rank order of the corresponding error rates ($r_s = -.10$, with $n = 5$). Thus, we can reject the notion that the failure to find an effect of complexity on rate of rotation resulted from reduced representations of the standard shapes. Indeed, the lack of relationship between complexity and both reaction time and error rates suggests that, even for the more complex forms, a good deal of the spatial structure of the form was preserved in its corresponding internal representation.

Table 6.2
Error Rates to Test Forms at the Five Levels
of Visual Complexity, for the Group Data
and for the Two Types of Subjects

Level of visual complexity	Group data	Type I (fast) subjects	Type II (slow) subjects
6-point form	11.58%	11.11%	11.80%
8-point form	5.62%	6.14%	5.35%
12-point form	7.52%	7.18%	7.69%
16-point form	11.27%	11.60%	11.11%
24-point form	10.95%	14.30%	9.19%

Note. For group data, $N = 6$; for Type I subjects, $N = 2$; for Type II subjects, $N = 4$.

Another related possibility is that during the course of the experiment subjects learned which features of the forms were maximally useful in distinguishing standard shapes from highly similar perturbations. Presumably, a representation of just these discriminating features and, perhaps, a highly schematic representation of any given standard shape was mentally transformed during the preparation interval and then used for comparison with the test form. Again, this account is based on the notion of a reduced representation and, hence, makes predictions not supported by the data. Furthermore, this strategy is rather unlikely on a priori grounds. During the preparatory mental rotation, the subject was in a state of uncertainty as to the nature of the upcoming test form. Representing and mentally transforming only a few features of the standard shape, features that served to distinguish it from a particular perturbation, would certainly be sufficient to achieve the correct response *if* that perturbation then appeared as the test probe. However, the transformed internal representation would not necessarily contain sufficient structural information for comparison with another perturbed probe that itself was similar to the standard. (Note from Figure 6.1 that, owing to the random method of generating the perturbations, the features which distinguish standard shapes from similar *different* probes—for example, D1, D2, D3—are seldom in the same general section of the shape.)

A final alternative account attributes the failure to find a complexity effect to the substantial previous experience which subjects in the present experiment had with variations of this rotation task. However, it is difficult to see how practice would eliminate a complexity effect—except by the formation of a more accurate holistic representation of each form. Moreover, a t test for a difference between the slope of the RT_1 function in the present experiment and the slope of the reaction time function in the Cooper (1975) experiment—from the data for just the six subjects and just the five standard shapes used in the present experiment—revealed no significant effect of the additional practice ($t_5 = 1.39$, $p > .20$). (The respective estimated rotation rates are 589° per sec and 524° per sec.)

Thus we can conclude that the rate of mental rotation is not systematically related to the complexity of the internal representation undergoing this rotation. In addition, the failure of explanations based upon reduced representations of the visual stimuli indicates that the internal representations being mentally transformed preserved much of the spatial structure of their external counterparts. These conclusions are, of course, appropriate only for the definition and range of complexity employed in the present experiment. In addition, these conclusions may be limited by the fact that, in the present experiment, only a single form from each of the five levels of complexity was used.

Nonetheless, the failure to find an effect of form complexity on rotation rate, even within the limited range of complexity examined here, poses problems for the sort of simple propositional model outlined earlier. In particular, this finding permits rejection of the entire class of propositional models that assume that rotation of an internal representation is performed feature-by-feature, or on successive subparts of the representation one at a time. Thus, the lack of complexity effects places significant constraints on the nature of propositional models of the representations and processes underlying the rotation task.

Recently, a different class of propositional models have been proposed that can accommodate the data reported here (see Bobrow, 1975; Palmer, 1975). The general characteristic of these representations is that orientation can be changed by one simple operation that automatically changes the orientation of all subparts of the representation. An example of such a model would have a single reference line with all subparts of the representation related to this reference line. Rotation of the entire representation would be accomplished by changing the orientation value of the reference line. Such a representation is virtually indistinguishable from an analog representation of the sort described above (cf. Cooper & Shepard, 1973; Metzler & Shepard, 1974; Shepard, 1975), particularly in that all of the information concerning the spatial structure of a visual object could be preserved and integrally transformed in either representation.

Subject differences. Examination of the data of each of the six individual subjects revealed totally unexpected but reliable qualitative differences in the pattern of reaction times. These subject differences emerged only in the discriminative reaction time (RT_2) data. Analyses of variance on the preparation-time (RT_1) data revealed that for each of the six subjects the main effect of angular departure from the trained orientation was highly significant ($p < .001$ in all cases). For all subjects, polynomial regressions revealed highly significant linear components in the RT_1 data and no significant quadratic or higher-order effects. The subjects did differ, quantitatively, in the slope of the RT_1 functions. Slope values for individual subjects ranged from 1.13 to 2.75, corresponding to rotation rates of 885° per sec to 364° per sec. None of the subjects showed a reliable monotonic increase in reaction time with form complexity.

In Figure 6.3, preparation-time and discriminative reaction time data are plotted separately for two groups of subjects. These plots represent a subdivision of the group data shown in the left-hand panel of Figure 6.2. The left-hand panel of Figure 6.3 shows the data for the two subjects with the fastest discriminative reaction times, and the right-hand panel shows the data for the four slower subjects. The six subjects were divided into these two groups on the basis of qualitative differences in reaction time data, which are presented

below, as well as differences in overall response speed.[2] The two
fastest subjects are referred to as "Type I" subjects, and the four
slower subjects are referred to as "Type II" subjects. The qualitative and quantitative differences between these two groups of subjects are reflected by the data of all of the individual subjects within
each of the groups.

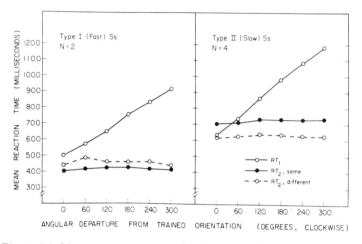

Figure 6.3 Mean preparation time (RT_1) and discriminative reaction
time (RT_2) as a function of angular departure of the test form from the
trained orientation, plotted separately for the two groups of subjects.
(The functions for the two types of subjects correspond to the group
functions illustrated in the left-hand panel of Figure 6.2.)

For both types of subjects shown in Figure 6.3, two central features of the group data (Figure 6.2, left-hand panel) are apparent,
namely, the striking linearity of the RT_1 function and the flatness
of both *same* and *different* RT_2 functions for all test stimulus orientations. In the case of the Type II subjects, the group tendency for
same responses to be longer than *different* responses is accentuated.
The Type I subjects, however, show a reversal of this *same-different*
ordering, with *same* responses an average 40 msec faster than *different* responses.

Further striking differences between these two groups of subjects are displayed in Figure 6.4. Mean discriminative reaction time,
averaged over subjects within groups and form complexity, is plotted
separately for the Type I subjects (left-hand panel) and the Type II
subjects (right-hand panel). Both plots correspond to the group data
in the right-hand panel of Figure 6.2. The four Type II subjects exhibit a sharp monotonic decrease in *different* RT_2 with increasing
dissimilarity between the standard form and the test probe. Mean
same responses and *reflected* responses are of intermediate speed.

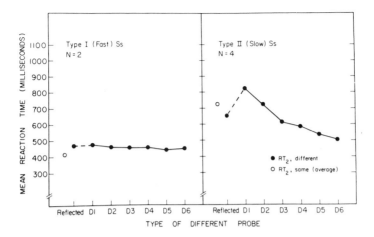

Figure 6.4 Mean *different* reaction time as a function of type of different probe, plotted separately for the two groups of subjects; mean *same* reaction times are also shown for purposes of comparison. (The functions for the two types of subjects correspond to the group functions illustrated in the right-hand panel of Figure 6.2.)

For the two Type I subjects, *different* RT_2 is virtually constant, regardless of the similarity between the standard and the test form. *Same* responses are faster than *different* responses to all seven classes of test probes.

Despite the striking difference in the reaction time data of these two groups of subjects, the error rates shown in the right-hand columns of Tables 6.1 and 6.2 give virtually no indication of a difference. And Table 6.2 indicates that for neither group of subjects are error rates systematically related to form complexity.

Several simple explanations for the differences in performance of these two types of subjects can be rejected at the outset. The possibility of a "floor effect" explaining the flat RT_2 *different* function for the fast Type I subjects (cf. Figure 6.4) can be eliminated because the *same* responses of these subjects are even faster than their *different* responses. The possibility that a speed-accuracy tradeoff might somehow explain the subject differences in unlikely, for while the two types of subjects differ qualitatively in the patterns of their RT_2 data, their error rates associated with each class of the test forms are quite comparable (cf. Table 6.1).

It is tempting to suppose that these two types of subjects differ in the way in which they compare an internal representation with an external stimulus. The faster Type I subjects might adopt a holistic comparison process, whereas the Type II subjects might use a more analytic mode of comparison. Thus, the Type I subjects might attempt to match in parallel a memory representation with a visual test probe, seeking to verify that the two representations are the same. If this holistic comparison fails to produce a match, then the response "different" is made by default.

The Type II subjects might analytically compare a visual memory representation with a test probe (either serially or in parallel), checking for a difference between the two representations. As the similarity between the memory representation and the visual test stimulus becomes greater, the probability of quickly finding a difference becomes smaller, so more time is eventually required to reach the decision that the two representations are different (cf. Figure 6.4). This suggestion gains support from the general agreement between the RT_2 *different* data of the Type II subjects and previous literature on *same-different* visual comparison of multidimensional stimuli (e.g., Egeth, 1966; Hawkins, 1969; Nickerson, 1967). The general interpretation of these studies is that the "different" response is the outcome of an analytic comparison of the attributes or features of the two visual representations.

The Type I–Type II performance differences have recently been replicated on a larger number of subjects under a variety of experimental conditions (Cooper, 1976b). Current investigation is directed toward determining the nature of the processes that produce these marked performance differences and examining the implications of such differences for models of *same-different* visual comparison.

Summary

The principal objective of the present experiment was to explore the relationship between stimulus complexity and rate of mental rotation. Complexity did not systematically affect preparation (rotation) time, discriminative reaction time, or discrimination accuracy. These findings challenge models of the processes and representations underlying the rotation task which hold that (a) the process of mental rotation is applied to a reduced or schematic representation of a visual object, and/or (b) the process of mental rotation is carried out successively on individual features of an internal representation of a visual object.

In addition, individual differences in both *same* and *different* discriminative reaction times were found, suggesting qualitative differences in the nature of the visual comparison processes of the two types of subjects.

7 | Demonstration of a Mental Analog of an External Rotation

Originally authored by Lynn A. Cooper

Subjects imagined a designated two-dimensional shape rotating within a blank, circular field at a self-determined rate. At some point during the mental rotation, a test shape was presented at one of twelve picture-plane orientations, and the subject was required to determine as rapidly as possible whether the test-shape was the same as the originally designated shape or was its mirror image. When the test shape was presented in the expected orientation (the orientation assumed to correspond to the current orientation of the rotating internal representation), reaction time was short and constant, regardless of the angular departure of that orientation from a previously trained position. This was true even when the test shape was presented in an orientation which had not previously been tested. When the test shape was presented at some other, unexpected orientation, reaction time increased linearly with the angular difference between the expected orientation and the orientation of the test shape. It is argued that these results provide a demonstration of the "analog" nature of mental rotation.

Recently, several investigators have reported that the time required to determine whether two visual stimuli are the same in shape or mirror images increases linearly with the angular difference between the orientations of the visual stimuli (Cooper, 1975; Cooper & Shepard, 1973; Metzler, 1973; Metzler & Shepard, 1974; Shepard & Metzler, 1971). This linear relationship between reaction time and angular difference in orientation has led these investigators to suggest that subjects perform the task by "mentally rotating" an internal representation of one of the visual stimuli into congruence with the orientation of the other stimulus and then comparing the two representations for a match or a mismatch in shape.

Cooper and Shepard (1973), Metzler and Shepard (1974), and

Reprinted by permission from *Perception & Psychophysics*, 1976, *19*, 296–302.[1]

Shepard (1975) have viewed this process of mental rotation as an internal analog of the process that occurs when the rotation of an external object is perceived. (See above, Chapters 3 and 4.) Central to these investigators' notions is the idea that, during a mental rotation, the internal process passes through a pathway or a trajectory. This trajectory can be viewed as a series of intermediate states, between the beginning and the end of the process, which have a one-to-one correspondence to the intermediate stages in the external rotation of an object. This one-to-one correspondence between the intermediate states in a mental rotation and a rotation of an external object need not be one of structural isomorphism between the internal representation undergoing the mental rotation and the external object undergoing the physical rotation. Rather, the correspondence may entail only that, during a mental rotation, the internal process passes through a series of states at each one of which the subject is especially prepared for the presentation of a particular external object in a particular orientation.

The linear relationship between reaction time and angular difference in orientation, obtained in the studies mentioned above, is one form of evidence that the internal process underlying the observed reaction times is passing through an ordered series of stages. That is, the linear reaction-time function indicates that the time needed to compare two visual objects presented at orientations A and C is an additive combination of the time needed to compare those objects presented at orientations A and B and the time needed to compare those objects presented at orientations B and C. This finding is indirect evidence for the claim that the internal process underlying comparison of the objects presented in orientations A and C passes through an intermediate state corresponding to orientation B.

The objective of the present experiment is to provide additional, more conclusive evidence that the internal process underlying comparison of visual objects differing in orientation is specifically one of rotation, in that the successive states in the trajectory through which the process passes have a one-to-one correspondence to the successive stages in the rotation of an external object. This evidence consists of demonstrating that, while mentally rotating an internal representation of a visual shape from orientation A to orientation C, the most rapid discriminative responses are obtained to an external test shape presented in an intermediate orientation B.

The present experiment incorporates and expands upon features of two previous studies designed to demonstrate this sort of correspondence between a mental rotation and an external rotation of a physical object (see Cooper & Shepard, 1973, Experiment II; and Metzler, 1973). Specifically, subjects are instructed to imagine a designated visual shape rotating within a circular field at a self-determined rate (cf. Metzler, 1973; Metzler & Shepard, 1974). At some randomly determined point during the mental rotation, a test probe is presented and the subject is required to determine as rapidly as possible whether the test form is the same as the originally designated shape or its mirror image. On a portion of the trials, the test probe is presented in the "expected" orientation—viz. the external orientation assumed to be congruent with the orientation of the rotating internal representation of the designated shape (cf. Cooper & Shepard, 1973, Experiment II). On the remainder of the trials, the test probe is presented in some other "unexpected" orientation. The points in time during the mental rotation at which test probes are presented are based on estimated rotation rates for the present subjects and present stimuli from a previous study (Cooper, 1975; Chapter 5, here).

The significant novel feature of the present experiment is that on a small proportion of the trials, test probes are presented at intermediate orientations which are unfamiliar to the subjects. In the Cooper (1975) experiment, the present subjects viewed test forms at six equally spaced orientations about the circle. In the present experiment, test probes are introduced at orientations *between* these six familiar positions. If reaction times to "expected" probes presented in these intermediate orientations are as rapid as reaction times to "expected" probes presented at previously experienced orientations, then evidence for the analog nature of mental rotation, in the sense outlined above, is provided. Such an outcome would demonstrate that, in rotating from orientation A to orientation C, the internal process does pass through an intermediate state corresponding to orientation B.

Method

Subjects. The six subjects were all students and staff at Stanford University. This group of subjects consisted of all of the original participants in a set of earlier, related experiments (Cooper, 1975) who were still residing in the Stanford area.

Stimuli. The stimuli were the eight random, angular shapes used by Cooper (1975). These two-dimensional shapes varied in the number of angles or points determining inflections on the perimeter, from a minimum of 6 points to a maximum of 24 points. For each shape, both an arbitrarily selected "standard" version and its mirror image or "reflected" version were included in the stimulus set.

Advance "identity" cues were also presented. Identity information consisted of an outline drawing of the standard version of the upcoming test form, displayed in a previously learned orientation. In the Cooper (1975) experiments, the present subjects had learned to discriminate standard versions of the shapes from reflected versions at one of six picture-plane orientations. This orientation constituted the previously learned or "trained" orientation in which the identity cue was presented. All stimuli were presented in an Iconix three-field tachistoscope and appeared centered within an illuminated circular field with a black surround. Luminance of the circular field was 68.5 cd/m^2, and it subtended a visual angle of 4°. Both the test form and the identity cues subtended an angle of about 2°.

In order to reduce the number of trials per subject, each subject was tested with only three of the eight possible shapes. Forms were assigned randomly to individual subjects, with the constraint that the eight forms be represented approximately equally across subjects.

Procedure. Prior to the experimental trials, each subject was refamiliarized with both standard and reflected versions of the test shapes and completed 36 practice trials using the standard experimental procedure.

The sequence of events on each experimental trial was as follows: The subject was told that the trial was beginning, and the identity cue was displayed for 2 sec. The identity cue informed the subject as to the standard shape for that trial, and it was always presented in the trained orientation. Immediately following the offset of the identity cue, there was a 100-msec blackout. This brief blackout informed the subject that it was nearly time to imagine the standard shape which had been presented as the identity cue rotating in a clockwise direction. A blank, circular field was then presented, and the subject began the mental rotation. At some preselected time after the initiation of the mental rotation, a test form was presented at one of 12 equally spaced orientations within the circular field. The subject determined as rapidly as possible whether the test shape was the same as the identity cue (a standard version) or its mirror image (a reflected version). "Standard" responses were signaled by pushing a right-hand button, and "reflected" responses were signaled by pushing a left-hand button. This response assignment was reversed for the one left-handed subject, so the preferred hand was always used to respond "standard."

There were two types of experimental trials—"probe-expected" trials and "probe-unexpected" trials. On "probe-expected" trials, the test form was presented in the expected orientation, i.e., the orientation assumed to be congruent with the current orientation of the rotating internal representation of the identity cue. This was accomplished in the following manner: For each subject and each standard shape, rotation rates were computed from the data of Cooper's (1975) Experiment II. (These rates were determined by plotting mean reaction time as a function of angular departure of the test form from the trained orientation for each individual subject and each test shape. The slope of the best-fitting straight line was computed for each reaction-time function, and the reciprocal of the slope provided an estimate of rotation rate, expressed as degrees per millisecond.) Each rotation rate was then used to determine the duration of the blank, circular "rotation" field for a test form presented at a given orientation. Durations were thus computed for each individual subject, each standard shape, and each test-form orientation. Consider, for example, a subject whose estimated rotation rate for a particular standard shape was 1.5°/msec. For this subject, on a "probe-expected" trial on which the test form was presented at 120° of clockwise rotation from the trained orientation, the duration of the blank, circular "rotation" field would have been 80 msec.

On the majority of the "probe-expected" trials ("probe-expected, familiar" trials), the test form was presented in one of six equally spaced orientations around the circle (in 60° steps of clockwise rotation, starting from the trained orientation). The subjects were familiar with viewing the test forms in these positions, as only these six orientations were used in the Cooper (1975) experiments. On the remainder of the "probe-expected" trials ("probe-expected, unfamiliar" trials), the test form was presented at an orientation in which the subjects had never before viewed the form. These unfamiliar orientations were the six intermediate 30° steps between the familiar six 60° steps of clockwise rotation. Thus, the unfamiliar orientations consisted of 30°, 90°, 150°, 210°, 270°, and 330° angular departures from the trained orientation, and familiar orientations consisted of 0°, 60°, 120°, 180°, 240°, and 300° angular departures from the trained orientation.

On "probe-unexpected" trials, the test form was presented in an orientation departing from the assumed current orientation of the rotating internal representation of the identity cue. Only the six familiar orientations were used on these "probe-unexpected" trials. The duration of the blank, circular "rotation" field and the angular departure of the test form from the expected orientation were computed from the rotation rates described above. Consider, again, the subject whose rotation rate for a particular shape was 1.5° msec. For a "probe-unexpected" trial on which the test form was presented at 120° of clockwise rotation from the trained orientation *and* at a 120° counterclockwise angular departure from the expected orientation, the duration of the blank, circular "rotation" field would have been 160 msec.

Instructions to the subjects emphasized both speed and accuracy of the discriminative "standard-reflected" response. Subjects were instructed to begin the mental rotations as soon as the blank, circular "rotation" field appeared, and they were encouraged to perform the mental rotations at a natural, comfortable rate. Subjects were not told that test forms would sometimes appear in unfamiliar orientations.

General experimental design. Each of the six subjects completed 108 "probe-expected, familiar" trials, 36 "probe-expected, unfamiliar" trials, and 108 "probe-unexpected" trials. The "probe-expected, familiar" trials consisted of three presentations of each of the three standard shapes at each of the six familiar orientations in both standard and reflected versions. The "probe-expected, unfamiliar" trials consisted of one presentation of each combination of standard shape, unfamiliar orientation and test-form version. Thus, each of the "probe-expected, unfamiliar" trials was unique.

The "probe-unexpected" trials consisted of three presentations of each of the three standard shapes at each of the familiar orientations in both standard and reflected versions. The three presentations consisted of one presentation at each of three angular departures from the expected orientation. For any given expected orientation, the three angular departures were $60°$, $120°$, and $180°$. Both standard and reflected versions were presented as test probes for $180°$ departures from the expected orientation. For $60°$ and $120°$ departures, the trial composition was more complex. Since $60°$ and $120°$ departures could be in either a clockwise or a counterclockwise direction, one direction of angular departure was selected for presentation of the standard test form, and the other direction of angular departure was selected for presentation of the reflected test form. Assignment of test-form version to direction of angular departure was done as follows for each of the six subjects: For two of the test forms, standard test probes were presented at $60°$ clockwise departures and at $120°$ counterclockwise departures. Reflected test probes were presented at $60°$ counterclockwise departures and at $120°$ clockwise departures. For the third test form, this assignment of standard-reflected version to direction of angular departure was reversed. The above assignment resulted in an equal number of standard and reflected test probes at each angular departure from the expected orientation, and it also permitted equal presentation of each of the three test forms in both standard and reflected versions at each of the six familiar orientations.

For each subject, the 252 experimental trials were presented in a random order and required approximately three 1-hr. sessions. Trials on which errors were made were retaken, interspersed with additional filler trials.

Results

Reaction times. The average results for the subjects are illustrated in Figure 7.1. In the left-hand panel, mean reaction time—averaged over subjects, test forms and standard-reflected versions—is plotted as a function of angular departure of the test form from the trained orientation for "probe-expected" trials only.

Note, in particular, two features of these data: (a) On "probe-expected" trials, average time required to discriminate standard from reflected test forms is virtually constant, regardless of the angular departure of the test form from a previously learned orientation. (b) Mean reaction times to test probes presented in unfamiliar orientations (30° probes) are approximately equal to mean reaction times to probes presented in familiar orientations (60° probes). The range of mean reaction times plotted in the left-hand panel of Figure 7.1 is only 32 msec, and mean reaction time to unfamiliar probes is not significantly different from mean reaction time to familiar probes (t_{10} = .74, $p >$ .20).[1] In addition, though not illustrated in Figure 7.1, "standard" responses were faster than "reflected" responses at all test-form orientations. This standard-reflected difference averaged about 65 msec for unfamiliar probes and 60 msec for familiar probes.

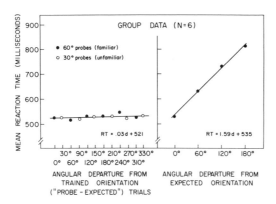

Figure 7.1 Reaction-time results for the group data. In the left-hand panel, mean reaction time is plotted as a function of angular departure of the test probe from the trained orientation for "probe-expected" trials only. Open circles represent unfamiliar test probes, and solid circles represent familiar test probes. In the right-hand panel, mean reaction time is plotted as a function of angular departure of the test probe from the expected orientation for "probe-unexpected" trials.

In the right-hand panel of Figure 7.1, mean reaction time is plotted as a function of angular departure of the test form from the expected orientation. The 0° point represents an average of all "probe-expected" trials (i.e., all of the data points plotted in the left-hand panel). The 60°, 120°, and 180° points are averaged over subjects, test forms, angular departure from the trained orientation, standard-reflected versions, and clockwise and counterclockwise angular departures.

In marked contrast to the flat reaction-time function for "probe-expected" trials (cf. Figure 1, left-hand panel), mean reaction time to unexpected probes increases quite linearly with the angular departure of the test form from the expected orientation. A polynomial regression computed on this reaction-time function revealed a highly significant linear component [$F(1,2)$ = 1963.69, $p < .001$] and no significant quadratic or higher order effects. The slope of this reaction-time function, shown in the right-hand panel of Figure 7.1 (viz., 1.59) is not significantly different from the slope found in the previous experiment (Cooper, 1975) for just these six subjects (viz., 1.74). Finally, though not shown in the right-hand panel of Figure 7.1, "standard" responses were an average 52 msec faster than "reflected" responses on "probe-unexpected" trials.

Separate analyses of variance, performed on data for each of the trial types, viz., "probe-expected, familiar" trials, "probe-expected, unfamiliar" trials, and "probe-unexpected" trials, confirmed the results for the group data shown in Figure 7.1. For "probe-expected" trials, whether "familiar" or "unfamiliar," the main effects of subjects and standard-versus-reflected versions were significant, but the main effect of angular departure for the trained orientation was not significant. For "probe-unexpected" trials only the main effects of subjects and angular departure from the expected orientation were significant. Note, in particular, that the main effect of "angular departure from the trained orientation" was not significant [$F(5,25)$ = 2.04, $p > .10$].

The data for each of the six individual subjects are illustrated in Figures 7.2 and 7.3. In Figure 7.2, mean reaction times for "probe-expected" trials are plotted as a function of angular departure of the test form from the trained orientation, corresponding to the group data shown in the left-hand panel of Figure 7.1. The central features of the group data are reflected in the data of each of the individual subjects. For all six subjects, reaction time to expected test probes is nearly constant for all test-form orientations. Best-fitting straight lines for each of the six reaction-time plots in Figure 7.2 show an appreciable positive slope for only one subject (Subject 2). In addition, mean reaction times to test probes presented in unfamiliar orientations are virtually indistinguishable from mean reaction times to test probes presented in familiar orientations. Mean reaction times to familiar and unfamiliar test probes were significantly different for only one of the individual subjects (for Subject 5, t_5 = 2.30, $p < .025$).

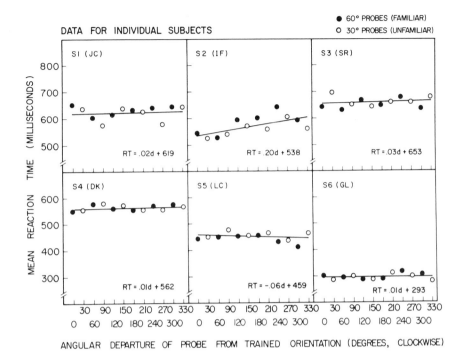

Figure 7.2 Mean reaction time to unfamiliar and familiar expected probes, plotted as a function of angular departure from the trained orientation, for each of the six individual subjects. The functions for the individual subjects correspond to the group function illustrated in the left-hand panel of Figure 7.1.

In Figure 7.3, mean reaction times for "probe-unexpected" trials are plotted as a function of angular departure of the test probe from the expected orientation, corresponding to the group data shown in the right-hand panel of Figure 7.1. Again, the data for each of the individual subjects capture the essential features of the group data. For all six subjects, mean reaction time increases in a strikingly linear fashion with angular departure of the test form from the trained orientation. Though not illustrated in Figures 7.2 and 7.3, "standard" responses were faster than "reflected" responses for each of the six subjects and for both "probe-expected" and "probe-unexpected" trials.

Errors. Error rates for individuals ranged from 1.6% to 7.4%, with a group average of 4.9%. Average error rates for "unexpected, familiar" and "unexpected, unfamiliar" probes were approximately equal—3.7% and 4.4%, respectively. Average error rate for "unex-

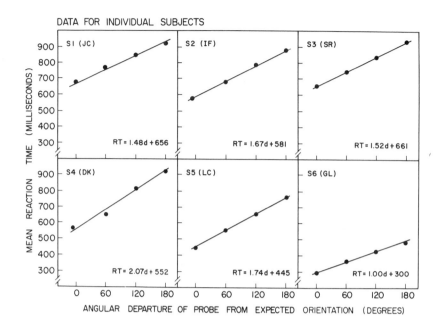

Figure 7.3 Mean reaction time to unexpected test probes, plotted as a function of angular departure of the test probe from the expected orientation, for each of the six individual subjects. The functions for the individual subjects correspond to the group function illustrated in the right-hand panel of Figure 7.1.

pected" probes was 6.2%. For both expected and unexpected probes, errors were distributed approximately equally over angular departures from the trained orientation. For unexpected probes, error rates increased monotonically with angular departure from the expected orientation.

Discussion

The first significant feature of the data from the present experiment is the virtually constant reaction time to test probes presented in the expected orientation, regardless of the angular departure of that orientation from the previously trained position (see Figure 7.1, left-hand panel, for the group data and Figure 7.2 for the data of individual subjects). These flat reaction-time functions can be compared with the striking increase in reaction time with angular departure from the trained orientation obtained by Cooper (1975; reproduced here in Chapter 5) for these same subjects and same test forms. The difference between these two situations is that the procedure used in the present experiment permitted presentation of the test probe at an orientation for which the subject was maximally prepared and, hence, yielded essentially constant reaction times to probes at all angular departures from the trained orientations. Thus, the flat reaction-time function indicates that, during the mental rotation, the internal process passed through an ordered series of states which consisted of a sequence of "readinesses" to respond discriminatively to a particular stimulus presented in a particular external orientation.

The second and perhaps most significant aspect of the data presented in Figures 7.1 and 7.2 is that reaction times to familiar (60° step) expected probes were no faster than reaction times to unfamiliar (30° step) expected probes. This result provides evidence that the internal process which the subjects were carrying out in accordance with instructions was specifically one of rotation, in that the process passed through a trajectory of states which had a one-to-one correspondence to the intermediate stages in the rotation of an external object. That is, the near equivalence of reaction times to familiar and unfamiliar expected test probes indicated that in rotating from a familiar orientation, A, to another familiar orientation, C, the internal process passed through an intermediate state corresponding to an unfamiliar orientation, B, at which the subject was most prepared for the presentation of a visual stimulus which he had never before viewed in that particular external orientation. If subjects were using some process other than a mental rotation such as, for example, successively generating representations of the standard shape in the familiar 60° positions only, *then we should expect reaction times to familiar probes to be uniformly shorter than reaction times to unfamiliar probes presented in intermediate orientations.* [2]

In marked contrast to the flat reaction-time functions obtained for "probe-expected" trials, reaction times to unexpected test probes increased linearly and quite sharply with angular departure of the test probe from the expected orientation (see Figure 7.1, right-hand panel, for the group data and Figure 7.3 for the data of individual subjects). These linear reaction-time functions suggest that subjects used a process of mental rotation in determining the "standard-reflected" version of unexpected test probes. In this case, subjects could have undertaken a correctional "poststimulus" rotation (cf. Cooper, 1975) in order to achieve congruence between the orientation of the external, unexpected test probe and the expected orientation. The representation of the standard shape presented as the identity cue could have been rotated, in a clockwise or counterclockwise direction, into the orientation of the test probe, and the two representations could then have been compared for a match or mismatch in shape. Alternatively, a representation of the test probe could have been rotated into the expected orientation. Additional evidence that a correctional "poststimulus" rotation was used on "probe-unexpected" trials derives from the fact that the values of the slopes of the reaction-time functions in Figure 7.3 are quite close to the slope values estimated for each of these six subjects in the rotation experiments by Cooper (1975; and Chapter 5).

The linear increase in reaction time with angular departure from the expected orientation on "probe-unexpected" trials has a further implication. In the absence of these data, any interpretation of the constant reaction times obtained on "probe-expected" trials would be somewhat problematic. That is, one could argue that the experienced subjects in the present experiment had learned to identify rotationally invariant features of the test shapes which served to distinguish standard from reflected versions. This explanation could account for the equivalence of reaction time to expected probes presented at all angular departures from the trained orientation; however, it also predicts that reaction time to *unexpected* probes should be rapid and independent of orientation. Thus, the flat reaction-time function obtained for "probe-expected" trials, *in conjunction with* the linear increase in reaction time obtained for "probe-unexpected" trials, provides strong support for the claim that a process of mental rotation was used both in preparing for the presentation of a test probe and in determining the version of a test probe presented in an unexpected orientation.

In summary, the results of the present experiment provide a demonstration of the analog nature of mental rotation. In particular, these results show that, during a mental rotation, the internal process passes through a trajectory of intermediate states that have a one-to-one correspondence to the intermediate stages in an external rotation. Each intermediate state through which the internal process passes consists of a readiness to respond discriminatively to a particular object in a particular external orientation, if such an object were actually to be presented (cf. Cooper & Shepard, 1973; Shepard, 1975).

On the basis of the data from the present experiment, it is not possible to determine whether the process of mental rotation is strictly continuous in nature or proceeds in a series of small, discrete steps. Experimental discrimination between these alternatives seems, at present, unfeasible. The equivalence of reaction times to familiar and unfamiliar expected probes suggests that the internal process may be continuous and, at the very least, indicates that the size of any discrete, component steps must be rather small (a maximum of $30°$). In addition, the above result indicates that a mental rotation of at least $60°$ is analog, in the sense that the process has an intermediate state which has the required one-to-one relationship to an intermediate stage in the rotation of an external object.

8 | Epilogue to Part 1

Mental Rotation

The chapters of Part I have presented our own and our collaborators' empirical and theoretical work on mental rotation published from 1971 to 1976. In this chapter, we discuss more recent studies of mental rotation done by ourselves and others. The discussion is divided into two parts. In the first, we consider a selected sample of new and significant empirical investigations and methodological contributions. In the second, we consider the implications of both this new work and our own original findings for persisting theoretical issues concerning the internal representation and processing of spatial information.[1]

During the past five years, the process of mental rotation has been a subject of active empirical investigation, undoubtedly because of the implications of this process for the nature of nonverbal internal representation. In this chapter, we briefly review recent contributions to the literature on mental rotation. Our coverage of this literature is selective rather than comprehensive. In particular, we emphasize those studies that have provided empirical evidence that bears significantly on unresolved theoretical issues. We also consider methodological advances that have permitted the acquisition of data that permit the construction of more detailed models of the process of mental rotation. Finally, we review briefly the current status of theoretical controversies concerning the nature of this process.

Empirical and Methodological Developments

Analysis of eye movements during mental rotation. One of the most illuminating methodological advances that has occurred in the past several years is the recording of eye fixation patterns, in conjunction with reaction-time data, in interpreting the nature of a variety of cognitive processes, including mental rotation. The assumption behind this sort of analysis is that the eye fixates the portion of a visual display currently being processed and, hence, the entire pattern of eye fixations observed on a particular trial of a cognitive task can provide a rich source of evidence concerning the microstructure of the underlying information-processing operations.

Informal observations reported by Metzler and Shepard (Chapter 3, p. 68) for the case in which two simultaneously presented objects are to be compared for shape indicated that subjects look back and forth between the two objects while performing a mental rotation. This observation has been confirmed and greatly elaborated in the systematic analysis of eye movement patterns during mental rotation by Just and Carpenter (1976) and Carpenter and Just (1978). Using a computer-controlled corneal reflectance eye-tracking system, these investigators have been able to monitor the general locus and precise duration of individual eye fixations on particular trials of mental rotation experiments. They have used these data as evidence for (a) a three-stage model for the mental rotation task, and (b) a detailed specification of the nature of the processing within each stage. More recent work from their laboratory has also provided evidence for individual differences in spatial transformation tasks similar to those of mental rotation (Carpenter & Just, 1981).

In general agreement with the reports by subjects in the original Shepard and Metzler task (see Chapter 3, p. 53), Just and Carpenter (1976) proposed that information processing proceeds through three successive stages. The first stage is one of *search*, in which sections of the two figures that potentially correspond to each other are located. The second stage, called *transformation and comparison*, is the one that we would associate with the process of mental rotation itself. In this stage, the segments that are taken to correspond in the two figures are mentally rotated, while a sequence of comparisons is made to determine just when the orientations of these segments are congruent. The final stage, *confirmation*, is devoted to determining whether other segments of the figures, also, are congruent as a result of the mental rotation.

Figure 8.1 illustrates a typical pattern of eye fixations during a trial in a mental rotation experiment on which the orientations of the figures differed by 80° and the subject correctly determined that they were the same in shape. According to Just and Carpenter's (1976) analysis, fixations 1 through 4 correspond to the search stage in which the subject located the general region of the right-hand object (4) that corresponded to the initially fixated (upper) region of the left-hand object (1 and 2); fixations 5 through 8 correspond to the transformation-and-comparison stage in which the corresponding upper portions of the two objects were brought into congruence by mental rotation; and fixations 9 through 12 illustrate confirmation

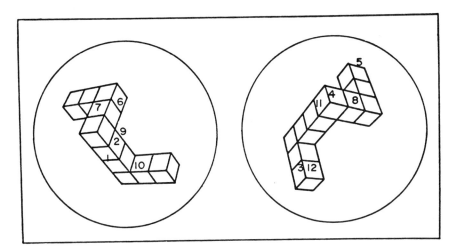

Figure 8.1 Sequence of eye fixations on a "same" trial in which the angular disparity between the visual objects was 80 degrees. (From Just & Carpenter, 1976.)

in which attention was shifted to the lower portions of the objects (9 to 10 on the left-hand object, and 11 to 12 on the right-hand object) to verify that the lowest segment was properly oriented following the mental rotation.

By cumulating the durations of the recorded fixations associated with each processing stage identified in this way, Just and Carpenter (1976) have been able to decompose the total reaction time on any given trial into latencies attributable to search, transformation-and-comparison, and confirmation operations. Figure 8.2 shows such reaction-time results, plotted as a function of angular difference between two visual figures and averaged over all "same" responses, for each stage separately. Notice that processing time increased with

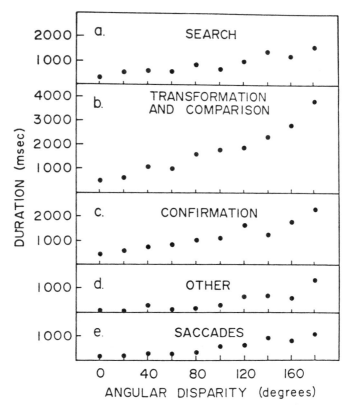

Figure 8.2 Mean duration of various processing stages in "same" trials for the mental rotation task as a function of angular disparity. (From Just & Carpenter, 1976.)

angular disparity during each of the three stages. The most substantial increase, however, is in the transformation-and-comparison stage, which is associated with the process of mental rotation.

Another aspect of their data on the pattern of switches in eye fixation between the two visual figures has led Just and Carpenter (1976; see also Carpenter & Just, 1978) to propose an account of the nature of the process of mental rotation that differs somewhat from our own (Chapters 2 through 7; in particular, Chapters 4 and 7). Just and Carpenter (1976) have noted that the majority of switches in fixation generally occur during the transformation-and-comparison stage and, further, that during this stage there is about one additional switch in fixation for each additional 50° increment in angular disparity between the two visual objects. These data have led them to suggest that the transformation-and-comparison process operates on a schematic internal representation, consisting of individual portions of visual figures in discrete steps of about 50°. This view departs from our notion of mental rotation as an analog process operating on holistic internal representations of visual objects. However, Just and Carpenter (1976) acknowledge that their model of mental rotation fulfills our criterion for an analog process in that during a rotation of, e.g., 150°, the internal process passes through intermediate stages corresponding to intermediate external orientations of 50° and 100°. Later in this chapter, we consider the additional possibility that the nature of information processing during mental rotation may change with variations in experimental procedure. Specifically, experiments in which individually presented, well-learned stimuli must be compared with a long-term memory representation (e.g., Chapters 4 through 7) may encourage analog processing of integrated internal representations, whereas experiments involving simultaneous comparison of unfamiliar visual objects may sometimes encourage more discrete, feature-based rotational processing.

There is a further finding from the Just-Carpenter experiments that is highly relevant to our later discussion of the effects of stimulus complexity and that nicely illustrates the analytic power of combining eye-movement and chronometric methodologies. In one of their experiments, Carpenter and Just (1978) examined the effects of stimulus attributes on eye movements during mental rotation by comparing results obtained with the original Shepard-Metzler figures (the perspective drawings of three-dimensional objects) with those obtained with simpler, two-dimensional versions of similar objects. Overall, reaction time in both cases increased with increasing angular disparity between the two objects in the pair. However, the slope of the reaction-time function was greater for the three-dimensional objects than for the simpler two-dimensional versions.

This might at first appear to constitute strong evidence for an effect of stimulus complexity on the rate of mental rotation, with more complex objects entailing slower transformational rates. When Carpenter and Just decomposed the reaction-time data into the three stages of processing via their eye-fixation analysis, a most interesting result emerged. A comparison of results for just the transformation-and-comparison stage showed no difference in rotation rate for two- and three-dimensional visual displays. This was because there was virtually no increase in processing time with increasing angular disparity for search and confirmation in the case of the two-dimensional objects, whereas the increase in these non-rotational stages was appreciable in the case of the three-dimensional objects (cf. Figure 8.2). Carpenter and Just (1978) suggest that the invariance of processing time in the search and confirmation stages for two-dimensional objects may be due to greater discriminability of segments of the two-dimensional than of the three-dimensional objects. In any event, the experiments by Carpenter and Just and others lead us to conclude that an analysis of eye fixations provides a powerful tool for evaluating detailed models of the processes underlying performance in tasks requiring spatial transformations.

Rate of mental rotation: Effects of stimulus attributes. A recurrent puzzle in the literature on mental rotation concerns the determinants and potential significance of differences in the rate of mental rotation. As we have seen in the chapters of Part I, the rate of rotation has been found to differ among individual subjects, and across experiments using different experimental procedures and stimulus materials. Of particular contention is the role of stimulus factors in the rate of mental rotation. For, Pylyshyn (1979) and others have argued that any finding suggesting that a stimulus variable affects the rate of mental rotation indicates that the process is "cognitively penetrable" and hence does not qualify as an analog operation performed on a holisitic internal representation. And, the absence of an effect of stimulus complexity on rotation rate found in the Cooper-Podgorny experiment (Chapter 6) was taken as evidence against a particular version of a feature-based propositional model of the transformational process. Recently there have been several reports of systematic effects of stimulus factors on the rate of mental rotation and additional procedural criticisms of the Cooper-Podgorny experiment. Hence, a review of the status of these findings and arguments and an evaluation of their significance for theories of the nature of mental rotation seems in order.

The chief procedural objection to the Cooper-Podgorny experiment has come from Anderson (1978). His criticism is directed toward claims concerning the nature of the comparison process following mental rotation, but it can easily be extended to claims concerning the effects of complexity on the mental rotation process itself. To quote Anderson (1978):

> Consider the experiment by Cooper and Podgorny (1976) on recognition of Attneave polygons: They varied the number of points in the polygons from 6 to 24 and obtained no effect of this measure on recognition time. As distractors, they used transformations of the target polygons with some of their points perturbed. There were no more errors made to distractors for polygons of greater complexity. This was used as evidence against the possibility of a less careful processing of the more complex shapes. However, the more complex distractors also had more points perturbed. Therefore, one would have to remember a smaller portion of the points

from the more complex figures to achieve the same probability of detecting a distractor.   (p. 262)

Anderson's objection applies equally well to the effect of the complexity manipulation on the nature of the internal representation undergoing mental rotation. Presumably, since more complex standard shapes were associated with distractors having more points perturbed (in order to achieve equality across complexity levels in similarity of distractors to standard shapes), less information would have to be internally represented and mentally rotated for purposes of eventual comparison, thus rendering the complexity manipulation ineffective.

It is difficult to evaluate the force of this objection in the absence of the experiment Anderson calls for—one in which complex shapes are associated with more similar distractors than are simple shapes. However, consider the following counterargument: During the mental rotation preceding the visual comparison, subjects had no advance knowledge concerning just which distractor would be presented. And, the distractors were random and often subtle distortions of the standard shapes. Under these conditions, the most effective strategy would be to preserve as much information as possible in the internal representation undergoing mental rotation. Presumably, then, more information would be preserved for more complex shapes, thus rendering the complexity manipulation effective.

Perhaps more disturbing than Anderson's objection to the Cooper-Podgorny study are recent experimental reports of effects of stimulus variables similar to complexity on the rate of mental rotation. For example, Pylyshyn (1979) has purported to demonstrate that figural integrity or "goodness" systematically affects the rate at which mental rotation occurs, with less structurally coherent figures producing slower rotation rates. It is difficult to assess how seriously this finding challenges the Cooper-Podgorny result because of substantial procedural differences between the two experiments. In the Cooper-Podgorny study, subjects were required to rotate mentally a representation of a single, well-learned stimulus in preparation for an identical or different test probe. Separate estimates were derived for rotation time and comparison time (see Chapter 6 for details). In the Pylyshyn experiment, a visual figure and a test probe were presented simultaneously, in different orientations, and subjects were required to determine whether or not the test probe was a part of the figure. The goodness of the probe as a part of the figure was manipulated, and it was this stimulus factor that produced variations in the slopes of the reaction-time functions.

Pylyshyn's finding must be interpreted with caution, and it does not provide conclusive evidence that the stimulus factor of goodness affects the rate at which the process of mental rotation is carried out. Because of the conditions of presentation employed by Pylyshyn and the nature of the judgment required of the subjects, the measured reaction times include not only a component attributable to rotation, but also other components associated with operations such as encoding and comparison. Thus, it is not possible to determine in precisely which information-processing stage the effect of figural goodness resides. Hochberg and Gellman (1977) have reported an experiment similar to Pylyshyn's in which visual figures were presented simultaneously and more complex figures produced slower rotation rates than simpler figures. Again, because of the conditions of presentation, it is difficult to determine whether the complexity effect derived from the operation of rotation or from other operations like search, encoding, or comparison. Nevertheless, it does seem likely that rates of mental rotation may be reduced for objects that are both more complex and (unlike those in the Cooper-Podgorny experiment) relatively unfamiliar to the subject—if only because such objects, lacking full mental integration, may have to be mentally rotated piece by piece. (Some evidence for such an interaction between complexity and familiarity in mental rotation has been obtained in as yet unpublished experiments by Bethell-Fox and Shepard—see Chapter 12 of Part II.)

Another stimulus factor that has often been thought to produce differences in rate of mental rotation is the dimensionality of the visual objects depicted. And there was, of course, a marked difference between the 60° per second rate estimated by Shepard and Metzler (1971, also Chapter 3) for perspective drawings of three-dimensional objects and the approximately 500° per second rate estimated by Cooper (Chapter 5) for two-dimensional random polygons. This difference must also be interpreted with caution, however, as most studies employing three-dimensional objects as stimuli have used simultaneous presentation whereas most studies employing two-dimensional objects have used comparison of a single visual stimulus with a memory representation. We suspect that it is this procedural difference rather than the difference in dimensionality that is the principal determiner of rate of mental rotation.

Recently, several investigators have explored the effects of stimulus dimensionality on rotation rate while holding conditions of presentation constant. As we already noted, the findings of Carpenter and Just (1978) indicate that dimensionality affects the search and confirmation stages, but not the transformation-and-comparison stage, of the mental rotation task under conditions of simultaneous presentation. Podgorny (1975) also compared rotation rates for

Shepard-Metzler stimuli and two-dimensionalized versions of those same objects and found no differences. Interestingly, Podgorny's experiment also contrasted simultaneous and successive presentation conditions, and he found that both the slope and the intercept of the reaction-time function were greater with simultaneous than with successive presentation.

In an unpublished series of experiments, Cooper and Farrell attempted to manipulate object dimensionality while holding object complexity—defined as the number of line segments in a visual object—constant. In some experiments, the two-dimensional objects were hexagonal shapes divided into six equal sections, with simple geometric symbols in three of the adjacent sections. The three-dimensional objects were perspective drawings of cubes, with geometric symbols on three faces of each cube. Figure 8.3 provides an example of these stimuli. On each trial, two figures of either type were presented in different orientations, and subjects were required to determine whether the configuration of symbols on the faces or sections of the two objects was the same or different. The results from this experiment are shown in Figure 8.4, and it is clear that the estimated rate of mental rotation does not change with the depicted dimensionality of the visual figures.

In summary, there is as yet no conclusive evidence for effects of stimulus factors on the rate of mental rotation—at least for psychologically well-learned, integrated objects. In the case of the variable of depicted stimulus dimensionality, the absence of differences found in the experiments of Carpenter and Just (1978), Podgorny (1975), and Cooper and Farrell (unpublished) seem reasonably compelling. In the case of the variables of stimulus complexity and coherence or goodness, the presence of differences found in the experiments of Pylyshyn (1979) and Hochberg and Gellman (1977) are suggestive but must be interpreted with caution. This is because the procedures used by these investigators do not permit separate assessment of the effects of stimulus factors on the various information-processing stages underlying performance on the rotation task. What does seem clear is that the rate of rotation can be dramatically affected by methods of experimental procedure. Specifically, rotation rates are faster when a single external stimulus must be compared with a well-learned memory representation than when two external stimuli must simultaneously be matched. A possible explanation for this finding may be that simultaneous presentation induces a strategy of part-by-part rotation and comparison (cf. Carpenter & Just, 1978) which is slower than rotation of a single, well-integrated internal representation followed by comparison with a representation in memory. (See related differences shown on pages 250 and 256).

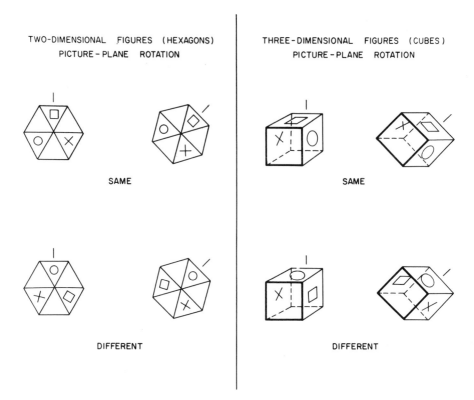

Figure 8.3 Examples of the two-dimensional and three-dimensional stimuli used by Cooper and Farrell (unpublished) for both "same" and "different" trials.

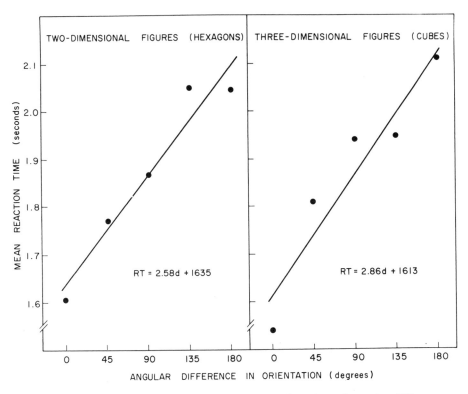

Figure 8.4 Mean reaction time plotted as a function of angular difference, separately for two- and three-dimensional stimuli, from the Cooper and Farrell experiment.

Differences in mental rotation between special populations, age groups, and individual subjects. Chronometric results indicating the use of mental rotation have been obtained for children (Marmor, 1975) and for elderly adults (Gaylord & Marsh, 1975), but the estimated rates of rotation are slower than those found in the usual adult population. Another special population that has been examined is the blind (Carpenter & Eisenberg, 1978; Marmor & Zaback, 1976). In these experiments, blind subjects were presented with two tactual objects in different orientations and were required to determine whether the objects were the same or different in shape. Reaction time increased linearly with angular difference between the orientations of the objects, suggesting that mental rotation was used to make the determination. Apparently mental rotation is not a specifically visual process, but rather can be abstract and amodal in nature.

The experiments reported in Chapters 3 through 7 have shown reliable, linear reaction-time functions for individual subjects as well as for average data. However, estimated rotation rates differ considerably among the individual subjects. For example, in Cooper's (1975; Chapter 5) study using random polygons, estimated rates of rotation for individuals ranged from 320° to 840° per second. Pellegrino, Mumaw, Kail, and Carter (1979), using two-dimensional stimuli, and Lansman (1981), using three-dimensional objects, have related such differences in rotation rates to psychometric measures of spatial aptitude. As might be expected, subjects who scored poorly on paper-and-pencil tests of spatial ability showed slower rates of mental rotation, as estimated from their performances in laboratory tasks of the sort we have been considering in Part I. A paper-and-pencil version of the Shepard-Metzler mental rotation task, prepared by Vandenberg (1971), has been widely used to assess some of the possible sources of individual differences in performance on spatial tests (e.g., see McGee, 1979). However, Vandenberg (1975) found that sex differences, often reported in this work, are reduced if the subjects are first given some practice on such spatial tasks.

Especially interesting to us is Carpenter and Just's (1981) finding that low spatial ability and high spatial ability subjects differ in their patterns of eye fixations while solving problems of the Shepard-Metzler variety. Specifically, low spatial subjects spend more time in the initial search stage than do high spatial subjects, they often repeat transformation-and-comparison episodes, and they are more likely to rotate two non-corresponding sections of visual figures into congruence. This sort of an eye fixation analysis promises to lead to a rich account of the information-processing skills underlying individual differences in spatial aptitude.

Conditions influencing the occurrence of mental rotation. In the experiments described in Part I, subjects were required to distinguish between visual forms and structurally equivalent mirror images (with the exception of certain conditions of the Cooper-Podgorny experiment, Chapter 6). The question arises as to whether a process of mental rotation is needed to make other sorts of spatial decisions concerning disoriented stimuli. Corballis and Roldan (1975) have shown that mental rotation is not limited to the discrimination between objects and their mirror images, but is also used to determine whether or not disoriented patterns of dots are symmetric about some axis. Hintzman, O'Dell, and Arndt (1979) have conducted a series of experiments asking whether mental rotation is required in judging the direction from the self of a particular object in a layout of objects when the self's imagined orientation with respect to the layout changes. Their results are rather surprising, and we can offer no simple explanation. In one set of experiments, subjects were presented with a circular display consisting of an arrow and a dot at different locations around the perimeter of the circle. Subjects were required to indicate the direction from themselves that the target dot would be if they were in the orientation indicated by the arrow. Reaction time for making this decision increased with the angular difference between the orientation of the arrow and the canonical upright position. This finding suggests that the direction of the dot was determined by mentally rotating the visual display until the arrow reached the upright position and then indicating the transformed orientation of the dot. However, when the task was modified by having subjects learn the location of objects in a room and by then using one object as the orientation indicator (analogous to the arrow in previous experiments) and another object as the target whose direction was to be determined (analogous to the dot in the earlier studies), no evidence indicating mental rotation was obtained.

Results of an as yet unpublished study by Shepard and Hurwitz (1981) show a difference between conditions that may be related to the difference reported by Hintzman, et al. (1979). The Shepard-Hurwitz experiment was designed to explore the possible role of mental rotation in the interpretation of bends in lines as left or right turns in reading a map presented in different orientations. A long line appeared on a CRT display screen, coming in at some angle and terminating in the center of the display screen. Following some delay, a shorter line segment was then added at some angle to the (central) end of the longer line. Subjects responded as quickly as possible to indicate whether the shorter line represented a left or a right turn from the longer line. In all conditions, reaction time increased monotonically with the departure of the longer line from the vertical orientation in which the central end pointed straight up.

Indeed, the dependence of reaction time on departure from this vertical orientation was strikingly similar in shape (from 0° to 180°) to the dependence found by Cooper and Shepard (1973a) for discrimination between normal and reflected alphanumeric characters displayed in various departures from upright (see Chapter 4, here, particularly Figures 4.5 and 4.6).

However, the availability of the orientation information provided by the longer line for as much as one second prior to the presentation of the shorter line generally did not flatten the reaction-time function unless subjects were explicitly instructed to form a preparatory visual image of the pattern that the shorter line should form with the already presented longer line if it were to constitute, say, a right turn. Without such imagery instructions, most subjects apparently waited to carry out any mental rotation until after the shorter line appeared. Their functions were lower when the shorter line was delayed (presumably because their reaction time no longer included the time needed to interpret the orientation of the longer line); but their functions were often just as steep as when the shorter line was not delayed. These results are reminiscent of those of Cooper and Shepard (Chapter 4) in which advance orientation information was not accompanied by advance information as to the identity (or shape) of the disoriented object and in which there was, also, no flattening of the reaction-time function and hence, presumably, no advance rotation.

Related to the question of the conditions under which mental rotation occurs is the issue of whether such a rotational transformation—when it occurs—is carried out to achieve congruence with retinal or with gravitational upright, when these two orientations are different. Work by Corballis and his associates indicates that the answer to this question depends on the nature of the stimuli being mentally transformed. In one experiment, Corballis and Roldan (1975) found that reaction time for detecting the symmetry of disoriented visual patterns depends primarily on angular departure of the patterns from the upright orientation defined retinally, when retinal and gravitational upright are dissociated by means of head tilt. However, when the visual patterns are familiar objects with canonical orientations in the external world (e.g., alphanumeric characters), rotation appears to be carried out to achieve congruence with environmental, as opposed to retinal, upright (Corballis, Zbrodoff & Roldan, 1976).

Theoretical Issues

In concluding Part I, we turn to a consideration of the current status of the central theoretical issues raised in the preceding chapters.

We have argued in those chapters that the process of mental rotation is an analog one in that intermediate states in the process have a one-to-one correspondence with intermediate stages in the external rotation of an object. We have argued, further, that the internal representation upon which mental rotation operates is holistic in that the representation preserves the essential spatial structure of its corresponding external referent. These claims have not gone unchallenged, and they have been instrumental in generating the so-called "analog/propositional" controversy which has been vigorously debated in cognitive psychology for nearly a decade. A central issue in the ongoing debate concerns whether it is necessary to postulate special types of representations and processes—viz., analog ones—for spatial information in addition to the discrete, symbolic representations that have been successful in characterizing knowledge of verbal/linguistic information.

The precise nature and focus of the debate has changed over the past few years, sometimes in rather subtle ways. Early criticisms of the use of analog representations as explanatory constructs pointed to the incoherence of the "picture metaphor" for mental imagery and to the necessity for postulating a single underlying symbolic representational system for translating between spatial and linguistic concepts (see, in particular, Pylyshyn, 1977). Another line of attack has consisted of showing that symbolic representations and processes can be made to imitate the phenomena—such as those presented in Chapters 3 through 7 and those reported by Kosslyn (1980) and his collaborators—generally used to support the need for analog representations and operations (see Anderson, 1978, and, for a counterargument based on the naturalness of a proposed representational system for the phenomena that are to be explained, Kosslyn & Pomerantz, 1977).

More recently, Pylyshyn (1979; 1981) has voiced a rather different set of objections to the research and the theoretical efforts of proponents of the analog position. One part of Pylyshyn's argument is an attempt to discredit analog accounts of the process of mental rotation by demonstrating that the results of rotation experiments can be influenced by factors such as practice, and in particular, properties of stimulus structure (Pylyshyn, 1979). Hence, the process of mental rotation is "cognitively penetrable" in that the properties of the underlying operation are not fixed. Regardless of whether or not Pylyshyn's criterion of cognitive penetrability is accepted, it is still the case that the results of his experiments do not conclusively demonstrate that the rate of mental rotation is affected by stimulus- or knowledge-based factors. Recall from our discussion above of effects of complexity on rate of rotation that Pylyshyn's critical experiment used conditions in which the duration of stages other than just the rotation operation entered into the measured reaction times. Thus, it is not possible in his experiment to determine which internal operation(s) is/are affected by experimental manipulations if such effects are found.

A second suggestion that Pylyshyn (1981) has made is that the results of experiments on mental transformation may be accounted for by subjects' use of tacit knowledge concerning the nature of physical transformations and their interpretation of experimental situations as inviting the simulation of what they know the appropriate physical transformation to be. This is in contrast to the view that analog operations are situation-independent properties of internal mechanisms that are used to solve problems involving spatial transformations. We do not view this as a serious objection to our interpretation of the experimental results reported in Chapters 3 through 7. For, in many of those experiments subjects were not explicitly instructed to generate mental images or to engage in imagined rotational transformations. Rather, the use of mental rotation appeared to be the natural way of solving certain spatial problems.

In summary, our view of the nature of the process of mental rotation has not changed fundamentally as a result of new directions in the "analog/propositional" controversy. We do acknowledge that variations in experimental procedure may encourage changes in representational and processing strategies. In some unpublished experiments, which have been put forward to us as failing to replicate our findings on mental rotation, the stimuli have been so restricted or especially chosen that the subjects could easily base their discriminative reponses on superficial cues peculiar to those particular stimuli and so did not have to carry out a mental rotation. Likewise, as we have already noted, whereas experiments in which a single, well-learned stimulus is mentally rotated may encourage the subject to maintain a holistic, integrated internal representation, experiments involving simultaneous presentation of two less familiar and incompletely integrated visual objects may result in more schematic representations and more piece-by-piece processing. Of course it is surely possible to simulate a process that according to our criterion is an analog one by a system that operates at its fine-grain level by discrete operations on discrete symbols—or vice versa, for that matter. However, while there is no a priori reason for a discrete or propositional system to behave in an analog manner, our experiments indicate that the human cognitive system does tend, under appropriate conditions, to operate in that way. It is for this reason that we still find the experimental results in Chapters 3 through 7 to provide persuasive evidence that what we have called mental rotation is in a significant sense an analog simulation of an actual physical rotation.

II | Other Transformations

Introduction to Part II

As explained in Chapter 1, in undertaking the investigation of the mental simulation of spatial transformations, we had reasons for beginning with simple, rigid rotations. Nevertheless, as evidence accumulated in support of the notion that discriminative responses to objects differing by a single rotation about a fixed axis were mediated by a mental analog of a rigid rotation, we felt emboldened to see whether discriminative responses to objects transformed by other, possibly more complex spatial operations or sequences of operations were similarly mediated by mental analogs of those other operations.

Inspired in part by paper-and-pencil test of mental "paper folding" and "surface development" that had long been used for assessing spatial abilities (e.g., French, Ekstrom, & Price, 1963; Smith, McFarlane, 1964), Shepard and Feng (1972) understood the first of these chronometric studies of the analog nature of more complex spatial processes. The ensuing Chapter 9 describes two of these studies. Each individual operation that a subject mentally performed, being a fold, could still be regarded as a rotation, but there were two differences from the rotations considered in Part I: In this new task, each rotation (a) was a rigid rotation of only one piece of the object relative to the rest, rather than a rotation of the entire object as a rigid whole, and (b) was just one in a sequence of such operations that had to be completed before the required discriminative response could be made.

Next, Chapter 10 represents an extension of our earlier studies (described in Chapter 4) of the discrimination between standard and backward (mirror-image) alphanumeric characters presented in rotated orientations. We had concluded from those studies that although the recognition of a certain stimulus as a particular, familiar character (e.g., the letter "R") can be done about as quickly in any orientation, the discrimination between its two enantiomorphic or mirror-image versions, when presented in a rotated orientation, requires a compensating mental rotation. This chapter reports an experiment (Cooper & Shepard, 1975) in which we found similar evidence that although a human hand can be recognized as such in any orientation, the identification of whether it is a left or a right hand is accomplished by imagining one's own right or left hand moved into the displayed orientation and then checking for a match or mismatch. The mental transformations in this experiment, also, do not always correspond to a single rigid rotation; they may consist of at least two rotations or equivalently, of a rotation together with a reflection. Moreover, in both this experiment and the experiment on mental folding, subjects often reported a noticeable component of kinesthetic as well as visual imagery.

Chapter 11 goes on to describe a chronometric investigation of the mental joining of rigid pieces (squares and triangles) into a spatial whole (Glushko & Cooper, 1978). One way in which this study of mental assembly goes beyond the earlier study of mental folding of squares (Chapter 9) is that match-mismatch reaction times to a pictorial probe are used to establish that following the mental assembly of the parts, subjects do indeed have a visual representation of the resulting spatial structure that is simultaneously available as a structural whole.

The epilogue to Part II (Chapter 12) briefly reviews some subsequent results on mental folding and assembly of parts into wholes, as well as some of the corroborative findings that have been obtained by other investigators concerning still other spatial transformations, such as translations, changes of scale (dilatation), combinations of these with rotations, and even nonspatial transformations that may serve similar normalizing functions.

9 | A Chronometric Study of Mental Paper Folding

Originally authored by Roger N. Shepard and Christine Feng

On each trial subjects viewed one of the patterns of six connected squares that result when the faces of a cube are unfolded onto a flat surface. The subjects tried, as rapidly as possible, to decide whether two arrows, each marked on an edge of a (different) square, would or would not meet if the squares were folded back up into the cube. The time required to make such decisions increased linearly (from 2 to about 15 sec) with the sum of the number of squares that would be involved in each fold, if those folds were actually performed physically.

In a recent study of "mental rotation of three-dimensional objects," Shepard and Metzler (1971) found that the time required to recognize that two-perspective drawings portray objects of the same three-dimensional shape increased linearly with the angular difference in the portrayed orientations of the two objects. The marked linearity of this increase (from 1 sec at 0°, to 4 or 5 sec at 180°), together with other aspects of the data, suggested that the comparison in shape was accomplished by first carrying out some sort of purely mental analog of an actual physical rotation of one of the two objects into congruence with the other in three-dimensional space.

The question naturally arises as to whether evidence can be found for a similar sort of isomorphism between physical operations and their purely mental analogs when the relevant physical operations are of a more complex nature and require, for example, a sequence of quite distinct spatial manipulations. We report, here, an attempt to obtain such evidence using a specially designed variation of the kind of "paper-folding" or "surface-development" tasks that are often

Reprinted by permission from Cognitive Psychology, 1972, *3*, 228–243 (copyright © 1972 Academic Press, Inc.).[1]

used in tests of spatial abilities (French, Ekstom, & Price, 1963; Smith, McFarlane, 1964), that appear to be extremely difficult to perform by purely verbal processes and, indeed, that have recently been found to be most effectively performed by the linguistically inferior right hemisphere of the brain (Sperry & Levy, 1970).

Our approach departs from earlier studies of spatial abilities using tasks of this kind, however, for our concern is not with discrimination between individual subjects (or hemispheres) on the basis of their overall time to complete a series of varied problems of such a general type. Rather, our concern is with the dependence of the time to solve *individual* problems upon identifiable parameters of those problems (or of certain subtypes to which they belong), and with what this can tell us about the nature of the underlying mental process.

EXPERIMENT I

In both of the experiments to be reported here, subjects were visually presented with patterns of six connected squares such as result when the faces of a cube are unfolded onto a flat surface. For each such pattern, the times were recorded for Subjects to determine whether the two arrows marked on this pattern would or would not meet if the squares were to be folded back up into a cube. In this first experiment a large number of potentially relevant factors (concerning the arrangement of the squares and the placement of the two arrows) were varied in an exploratory attempt to discover which factors have an important effect on reaction time.

Method

Subjects. Ten undergraduate students (six male and four female), recruited from the introductory psychology course at Stanford, were individually run as subjects.

Stimuli. Each problem was visually presented in the form of a two-dimensional ink drawing of the six connected faces of an "un-folded" cube (as is illustrated within each of the circles in Figure 9.1). In each such drawing one face was shaded (to represent the fixed base of the cube), and two arrows were marked—each centered on one edge of two different squares (as shown). All 11 structurally distinct patterns of squares that represent such an unfolding of a cube were included among the stimuli, as were all structurally distinct arrangements of two arrows that would be brought together only by folding it back up. (By "structurally distinct," here, we mean arrangements that cannot be transformed into each other merely by rigidly rotating or reflecting the entire pattern.) Altogether 164 such drawings were presented to each subject. Half of these were "match" cases in which the two arrows would in fact meet, if the squares were folded back up into a cube (as in A of Figure 9.1). The other half were "non-match" cases in which the two arrows could not be made to meet by folding (as in B). Each of the 164 drawings was glued to a separate 5 × 8 inch card for indivdual presentation behind a 3 inch circular aperture (that corresponded in relative size to the circles shown in Figure 9.1, and that subtended a visual angle of approximately 6°).

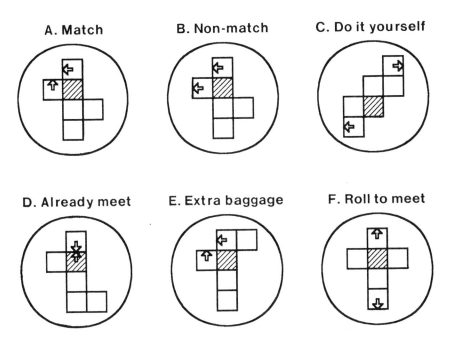

Figure 9.1 Six illustrative problems.

Procedure. Following a brief warning signal, each trial was initiated by illuminating and thus displaying the stimulus selected for that trial behind a half-silvered mirror and, simultaneously, starting the reaction-time clock. The subject, whose hands were already resting on two levers, then proceeded to pull the right-hand lever when able to determine that the two arrows would meet, or to pull the left-hand lever when able to determine that the two arrows would not meet, if the squares were to be folded up into a cube (with the shaded square taken as the fixed base). The actuation of either lever stopped the clock, recorded the response, and terminated the display.

All 164 stimuli were presented in a different random order to each subject and, so, a random half of the presentations consisted of match cases (in which the right-hand response was correct) while the other half consisted of nonmatch cases (in which the left-hand response was correct). No feedback was provided as to the correctness of each response. However, prior to the first recorded trial, each subject was given a few practice trials with feedback, following a through explanation of what to do—including a demonstration with two cut-out and flattened cubes that actually *were* then folded up, physically, to show that the two arrows did meet in the one case, and that they did not meet in the other. Subjects were asked to respond as rapidly as possible on each trial, while keeping errors to a minimum. For a typical subject, the entire session took between 45 and 60 min.

Results

Errors. As we have come to expect for tasks involving spatial abilities, there were wide differences among the performances of individual subjects. Of the ten subjects, three (one male, two female) had error rates (ranging from 16—29%) that were so high—particularly on the most difficult problems—that it seemed best to exclude their data in computing the mean reaction times presented below. In fact, however, the addition of their data has subsequently been found to have no noticeable effect on the plotted functions. In any case, the seven subjects whose data *are* averaged below all had overall error rates of less than 10%.

Reaction time as a function of number of individual folds. If the subjects were making their responses by performing operations mentally that are at all analogous to what they would do in actually folding up a cube physically, then we should expect that their reaction times would increase with the number of separate physical operations that would have to be performed in sequence in order to bring the two arrows into physical coincidence. In order to test this expectation, the 82 match cases were divided into five groups depending upon whether the least number of individual 90° folds that would have to be made in order to bring the two arrows into 90° coincidence at one edge of the cube (without moving the shaded base) was 1, 2, 3, 4 or 5. (On the basis of the results for both of the present experiments, the case in which the two arrows were already in coincidence (Figure 9.1 D) is interpreted as still requiring one fold—presumably in order to achieve the 90° angle between the squares containing the two arrows.)

Since there was only a weak correlation, over the seven subjects, between number of errors made and mean reaction time on the 40 problems for which no errors were made by any subjects ($r = -.28$), no serious bias should be introduced by presenting the averages of reaction times for correct responses only. This is done in the following figures. (However, it has also been established that inclusion of reaction times for incorrect responses does not appreciably affect the results. See, for example, p. 202 and Figure 9.7.)

For each number of individual folds, the interquartile ranges and the means are separately plotted in Figure 9.2 for certain subgroups (to be described shortly) of the means (over the seven subjects) for individual stimulus figures. Overall, there is a quite linear increase in (correct) reaction time with this simple measure of minimum number of separate operations (whether physical or purely mental) that would be required to achieve the 90° coincidence. However it is also evident that different cases involving the same number of individual folds (e.g., 3) vary widely in mean reaction time, and that the means of some subgroups (e.g., the two shown for the case of two individual folds) may depart systematically from the overall linear trend.

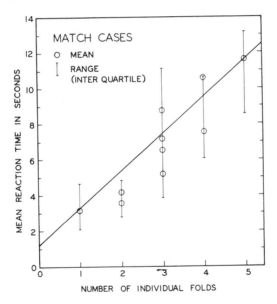

Figure 9.2 Latency of correct "match" responses in Experiment I as a function of the number of individual folds that would be needed to bring the two arrows into 90 degree coincidence with each other (for each of ten different types of problems).

Reaction time as a function of sum of number of squares carried along for each fold. A closer examination of the detailed results revealed that, for each of the five major groups distinguished by the number of individual folds, there were subgroups of stimulus figures

that could be distinguished from each other on the basis of other
structural features of the stimuli and, moreover, that appeared to
differ from each other consistently in terms of observed reaction
times. Indeed it appeared that the 82 match cases could be divided
into some ten different figure types (see Figure 9.4) such that (a)
the shaded "base square" together with just those squares that would
have to be folded in order to join the two arrows formed essentially
the same subconfiguration except for reflections and/or rotations of
that flattened subconfiguration in the two-dimensional plane, and
such that (b) the reaction times were relatively homogeneous within
each such type. Moreover it then became clear that, for types involving the same numbers of individual folds, the reaction times varied
systematically with the number of squares involved or carried along

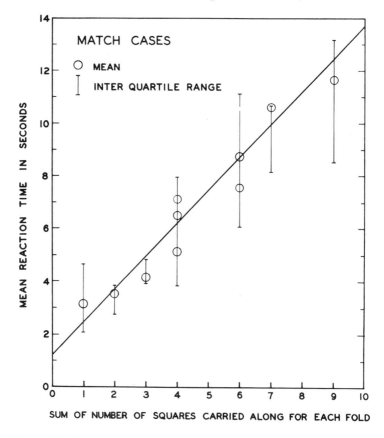

Figure 9.3 Latency of correct "match" responses in Experiment I as a
function of the sum of the number of relevant squares carried along for
each fold—in the sequence of folds needed to bring the two arrows into 90
degree coincidence with each other (for the same ten types of problems).

with each fold. Thus, although Types B and C (Figure 9.4) both require two folds, if the shaded square really is treated as fixed, in Type B only one square need be moved in each of the two folds, whereas in Type C *two* squares must be carried along together on the first fold followed by one square on the second fold (hence the indicated code, "2 + 1"). And, indeed, reaction times to figures of Type C were consistently slower than those to figures of Type B.

Accordingly, the same data already plotted in Figure 9.2 are replotted in Figure 9.3 using "the sum of the number of squares carried along for each fold" as an independent variable in place of the earlier and simpler "number of individual folds." In the case of the pattern shown in Figure 9.1 C (a variant of Type L in Figure 9.4), for example, we now take account of the fact that, although the number of individual folds required is five, the first, second, and third folds of the squares above the shaded square carry along 3, 2, and 1 squares, respectively, while the first and second folds of the squares to the left carry along 2 and 1 squares, respectively. For this pattern the "sum of the squares carried along" in the folding process is therefore $(3 + 2 + 1) + (2 + 1)$ for a total of 9. Apparently, by using this refined independent variable—which takes into account both the number of operations to be performed *and* the memory load associated with each operation—we are able to provide a somewhat tighter account of the observed reaction times for the 82 match cases.

Other aspects of the results. Close examination of the reaction times also disclosed some other subtle effects that were not explicitly anticipated. One quite consistent effect concerns what we refer to as "extra baggage." Notice that the relation of the two arrows to each other and the shaded base in Figure 9.1 E is identical to that shown in Figure 9.1 A. Nevertheless, if the minimum folding needed to join the two arrows were actually carried out, an extraneous square (attached at the top right) would be carried along in the case of Figure 9.1 E but not in the case of Figure 9.1 A. Comparison of a number of such corresponding cases revealed that the presence of such "extra baggage," although it is in a sense irrelevant to the task of joining the two arrows, generally added from ½ to 1 sec. to the overall reaction time. (However, this contribution is apparently less than the roughly 1.3-sec. delay entailed by each *relevant* square that must be carried along and, unlike the case of such relevant squares, appeared not to increase systematically with the *number* of irrelevant squares in the "extra baggage.")

A second type of case, in which the reaction times were actually shorter than would be predicted solely on the basis of the chosen independent variable (rather than longer, as in the case of "extra baggage"), is illustrated in Figure 9.1 F. In all cases in which the two arrows pointed away from each other at opposite ends of a straight string of four squares containing the shaded square, the reaction times were consistently shorter than predicted (by the $2+1+1$ code assigned to those cases). Introspectively, it seems that the squares in such a string are not folded up one-by-one in the kind of discrete, sequential manner that we have supposed but instead are "rolled up" by a single more continuous, integrated, and apparently faster maneuver. In the entire population of figures used, however, only a few were of this special type.

EXPERIMENT II

The findings of Experiment I (together with the identification of the basic "types" of cases) seem to provide a basis for designing a more tightly controlled second experiment. The principal short-comings of the first experiment that appeared, retrospectively, to call for correction were the following: (a) Since the different types of cases were identified *post hoc* in the first experiment, the number of cases of each type were very unequal and, hence, the individual means shown in Figure 9.3 are based on very different numbers of observations. (b) Likewise, the cases involving "extra baggage" (Figure 9.1 E) and the few cases in which the folding operations evidently did not have to be performed in a strictly sequential manner (Figure 9.1 F), were represented very unequally in the different types. (c) Finally, owing to the complete sampling of arrow positions, there were many cases in which the number of folds required to verify a *non*-match depended on which arrow was folded up first and, so, there was no unambiguously defined way to plot functions (such as are shown in Figures 9.2 and 9.3) for the nonmatch cases. Experiment II was designed to correct these and other, more minor difficulties (but at the expense of excluding some of the original variables—such as that of "extra baggage").

Method

Subjects. As before, ten undergraduate students in introductory psychology (this time five male and five female) were run individually.

Stimuli. The figures were of the same general sort as those presented in Experiment I but, this time, they were chosen so that (a) there were exactly eight match and eight nonmatch examples of each of the ten basic types labeled A—X in Figure 9.4, (b) there were no cases that involved the complicating factors of "extra baggage" or nonsequential "rolling up,"and (c) the number of folds necessary to verify a nonmatch was always the same regardless of which arrow was folded up first.

The presented figures always included all six faces of the cube (as shown in the right-most column in Figure 9.4). However, for purposes of analysis, they have been classified as to type on the basis of just the subconfiguration of squares to be folded, together with the shaded base (as shown in the column headed "figure type"—but without regard to the overall orientation of this subconfiguration of relevant squares). Each nonmatch case differed from a corresponding match case simply by the displacement of one arrow to an adjacent edge of its original square. Finally, one type, X, was made much more difficult than any type included in the first experiment by moving the shaded square to an extreme end of the entire configuration of squares.

	CODE	FIGURE TYPE	EXAMPLE
A	I		
B	I+I		
C	2+I		
F	2+I+I		
G	3+I+I		
H	3+2+I		
I	3+2+I		
K	3+2+I+I		
L	3+2+I+2+I		
X	5+4+3+2+I		

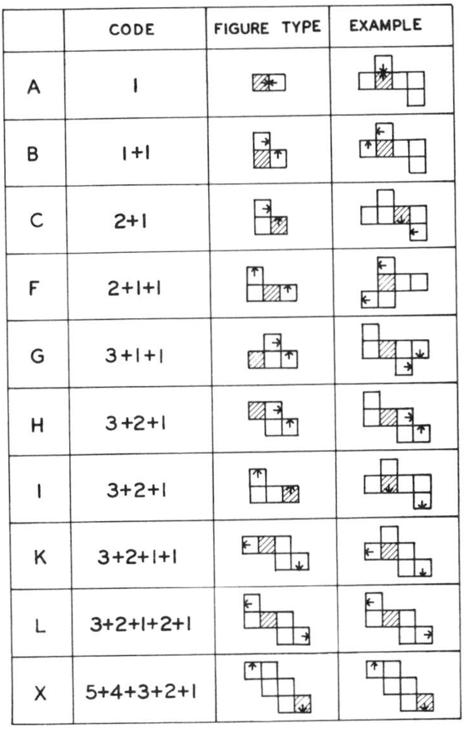

Figure 9.4 The ten structurally different types of problems used in Experiment II. (The missing letters, D, E, J, refer to types eliminated on the basis of results from Experiment I.)

Procedure. The procedure was exactly the same as that already described for Experiment I with the one exception that the instructions gave more explicit emphasis to the requirement that subjects should treat the shaded square as a fixed base and that they should imagine folding up the unshaded squares only.

Results

Errors. As before there was considerable variation among subjects. Nevertheless, if we disregard the one, newly added and much more difficult problem type (X), all but one of the ten subjects (a male) maintained overall error rates below 7.5%. Moreover even that one subject (despite an overall error rate of 15%) yielded reaction-time data that were closely comparable to those for the remaining nine subjects, whose error rates averaged to only 4.2%. Therefore it appeared safe, this time, to include the data from all ten subjects in analyzing reaction times.

Reaction times for the match cases. For each of the ten basic types presented, the mean and total range of the correct reaction

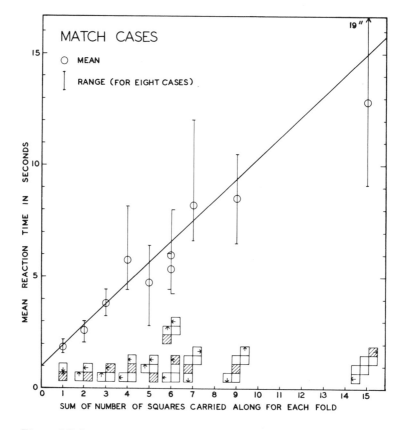

Figure 9.5 Latency of correct "match" responses in Experiment II as a function of the sum of the number of squares carried along for each fold—in the sequence of folds needed to bring the two arrows into 90 degree coincidence with each other (for the ten types of problems shown in Figure 9.4).

times for the eight match cases of that type are separately plotted, in Figure 9.5, as a function of the refined independent measure: "sum of number of squares carried along for each fold." The resulting trend is still quite linear and, this time, the *total* ranges are no larger than the interquartile ranges plotted before (in Figure 9.3). The over sixfold linear increase in reaction time (from 2 to about 15 sec) appears to provide further support for the notion that the subjects were carrying out sequences of imagined operations that varied greatly in terms of number and/or difficulty of steps. If, as we suggest, each step consisted of imagining a certain connected group of squares folded together, then the slopes of the plotted lines indicate that roughly one second of additional time was required for each additional square in any group thus "folded."

Reaction times for the nonmatch cases. For each of the same ten basic types, the mean and the total range for the eight nonmatch cases of that type are presented in the same way in Figure 9.6. Again a generally good fit to a linear function is obtained—particularly for the easier cases in which the independent variable takes on values from 1 to 5, only. However one type (the nonmatch version of Type I in Figure 9.4) seems consistently, if inexplicably, to have taken longer than its code $(3 + 2 + 1)$ would predict. As the codes do predict, though, the slopes of the functions fitted to the match cases (Figure 9.5) and to the nonmatch cases (Figure 9.6) are identical. The nonmatch function is elevated throughout, however, by an approximately half-second additive constant. Although in the present case this may in part reflect a tendency to respond somewhat more slowly with the nonpreferred left hand, introspective reports and similar results in other experiments (e.g., in which we have reversed the roles of the two hands) suggest that it is primarily a matter of being set to register a match and of then having to take additional time to "switch" to the other response if the sought for match fails to occur. This may, then, be another instance conforming to the general principle of "congruence" advocated by Clark and Chase (1972).

Reaction-time functions for individual subjects. The question remains as to whether the linear trend evident in all these figures is representative of the performance of individual subjects or whether it is merely an artifact of averaging the data from subjects who may individually have been using quite different strategies or methods. In an effort to answer this question, mean reaction times were plotted separately for each of the ten subjects in Experiment II (Figure 9.7). In view of the relatively great variability of the reaction times and the relatively small number of correct responses for the two most difficult problem types (L and X) and in order to achieve a

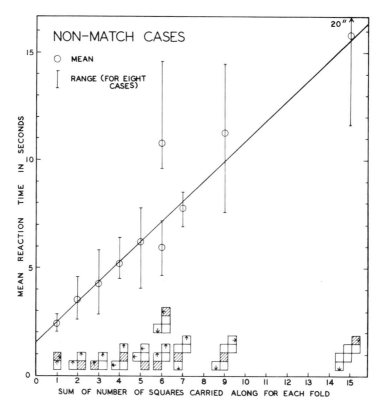

Figure 9.6 Latency of correct "non-match" responses in Experiment II as a function of the sum of the number of squares carried along for each fold—in the sequence of folds needed to verify that the two arrows do not meet (for the nonmatch variants of the ten types of problems shown in Figure 9.4).

reasonably compact display, points are included in this figure only to a value of 7 for the measure of predicted difficulty ("sum of number of squares carried along for each fold").

Each plotted point (+ or –) represents the mean, for the designated subject, of the reaction times for all eight problems of the indicated type (match or nonmatch)—regardless, this time, of whether the responses were correct or incorrect. (To base the means upon correct responses only would considerably reduce the number of observations in some cases though, again, the overall picture would not be changed in any important way.) As in Figures 9.5 and 9.6, there are two problem types with difficulty level 6. These are distinguished in the figure by attaching the appropriate letters, H or I, to the plotted points for this difficulty level. Finally, an overall average curve is

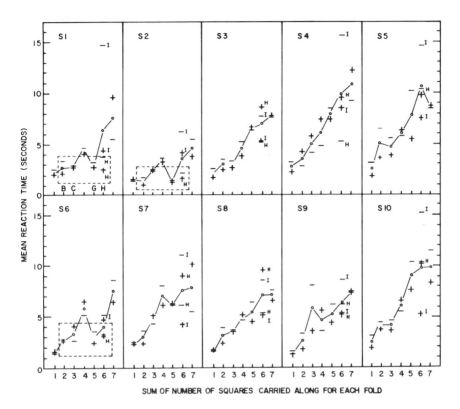

Figure 9.7 Reaction-time functions for each of the ten individual subjects in Experiment II. (Means for the match and nonmatch cases are separately plotted as pluses and minuses, respectively. The dashed-line boxes included in the plots for subjects 1, 2, and 6 are explained in the concluding discussion section.)

plotted for each subject by connecting, by straight line segments, the means (indicated, where appropriate, by small circles) of the + and – points, computed separately for each predicted difficulty level.

Inspection of this figure suggests that subjects 1, 2 and 6 may indeed have been solving the problems in a different way from the remaining seven. With the exception of the mean curves for those three, however, the curves do not appear to depart systematically from a linearly increasing function. Hence the data from seven of the ten subjects, although rather variable owing to the small number of reaction times included in each point, are in satisfactory agreement with the preceding curves obtained by averaging over all ten subjects. In contrast to these, however, the curves for subjects 1, 2 and 6 all exhibit a marked reversal in which reaction times are consistently shorter to problems of predicted difficulty level 5 than to those of level 4. A strategy that appears to explain this deviant pattern of reaction times rather simply will be proposed in the ensuing discussion.

DISCUSSION AND CONCLUSIONS

Despite the generally linear increase in the reaction-time functions for most subjects, it is possible that the decisions were sometimes, or even always, mediated by a process that is not really analogous to one of folding up the cube in physical space. Their decisions might for example have been based on some (largely verbal) process of analysis of the purely two-dimensional pattern—such as, perhaps, a process of counting the number of outside edges separating the two arrows in order to see whether that number is even or odd. And, indeed, that alternative explanation can account for the relatively long reaction times for the most difficult types (K, L, X, in Figure 9.4), in which the two arrows are generally further apart in the presented two-dimensional configuration. However there are at least three considerations that appear to weigh against such an alternative explanation.

One is that of "extra baggage." For, although the extraneous squares to which this term refers do not affect the relation between the two arrows as such, when they were included (in Experiment I) they generally did increase the reaction time by somewhere between ½ and 1 sec. If, as we propose, subjects attempted a mental folding of the cube, it seems plausible that the presence (even if not the number) of extraneous squares that were directly affected by the folding would contribute to the burden on short-term memory and, hence, to processing time.

A second consideration, which seems to run even more strongly against any alternative explanation based merely on some (perhaps verbal) analysis of the relations just between the two arrows, is that, whereas the position of the shaded square should be entirely irrelevant for any strategy of this alternative type, the choice of square to be used as a base (during the mental folding) had a marked effect on average reaction time. Consider, for example, the four types B, C, G and H (in Figure 9.4). In all four of these types the two arrows bear exactly the same geometrical relation to each other in the presented two-dimensional pattern. The only thing that distinguishes these four types is the relation that the two arrows together bear to the shaded base. Yet (if we average the mean reaction times for the match and nonmatch cases for all ten subjects in Experiment II) we find that the overall means for Types B, C, G and H—far from being constant—take on the steadily increasing values 3.1, 4.0, 5.5 and 6.0 sec, in rather close linear correspondence to the predicted difficulty levels

(2, 3, 5 and 6) derived from their respective "codes." Indeed for both the match and nonmatch cases separately, there is not even any overlap between the eight means for the easiest (Type B) and the eight means for the most difficult (Type H) of these four types. This appears to provide rather strong support for the notion that most of the subjects made their decisons by mentally folding up the relevant unshaded squares while leaving the shaded square fixed—as requested in the instructions.

Notice, moreover, that this second consideration appears at the same time to furnish us with a straightforward explanation for the deviant pattern exhibited in Figure 9.7 by subjects 1, 2 and 6. For, if these three subjects did not imagine the squares folded up from the shaded square—taken as a fixed base, then Types B, C, G and H should all have the same short reaction times. But this is essentially what has happened for these three subjects, as is indicated by the dashed rectangles drawn around the datum points for just these four types. Indeed, with regard to predicted difficulty level 6, it is true of all and only these three subjects that both the match and nonmatch versions of Type H are always below both the match and nonmatch versions of Type I. It appears, then, that these three did not, as the other seven, follow the instructions to imagine the squares as folded up from the shaded base. Whether these nevertheless did solve the problems by a process of mental folding (but without, as the other taking the shaded square as the fixed base), or whether they resorted to some more verbal process cannot be definitely settled on the basis of the reaction times alone. The following consideration seems, however, to favor the former interpretation.

In the postexperimental introspective reports elicited from the subjects themselves, all ten subjects claimed that they did indeed imagine going through the steps of folding up the relevant squares in order to determine whether or not the two arrows would meet. Some subjects described this imagery process as being primarily visual others spoke, as well, of a strong kinesthetic component in which they imagined folding up the cube with their own hands—while in reality, of course, their physical hands remained ready to actuate the two response levers. (Cf., the following Chapter 10, for further indications of a kinesthetic component in imagery.)

But just what does it mean to speak of a purely mental process as being "analogous" to some external physical process—in this case the actual folding up of the flattened squares into the form of a cube? Theoretically, it could be interpreted, in accordance with a principal of "second-order isomorphism" (Shepard & Chipman, 1970), to mean that—whatever neurophysiological events are taking place while one is merely *imagining* the external process in question—these events have much in common with the internal events that occur when one is actually *perceiving* the external process itself. As an empirically testable corollary, it implies that while one is in the course of imagining the external process, one passes through an ordered set of internal states of special relation to or readiness for the successive states of the external process. In collaboration with Lynn Cooper, we are presently attempting some direct experimental tests of this corollary. (The result of those experiments are given in the earlier Chapter 4 of this volume.)

10 | Mental Transformations in the Identification of Left and Right Hands

Originally authored by Lynn A. Cooper and Roger N. Shepard

Subjects determined as rapidly as possible whether each line drawing portrayed a left or a right hand when the drawings were presented in any of four versions (palm or back of either hand) and in any of six orientations in the picture plane. Reaction time varied systematically with orientation and, in the absence of advance information, was over 400 msec longer for the fingers-down orientation. However, when subjects were instructed to imagine a specified (palm or back) view of a specified (left or right) hand in a specified orientation, reaction times to test hands that were consistent with these instructions were short (about 500 msec), independent of orientation, and unaccompanied by errors. It is proposed that subjects determine whether a visually presented hand is left or right by moving a mental "phantom" of one of their own hands into the portrayed position and by then comparing its imagined appearance against the appearance of the externally presented hand.

Human subjects are able to identify a visually presented hand as a left or a right hand even in the absence of extraneous correlated cues (such as wristwatches, wedding rings, or writing instruments) and even though the hand may be presented in any of a vast number of different positions.

The basis for making this identification is not obvious, since the two hands do not differ with respect to any simple visual feature inherent in one or the other. Rather, they differ only with respect to the overall structures of the two hands which, as Kant long ago noted, are identical except for a reflection in three-dimensional space (e.g., see Gardner, 1969; Nerlich, 1973). In view of the enormous variety of ways in which either three-dimensional hand can project onto the retina, it seems unlikely that each such two-dimensional projection is identified as right or left by comparison against "right-

Reprinted by permission from *Journal of Experimental Psychology: Human Perception and Performance*, 1975, *104*, 48—56.[1]

hand" and "left-hand" templates stored individually for all possible projections.

Our introspections as well as the verbal reports of many of our subjects suggest that this determination is generally made by imagining one's own preferred hand in the position of the visually presented hand and, then, by testing for a match or mismatch between the appearance of the externally presented hand and the internally transformed visual–kinesthetic image of one's own hand. Thus, without having either to preserve or to search through a store of fixed two-dimensional templates corresponding to all possible retinal projections, the desired discrimination may be made more economically by retaining a single internal representation or "phantom" for each hand. This phantom can then be mentally maneuvered into any position, where it can serve as a sort of template for comparison against a visually presented hand. The present experiment is primarily concerned with two empirically testable consequences of this account of the identification of hands.

1. When a hand is presented in just the position in which the subject is expecting it, the subject need merely compare the external stimulus against his or her previously prepared mental template. Such a comparison should be quite rapid and independent of the correctly anticipated orientation of the test hand (cf. Cooper & Shepard, 1973a, 1973b).

2. However, when the position of the visually presented hand departs from a standard reference position or from some other specifically expected position, a subsequent transformation of the internal representation will be needed before it can be matched against the externally presented hand. In this case, the time to make the left–right determination should increase monotonically with the departure of the test hand from the standard or expected position (cf. Cooper & Shepard, 1973a, 1973b; Shepard & Metzler, 1971).

Our desire to evaluate these proposals has two principal sources: (a) the intrinsic interest of the particular problem of how people identify left and right hands, and (b) the implications of this particular problem for general theoretical arguments concerning the importance of holistic analog operations in human perception and thought recently developed by Shepard (1975), Cooper and Shepard (1973a), and Metzler and Shepard (1974).

Method

Subjects. The eight subjects, five males and three females, were students and staff at Stanford University. All subjects were right-handed.

Stimuli. The four alternative test stimuli, displayed in the 2 × 2 array in Figure 10.1, were line drawings of each of the two sides (palm and back) of each of the two opened-out human hands (right and left). On a given experimental trial, any one of these four alternative versions of a human hand could be presented in any one of six equally spaced orientations around a circle in the two-dimensional picture plane. The six possible orientations corresponded to 60° steps (measured clockwise) from the 0° orientation, which was defined as the orientation in which the fingers pointed straight up. This 0° orientation is illustrated for each of the alternative test hands in Figure 10.1.

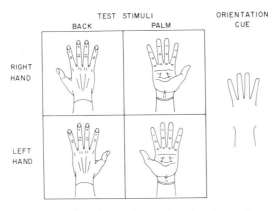

Figure 10.1 The four alternative hand versions that could appear as test stimuli are exhibited in the 2 × 2 array in the zero-degree orientation. (The partial outline used to indicate only the orientation of the upcoming test stimulus is illustrated at the right.)

In addition to the four test stimuli, a thumbless outline of the hand (illustrated at the right in Figure 10.1) was used whenever advance information concerning the picture-plane orientation of the upcoming test stimulus was to be provided. Since this partial outline included the wrist and four fingers, the rotational position in which it appeared furnished complete information regarding the orientation of the ensuing test stimulus. However, since the thumb and all of the internal markings that differentiate the palm from the back were omitted, and since the thumbless outline was constructed as completely symmetrical about the natural axis of the hand, the advance orientation cue provided no information as to *which* of the four possible alternative test stimuli would appear in that orientation. (In order to be consistent with this thumbless outline, all four drawings of complete hands were constructed, with a small distortion of the appearance of real hands, so that with the exception of the thumb, each picture was exactly symmetric. Thus, the "little finger" was depicted as identical in size to the opposite index finger.)

Structure of individual trials. All of the visual stimuli were presented in an Iconix three-field tachistoscope. On each trial the subject was required to determine, as quickly as possible, whether the visually presented test stimulus represented a right hand or a left hand, regardless of which side of the hand (palm or back) was portrayed and regardless of its orientation in the picture plane. "Right-hand" responses were signaled by pushing a right-hand button, and "left-hand" responses were signaled by pushing a left-hand button. The reaction time recorded on each trial was always the time from the onset of the actual test stimulus to the first depression of one of the response buttons. Each test stimulus remained illuminated until the subject had made such a response.

The onset of the test stimulus coincided either with the offset of a 2,000-msec blank warning field (if no advance orientation cue was provided), or with the offset of a 2,000-msec field containing the thumbless outline used as an advance orientation cue. In the latter case, the advance cue and the ensuing test stimulus always appeared in the same picture-plane orientation.

The sequence of visual stimuli appeared centered in a white circular field with a black surround. The luminance of the circular field was about 68.5 cd, and it subtended a visual angle of 4°. The test hands and the thumbless orientation cue subtended an angle of about 1.5°.

The six experimental conditions. When the presentation of the test stimulus was not to be preceded by any orientation cue, the subject was instructed simply to determine as rapidly as possible whether the test stimulus was a right hand or a left hand—regardless of the position in which the test hand might appear. However, when the test presentation was to be preceded by the thumbless outline, the subject was first given one of five different instructions on how to use that cue in preparing for the ensuing stimulus. These five alternative instructions, together with the "no advance information" condition, constitute the full set of six experimental conditions.

In four of the five advance-information conditions, the subject was given explicit instructions on the strategy to be used in preparing for the upcoming test stimulus. Specifically, the subject was asked to imagine one particular version of a human hand in the orientation designated by the thumbless outline during the 2,000-msec advance-information interval. For example, in one such condition, the subject was instructed to imagine the back of the right hand superimposed on the thumbless outline during its 2,000-msec duration. Similarly, in the three other "imagery instruction" conditions, the subject was requested to imagine the palm of the right hand, the palm of the left hand, or the back of the left hand in the designated orientation.

Regardless of the specific instruction given to the subject, in all four of these conditions the actual test stimulus could be any of the four alternative versions of a human hand (always appearing in the orientation indicated by the thumbless outline). Thus, in each of these four separate imagery instruction conditions, the probability that the specific version of a hand that the subject was requested to imagine in advance would be identical to the actual test stimulus, when presented, was only .25.

In the fifth advance-information condition, no specific strategy instructions were provided. The subject was simply encouraged to make use of the orientation cue in whatever way possible, but to try not to imagine any *specific* version of a hand during the 2,000-msec duration of the thumbless outline.

General experimental design. A within-subject factorial design was used such that each of the eight subjects saw each of the four alternative hand versions (back and palm of the right and left hands) in each of the six orientations (0°–300° in 60° steps) under each of the six experimental conditions. Thus, 144 experimental trials per subject were required to obtain one observation for each cell of the design.

Following an initial practice session consisting of 36 trials, each subject participated in two experimental sessions. The trials were blocked by conditions such that within each session six blocks were completed. Each within-session block corresponded to one of the six experimental conditions. Within each of these six blocks, 12 experimental trials—selected randomly from the complete set of 24 trials for each condition—were presented. The order of conditions within a session was balanced over subjects and over the two sessions.

Trials on which errors were made were later retaken in order to obtain for each subject an errorless reaction time for each combination of test-hand alternative, orientation, and experimental condition.

Results

Reaction time as a function of the relationship between the imagined and presented hands. Mean reaction times averaged over all eight subjects and over all four versions of the test hand are displayed in Figure 10.2. The filled circles and solid lines were obtained by also averaging over all six orientations in the picture plane. The open circles and dashed lines (which will be considered later) were obtained by averaging only over the 0° and ± 60° orientations. Each of the four data points connected by line segments represents a particular relationship between the hand that the subject had been instructed to imagine and the hand that was actually presented.

For the first or leftmost point ("same side, same hand"), the imagined and presented hands were identical with respect to hand identity,

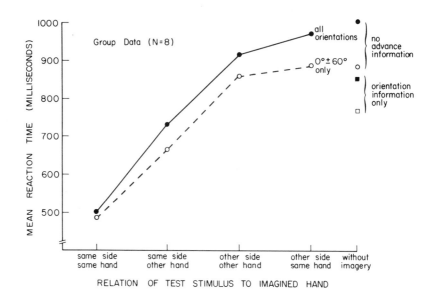

Figure 10.2 Mean reaction time for each of the four possible relationships between the hand the subject was instructed to imagine and the hand actually presented as the test stimulus (connected points). (Mean reaction times for the two conditions in which no specific hand was to be imagined are displayed as separate points at the right. The filled circles plot averages over all six orientations, while the open circles plot averages over only the more upright orientations of zero degrees ± 60 degrees.)

side, and orientation. For the second point ("same side, other hand"), the imagined and presented hands differed only with respect to hand identity. That is, although the presented hand showed the same (palm or back) side in the same (picture-plane) orientation as the imagined hand, the thumb appeared on the opposite side. Thus, the (left-right) identity of the presented hand was opposite to that imagined. For the third point ("other side, other hand"), the presented and imagined hands differed with respect to both hand identity and side. In this case the thumb position and the entire outline of the presented hand agreed with what was imagined, but the internal markings that distinguish the palm from the back differed. For the last point ("other side, same hand"), the presented hand and the imagined hand differed with respect to both thumb position and palm–back markings. These two discrepancies resulted in a presented hand that was the same in left–right identity as the imagined hand—only displayed as flipped over to the other side.

At the right in Figure 10.2, are the corresponding pairs of points for the two remaining conditions in which no specific imagery instructions were given. The higher points represent the condition in which no advance information was provided, and the lower points represent the condition in which the orientation cue was provided and the subject was requested to use that cue without imagining either hand in the indicated orientation. As before, the filled points are averaged over all six orientations, and the open points are averaged over just the upright orientation and $\pm 60°$ from upright.

As these group data indicate, subjects responded quite rapidly whenever the presented hand was identical to the hand imagined in advance. An additional 200 msec were required (to make the opposite response) when the same side of the opposite hand was presented instead. Still another 200 msec were required when the opposite side of *either* the same or the opposite hand was presented. Mean reaction times in this last case approximated the reaction times when *no* information as to hand, side, or orientation was provided in advance.

Statistical tests indicate that all pairwise differences among the mean reaction times connected by solid lines in Figure 10.2 are reliable, with the exception of the differences between the last two points on the right.[2]

The same pattern emerged consistently in the data of each of the eight individual subjects. For every subject the first three of the four connected points (cf. Figure 2) increased monotonically and approximately linearly. However, five of the eight subjects exhibited an appreciable increase in reaction time from the third to the fourth points, while three subjects exhibited a reversal for these last two points. As we shall suggest below, these two groups of subjects may have used somewhat different strategies.

Reaction time as a function of test-stimulus orientation under different conditions. Figure 10.3 presents mean reaction time as a function of orientation of the test stimulus (expressed in degrees of clockwise rotation from the orientation in which the fingers point straight up) for the four imagery instruction conditions. The four separate reaction time functions correspond to the four possible relationships between the imagined stimulus and the actual test stimulus distinguished in Figure 10.2. The plotted points are averages, within the four types of relationships between the imagined hand and the test hand, taken over the eight subjects, the four imagery instruction conditions, and the four specific palm–back and left–right test-stimulus combinations. All of the points plotted in Figure 10.3 are independent, with the exception of the points at $360°$, which are duplicates of the points at $0°$.

The differences among the overall heights of the four reaction time functions correspond to the differences among the mean reaction

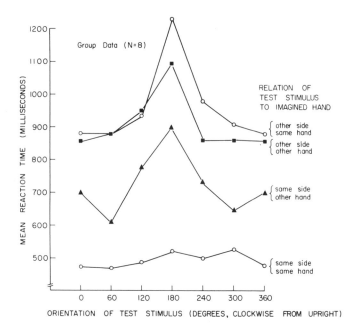

Figure 10.3 Mean reaction time plotted as a function of
test-stimulus orientation, expressed as degrees of clockwise
rotation from the zero-degree (fingers pointing up) position.
(The four separate functions correspond to the possible
relationships between the imagined hand and the test hand.)

times plotted in Figure 10.2. Our concern now is with comparisons
among the shapes of these four functions. For all of the cases in
which the imagined stimulus and the test stimulus differ in some way,
reaction time generally increases as the orientation of the test stimulus departs from the 0° (fingers up) orientation. The reaction time
increase is particulary marked as the maximum departure is approached at the completely inverted (fingers down) orientation of
180°. In striking contrast, when the imagined hand and the presented
hand are identical in all respects, the function relating time and test-
stimulus orientation is virtually flat.

With respect to both its flat shape and its low absolute level (of
only about 500 msec), this reaction time function is reminiscent of
the function obtained by Cooper and Shepard (1973a, 1973b)
when subjects were informed sufficiently in advance as to the identity
and the orientation of an upcoming rotated letter or numeral. As in
that previous experiment, we conclude here that subjects prepared
for the upcoming test hand by imagining the appropriate hand version rotated into the indicated orientation. If the test hand, when

presented, was identical to the imagined hand, then subjects could rapidly indicate that the two representations matched, regardless of the picture-plane orientation of the test hand.

In Figure 10.4 mean reaction time (over subjects and test-hand versions) is plotted as a function of orientation of the test stimulus for the two experimental conditions in which subjects were given no specific instructions as to how to use the thumbless orientation cue (if it was presented at all). In both conditions, reaction times are (a) generally longer than in the case of the imagery instruction condition, and (b) markedly dependent on orientation.

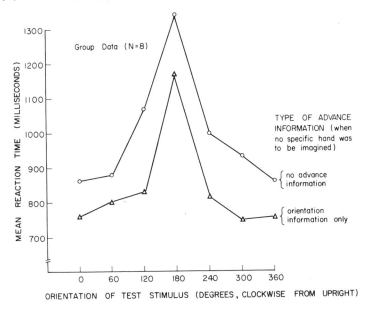

Figure 10.4 Mean reaction time plotted as a function of test-stimulus orientation for the conditions in which no advance information or only orientation information was provided.

From Figure 10.4 we see that when *no* information is provided in advance of the presentation of the test stimulus, reaction time increases rapidly as that test stimulus approaches the completely inverted, 180° orientation. When information concerning the orientation of the upcoming test hand is provided, but the subject does not know *which* concrete stimulus to expect, mean reaction times are some 100–150 msec faster than in the no-advance-information condition at all orientations alike. These new results provide further support for two of our earlier (Cooper & Shepard, 1973a) conclusions: (a) Subjects *cannot* effectively prepare for a rotated stimulus by "mentally rotating" only an abstract frame of reference. (b) The presentation of advance information concerning only orientation reduces total reaction time by an amount that would otherwise be needed to determine the orientation of the test stimulus itself *before* any further processing, such as mental rotation, can be initiated.

Errors. All trials on which errors were made were retaken during the experimental sessions. Error rates ranged from 2.1% to 9.2% for individual subjects, with an average error rate of 5.6%. In addition, error rates correlated positively with mean reaction times. It is noteworthy that no errors were made by any one of the eight subjects on those trials in which the hand version that the subject had been instructed to imagine was then presented as the test stimulus.

Discussion

Evidence that identification is based on an internal analog transformation. The above results confirm the two testable consequences initially derived from our notion of how subjects determine the left-right identity of a visually presented hand. (a) When subjects were given complete, veridical information as to the version and orientation of the to-be-presented hand, they responded rapidly and entirely without error regardless of the designated orientation. The uniform speed and accuracy of these responses suggests that they were based on the outcome of a holistic template-like comparison between an internally readied representation and the ensuing external stimulus. (b) When the advance information was either incomplete or nonveridical, reaction times were 200–700 msec slower, and they depended systematically on both the orientation of the test hand and the relation of the test hand to the imagined hand. This finding is consonant with the notion that, in order to achieve a match and hence identification, an internal representation of the corresponding hand had to be transformed from some standard, canonical position into the palm-back and picture-plane orientation actually presented—with more extensive transformations requiring more time.

If there is one "canonical" orientation shared by all subjects, then our results suggest that it is the orientation with the fingers pointing upward. This is certainly consistent with the fact that in either viewing or displaying one's own hands (as in presenting a finger count), one generally tends to hold the hands with the fingers pointing up.

However, in view of both the relative flatness of the reaction time functions in the vicinity of 0° and the fact that one often views or displays the hands in positions tilted somewhat from the 0° orientation, it is quite possible that subjects could have canonical internal representations corresponding to different, somewhat tilted orientations.

Nevertheless, identification time increased sharply for all subjects as the presented hand approached the 180° orientation in which the fingers point straight down.[3] Some subjects emphasized the kinesthetic component of their mental imagery in this task and claimed that the marked increase in reaction time at this orientation was due to the physical awkwardness of positioning one's own (right or left) hand in that inverted orientation—even though the positioning is performed only mentally. The increase may also be attributable to the related fact that we less frequently see our own physical hands in this rather awkward position. In any case, since subjects *can* prepare in advance for a hand presentation at any such inverted orientation under appropriate conditions (cf. Figure 10.3), the dependence of reaction time on orientation in the *absence* of appropriate advance information presumably reflects two facts: (a) We do not ordinarily expect to be presented with hands in inverted positions. (b) Extra effort and time are required to prepare for a rapid match against a hand in an "awkward" orientation.

A proposed information-processing model. The data from this one experiment are not sufficient to determine the precise sequence of internal processes that underlie the determination of the left-right identity of a visually presented hand. Nevertheless, we tentatively propose that on a trial in which the subject is asked to imagine a particular side of a particular hand in the predesignated orientation, the subject proceeds through the following self-terminating sequence of steps:

1. Following the instruction to imagine a particular side of a particular hand in a particular orientation, the subject prepares for the upcoming test stimulus by first imagining the designated hand moved into the designated position (of side and picture-plane orientation), and by then readying his or her corresponding physical hand to respond if the imagined hand matches the ensuing test hand.

2. Immediately upon its external onset, the test stimulus is compared in a holistic, template-like fashion with the preparatory mental image. If the two representations match, the prereadied response is executed and the recorded reaction time (of about 500 msec) is the sum of (a) the time to process the test stimulus and detect the match and (b) the time to execute the response.

3. If the attempted match fails, an internal representation of the opposite (nondesignated) hand is mentally moved into the designated position (of side and orientation), and response readiness is switched to the corresponding (nondesignated) physical hand.

4. As before, a holistic comparison is attempted between the mentally transformed internal representation and the external stimulus. If a match is achieved, the currently readied response is executed. The

additional 200 msec (at 0°)–400 msec (at 180°) in the recorded reaction time is the sum of (a) the time to carry out the mental positioning (200 msec at 180°), (b) the time to switch control to the opposite hand (about 100 msec according to Cooper & Shepard, 1973a), and (c) the time to complete the holistic comparison.

5. If this second attempted match fails, the current internal representation (i.e., the image of the nondesignated hand) is mentally flipped over to its opposite (palm or back) side.

6. A third holistic comparison is then made between this previously rotated and, now, flipped representation of the nondesignated hand and the external test stimulus. If a match results, the readied response (still of the nondesignated physical hand) is executed. The additional 200 msec in the recorded reaction time is the sum of (a) the time to carry out the mental flip and (b) the time to complete this third holistic comparison.

7. If this last attempted match fails, then by elimination, readiness is switched to the originally designated hand before executing the "same hand" response.

This processing model yields a satisfactory account of the major features of the data displayed in Figures 10.2 and 10.3. However, as mentioned above, for three of the eight subjects, reaction times to the opposite side of the opposite hand (from that imagined) were *longer* than reaction times to the opposite side of the same hand (i.e., the third and fourth points plotted in Figure 10.2 were reversed for these subjects). We might speculate that these subjects retained, in some state of secondary readiness, the prepositioned representation of the designated hand (from Step 1) during the subsequent transformation and comparison involving the opposite hand (Steps 3 and 4). They might then be able to use that representation of the originally designated hand in performing the flip and comparison of Steps 5 and 6. This proposal, though highly speculative, would produce the observed reversal in reaction time of the last two points for these three subjects.

In any case, the first four of the seven steps proposed above are strongly suggested by the data for all eight of the subjects. The flat shape and low height of the bottom function in Figure 10.3 establish that subjects first attempted a holistic match with a representation of the predesignated hand that had been mentally maneuvered into the predesignated position. The peaked shape and intermediate height of the next higher function indicates that subjects next attempted a match with a representation of the opposite, nondesignated hand that had *not* previously been mentally maneuvered into the designated position.

Concluding observations. The last three of the seven steps proposed are much less certain than the first four—particularly in view of the inter-subject differences. Other more quantitative details also remain uncertain. For example, is the time required to complete a mental flip from one side to the other of an imagined hand at all dependent on the orientation of that hand in the picture plane? The approximate parallelism of all but the bottommost curve in Figure 10.3 suggests that any such dependence is relatively slight.

A related quantitative question concerns the curves plotted in Figure 10.2. The shape of the solid curves is potentially misleading, as the plotted points are averages over all six picture-plane orientations. For, recall that reaction time varied markedly with orientation in the case of the three points on the right in Figure 10.2, but was essentially flat in the case of the point on the left (cf. Figure 10.3). Since reaction time was approximately flat in the $-60°$ to $+60°$ range around the normal, upright orientation for all curves in Figures 10.3 and 10.4, the dashed line (with open points) in Figure 10.2 is largely free of this artifact. The effect of this correction is to lower all except the first point by 50-100 msec. Thus, the shape of the curve is changed very little; however, the increase exhibited by the first three points becomes, if anything, even more linear.

Whether this linearity is theoretically significant or coincidental is not yet known. In terms of the tentatively proposed model, the time required to rotate the image of a hand from the upright to the inverted orientation (included in the difference between the first two points in Figure 10.2) approximately equals the time to flip the image from one side to the other (included in the difference between the second two points). Certainly both operations amount to $180°$ rotations about some axis in three-dimensional space (cf. Shepard & Metzler, 1971).

One of our intents in reporting this experiment has been to make plausible the claim that identification of "isomeric" objects is accomplished by a sequence of analog mental transformations and holistic matches. Alternatively, one might consider a "two-stage" or "dual-process" model in which failure of the initial holistic match (Step 1) is followed by a series of local tests against individual features rather than by holistic operations throughout (cf. Bamber, 1969; Sekuler & Abrams, 1968; Silverman, 1973; Smith & Nielson, 1970). In the present case, such individual features would include palm-versus-back markings, position of the thumb, etc. However, any account based on local feature tests has difficulty explaining the strong dependence of reaction time on test-stimulus orientation exhibited in all but the bottommost curve in Figure 10.3. (One might argue that individual features take longer to detect when they appear in the unfamiliar, upside-down orientation. But this argument is difficult to reconcile with both the approximate parallelism of the obtained curves and with the introspective impression that discrimination of palm-versus-back markings should not increase in difficulty with departure from the upright position.) It may be that with more extensive practice in distinguishing left from right versions of unadorned hands, subjects could learn to achieve the discrimination by a series of feature tests. However, in the case of the present experiment, such an interpretation seems unlikely.

In conclusion, we interpret our results as supporting the notion that subjects determine the left-right identity of a presented hand by first imagining one of their own hands moved into the position of the presented hand, and then testing for a match or mismatch. Only the general analog and holistic character of these operations are dictated by this sort of model. The precise sequence of these operations under any given condition has been inferred entirely from the obtained data. In particular, the specification (in Steps 3 and 4 above) that a failure of the first holistic match is always followed by a test with the same side of the opposite hand *before* a test with the opposite side of the same hand was determined solely by the outcome of the empirical data—not by any requirement of a theory based on analog transformations and holistic matches. Thus, a remaining question of interest is whether subjects could be induced, by means of appropriate instructions and/or practice, to perform some of these operations in a quite different order.

11 | Spatial Comprehension and Comparison Processes in Verification Tasks

Originally authored by Robert J. Glushko and Lynn A. Cooper

Two experiments used the sentence-picture verification paradigm to study encoding and comparison processes with spatial information. Subjects decided whether a description of a geometrical figure matched a visually presented figure. When the two displays were presented successively and subjects took as much time as they needed to prepare for the test figure, verification time was not affected by the pictorial complexity of the test figure or by the markedness of the relational terms used in the descriptions, and "same" responses were faster than "different" responses. When subjects had less time to study the description before the test picture appeared, effects of complexity and lexical markedness emerged and were largest when the two displays appeared simultaneously; concurrently, "differents" became faster than "sames." Evidently, when given enough time, subjects could mentally assemble the component triangles, squares, etc. of the described figure into a coherent image (a) that no longer reflected the linguistic features of the verbal description and (b) that could then be matched against the ensuing visual test figure by a uniformly rapid, parallel process.

A major goal of cognitive psychologists is to understand the nature of the internal representations and processing operations that mediate the comprehension of spatial information. Two general experimental approaches characterize much of the research on spatial comprehension. In studies using the "sentence verification" paradigm the subject determines whether or not a sentence or name correctly describes a spatial display (e.g., Carpenter & Just, 1975; Clark, Carpenter, & Just, 1973; Clark & Chase, 1972, 1974; Just & Carpenter, 1975; Seymour, 1973a, 1974a, d, 1975; Tversky, 1975). This kind of task is typically used by psycholinguists to study the effects of variables such as syntactic complexity, negation, and lexical markedness

Reprinted by permission from *Cognitive Psychology*, 1978, *10*, 391-421 (Copyright © 1978 Academic Press, Inc.).[1]

(see Clark, 1969) on verifying spatial sentences. In "description matching" studies, experimenters primarily interested in memory processes compare matching a spatial description to a subsequently presented visual figure with matching two sequentially presented visual figures (e.g., Cohen, 1969; Nielsen & Smith, 1973; Santa, 1977; Seymour, 1973b, 1974b, c; Smith & Nielsen, 1970; Tversky, 1969). These researchers study the temporal properties of picture and sentence representations and investigate the possibility of translating or recoding one representation into the other.

The sentence verification and description matching paradigms resemble one another, and researchers in each tradition have proposed models for their particular task and have suggested that these models might be extended to the other paradigm as a general model of spatial comprehension and comparison. The two most influential attempts at characterizing the comprehension of spatial information have resulted in the *propositional* and *dual code* models. Unfortunately, the typical patterns of results from the two approaches are somewhat inconsistent, and neither class of model seems capable of unifying the two lines of research.

Propositional models were proposed in a number of sentence verification studies to account for a regular cluster of linguistic effects on verification latency. In general, descriptions that are linguistically complex (e.g., descriptions that contain negatives) take longer to verify than simple affirmative descriptions. The most reliable result is that sentences containing lexically marked spatial relations like BELOW take longer to verify than sentences containing their lexically unmarked counterparts like ABOVE.

Propositional models propose a single abstract propositional format for both sentence (description) and figure representations. This common representation consists of embedded relational predicates, each containing one or more arguments. For example, the propositional model presented by Clark and Chase (1972, 1974) holds that simple pictures of some shape "A" depicted above another shape "B" are encoded either as ABOVE (A,B) or as BELOW (B,A). Similarly, the two descriptions that A is ABOVE B and that B is BELOW A are represented as ABOVE (A,B) and BELOW (B,A), respectively. When sentences and pictures are compared, the verification latency depends on the number of operations needed to compare the corresponding constituents of the two representations. This constituent comparison process (Carpenter & Just, 1975) is serial rather than holistic, and the constituents are compared from the "inside out," that is, from the most embedded to the least embedded constituent of the representation.

Researchers using the description matching paradigm typically report two results that are at odds with the description complexity and lexical markedness effects from the sentence verification paradigm. First, the effects of description complexity often vary with the retention interval between the presentation of the description and the subsequent presentation of the test figure (e.g., Nielsen & Smith, 1973). Second, description matching studies often fail to find effects of lexical markedness on the time to make a sequential description-figure comparison (e.g., Seymour, 1974a, 1975).

Dual code models have been primarily concerned with the asymmetry in the effects of figure-figure and description-figure matches over time. The common feature of these models is that the proposed representations of figures and of spatial descriptions are qualitatively different. Nielsen and Smith's dual code model holds that a figure is represented as an integral image, while a description is initially encoded as a list of features with verbal properties. Their model proposes that the effects of description complexity disappear over time because subjects recode the verbal feature list into a more integral form if they expect an integrated test figure.

We report two experiments that employ features of both the description matching and sentence verification paradigms. As in the description matching paradigm, we compare reaction time for matching an initially presented spatial description to reaction time for matching two sequentially presented visual figures. As in the sentence verification paradigm, we systematically manipulate properties of the initially presented descriptions.

Our purpose in reporting these experiments differs from that of many previous researchers. We neither test models nor propose or support a particular model of spatial comprehension and comparison. Instead, we present our studies as *demonstrations* that certain experimental methods lead to results which characterize the task more than indicate representational or processing invariants.

EXPERIMENT I

In the first experiment, we study the process of constructing an internal representation from a figure or from a verbal description of the figure. We generalized the spatial comparison task by using descriptions and figures at several levels of linguistic and pictorial complexity. In addition, we separated encoding and comparison time with a successive rather than a simultaneous presentation of the two displays. After subjects were presented with either a visual figure or a verbal description, they were allowed as much time as necessary to "prepare" for the test figure. Following this preparation interval, a test figure was presented, and subjects were asked to judge as rapidly

as possible whether the test figure was the same as or different from
the initially presented figure or description.

Method

Subjects. Four subjects, all students and staff at the University of
California, San Diego, participated in the experiment for four two-
hour sessions and a single one-hour session.

Stimuli. Subjects were presented with two different types of visual
displays, geometric figures and verbal descriptions of geometric figures. Figure 11.1 shows sample figures and their corresponding descriptions. The figures could have three levels of complexity. That is,
they could be composed of two, three, or four component parts.
The component parts were always squares and equilateral triangles.

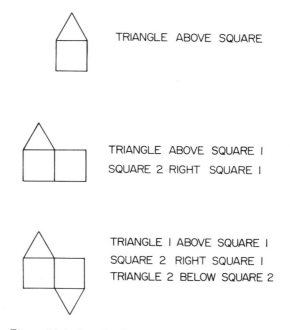

Figure 11.1 Sample figures and descriptions at the three
levels of complexity used in Experiment 1.

There were four different figures at each of the three levels of
complexity. The four 2-component figures consisted of a square and
a triangle, with the triangle above, below, or on the right or left sides
of the square. The four 3-component figures consisted of two adjacent squares and a triangle above or below one of the squares. Finally,
the four 4-component figures consisted of two adjacent squares and
two triangles. For two of these figures, the triangles were either both
above or below the two squares. For the other two figures, the

triangles were diagonally opposite one another, with one above and one below dfferent squares.

The verbal descriptions were one, two, or three lines in length. Each 3-word line contained the name of a component figure, a spatial relation, and the name of a second component figure. The relational terms used were ABOVE, BELOW, RIGHT, and LEFT. These relations were used in their "natural" meanings (see Fig. 11.1).

Two or more descriptions for each figure were used in order to study the effects on preparation and comparison times of different relational terms and the order in which different component parts were introduced and arranged. Each of the four 2-component figures was described by a pair of 1-line descriptions using either the ABOVE/BELOW or RIGHT/LEFT spatial relations. Each of the 3-component figures had four 2-line descriptions and each 4-component figure had eight 3-line descriptions. In all, 56 different descriptions were used in Experiment 1.

Procedure. On each experimental trial, two reaction times were recorded. The first reaction time (or preparation time, RT_1) consisted of the time needed to comprehend and encode the initial display. RT_1 was the time between the onset of the initially presented figure or description and the subject's foot-pedal response that denoted a request for presentation of the test figure. The foot pedal press resulted in termination of the first visual display and initiation of the test display sequence. The interval between the subject's preparation response (foot pedal press) and presentation of the test figure was either 0 or 3000 msec. The test figure appeared centered on the screen in the same spatial location as the first display.

The second reaction time (or comparison time, RT_2) consisted of the time needed to determine whether the test figure was the same as or different from the figure initially presented or described. This comparison time was measured from the onset of the test figure to the subject's indication of "same" or "different" by pressing one of two response buttons. After subjects responded, they received feedback from a light over the correct response button. A "same" test figure was identical in all respects to the one initially presented or described. "Different" figures were one of the other three figures from the same level of complexity as the "same" form. This constraint on the "different" set precluded responses based solely on the number of components in the test figure. In addition, the nature of the 4-component figures discouraged subjects from adopting a strategy of encoding a single feature from the initial display and responding "same" or "different" depending on whether or not the feature was present in the test figure.

There were four experimental conditions: figure–figure (F–F) and description–figure (D–F) trials at each of the two interstimulus intervals, 0 and 3000 msec. In each experimental session, trials were blocked by each of the four conditions in 96-trial blocks, and all four conditions were run in each session for a total of 384 trials per session. The order of the four blocks was balanced within each session and randomly assigned between subjects, with the constraint that F–F and D–F blocks alternate. Within each session and condition, trials were randomly selected from the three levels of figure or description complexity.

Results

Preparation time (RT_1). Figure 11.2 illustrates mean RT_1 for trials on which subjects responded correctly, averaged over interstimulus interval, and plotted separately for the F–F and the D–F conditions.

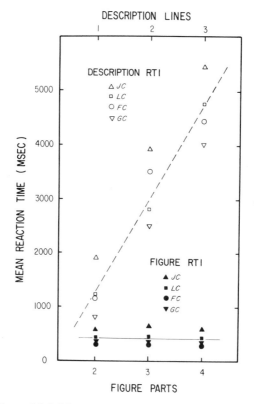

Figure 11.2 Mean preparation or comprehension time (RT_1) as a function of complexity for the description and figure conditions of Experiment 1. Symbols are the means for individual subjects, with the best-fitting straight lines for the group data.

The most striking features of the data are the differences in the time required to prepare for a test figure in the two presentation conditions. In the F-F condition, approximately 400 msec are needed to encode an initially presented visual figure, and this time is not affected by the complexity of the figure. In the D-F condition, the time needed to construct a memory representation from a description increases linearly with the complexity of the description.

In order to examine any effects on preparation times of different relational terms and alternate descriptions of the same figure, separate analyses of variance were performed on the D-F RT_1 data for each level of description complexity. Previous investigators (e.g., Clark & Chase, 1972; Olson & Laxar, 1973) have reported that sentences using ABOVE or RIGHT are comprehended faster than semantically-equivalent sentences with their "marked" counterparts BELOW and LEFT. However, for our 1-line, 2-component descriptions, there was no overall effect of relational terms. In fact, there were no significant differences between any pair of relational terms means.

Comparison time (RT₂). Figure 11.3a presents mean correct RT_2 averaged over subjects, interstimulus interval, and responses. Means for the F-F and D-F conditions are plotted separately as a function of the complexity of the test figure. Figure 11.3a clearly shows that, while the F-F means are about 60 msec faster than the D-F means, neither reaction time function is affected by the complexity of the test figure. In addition, though not shown in the figure, "same" responses are reliably faster than "different" responses in both the F-F and D-F conditions. The constant difference between the F-F and D-F matching times, the absence of an effect of test-figure complexity, and the greater speed of "same" responses were also apparent in the data of each of the four subjects.

Figure 11.3b presents mean correct RT_2 as a function of interstimulus interval, plotted separately for the D-F and the F-F conditions. In the analysis of variance on the group data, the main effect of Interstimulus Interval was not significant, primarily because the Subjects × Interstimulus Interval and Presentation Condition × Interstimulus Interval interactions were both significant sources of variance. However, analyses of the data of individual subjects indicate that the overall interaction shown in Figure 11.3b represents a very reliable increase in F-F matching time with increasing interstimulus interval, and a somewhat uncertain effect in the opposite direction for D-F matches. A planned comparison confirmed that the overall interaction was located in the increase in F-F matching time.

Separate analyses of variance on the group RT_2 data for each level of description complexity examined possible effects of using alternate spatial relations or syntactic structures on matching time. In none of these analyses were the effects of Figures or Descriptions significant, nor did these factors interact with each other or with any other factor. In addition, we tested specific hypotheses of markedness effects over the eight 1-line description means, but found no significant differences. The two descriptions using ABOVE (399 msec) were verified no faster than the two with BELOW (401 msec), and those with RIGHT (413 msec) did not differ from those with LEFT (422 msec).

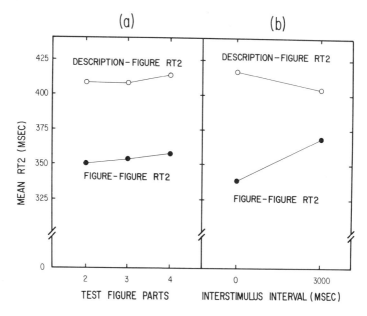

Figure 11.3 (a) Mean correct comparison time (RT_2) as a function of test-figure complexity for the description-figure and figure-figure conditions of Experiment 1. (b) Mean correct RT_2 as a function of interstimulus interval for the description-figure and figure-figure conditions of Experiment 1.

Errors. Error rates were low, ranging from 2.6% to 6.4% for individual subjects, with an average rate of 3.7%. Errors occurred with equal frequency in the F-F and the D-F conditions, and were equally likely for displays at each level of complexity. However, errors were more frequent when the interstimulus interval was 0 msec (4.8%) than when it was 3000 msec (2.5%). This effect may be due to some difficulty in making two responses in rapid succession.

Discussion

Two central features of the results of Experiment 1 conflict with those reported in similiar sentence verification and description matching experiments. First, the comparison time functions for both F-F and D-F conditions shown in Figure 11.3a are qualitatively alike in that neither function is affected by the complexity of the test figure or the length of its initial description. Second, the particular spatial relation (ABOVE, BELOW, RIGHT, or LEFT) used in a description line does not influence D-F comparison time.

Dual code models have been proposed to account for asymmetric effects of complexity on figure and description matching, and no such differences were found in the present experiment. Propositional models also predict effects of description complexity on comparison time. For example, Carpenter and Just's (1975) constituent comparison model proposes a serial comparison of corresponding parts of the initial and test representations. Such a model should certainly predict an increase in RT_2 with complexity in our D-F condition, unless the time to find and compare each constituent can be extremely short or the size of each constituent is variable. The absence of effects of relational terms on comparison time is also problematic for propositional models of spatial comprehension. For example, the serial comparison model of Clark and Chase (1972) is based in part on effects of lexical markedness of the particular spatial relations used to describe a figure.

The failure to find any effects of lexical markedness or description type on comparison time is consistent with the claim that the figures and descriptions are ultimately represented in the same way. Thus, while the representation may have contained information regarding the original form of the display, this information was not directly utilized in the comparison process. The absence of a complexity effect on comparison time in both the initial figure and the initial description conditions supports the related claim that all parts of the representations are at once available to the comparison process or else retrieved and compared in parallel. Subjects may have tried to verify that the two displays were the same and then made a default response of "different" if this holistic or parallel comparison failed to produce a match. This analysis is consistent with the advantage of "same" matches over "different" matches.

However, this interpretation of Experiment 1 depends on the assumption that the internal representation in the comparison process preserves the complexity of the initial description or figure. Another possibility is that subjects construct a representation from a description that *initially* reflects its complexity (which would produce the increase in description RT_1 with complexity), but then abstract some simpler representation for verification that is independent of complexity. Specifically, it may be possible on some trials for subjects to make a correct "same" or "different" judgment on the basis of a single stimulus feature, such as the direction that a triangle points. One purpose of Experiment 2 is to evaluate this possibility.

In summary, our results are at odds with previous research on spatial comprehension. The data suggest that in our task, subjects construct spatial representations and use parallel or holistic verification operations. These results and interpretations are different from those proposed by propositional and dual code theorists, even though their experiments used paradigms quite similar to ours. We attribute much of this discrepancy to methodological differences between the procedures used in Experiment 1 and those used by other researchers. The two most salient methodological differences are (a) the use of subject-controlled instead of fixed duration displays, and (b) the use of successive instead of simultaneous presentations. The primary goal of Experiment 2 is to study spatial matching and verification processes in a number of experimental situations that span these different methodologies.

EXPERIMENT II

In this experiment, we study four tasks along a continuum from simultaneous presentation of the description and figure displays, through "deadline" conditions with successive displays, and finally to a subject-controlled condition where the onset of the test figure is completely determined by the subject. From the first experiment and from some logical considerations, we can generate a number of predictions about how encoding and comparison processes might change along with the structure of the verification task in Experiment 2.

In the subject-controlled condition, subjects presumably take the time to construct the optimal representation for the successive verification task. This representation allows subjects to decide rapidly whether the test figure is the one that they expect. Since the subject-controlled procedure separates the encoding of the description from the encoding of the test figure, this representation of the initial description should be capable of distinguishing the described figure from any member of the entire class of distractors in the experiment. The description representation that subjects constructed in Experiment 1 to expedite comparison with a pictorial display could be verified equally rapidly for figures of differing complexity without effects of the particular linguistic elements in the descriptions.

One reasonable tack for subjects in the deadline conditions would be to continue processing the description to generate this optimal representation even after the test figure is presented. On the other hand, once the test figure appears, subjects might use some information about its structure to facilitate the encoding of a representation from the description. Thus, in these conditions, and in the simultaneous condition as well, processing of the description might be contingent on particular features of the figure against which the description must be verified. The subject-controlled task is unique in that it alone requires the encoding of the description to be completed prior to the encoding of the test figure.

Contingent processing of the description in the deadline or simultaneous condition might have several effects. First, subjects might be able to detect a difference between the test figure and a partially encoded description. Thus the representations of the description and the figure might be less complete in conditions other than the subject-controlled where there is no opportunity for contingent processing. If subjects construct the minimal representations of the two displays that will suffice on a given trial, then we might expect effects of display complexity on verification time. Finally, if some characteristics of the test figure are known while the description is being encoded, it may be desirable to preserve specific information about the description in its representation. This information could then be used in the verification procedure to direct scanning or testing operations toward features that are mentioned in the description. Effects of lexical markedness might be generated in the use of this specific lexical information.

In the simultaneous condition, subjects have no time to generate expectations about the test figure before it appears. Even more than in the deadline conditions, subjects may use features of the accompanying test display to eliminate unnecessary encoding and comparison processing (i.e., to construct minimal representations that are optimal for particular test figures on a given trial). Despite these considerations, most of the current models of spatial comprehension characterize simultaneous sentence-picture comparison as a sequence of *independent* stages consisting of (a) encoding the two displays, (b) comparing the two representations, and (c) executing a choice response (Clark & Chase, 1972, 1974; Carpenter & Just, 1975; Just & Carptenter, 1975). These models also assume that the comparison of the sentence and figure requires complete representations of each.

Method

Subjects. Four students at the University of California, San Diego, were paid for completing two experimental sessions which together took three hours. None of the subjects had been in Experiment 1.

Stimuli. We used 2- and 3-component figures with their corresponding 1- and 2-line verbal descriptions. There were eight different figures at each level of complexity. The component parts from which all displays were constructed were a square, a triangle, and a circle.

We introduced the third component to generate a more complex set of figures than the 2-component sets used in Experiment 1. For any figure in the stimulus set, there exists another that has all but one component in the same location and orientation; alternatively, for any component in a figure, another figure exists in the set that has that component in the identical location and orientation. This stimulus set makes a single-component comparison strategy inadequate. This thereby implies that display complexity is incorporated in the comparison representations.

The 2-component figures were the four arrangements of the triangle either above or below the square or the circle, the two vertical arrangements of the square and circle, and the two hoziontal arrangements of the square and circle. Each of these eight figures had two 1-line descriptions using either the ABOVE/BELOW or the RIGHT/LEFT pairs of spatial relations.

The 3-component figures were all composed of a square, a circle, and a triangle. All of these forms had the square and circle side-by-side with the triangle either above or below the square or circle. There were four such configurations with the circle on the right of the square and four with these positions reversed. Each of these eight figures had four 2-line descriptions. One of these descriptions used ABOVE and RIGHT, one used ABOVE and LEFT, one used BELOW and RIGHT, and one used BELOW and LEFT.

Procedure. The four tasks in Experiment 2 have a number of features in common but are qualitatively different in other respects. The subject-controlled and the two deadline conditions all used the two-reaction-time procedure of Experiment 1. In all three tasks, the test figure appeared when the subject pressed a button to indicate sufficient comprehension of the spatial description to enable a rapid and accurate "same" or "different" decision. However, in the two deadline conditions, the test figure came on after a certain amount of time had elapsed since the onset of the description even if the subject had not yet signaled the preparation was complete. Finally, in the simultaneous condition, the description and the test figure came on together, and only a single reaction time was recorded.

Subject-controlled condition. This task is primarily a replication of the description-figure (D–F) matching condition of Experiment 1. However, the addition of the third component in the figure set makes this condition a critical test of the interpretation from Experiment 1 that the description representation in the successive matching task incorporates spatial information in a form that preserves the complexity of the initial description.

6- and 2-sec deadline conditions. From pilot work, we chose the 6-sec deadline to create a spatial verification situation where subjects were not likely to have always completed their preparation from the more complex descriptions when the test figure appeared. However, 6 sec is almost certainly enough time to prepare a suitable verification representation for the 1-line, 2-component descriptions. Similarly, we chose the 2-sec deadline to be close to the average time that subjects need to adequately understand the 1-line, 2-component descriptions.

The two deadline conditions are somewhat similar to the fixed duration presentations often used in description matching studies. Both deadline and fixed display procedures place an upper limit on preparation time, the deadline procedure allows subjects to initiate the test sequence *before* that limit is reached if their preparation is completed before the deadline.

Simultaneous condition. This task is the one usually used by researchers who study spatial comprehension and verification. The description and test figure appear together, and the subject's task is to decide whether the sentence describes the test figure. Thus only one reaction time can be recorded.

The descriptions and test figures were presented on an oscilloscope display by a computer which also recorded the reaction times on each trial. The descriptions appeared at the top of the screen and remained on when the test figures appeared below them (note that the description and figure came on together in the simultaneous condition).

Each subject participated in all four experimental conditions. Trials were blocked by conditions, and subjects completed two of these blocks during each of the two experimental sessions. The order of these four blocks was balanced across subjects to control for practice effects.

Each condition included 192 trials. The first 64 trials in each block were treated as practice and not analyzed. The 128 experimental trials in each block consisted of 64 from each of the two levels of description and test figure complexity and were randomly ordered. Each of the 16 different 1-line descriptions (two for each of the eight 2-component figures) appeared four times. On half of these trials, the description was followed by the "same" figure, and on the other half, a "different" figure appeared. Each of the 32 different 2-line descriptions (four for each of the eight 3-component figures) appeared twice, once followed by a "same" figure and once by a "different" distractor. Thus each subject completed 512 experimental trials.

Results

Complexity effects on preparation time. Figure 11.4a presents mean RT_1, for trials on which subjects responded correctly, as a function of description complexity in the subject-controlled and deadline conditions. Three major features of the RT_1 results are apparent. First, in all three conditions, 2-line descriptions take longer to comprehend than 1-line descriptions. Second, the deadline conditions worked; the time taken to encode the descriptions in the subject-controlled conditions is greater than the time allowed in the deadline conditions. Finally, the difference in RT_1 between 1- and 2-line descriptions is largest in the subject-controlled condition, intermediate in the 6-sec deadline condition, and smallest in the 2-sec deadline condition.

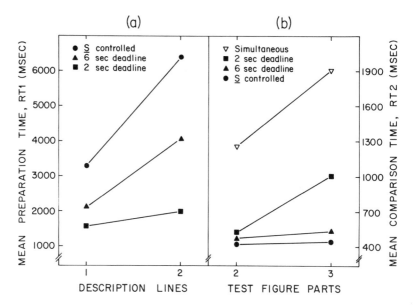

Figure 11.4 (a) Mean correct preparation time (RT_1) as a function of description complexity for the subject-controlled and deadline conditions of Experiment 2. (b) Mean correct comparison time (RT_2) as a function of test figure complexity for the four conditions of Experiment 2.

Markedness effects on preparation time. In RT_1, the advantage of ABOVE over its marked counterpart BELOW is consistent, averaging 209 msec for the two deadline conditions and the subject-controlled condition. However, the high variability in RT_1 left all three ABOVE-BELOW differences just short of significance. The RIGHT-LEFT difference was even less reliable.

Complexity effects on comparison time. Figure 11.4b presents mean correct RT_2 in each of the four conditions as a function of test figure complexity. If viewed in conjunction with the data for RT_1 in Figure 11.4a, this figure illustrates the most important aspects of Experiment 2. *Subjects respond increasingly faster to the test figure as preparation time increases from zero (in the simultaneous condition) to 3 sec and more (in the subject-controlled condition).* Second, subjects generally respond faster to 2-component test figures than to 3-component test figures. However, this feature of the RT_2 data is dominated by the interaction between this effect of complexity and the effect of preparation condition. *The size of the complexity effect steadily shrinks as subjects take more time to prepare for the test figure, and the effect disappears completely when subjects take as much time as they need in the subject-controlled condition.*

Responses. Not shown in Figure 11.4b but critical in the interpretation of Experiment 2 are the effects of responses. In the overall analysis of RT_2, the average time to make a "same" response did not differ from the time to respond "different." However, this main effect is diluted by large 2-way interactions between Condition and Responses and between Complexity and Responses, and by the 3-way interaction between Conditions, Complexity, and Responses. These interactions reflect the following findings: "Same" responses are faster than "different" responses in the subject-controlled and the 6-sec deadline conditions. The responses are equal in speed at the 2-sec deadline, and "different" responses are faster than "same" responses when the two displays appear simultaneously. There is an overall advantage for "sames" for 2-component test figures with the reverse advantage for "differents" for the 3-component test figures. The pattern of faster "different" responses for 3-component figures holds in every condition but the subject-controlled one, in which "sames" are faster than "differents" at both levels of test figure complexity.

Markedness effects on comparison time. The markedness effects change considerably in the different tasks. The ABOVE and RIGHT advantages are largest in the simultaneous condition; ABOVE is verified 130 msec faster than BELOW, and RIGHT is verified 169 msec faster than LEFT. The ABOVE advantage shrinks to 47 and 31 msec in the two deadline conditions, and finally to just 7 msec in the subject-controlled condition. The RIGHT-LEFT differences do not diminish according to such an orderly trend, but the advantage of RIGHT is a nonsignificant 25 msec in the subject-controlled condition.

Errors. Subjects made errors on 8.4% of the trials in Experiment 2, with individual error rates ranging from 5.9% to 15.2%. Errors were most frequent in the 2-sec deadline condition and least common in the simultaneous condition. Errors were more likely for 3-component test figures than for 2-component test figures in every condition except the simultaneous task. Finally, errors were equally frequent on "same" and "different" trials in every condition.

Subject-controlled condition. The results in the subject-controlled condition clearly replicate the description–figure (D–F) conditions of Experiment 1. Preparation time (RT_1) was strongly affected by the complexity of the verbal descriptions, with 2-line descriptions taking over 3 sec longer to understand than the 1-line descriptions. And, again, comparison time (RT_2) was not affected by test figure complexity. Most importantly, the theoretically critical absence of effects of linguistic markedness on comparison time (RT_2) was replicated in Experiment 2.

6-sec deadline condition. Complexity affected both RT_1 and RT_2 in the 6-sec deadline condition. In RT_1, 2-line descriptions were encoded over 2 sec faster than 2-line descriptions in the subject-controlled condition. This shortening of RT_1 for the more complex descriptions reflects the truncated preparation time distribution in a deadline condition. Any preparation activity that takes longer than 6 sec must carry over into RT_2 after the test figure is already present. Subjects had not finished their preparation by the 6-sec deadline on 15.6% of the 2-line descriptions and on 1.2% of the 1-line descriptions.

The differential carry-over from RT_1 in a deadline condition resulted in an effect of test figure complexity in RT_2. Two-component test figures took 465 msec to verify, but the large number of trials on which preparation of 3-component representations was not complete at the test figure onset inflated verification time for the more complex figures to 536 msec.

To test our notion of "spillover," we separated trials on which the subject initiated the test display from those on which the deadline was reached before preparation was completed. RT_2 for those trials on which the subject was not prepared when the 6-sec deadline was reached was 864 msec, while RT_2 for subject-initiated 3-component test figures was nearly as rapid as RT_2 for 2-component figures, just 483 msec.

2-sec deadline condition. As in the 6-sec condition, complexity affected both RT_1 and RT_2 in the 2-sec condition. Preparation of verification representations for 2-line descriptions was completed before the deadline on just nine of the 256 trials (3.5%), while preparation from 1-line descriptions beat the deadline on 167 of the 256 trials (65.2%).

Three-component figures took almost twice as long to verify as 2-component figures. The 2-sec deadline so severely limits RT_1

preparation for the 2-line descriptions that the spillover into RT_2 produces a larger complexity effect there than in RT_1. Again, however, on the small number of 3-component trials on which subjects were prepared for the test figure when the deadline was reached, the effect of test figure complexity is almost absent. For these nine trials, RT_2 for 3-component test figures was 540 msec, not much slower than the 514 msec that subjects took to verify 2-component figures when they had signaled preparation prior to the deadline. The complexity effect clearly results from the "unprepared" state; RT_2 for 3-component figures when subjects did not beat the deadline was 1023 msec.

Simultaneous condition. The complexity and markedness effects in the simultaneous condition replicate earlier sentence verification work using this procedure. When the description and the test figure appear simultaneously, the time to decide whether the description describes the figure is longer for the more complex displays. One-line descriptions using ABOVE take 130 fewer msecs to verify than those using BELOW, and this markedness effect is highly reliable. The advantage of RIGHT over LEFT was just short of significance.

Discussion

We conducted Experiment 2 for two reasons. First, we wanted to demonstrate that the description representatons in our subject-controlled comparison task preserved spatial complexity without producing a complexity effect. Second, we sought to understand the effects of methodological variation in spatial matching and verification tasks and their implications for a general model of spatial comprehension.

Replication of Experiment 1. In the subject-controlled condition, 2-line descriptions took no longer to verify than 1-line descriptions, even though they initially took almost twice as long to comprehend. Since the use of three possible components for the figures makes it likely that the verification representation incorporates the display complexity, one plausible interpretation is that subjects construct description representations which preserve information about the spatial arrangement of all the component parts. Moreover, this representation and its associated processes do not maintain information about the initial linguistic elements in the description, since RT_2 is not affected by the linguistic markedness of the relational terms. We thus conclude that this representation is more spatial than linguistic in terms of its functional properties in the comparison process.

Effects of task differences. There are three results in each of the four conditions of Experiment 2 that together characterize the information included in the internal representations and the nature of the comparison and verification processes that operate on the representations. These results are (1) the effects of description and test figure complexity on preparation time and comparison time, (2) the relative speed of "same" and "different" responses, and (3) the effects of linguistic markedness of the relational terms in the descriptions on comparison time.

Complexity effects. The effect of description complexity on RT_1 is trivial; subjects take longer to understand two sentences than one sentence. However, since subjects take about 3 sec to study each sentence in a description in the subject-controlled condition, the much smaller complexity increments in the deadline conditions require interpretation.

In the deadline conditions, subjects might try to use the same representations and processing strategies that they chose in the subject-controlled task. They might continue to process the description to construct a complete representation for verification even after the test figure was presented. This strategy would inflate RT_2 by the difference between the deadline RT_1 and the RT_1 in the subject-controlled condition (less the few hundred msec saved by not making the response to initiate the test figure). Figure 11.4 shows a tradeoff between preparation and comparison time, but the pattern is not as simple as the preceding strategy would predict. As preparation time is reduced, verification takes more and more time and is slower by increasing amounts for the more complex test figures. But large decreases in preparation time produce considerably smaller increases in comparison time.

A clear demonstration that the information processing changes considerably as the verification task varies comes from comparing the subject-controlled and the simultaneous conditions. If subjects performed the same processing of the description and test figure in these two tasks, then total processing time ($RT_1 + RT_2$) for the two tasks should only differ by the time needed to signal completed preparation in subject-controlled RT_1. In addition, the difference between the more complex and less complex displays should be the same in both conditions. Neither of these predictions is confirmed by the data.

If encoding and comparison operations were serial and independent in the deadline and simultaneous tasks, then this RT_1 versus RT_2 tradeoff would be nearly additive. Instead, the marked nonlinearity suggests that rather than completing their "normal" preparation by comprehending the description in isolation, subjects begin processing the test figure and thereby eliminate the need to construct complete representations of the initial description. In general, complexity effects in RT_2 signify that subjects are constructing the minimal representations of the description and test figure that will suffice for a particular trial.

Response effects. As subjects have less time to prepare for the test figure, one clear sign of the corresponding changes in their representations and comparison strategies is the transition from faster "same" responses to faster "different" responses. In the subject-controlled condition, subjects are instructed to construct a representation of the description that allows them to decide rapidly whether the test figure is the one they expect. A reasonable interpretation of the faster "same" responses in this condition is that subjects attempt to verify that the test figure is the one described and respond "different" if this matching attempt fails. At the other end of the task spectrum, the simultaneous condition, subjects have no time to generate expectations about the test figure. The faster "different" responses in this condition imply that subjects process the description and test figures at the same time and respond "different" as soon as a mismatch is detected.

The transition from a strategy of verifying "sames" in the subject-controlled condition to detecting "differents" in the simultaneous task necessarily implies an interaction with description complexity. Detecting "differents" seems to be the strategy of last resort that subjects adopt when they have insufficient time to prepare completely for the test figure. Since 1-line descriptions take less time to comprehend than 2-line descriptions, they are less affected by deadlines. Thus, subjects spend more time in the "prepared" state for the simpler descriptions and "sames" remain faster than "differents" for 2-component figures in conditions that produce the reverse for the 3-component figures.

Lexical markedness effects. The pattern of markedness effects on comparison time (RT_2) is highly informative. There is a clear trend for the effects of linguistic markedness to decrease as RT_2 gets faster; and RT_2 gets faster when subjects take more time to prepare for the test figure. In the subject-controlled condition, subjects take the time to construct representations with properties that expedite comparison with a pictorial display, and therefore abstract spatial information away from the particular form in which it is presented. Such abstract spatial information is desirable if no knowledge of the particular test figure is available while the verification representation is being constructed. On the other hand, if some characteristics of the test figure are known while the description is being processed, it may be desirable to preserve specific information about the description. Thus with short (or zero) advance preparation time, description representations inevitably contain more information about the actual lexical items in the description, and markedness effects are generated in the use of this information.

GENERAL DISCUSSION

In Experiment 1 we extended the typical description matching and sentence verification experiments to more complex displays with subject-controlled presentations. Our results were not consistent with any of the models for spatial comprehension. We concluded that figure and description representations in this task preserved spatial information in a form that can be compared with a figure display in some holistic or parallel fashion. Nevertheless, we did *not* wish to propose this as a general model of how spatial information is represented and compared. Instead, we have studied a number of experimental situations which comprise a family of spatial comparison and verification tasks.

Three critical features in Experiment 2—complexity effects, the relative speeds of "same" and "different" responses, and lexical markedness effects—had changing outcomes across the four tasks that illustrated how the structure of the task determined the results. What may appear to be minor modifications of procedure from fixed to subject-controlled display durations or from simultaneous to successive presentations completely eliminate the usual large effects of complexity and the small but critical effects of linguistic markedness. Rather than indicating representational or processing invariants, configurations of these effects characterize specific tasks.

In most previous description matching studies, the initial descriptions or figures were presented for fixed periods of time, instead of allowing the subject to determine the optimal encoding time as in Experiment 1 and in the subject-controlled condition of Experiment 2. In these experiments, description complexity and lexical markedness effects were found, and these effects were more pronounced when the interval between the offset of the initial display and the onset of the test display was relatively short.

We believe that the difference between these results and our own lies in the use of fixed presentation times which differed between experiments. Subjects in previous experiments may have attempted to generate an integrated verification representation from the separately described parts, but may not have had sufficient time to generate this optimal representation.

The other methodological dimension along which we varied the tasks in Experiment 2 is that between successive and simultaneous presentation of descriptions and figures. Most of the current models for sentence-picture verification were developed in studies using the simultaneous procedure (e.g., Clark & Chase, 1972, 1974; Carpenter & Just, 1975; Just & Carpenter, 1975). These models propose a sequence of independent encoding, comparison, and response stages whose durations are typically estimated by using a set of reaction-time tasks which presumably differ only in the presence or absence of the to-be-estimated stages. The models developed using the subtract-and-estimate methodology make assumptions which may not be warranted when the sentence and picture displays are presented simultaneously. The nonlinear tradeoff between RT_1 and RT_2 in Experiment 2 argues against the independence assumption in the simultaneous condition.

A second questionable assumption of most stage models is that the comparison of the two displays requires complete representations of each. Such complete encoding may not be necessary when the two displays appear together or when the alternative displays are known. In Experiment 2, the transition from faster "same" responses in the subject-controlled condition to an advantage for "different" responses in the simultaneous condition suggests that subjects in the latter task forego attempts to construct complete description representations to verify "sames" and instead use a strategy of detecting "differents" via contingent and partial processing of the test figure.

Concluding remarks. Evidently, processes of spatial comprehension and comparison are strongly affected by the structure of the sentence verification or description matching task in which they are usually studied. Our central results (the changing configurations of complexity and markedness effects and the speed of "same" and "different" responses) place constraints on a general account of spatial comprehension. In subject-controlled verification tasks, the sentence and figure representations preserve spatial information in an abstract form that can be used by the associated comparison operations in a holistic or parallel fashion. Thus our results exclude as a general representation for spatial comprehension any data structure that can not use spatial relations as parallel access paths (such as strictly-serial list structures, serial production systems, or procedural systems without parallel computation). The changing configurations of representational properties in Experiment 2 also exclude iconic or otherwise uninterpreted image representations as well.

Nevertheless, our results do not discredit the earlier models as analyses of the properties and processing most useful in particular task environments. While subjects can generate many representations for a given display, a particular experimental task makes one kind optimal. The demands of the verification task (such as the number of alternatives, their complexity or their similarity to one another) greatly influence the usefulness of different kinds of information and affect the way in which this information is embodied in a representation. The fact that qualitatively different sorts of representations and processes may be required for different tasks simply underscores the flexibility of the human information processor in dealing with spatial information.

But the purpose of studying individual tasks should be to discover constraints that operate across tasks; a general model must relate the results from several experimental approaches. Therefore, a unifying account should be concerned not so much with specific tasks as with the structures of tasks that make particular representations and processing most appropriate. In this framework, we conclude that the nature of spatial comparison processes is mutable, task-constrained, and *not* a basic unchanging aspect of human cognition.

12 | Epilogue to Part II

Other Transformations

Since our original studies of mental rotation (Part I), a number of colleagues and associates have extended essentially the same type of chronometric paradigm to the investigation of a variety of other spatial transformations, including translations, expansions and contractions, combinations of these with rotation, and, as in the preceding chapters of Part II, sequences of foldings and joinings of rigid parts into a spatially structured whole. In this chapter we review an illustrative sample of the results that have emerged from these further experiments, including some that have not previously been published. We conclude with brief discussions of the possible significance of still more general mental transformations such as topological transformations and even nonspatial transformations that may nevertheless be analogous in some way to spatial transformations. [1]

Whereas in Part I we focused exclusively on the mental simulation of rigid rotations of an object as a whole, in Part II we have turned to a consideration of the mental simulation of a variety of other spatial transformations, including sequences of rigid motions (Chapter 10) and the rigid movement of parts relative to a whole (Chapters 9 and 11). Basically, however, there has been no change in the experimental paradigm: Throughout, we have based our conclusions principally on the times that subjects take to carry out a particular mental transformation and/or on the times that they take to match the result of such a mental transformation against an external test stimulus. In this chapter we consider, more briefly, a few further studies in which this same sort of paradigm has been extended to still other spatial transformations or combinations or sequences of such transformations.

Types of Spatial Transformations

In view of the special importance of rigid transformations, it seems convenient to distinguish between three general cases of spatial transformations: (a) strictly rigid transformations, such as rotations, translations, and reflections or combinations or sequences of these, in which the object as a whole retains its rigid structure throughout; (b) what we might call "semirigid" transformations, such as foldings or joinings of discrete parts, in which each of those parts, though not the whole constellation of them, retains its separate rigid structure; and (c) nonrigid transformations, such as plastic deformations, in which the topological structure of the object is globally preserved but in which every part or region may be subject to differential, locally affine stretchings and compressions.

Even in speaking of a strictly rigid transformation, whether of the object as a whole or only of some part thereof, we need to distinguish, further, between that object or part as it is three-dimensionally interpreted and the two-dimensional projection of that rigid object or part as it is available at the sensory surface. For, the two-dimensional projections of a strictly rigid object may not itself be at all rigid: As a three-dimensional object advances and rotates around any axis except the line of sight, the projection undergoes nonrigid expansions, deformations, and even topologically discontinuous alterations. Conversely, such an expanding and deforming two-dimensional display may be perceived as an object that is rigidly advancing and rotating in space. Indeed as we noted in the introduction (Chapter 1), a three-dimensional object that is only rectilinearly translating in space will typically give rise to a two-dimensional projection that is nonrigidly expanding, contracting and, also, deforming just as under a relative rotation.

In reviewing some of the results that our colleagues and associates have obtained from their investigations of mental transformations of various types (other than the pure rotations covered in Part I), we begin with the simplest cases, such as rigid translations in the two-dimensional plane; and work up through more complex rigid transformations in space, to semirigid transformations (particularly foldings and joinings) and, briefly, nonrigid or topological transformations (which have as yet been little studied) and, finally, transformations that are spatial, if at all, only by analogy.

Mental Translation

Translation of a specific mental image. With respect to the relation between the distal object and its proximal projection, probably the simplest type of spatial transformation is rectilinear translation across a two-dimensional frontal plane. Under small translations, in particular, the sizes and orientations of the projections of all figures and their parts (edges, vertices, etc.) are essentially preserved. This simplicity is to some extent lost for large displacements, which necessarily induce, towards the periphery, a locally affine compression of the projection, or, as we have noted, for displacements of three-dimensional objects, which necessarily entail, in effect, a relative rotation in the projection.

Anyway, for even the simplest case of small displacements in the frontal plane, we know of no published experiments on mental translation that are directly analogous to our studies of mental rotation. In the spirit of the early work by Michotte (1955) on "amodal completion," Rosenbaum (1975) has reported on the ability of subjects to extrapolate the continuous motion of an object following its disappearance behind an occluding screen. But his experimental method was not designed to provide evidence that the location at which the subjects were most prepared to respond discriminatively to the reappearance of the object (as opposed, say, to the emergence of some altered object) was correspondingly translating in space. Closer, in chronometric methodology, to our experiments are those by Hartley (1977, 1981), which have yielded reaction times suggesting that in judging the length of a line, subjects mentally "lay off" (i.e., translate) a standard line segment along that line. Experiments that are still more closely analogous to ours on rotation have also been undertaken by Pinker (personal communication, 1981).

With regard to mental rotation, there evidently is not a complete psychological equivalence between the case in which subjects imagine an object rotated with respect to themselves (Part I, especially Chapter 3, here) and the case in which they imagine themselves moving about or rotating with respect to a fixed object (Huttenlocher & Presson, 1973, 1979; cf., also, Hintzman, O'Dell, & Arndt, 1981). Nevertheless, with regard to mental translation, there may be some connection between the case in which subjects imagine the translational displacement of a rigid image, as just considered, and the case in which they imagine themselves, or, more accurately, their focus of attention shifted with respect to a fixed image. However, experiments of this latter type have most typically required subjects merely to reach a specified target location or to make a simple visual detection there; they usually have not required subjects to discriminate a particular test stimulus at that location from other, similar alternatives. Accordingly, we discuss such attentional shifts in the following two separate sections concerning translations of generalized attention as opposed to translations of a specific image.

Translation of visual attention across a two-dimensional plane. Kosslyn and his collaborators, especially, have carried out a number of experiments in which the time to shift visual attention from one location to another along an imagined object (Kosslyn, 1973) or across a memory image of a two-dimensional field or map (Kosslyn, Ball, & Reiser, 1978) increased linearly with the spatial distance between the initial and target locations (also see Kosslyn, 1981; Kosslyn, Pinker, Smith, & Shwartz, 1979). Typically in these studies, the subjects were instructed to mentally scan across the image from the initial to the target location, and sometimes they were even explicitly asked to imagine tracking a small dot moving from the one location to the other. In such cases, the question might be raised as to whether subjects would similarly translate their attention across the intervening positions if not explicitly instructed to do so (cf. Lea, 1975; Mitchell & Richman, 1980).

However, Finke and Pinker (1981) have recently shown that the linear dependence of reaction time on distance can be obtained without any instruction to form images or to scan them. In their experiment, a two-dimensional field containing a random configuration of dots was replaced by a one-second blank field and then by a field containing a single arrow in some location and orientation. Subjects were instructed to indicate as soon as possible whether the arrow was or was not pointing directly towards the location in which some dot had appeared in the preceding visual array. Despite the absence of instructions to carry out any sort of linear scan, the time to detect that a dot had been located in the direction in which the arrow was pointing increased linearly with the distance from the arrow to the former position of such a dot. The rate of mental scanning inferred from the slope of the fitted linear function was similar to that obtained when explicit image scanning instructions were given and, incidentally, was considerably slower than the rate that would be expected if the scan corresponded to a physical eye movement.

Church (1974; also see Church & Church, 1977) recorded the times that a Class A chess player took to decide whether a black king was in check by a white piece (viz., the queen, a bishop, or a rook) when only the one black and one white piece appeared on a tachistoscopically presented chessboard. The remarkably linear dependence of reaction time on the number of squares separating the two pieces (reproduced here in Figure 12.12) appears to indicate that the decision was based on a linear scan along the relevant row, column, or diagonal. From the markedly different slopes of the two plotted functions, though, it appears that a greatly increased speed of scanning and/or a quite different strategy of search was possible when the two pieces were aligned vertically or horizontally, rather than on a diagonal. In subsequent experiments at Stanford, Milojkovic (1980) found a similarly linear dependence between the time to decide whether a designated chess piece was in a position to capture another piece even when the board position was available only in memory (the difference between the slopes for the diagonal and for the vertical or horizontal cases was not nearly as large for his subjects, however).

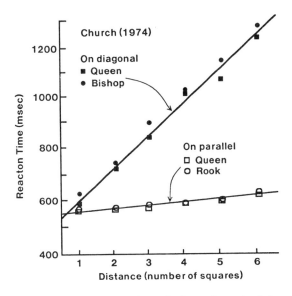

Figure 12.1 Mean time for a Class A chess player to determine whether a black king is in check by a white piece as a function of the number of steps separating the two pieces along a diagonal or along a row or column of the chessboard (from Church, 1974; replotted from Church & Church, 1977).

Translation of visual attention in three-dimensional space. If we accept the evidence that the time to shift attention from one spatial location to another increases linearly with the distance between the two locations, the following further question arises: Is the determinative distance the distance as projected on the retina (which is essentially equivalent to the angle through which the eye would have to rotate to fixate the one location and then the other), or is it the distance between the two locations in three-dimensional space? Such a question is analogous to the previously raised questions concerning the relative importance of proximal versus distal variables in mental rotation (Chapter 3) and in apparent motion (Chapters 13 and 16 of the following part III).

The results of several experiments reported by Pinker and Kosslyn (1978), Pinker (1980), and Pinker and Finke (1980) indicate that in the three-dimensional case, subjects can mentally scan either between two objects in three-dimensional space or between the visual projections of those two objects on a two-dimensional frontal plane. Depending on whether they are instructed to scan along the (imaginary) line connecting the two objects in space or to scan from the visual direction of one object to the visual direction of the other (as if through a rifle sight), scanning time linearly increased, respectively, with distance in three-dimensional space or with visual angle—which is essentially equivalent to distance in the two-dimensional projection.

Analog character of mental translation. The demonstrations that the time to shift attention from one location to another increases linearly with the distance between those two locations does not itself entail that the attention necessarily passes through intermediate locations. However, following our definition of an analog transformation as one that demonstrably does pass through such transformationally intermediate states (Cooper, 1976a; Shepard, 1975—see Chapters 1 and 7, here), Shulman, Remington, and McLean (1979) found that in shifting attention from one location to another in the visual field, subjects did pass through states in which their reaction times to visually presented probes were shortest at locations between the initial and final locations—even when there was no movement of the subjects' eyes. And Tsal (1981) has obtained other evidence for the analog character of such translational shifts.

Mental Size Scaling

Expansions and contractions of a mental image. Experiments that are more closely analogous (than those on mental translation) to our own chronometric studies of mental rotation are those that have investigated linear size scalings (also called dilatations or magnifications) of two-dimensional images. However, as we have noted, a linear expansion or contraction of an image on a two-dimensional frontal plane may well be interpreted by the subject as a rigid translation in depth; i.e., as an advance or recession, respectively (see Part III, especially Chapter 16; and Bundesen, Larsen, & Farrell, 1981a).

Sekuler and Nash (1972) required subjects to determine as rapidly as possible whether two successively presented rectangles were or were not of the same shape regardless of possible differences in size (or, indeed, orientation). The ratio of the linear sizes of the two rectangles could take on any of seven different values. Although such size differences were irrelevant to the required comparison of shape, discriminative reaction time increased approximately linearly with the size ratio of the larger to the smaller rectangle, providing perhaps the first clear indication that mental size scaling, like mental rotation, may be an analog normalizing process.

Bundesen and Larsen (1975) presented (simultaneously) pairs of random, two-dimensional polygons (similar to those used by Cooper —see Chapter 5-7 here) that differed over a five-to-one range in the ratios of their linear sizes. In three successive experiments, the time required to determine that the two polygons were of the same shape was again found to increase linearly with the size ratio of the larger to smaller polygon. Similar results were also obtained in further experiments reported by Larsen and Bundesen (1978), using successive rather than simultaneous presentation. In analogy with the reports of subjects in experiments on mental rotation, subjects in these experiments reported that when the second stimulus appeared, they scaled the memory image of the first stimulus up or down in order to bring it into the same size-format of the second stimulus and, thereby, facilitated the required determination of a match or mismatch in shape.

The results of several of the studies by Bundesen and Larsen are summarized in Figure 12.2. (These results have been further replicated by Bundesen, Larsen, & Farrell, 1981a). As in our own studies of mental rotation, the reaction times were appreciably longer when the two stimuli to be compared were presented simultaneously than when they were presented successively (and, hence, did not include the time to encode the first stimulus or to recheck it, during transformation, against its external counterpart). Also as in our studies, positive or "match" reaction times were longer than negative or "mismatch" reaction times by an amount that was constant and independent of the extent of the required mental transformation (approximately 75 msec in these studies). That the ratio rather than the difference of the sizes yielded the most linear trend in these studies is consistent with the general primacy of ratios in perception (Shepard, 1978d) and suggests that size scaling takes place along a logarithmic continuum of linear size (Bundesen, *et al.*, 1981a). Under some conditions, however, mental size scaling may not occur (Besner & Coltheart, 1976, in press; Kubovy & Podgorny, 1981).

Size scaling in the detection of small details of an image. Just as Kosslyn's experiments on mental scanning suggest that subjects may translate their attention across an image in order to verify the presence of a particular local feature (Kosslyn, 1973, 1980), other experiments that he has carried out on size scaling suggest that subjects may expand such an image in order to verify the presence of a fine-grain feature (Kosslyn, 1975, 1980). In his original dissertation experiments, subjects were asked to imagine a verbally designated animal (e.g., *cat*) and were then required to judge as rapidly as possible whether or not a particular property (e.g., *claws*) was appropriate for the imaged animal. Relative size of the imaged animal was manipulated both directly, by instructing subjects to imagine the animal as one of four designated sizes, and indirectly, by instructing subjects to imagine the animal standing next to a large or a small context animal. For both types of size manipulation, the time to determine whether or not the property was appropriate to the imaged animal decreased as the size of the imaged animal became larger, even when size and complexity were varied independently. These findings were interpreted as supporting the notion that detection of properties contained in relatively small images required a mental operation of size scaling, i.e., a mental magnification or "zooming in" on the critical portion of the imaged animal (Kosslyn, 1975). A number of subsequent experiments by Kosslyn and his associates have further supported and extended this interpretation (see Kosslyn, 1980).

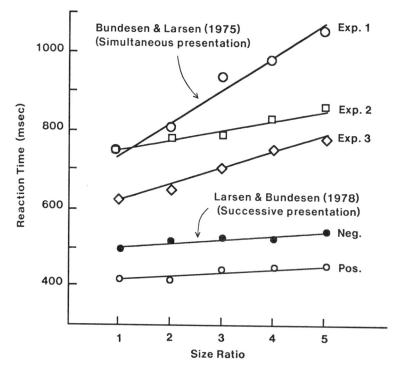

Figure 12.2 Mean time to determine whether two visually presented objects are the same in intrinsic shape as a function of the ratio of their linear sizes (replotted from several experiments by Bundesen & Larsen, 1975, using simultaneous presentation, and by Larsen & Bundesen, 1978, using successive presentation).

Combinations and Sequences of Mental Transformations

Combinations of size scaling and rotation. The already described study by Sekuler and Nash (1972) on size scaling included pairs of rectangles differing by a 90° rotation in the picture plane as well as by a disparity in size. In line with our own results on mental rotation, these investigators found that the addition of such an orientational disparity led to a systematic increase in the time required to compare the two rectangles with respect to shape. Moreover, this increase, which averaged about 70 msec for these rectangles, appeared to be essentially constant, independent of the disparity between the two rectangles in size. As Sekuler and Nash noted, this result suggests that the mental operations of size-scaling and of rotation may be essentially independent of each other.

More recently, Bundesen, Larsen, and Farrell (1981a) have carried out an extensive investigation of the way in which angular disparities and size ratios combine to determine the time needed to verify whether two planar figures match in shape. Their results provide further evidence that the two types of normalizing processes combine additively, though they presumably proceed simultaneously (cf. Chapter 16, p. 315). Again, however, the dependence of reaction time on difference in size is sometimes absent (Kubovy & Podgorny, 1981) or open to other interpretations (Besner, 1978).

Combinations of rotations and reflections. In an exploratory experiment by Shepard and Feng (see Shepard, 1975), subjects were asked to report, as quickly as possible, the results of performing a prespecified operation on a particular letter—which was then only named and not visually presented. Thus, on a particular trial the subject might be instructed to state "what results when you rotate 90° to the left the following capital letter—'N' ?" The time would then be recorded from the naming of the letter ("N") by the experimenter to the reporting of the result ("Z") by the subject. The following five operations were explored: reflection about the vertical axis, reflection about the horizontal axis, rotation of 90° counterclockwise, rotation of 180° (in the picture plane), and the double operation of reflection about the vertical axis followed by reflection about the horizontal axis. The letters used and the effects of the operations on these are shown in Figure 12.3. In some cases the letter turns into itself, in some cases it turns into another letter (or identifiable symbol), and in some cases it turns into a nameless design (in which case the subject reported "nothing"). Since the instructions were all presented in the auditory modality and no visual stimuli were presented, subjects could and, indeed, most did keep their eyes closed during this visualization task.

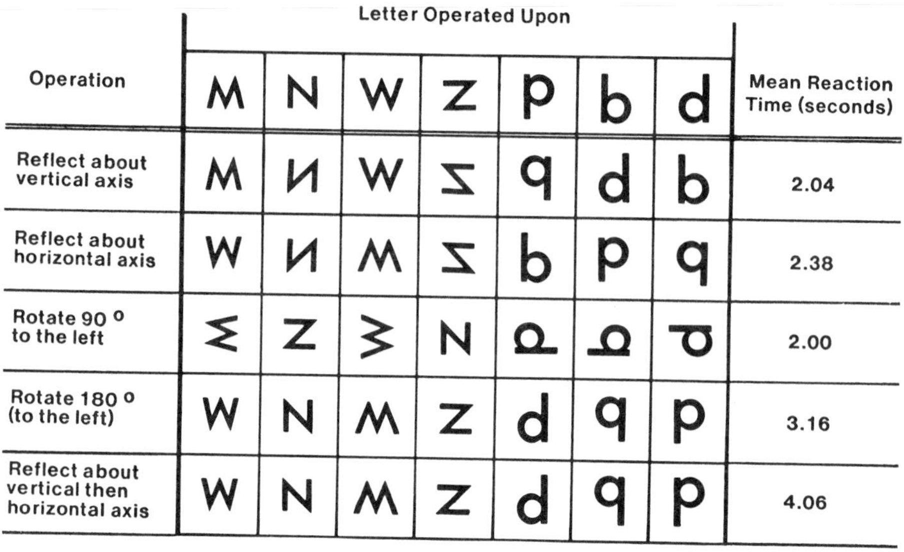

Operation	Letter Operated Upon							Mean Reaction Time (seconds)
	M	N	W	Z	P	b	d	
Reflect about vertical axis	M	И	W	ꙅ	q	d	b	2.04
Reflect about horizontal axis	W	И	M	ꙅ	b	p	q	2.38
Rotate 90° to the left	Ɛ	Z	Ɛ	N	ᴗ	ᴗ	ᴂ	2.00
Rotate 180° (to the left)	W	N	M	Z	d	q	p	3.16
Reflect about vertical then horizontal axis	W	N	M	Z	d	q	p	4.06

Figure 12.3   Results of applying each of five spatial operations on each of seven letters. For each operation, the numbers at the right give the mean times that subjects required, altogether, (a) to imagine the (orally) designated letter, (b) to imagine the designated operation performed on that letter, and (c) to identify and name the results of that operation (reproduced from Shepard, 1975).

The mean reaction times obtained in this pilot experiment are shown for the five different operations in the right-most column of the figure. These times all include, in addition to the time required to perform the operation itself, the times required to form the visual image and to "recognize" and then report the result of the operation on that image. Notice that these overall reaction times are shortest for the two single reflections and the 90° rotation (about 2 sec each), that the 180° rotation takes an appreciably longer time (about 3 sec), and finally that the double reflection takes the longest time of all (about 4 sec). The difference between these last two times is particularly interesting since, as can be seen in the table, both kinds of operations (the 180° rotation and the double reflection) yield identical images. The consistently longer reaction times for the double reflection indicates that the subjects *were* following directions and coming to their answers by carrying out the particular operations specified. It also indicates, again, that reaction time depends upon the particular trajectory of the subject's internal process, and not just on the relation between the initial and terminal states.

Sequences of rotations and reflections. A series of related experiments being carried out by Bethell-Fox and Shepard is still underway. Subjects are first presented with a square pattern formed by blackening in some subset of the nine cells in a three-by-three grid. That pattern is then removed and followed by a sequence of simple visual cues, each indicating which of eight spatial transformations is next to be performed on the memory image of the three-by-three pattern. Much as listed in Figure 12.3, these transformations include reflections about the vertical or horizontal axes, 90° rotations clockwise or counter clockwise, 180° rotation, and double reflections (about the vertical and then horizontal axes, or vice versa). The transformational cues consist of such things as a curved arrow to indicate rotation in a particular direction; a vertical or horizontal line, to indicate reflection about a vertical or horizontal axis; and crossed vertical and horizontal lines to indicate the double reflection (with one line dashed to indicate the axis of the reflection to be performed second).

The subject operates a switch to bring up each new transformational cue as soon as the last transformation has been mentally completed. At some point in this sequence a test stimulus appears (instead of another transformational cue), whereupon the subject makes a discriminative response to indicate whether or not that test stimulus matches the mental image resulting from the last-performed transformation. A record of the sequence of transformation times as well as the final discrimination time is recorded for each such sequence.

Many variables are being explored in these experiments, including the complexity, compactness, and symmetry of the stimulus patterns, the amount of pre-exposure to these particular patterns, and the pretested spatial abilities of the subjects. This work seems to be providing evidence, for example, that the independence of rate of mental rotation on complexity of the object rotated, reported by Cooper (see Chapters 5 and 6), may hold only when the object is sufficiently well learned. When the pattern in the three-by-three grid is still relatively unfamiliar to the subject, transformation time appears to increase significantly with the complexity of that pattern.

Most relevant here, is the confirmation that these experiments have already provided for some of the preliminary results obtained in the just described experiment by Shepard and Feng using alphanumeric characters as stimuli. In particular, double reflection has again been found to take significantly longer than 180° rotation— a further confirmation that it is the mental path to the final result and not the result itself that determines processing time.

Mental Manipulation of the Parts of a Whole

Folding of parts relative to a whole. In the original chronometric experiments by Shepard and Feng on the folding of squares into a cube (Chapter 9), the time that was measured was the total time to complete the required sequence of folds. No attempt was made in those experiments to measure, separately, the time required to carry out each individual fold in the sequence. As a result, the conclusions reached concerning the relative importance of certain structural variables such as the number of squares carried along with each fold were necessarily based on rather indirect inference. In a subsequent doctoral dissertation at Stanford, however, Emily Bassman (1978) undertook further experiments on the mental folding of the squares of a cube in which she recorded the times to perform individual folds having various structural properties.

In the one of Bassman's experiments that is most directly relevant here, subjects did not generally begin from a completely flattened-out pattern of squares as they did in the experiments by Shepard and Feng. Instead, from a set of pictures of already more or less folded cubes (Figure 12.4), Bassman presented two pictures that were so chosen that the structure portrayed in one picture could be transformed into the structure portrayed in the other by carrying out just one or two 90° folds. The picture of the more folded cube was exposed first in order to establish the target structure for the mental transformation, and the time was then recorded from the exposure of the picture of the second, less folded cube till the subject responded by pressing one of the two buttons to indicate whether that second structure could or could not be transformed into the target structure by making no more than two folds.

Figure 12.5 provides a comparison between Bassman's results and those from Shepard and Feng's second experiment, which was the one that included sequences of folds having from one to five squares carried along (the range covered by Bassman's experiment). There are of course major differences between the conditions under which the two sets of data were collected: First, for these small numbers of squares carried along, Shepard and Feng's data are only from early stages of folding, while Bassman's are sampled from all stages. And second, the amount of information that subjects had to maintain concerning which mental folds had already been made and which should be made next was greater in the experiment by Shepard and Feng, in which subjects had to carry out the entire sequence of folds without external support or confirmation of intermediate stages. We presume that this second difference accounts for the markedly flatter slope of the reaction-time function in Bassman's study (about 280

Figure 12.4 Portrayals of a pattern of six squares in various stages of being folded into a cube (reproduced from Bassman, 1978).

msec per square carried along in the mental folding) than in Shepard and Feng's study (about 900 msec per square).

In any case, Bassman's results for sequences of one and two folds having the same total numbers of squares carried along (either two or three) provide striking corroboration of Shepard and Feng's tentative and somewhat counterintuitive conclusion that it is the total number of squares carried along in the folding rather than simply the number of folds per se that determines the times needed to carry out the folds mentally. Indeed, the almost perfect coincidence between the linear functions fitted to Bassman's reaction times for pairs differing by one fold and for pairs differing by two folds indicates that each square that was carried along in any 90° fold required a constant additional time (of about 280 msec) and that over and above this, the number of folds as such had no appreciable effect.

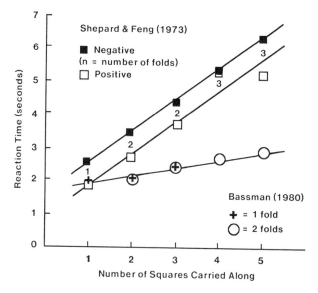

Figure 12.5 Time to carry out folds mentally as a function of the number of squares carried along in the folds, when there is no external support for intermediate stages (replotted from Shepard & Feng, 1973) and when there is (replotted from Bassman, 1978).

Bassman's experiments also went beyond Shepard and Feng's in showing that folding times were consistently longer for patterns of squares that were already about half folded than either for patterns that were as yet little folded (i.e., that were still largely flat) or for patterns that were nearly completely folded (i.e., that were close to a completed cube.) Since the configurations corresponding to intermediate stages of folding appear to be more complex (see Figure

12.4), the longer times at these intermediate stages is presumed to reflect the influence, with these incompletely learned patterns, of a greater perceptual complexity, memory load and, perhaps, difficulty in determining where the next fold is to be made.

Assembly of parts into a whole. Experiments like those described by Glushko and Cooper (Chapter 11), in which subjects mentally synthesized a structural whole out of separate parts appear to be capable of providing considerable information about the human ability to construct and to manipulate mental images and spatial concepts (an ability long ago remarked upon by Hume, as quoted in Chapter 1). Here, we briefly review some of the results reported by investigators who have carried out other, related experiments on mental synthesis. Generally, when the subject has formed an integrated internal representation from separate parts that have been either visually presented or verbally described, a test figure is presented, and the subject must determine as rapidly as possible whether or not the internally synthesized representation and the test figure match. Often, both the time needed to perform the mental synthesis and the time needed for comparison with the test figure are measured.

Evidence for some limitations on the ability of subjects to synthesize wholes out of parts was initially obtained by Klatzky and Thompson (1975), using schematic facelike forms containing either two or three individually meaningful features. The features in the first stimulus were either presented within a single facial outline or distributed over two or three outlines. Subjects had as long as they wished to attempt to combine the spatially distributed features into one integrated image. Then, following a variable interstimulus interval, a single test face was presented. *Same-different* reaction time increased with the number of facial outlines in the first display over which the to-be-integrated features were distributed. In this task, then, subjects were not entirely successful in synthesizing the individual components into a unified representation. However, subjects were successful in subsequent work by these same investigators. When meaningful but more abstract, geometrical objects such as triangles, rectangles, and trapezoids were to be mentally synthesized from less meaningful components such as line segments and corners, reaction time was essentially the same whether one, two, or three components were to be integrated (Thompson & Klatzky, 1978).

Exploring the role of figural goodness in mental synthesis, Palmer (1974) presented subjects with two spatially separated figures composed of three line segments that could be synthesized into a single figure composed of six segments. Examples of Palmer's displays are shown in Figure 12.6. As can be seen, the three-segment components differed in their goodness as structural units of the synthesized six-segment figure. (For a discussion of the figural goodness of the subparts see Palmer, 1974; and, for related empirical evidence of the importance of this factor, see Hinton, 1979; Reed, 1974; Reed & Johnsen, 1975.) As soon as a subject had synthesized a pair of three-segment figures into a single six-segment figure, he or she so indicated by pressing a button. Thereupon, a test figure was presented and the subject was required to determine as rapidly as possible whether the test figure was the same as or different from the mentally synthesized internal representation. The time required for mental synthesis was found to decrease with increasing goodness of the components to be synthesized. For at least one subject, moreover, discriminative reaction time to a whole test figure was independent of the figural goodness of the components from which it was synthesized, indicating (as for the group of subjects in the study by Thompson & Klatzky, 1978) that a complete mental synthesis could sometimes be achieved.

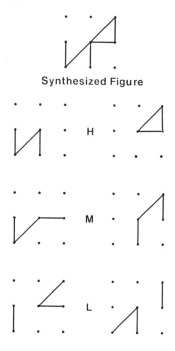

Synthesized Figure

Figure 12.6 Three-segment components of high, medium, and low figural goodness which, when synthesized, form the six-segment figure shown at the top (reproduced from Palmer, 1974).

Palmer (1974) proposed the following analysis of the mental operations required for the synthesis: First, the three-segment components are mentally translated into the same spatial location. Second, these mentally translated components are linked together. Finally, the linked representation is restructured into figurally good subunits. Presumably, goodness of the original three-segment components facilitates all three of these mental operations. Thus, pairs of three-segment components with high goodness values are easy to move, require few linkages, and need little if any restructuring. According to this analysis, mental synthesis includes, in addition to analog operations of spatial movement, discrete modifications in the resulting internal structure.

Although Palmer's subjects had to combine only two components to form the final structure, there is other evidence that the time to image a composite scene increases linearly with the number of component objects that must be combined (Beech & Allport, 1978). And, in what might be interpreted either as a limiting case of this or as another example of the earlier considered phenomenon of linear scanning along a mental image, Hartley (1977, 1981) found that when subjects were asked to estimate the length of a presented line in terms of a given small standard unit length of line, the time to make the estimate increased linearly with the number of such unit segments that would have to be laid off end-to-end to match the presented line.

More General Types of Mental Transformations

Topological deformations. We have argued that rigid or, at least, semirigid transformations are particularly easy to simulate mentally. However, we can also carry out other, more general types of mental transformations. Indeed, some types of problems appear to be difficult to solve, purely mentally, in any other way. Consider, for example the problem of characterizing the topological structure of the so-called "whole through a whole in a whole" illustrated in Figure 12.7A. As is well known, the topological structure of such a closed surface can be characterized in terms of a single integer, its "genus" (e.g., see Courant & Robbins, 1941), which corresponds to the number of "holes" that a torus-like surface (such as that shown in Figure 12.7F) must have in order to be topologically equivalent to it. A surface like that portrayed in Figure 12.7A is not immediately analyzable by passive visual inspection into an easily countable number of features such as "holes," however. Yet, by carrying out a more active process of imaging a suitable plastic deformation, as illustrated in the sequence between A and F, one can see that the original surface is in fact equivalent to a three-holed torus and, hence, is a surface of genus 3. In imagining such a plastic deformation, just as in imagining a rigid transformation, one presumably passes through representations of intermediate stages

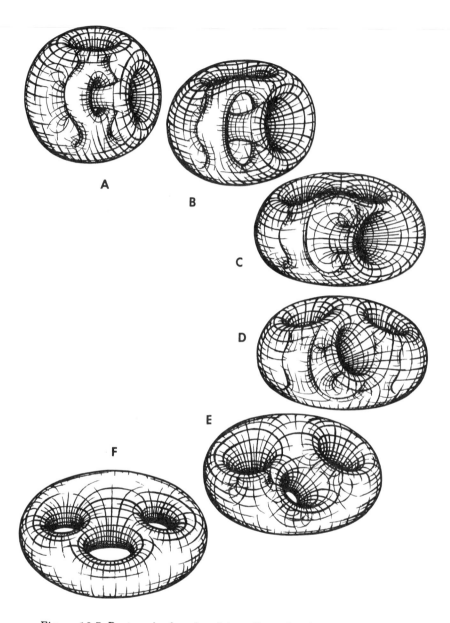

Figure 12.7 Portrayal of a closed two-dimensional manifold (A) and an imagined sequence of topological deformations (A through F) confirming that the original manifold is topologically equivalent to a "three-holed torus" and, hence, of genus 3.

(such as B, C, D, E, in the figure) with less time elapsing between neighboring stages (e.g., B and C) than between remote ones (B and E).

The maintenance of topological structure during such nonrigid mental transformations seems considerably more taxing than the maintenance of rigid structure—particularly if the object that is being mentally operated upon is very convoluted. This presumably, is why puzzles requiring, for example, the mental disentanglement or unknotting of ropes and the like are generally so difficult (see, e.g., Verplank, 1979). Also challenging is the maintenance of other intermediate structural constraints during mental manipulation, such as the length of a flexible rope, or the smoothness or differentiability of a curved surface. One of the most astonishing feats of mental simulation of the latter type appears to have been the construction of one method for the differentiable eversion of the sphere (in which the surface, in the extraordinarily involuted process of being turned inside out, is allowed to pass through itself, but not to be in any way torn or creased)—namely, that accomplished by a mathematician Bernard Morin, while blind! (see Max & Clifford, 1975; Phillips, 1966).

Normalizing transformations that are not literally spatial. Schemes for pattern recognition have sometimes required that a mechanism be included for normalizing images with respect to size, location or even orientation before comparing an externally presented stimulus against internally stored templates (e.g., see Minsky, 1961). Our own empirical studies of mental transformations indicate that such spatial normalizations may play a fundamental role in human perception, imagination, and spatial cognition generally. Indeed, the further possibility arises that more general normalizing operations that are spatial, if at all, only by metaphorical extension may play a comparably pervasive role.

In fact, just as many of us have found that the time to compare two objects increases linearly with the extent of a spatial transformation that is "irrelevant" to the comparison (Larsen & Bundesen, 1978; Shepard, 1978a), Dixon and Just have recently been finding that such comparison times increase in a similarly linear manner with other, not literally spatial disparities such as those of color (Dixon, 1978; Dixon & Just, 1978). On the basis of these new results, Dixon and Just advance the promising idea that all such results reflect the operation of mental "normalizing" transformations that quite generally precede mental comparison. Such preparatory normalizations cannot, in the case of discrepancies in color, be regarded as carried out over a path in the internal representation of concrete physical space, of course. They must be regarded as taking place in a more abstract representational or semantic space (Shepard, 1981).

Shifts of attention through semantic spaces. Ideas recently advanced by Lockhead and his students point toward a similar conceptualization (e.g., Hutchinson & Lockhead, 1977; Lockhead, Gaylord & Evans, 1977). They propose that attention travels, in the manner of a "spaceship," from one location in semantic space to another, and that wherever attention is located at a given moment, discrimination between alternative stimuli in that vicinity will be especially fast and accurate. Thus, stimuli used to prime the subject have their facilitative effect through bringing attention to the appropriate region of semantic space prior to the discriminative test. Our own findings of fixed rates of traversal of shortest transformational paths (also see Part III) and Dixon and Just's (1978) evidence for general "normalizing" operations, suggest the possibility that such shifts of attention may eventually be shown to have the analog characteristic of passing, at a definite rate, through an ordered set of stations that have demonstrably intermediate positions in an underlying semantic space.

Diagrammatic representation of analog transformations. The various mental transformations considered throughout this volume can be schematically represented by the diagram in Figure 12.8 (see Shepard, 1981). In establishing the equivalence of two objects, A and C, related by some physical transformation, the brain is considered to pass through a trajectory of intermediate states (such as B*) that have a one-to-one correspondence to intermediate physical states (B)—even when neither the latter nor their retinal projections (B') actually occur.

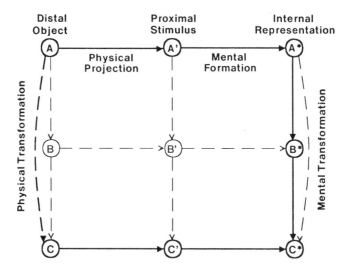

Figure 12.8 Diagrammatic illustration of the correspondence between mental and physical transformations (adapted from Shepard, 1981).

III | Apparent Motion

Introduction to Part III

When two views of the same rigid object are presented in a sequential alternation that is not too rapid, observers report the visual illusion of a single object moving rigidly and continuously back and forth between the positions displayed in the two views. Just as in mental rotation (Part I), the path of the transformation in such *apparent motion* tends to be a shortest or simplest path that preserves rigid structure—for example, a single rigid rotation about a unique fixed axis, when such an axis exists. A more detailed, quantitative comparison between mental rotation and the corresponding illusion of "apparent" rotational motion was tempting in view of two considerations: (a) the qualitative experience is very different in the two cases; whereas apparent motion is experienced automatically, effortlessly, quickly, and as a compellingly concrete perceptual illusion, mental rotation is generally optional, effortful, time consuming, and more intellectual, abstract, or schematic than concretely perceptual. (b) Yet the tendency in both cases seemed to be to follow the same shortest path of rigid transformation. Was it possible, then, that the same underlying perceptual machinery was constraining these two very different, externally driven and internally generated types of mental transformation?

Chapter 13 reports the first study in which we investigated this possibility by carrying out the closest possible analog of the original study of mental rotation of three-dimensional objects (Shepard & Metzler, 1971; see Chapter 3, here), using the different paradigm of apparent rotational motion (Shepard & Judd, 1975). Encouraged by the parallelism of the results, we then went on to seek more direct evidence that the internal process passes through representations of intermediate orientations and, so, satisfies our condition for an analog process in the case of apparent motion also. The results, obtained by requiring discriminative responses to visual probes presented during the course of apparent motion (Robins & Shepard, 1977), are presented in Chapter 14.

Chapter 15, then, reports a more recent experiment that demonstrates an intimate connection between visual shape and apparent motion, and that provides an indication as to the nature of the path of nonrigid motion that is experienced when the rate of alternation of two different views of an object becomes too rapid for the brain to construct the path of rigid transformation (Farrell & Shepard, 1981).

The epilogue to Part III (Chapter 16) briefly reviews some of the corroborative findings that have been obtained by other investigators using stimuli differing by transformations other than simple rotattions—such as (again) translations, size scalings (dilatations), and combinations of these with rotations. The epilogue also develops further the theoretical principles of path selection and object conservation that are presumed to govern these perceptual phenomena.

The book as a whole is then brought to a close with a more general, if speculative, consideration of the possible extension of such principles of path impletion to other cognitive domains of language and thought.

13 | Perceptual Illusion of Rotation of Three-Dimensional Objects

)

Originally authored by Roger N. Shepard and Sherryl A. Judd

Perspective views of the same three-dimensional object in two orientations, when presented in alternation, produced an illusion of rigid rotation. The minimum cycle duration required for the illusion increased linearly with the angular difference between the orientations and at the same slope for rotations in depth and in the picture plane. The similarity in pattern to the reaction times measured in the earlier task of mental rotation (Shepard & Metzler, 1971) suggests that the same mechanism may underlie subjects' performance in these two different tasks and, further, that holistic perceptual imagery, rather than discrete feature analysis and symbol manipulation, may play the principal role.

Shepard and Metzler (1971) found that the time required to determine whether two perspective views portray the same three-dimensional object is a linear function of the angular difference between the two orientations portrayed. The decision time is the same for rotations in depth and rotations in the two-dimensional picture plane. They proposed that subjects make the comparisons by carrying out a mental analog of the actual physical rotation of one object into congruence with the other and, further, that the mental representations that are internally transformed in this way are more akin to the three-dimensional objects portrayed than to the two-dimensional retinal projections of those objects.

To say that the internal process is a mental analog of an external process is, in part, to say that the internal process is similar in important respects to the perceptual process that would take place if a subject were actually to watch the corresponding physical rotation (see Cooper & Shepard, 1973; Metzler & Shepard, 1974—reprinted as Chapters 3 and 4, here). We investigated a perceptual illusion of apparent rotational movement in order to further explore the possible

---

Reprinted by permission from *Science*, 1976, *191*, 952-954.[1]

role of perceptual mechanisms in mental rotation. By alternately presenting two of the Shepard-Metzler perspective views of a three-dimensional object, we created the appearance of a single object rotating back and forth either (i) in depth about the vertical axis of the object or (ii) around a circle in the two-dimensional picture plane.

Presumably the rotational trajectory through which the object seemed to move as a result of these alternations is the same path through which subjects imagined one object moving into congruence with the other in the mental rotation task. The distinguishing factor is that, in the present case of apparent movement, the subjective experience is of a much more clearly perceptual nature. Instead of actively having to imagine one object rotated into the other, possibly step-by-step or even piece-by-piece, subjects effortlessly experienced the object rapidly and smoothly rocking back and forth as a rigid whole. This phenomenon of apparent rotation thus seems to be less readily accounted for in terms of theories—currently popular in cognitive psychology and artificial intelligence—that emphasize processes of sequential search, recoding, and discrete manipulation of symbolic or propositional structures.

In classical studies of apparent movement, a simple stimulus (for example, a luminous spot) alternately presented in each of two locations appeared to move back and forth without discontinuity. Moreover, as the spatial separation between the two presentations was increased, the temporal delay between the onsets of those presentations had to be increased in order to maintain optimum apparent movement—a relation known as Korte's third law (see Boring, 1942; Kolers, 1972). In our rotational extension of this perceptual illusion, the two alternating stimuli were presented in the same spatial location, and the difference between them was one of orientation. In a manner analogous to that of the classical studies, we determined, for each of several angular differences, the shortest delay between onsets for which the subject was still able to experience coherent rotational movement.

Method

Subjects. Ten students and staff members of Stanford University served as subjects.

Stimuli. Examples of the pairs of perspective views for the depth and picture-plane conditions are shown in Figure 13.1. The views were a subset of the computer-generated perspective projections of ten-cube objects originally used by Shepard and Metzler (1971). We chose two objects (one for each condition) which produced rotational illusions that were viewed from an easily interpretable

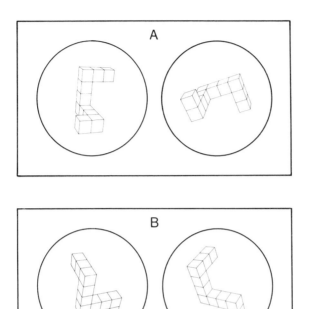

Figure 13.1 Pairs of perspective views of the three-dimensional objects,
illustrating an angular difference of 60 degrees in the picture plane (A) and
in depth (B).

perspective and moved with a minimum of ambiguity. The perspective
views were combined to construct pairs that differed in orientation
by 20°, 60°, 100°, 140°, or 180°.

At each of these angular differences, each of the ten subjects was
presented with one picture-plane pair and two depth pairs. We used
two different depth pairs in order to reduce the possibility that any
one pair would contain perspective views that would be particularly
difficult to interpret. In both conditions, the end cube nearest the
top of the object (when in standard upright position) was colored
yellow, which essentially eliminated the ambiguity in the mode of
apparent movement that otherwise occurred even at slow rates of
alternation of some pairs for which the perspective projections
appeared especially symmetrical.

The two views comprising each pair were presented in continuous
alternation in two fields of an Iconix tachistoscope. The termination
of one field coincided with the onset of the other. The duration of

the presentation of each field, always the same for both, ranged from 500 msec. to 40 msec. (Figure 13.2A).

Procedure. At the beginning of the experiment each subject was instructed and trained to rate the quality of the apparent rotation on a scale from 1 to 3, including ratings by tenths between the points. The three points on the scale were chosen to correspond to what seemed to be three distinct stages through which the phenomenal appearance passed as the rate of alternation increased. In the first stage, indicated by a rating of "1," the experience is strikingly similar to seeing an actual three-dimensional object rocking back and forth; the object seems to rotate as a rigid whole throughout its entire trajectory. In the second stage, rated as "2," there is also apparent movement, but of a nonrigid or noncoherent sort. For pairs differing by a large angle, different parts of the object appear to move independently or to deform into other noncorresponding parts (often yielding a sort of jumbling motion). For pairs differing only slightly in orientation, the motion takes on the quality of a vibration; motion is perceived but the object moves too rapidly to be followed as a rigid whole throughout its trajectory. In the final stage, rated "3," the two alternating views appear superimposed. There is flickering but no apparent movement.

The subject took as much time as needed on each trial to rate the quality of the apparent movement for a given pair at a particular rate of alternation. The trials were grouped into three equal blocks by condition, with half of the depth pairs preceding and half following the block of picture-plane pairs. Each subject rated a particular pair at all nine rates of alternation before proceeding to another pair with a new angular difference. The order of the five angular differences was counterbalanced across subjects, and the order of the nine rates of alternation within each angular difference was randomized separately for each subject.

Results

Although the subjects were not informed of either the angular difference or the randomly chosen rate of alternation for each successive trial, each subject gave consistent ratings, which generally changed monotonically with rate of alternation. Out of the 1350 ratings, there were only five violations of monotonicity. According to the subjects, the perceptual experience produced by a given rate of alternation of a given pair of views was quite distinctive and readily classified on the three-point scale.

For sufficiently slow alternations, ratings of "1" are consistently given, but beyond some critical rate, the rigid coherence of the apparent movement is lost and the ratings rather abruptly fall off toward "2," as is shown in Figure 13.2A. (Some subjects exhibit a short plateau at "2," which indicates that the experience of non-rigidity or noncoherence of the motion can occur over a range of rates.) Typically, as the angular difference is reduced, the drop occurs at shorter field durations; that is, for smaller angles, the appearance of rigid rotation of the object as a whole is maintained into more rapid rates of alternation.

As a quantitative estimate of the field duration at which the appearance of coherent rigid motion breaks down for each pair of views, we took the duration corresponding to the point at which the rating profile, starting from the level 1, first reached the level of 1.5, halfway between the ratings for rigid and nonrigid motion. For the rating profiles shown in Figure 13.2A, this crossing point occurred at durations (to within 5 msec.) of 100, 140, 180, 230, and 270 msec for angles of 20°, 60°, 100°, 140°, and 180°, respectively.

Although the results for individual subjects are more variable for this task than they were in the mental rotation task of Shepard and Metzler (1971), the mean results (Figure 13.2B) are parallel. Again we find that estimated time increases linearly with angular difference; the slope is virtually the same for differences in depth and in the picture plane. Statistical analyses indicated no significant departure from linearity in either of the two functions and no significant difference between their slopes. The fact that the absolute times were again slightly longer, overall, for the picture-plane pairs may be attributable, as in the earlier studies (see Metzler & Shepard, 1974; or Chapter 3, here), to properties peculiar to the particular objects and views chosen for the depth and picture-plane pairs.

The total range of times here of only 190 msec (from about 110 msec at 0° to 300 msec at 180°) is much less than the corresponding 3500-msec range (from 1 second at 0° to between 4 and 5 seconds at 180°) in the previous mental rotation task. Whereas the earlier range corresponded to an estimated rate of mental rotation of 50° to 60° per second, the present range corresponds to a vastly greater rate of nearly 1000° per second. The similarity between the patterns of these and the earlier results is consistent with the growing body of findings that corresponding processes of visual imagery generally proceed much more rapidly when (as in more perceptual tasks) they are driven externally than when (as in purely imaginal tasks) they must be generated internally (see, for example, Kosslyn, 1974; Posner, 1973, pp. 54-57; Weber & Castleman, 1970).

The finding of near equivalence between the breakdown times for apparent rotation in depth and in the picture plane adds to earlier evidence (Attneave & Block, 1973; Corbin, 1942) that phenomena of apparent movement are governed by relations in an internally constructed representation of something three-dimensional rather than by distances in the purely two-dimensional retinal image.

A. SUBJECT 1: DEPTH CONDITION

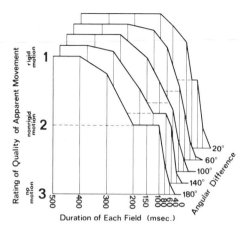

B. GROUP RESULTS: ALL TEN SUBJECTS

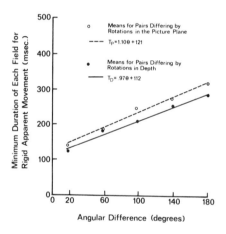

Figure 13.2 Results. (A) Profiles illustrating, for a typical subject, how ratings of apparent movement depended upon the duration of each of the two alternately presented views, for each of the five angular differences between the objects. Rating "1" is for rigid motion, "2" is nonrigid motion, and "3" is no motion. (B) Mean field duration at which rigid apparent rotation breaks down, plotted for the group of ten subjects as a function of angular difference between the two views, for pairs of objects differing by a rotation in depth (closed circles and solid lines) and in the picture plane (open circles and dashed lines). Straight lines have been fitted by the method of least squares to the plotted points. The slopes and intercepts of the best-fitting lines are 1.10 msec/deg and 121 msec, for the rotations in the picture plane, and 0.97 msec/deg and 112 msec, for rotations in depth. Breakdown of rigid rotation is defined in terms of the point at which a rating profile (A) crosses 1.5.

14 | Spatio-Temporal Probing of Apparent Rotational Movement

Originally authored by Clive Robins and Roger N. Shepard

A visual bar alternately presented in vertical and horizontal orientations appeared to rotate 90° through one of two pairs of opposite quadrants. Subjects judged whether a probe dot, interjected at some delay and angular deviation from the vertical bar, appeared before or after the bar "passed through" the corresponding angular orientation. When the motion was perceived in the probed quadrant, percent "before" responses dropped abruptly from near 100% to near 0% as delay increased, and the drop occurred at longer delays for probes at larger angular deviations. Under physically identical conditions, when the motion was perceived in an unprobed quadrant, percent "before" responses varied much less with delay and insignificantly with angular position. The accuracy of the judgments in the first case suggests the internal generation of an ordered sequence of intermediate representations during each apparent rotation.

Recent debate in cognitive psychology has concerned the nature of internal representations of real or imagined objects and of transformations on them. Many writers have favored discrete, symbolic, or propositional representations for visual as well as linguistic events, while others have presented evidence for more holistic or analogical representations of visual events—see Pylyshyn (1973) and Shepard and Podgorny (1978) for contrasting reviews of the alternative approaches. Taking the second type of approach, Shepard and Metzler (1971), Cooper and Shepard (1973), and their associates have suggested that imagined transformations of spatial objects bear important similarities to perceptions of corresponding actual transformations of externally presented objects—see Cooper and Shepard (1978) for a recent review.

Reprinted by permission from *Perception and Psychophysics*, 1977, *22*, 12-18.[1]

One promising line of attack on the representation problem has employed apparent movement, a phenomenon intermediate between merely imagined and veridically perceived transformations. Taking as their starting point Korte's (1915) third law of apparent movement that "an increase in the spatial separation between two stimuli must be accompanied by an increase in their temporal separation for an optimal appearance of movement to occur," Attneave and Block (1973) demonstrated that the critical spatial separation for Korte's law is the subjectively perceived distance in three-dimensional space and not the objective distance on the two-dimensional retina. More recently Shepard and Judd (1976) alternately presented Shepard and Metzler's (1971) pictures of three-dimensional objects differing in angular orientation. For appropriate time constants, they obtained a perceptual illusion of apparent rigid rotation even for views differing by as much as 180°. Moreover, Shepard and Judd found that the minimum onset-onset time necessary for the appearance of coherent rigid rotation increased linearly with angular difference and with the same slope for rotations both in the picture-plane and in depth. Despite marked quantitative differences in absolute overall level, the similarity in relative internal pattern between these findings and those of Shepard and Metzler (1971) suggests a possible commonality between purely imagined transformations and the perceptually experienced illusion of apparent movement. In any case, the more direct dependence of the phenomenon on distal relations in the external three-dimensional world than on proximal relations in the two-dimensional retinal image in both the experiments of Attneave and Block and of Shepard and Judd implicates relatively sophisticated internally constructed representations not readily explained in terms of two-dimensionally organized sensory mechanisms.

The present study investigates another respect in which the experience of apparent movement may partake of some of the functional richness of the perception of real movement. We ask subjects to judge whether a probe dot interjected at different temporal and spatial positions between the two stimuli appears before or after the apparently rotating image passes that point in space. If such judgments are made as a systematic monotonic function of the spatiotemporal position of the probe, this would constitute evidence for an analog nature both of the representation of the object and of its motion.

Possibly, of course, what goes on internally during such apparent movement has little or nothing in common with what goes on during the perception of a corresponding actual movement. As was originally suggested by Wertheimer (1912), the illusion that such a movement has occurred may represent a kind of retrospective neural "short circuiting" that follows the presentation of both stimuli, rather than any internal construction of a sequence of representations of intermediate orientations between the two stimuli. In this case, subjects might still be able to make the required judgments of "before" or "after" by a deductive inference based on the relative spatial position of the probe and its relative temporal position within the interstimulus interval. However, subjects should then perform similarly in a control condition in which, although the stimulus sequence is objectively identical, the path of apparent motion of the stimulus does not pass through the position of the probe. If, on the other hand, perceived rotation is rich enough to base the before/after judgment on a visual comparison of the image with the probe, while pure temporal estimation is relatively impoverished, then the judgments under the control condition should be closer to chance than those under the experimental condition.

To achieve these two physically equivalent conditions, we presented subjects with an inherently ambiguous alternation of a vertical and a horizontal bar with coincident centers. The motion was then seen either to pass back and forth through the northeast and southwest quadrants or through the northwest and southeast quadrants. The experimental and control conditions, respectively, were achieved by presenting the probe in a quadrant through which the movement currently was or was not being perceived by that subject.

Method

Subjects. Twelve students and staff members at Stanford University served as subjects in two sessions of one hour each.

Apparatus and stimuli. Subjects viewed the repeating sequence of stimuli in an Iconix 6192 four-channel tachistoscope. As illustrated in Figure 14.1A, a total cycle time of 760 msec was composed of the following displays, in this order: (1) a vertical white bar for 200 msec, (2) an empty black field for a variable preprobe interval (or ISI_1), called the *probe delay*, of between 30 to 130 msec duration (in steps of 20 msec), (3) a small yellow probe dot in one of the upper quadrants for 20 msec, (4) a postprobe black interval (or ISI_2) for between 30 to 130 msec so that the preprobe, probe, and postprobe intervals always totaled 180 msec, (5) a horizontal white bar for 200 msec, and (6) another black interval for 180 msec before the whole cycle was repeated, starting with (1), above. The white bars and yellow probe dot were presented against the same black background used for the blank intervals. The vertical and horizontal bars were positioned such that their centers, marked by small black dots, coincided at the center of the display. Each bar measured 8.9 x 1.3 cm, which, at the approximately 90-cm viewing distance, produced a visual angle of 5°40′. The 0.6-cm yellow probe dot subtended a visual angle of 25′, and always appeared in one of the two upper quadrants at an angular position of 30°, 40°, 50°, or 60° from vertical along a circular arc at 3.2 cm from the "pivotal" center of the display (as illustrated in Figure 14.1C for the right-hand quadrant).

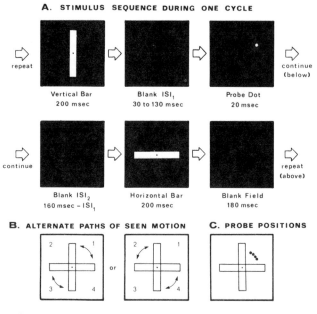

A. STIMULUS SEQUENCE DURING ONE CYCLE

repeat

Vertical Bar
200 msec

Blank ISI₁
30 to 130 msec

Probe Dot
20 msec

continue
(below)

continue

Blank ISI₂
160 msec – ISI₁

Horizontal Bar
200 msec

Blank Field
180 msec

repeat
(above)

B. ALTERNATE PATHS OF SEEN MOTION   **C.** PROBE POSITIONS

Figure 14.1 The sequence of visual fields presented during a single cycle (A), the two alternative paths through which the bar was virtually always seen to move (B), and the four angular positions in which the yellow probe dot might be presented—illustrated for one of the two upper quadrants only (C).

Procedure. The subjects were read the following instructions while they viewed binocularly the described sequence of stimuli: "This experiment is concerned with apparent movement. I will display a vertical bar and a horizontal bar, alternating in rapid succession. This may give the appearance of a movement through space of a bar, rocking back and forth. Do you see that? Through which quadrants does the bar seem to pass? Now a yellow dot should appear at some point in the bar's path, during the downswing of the top end. Your task is to say whether the dot appears before or after the bar passes the dot's place of appearance. If at any time the direction of rotation should change for you, please let me know and the dot position will be changed accordingly. You may find the judgment rather difficult and you should take as long as you need to feel really certain about it. Your response will not be timed. Please do not guess unless and until you have really tried to decide and cannot. Do not expect there always to be an equal number of 'before' and 'after' responses for any given dot position, indeed do not make any assumptions about their relative frequencies but judge each trial independently. After each block of 12 trials you may rest while I change the position of the dot. There will be two types of blocks of trials. In one case, the dot will appear in a quadrant through which the bar seems to pass, as you have just seen; in the other case, the dot will be in a quadrant through which the bar is not passing—like this. In this case you are to make the analogous judgment, that is, whether the probe appears before or after the bar would pass that point if it were rotating in the opposite direction, or if the probe were in the symmetrically opposite position."

We did not instruct subjects to fixate their eyes in any particular way. Every subject reported seeing apparent rotation when queried, though the rotation varied over subjects, almost always being seen as confined either to quadrants 1 and 3 or to quadrants 2 and 4, as shown in Figure 14.1B. Reported reversals in the quadrants of apparent movement occurred fairly infrequently, unexpectedly, and seemingly under little or no voluntary control.

Once we determined the quadrants through which rotation was being perceived by a given subject, we arranged to introduce the probe dot into the sequence in the one of the upper two quadrants appropriate to the experimental or control condition. If the quadrants of perceived rotation changed during a block of trials, the dot was shifted to the other side accordingly, such that the two main conditions were defined by a rotational direction/dot-location combination. For each of these conditions there were four blocks of 12 trials, one block at each probe position of 30°, 40°, 50°, and 60°. In a given block, each of the six permissible probe delays occurred twice, all trials being randomized independently for each block.

Each of the 12 subjects was run in two one-hour sessions of four blocks, the sequence of blocks in any session being determined by a randomization within subjects with the restriction that each of the eight subconditions be balanced to occur three times in each of the four order positions over the whole set of 24 sessions. Since the same range of probe delays was employed for all dot positions, the expected ratio of "before" to "after" responses is not equal to .5 and varied systematically with probe position. By our instructions to treat trials independently, we attempted to discourage possible guessing strategies that might utilize this dependence of expected ratio on probe position.

At the beginning of each session, we gave subjects six practice trials in each of the two main conditions, in a randomized order of conditions and trials within conditions. Following those, the four blocks were run in the same manner, with responses recorded. No feedback was given either during practice or data collection. We noted any trials on which the perceived motion switched into the other two quadrants. Subjects were questioned informally after each session about their experience in the task generally, and specifically about any such switches, and about the nature and relative difficulty of the judgments in each of the two main conditions.

Results and Discussion

At the top of Figure 14.2, the group data for the number of "before" responses are plotted as a function of probe delay for each of the four probe positions of 30°, 40°, 50°, and 60°. These four curves are plotted separately for the experimental condition, in which the probe was presented in the quadrant where the motion was being seen (Panel A) and for the control condition, in which the probe was presented in the opposite quadrant (Panel B). Of central interest are the different ways in which the frequency of "before" responses depends, in the two conditions, on probe delay and probe position.

Effect of probe delay. As is clear in the figure, the functional dependence of frequency of "before" responding on the delay of the probe was uniformly much stronger in the experimental than in the control condition; all four curves for the experimental condition (A) exhibit an abrupt, monotonic S-shaped decline from the maximum possible to zero "before" responses as probe delay increased, while all four curves for the control condition (B) are relatively much flatter and, indeed, never approach 100% or 0% responses.

For purposes of statistical analysis of the difference in dependence on delay in the two conditions, we computed the slope of the linear function of delay best fitting each subject's data after combining over all probe positions. For the experimental condition, all 12 of the subjects had negative slopes and the 95% confidence interval on the mean of these slopes was -.093 to -.077. For the control condition, 10 of the 12 subjects had negative slopes and the 95% confidence interval was -.048 to -.012. The slopes for the experimental condition were also significantly greater than for the control condition.

Effect of probe position. For the experimental condition (Figure 14.2A), the four individual curves appear, furthermore, to be systematically displaced farther and farther to the right as the angle of the probe's position is increased from 30° to 60°. But such a systematic shift with probe position is not present in the four curves for the control condition (except for what might be interpreted as a right-ward displacement of the 60° curve).

For purposes of statistical analysis this time, the number of "before" responses as a function of position was determined for each subject by summing over all probe delays. Again, slopes of these functions were computed for each subject under each condition. Of the 12 subjects, 11 had positive slopes in the experimental condition (and the remaining slope was zero), but only 8 of the 12 subjects had positive slopes in the control condition. Ninety-five percent confidence intervals on the mean of these slopes were .009 to .021 for the experimental condition and -.005 to .017 for the control condition. The slopes for the experimental condition were significantly different from zero ($t = 5.21$, $p < .001$), whereas the slopes for the control conditon did not differ significantly from zero ($t = 1.16$, $p > .20$).

These results are in agreement with the idea that subjects based their judgments in the experimental condition on a comparison between the probe and an internal representation of a bar rotating back and forth. Not only was there a virtually complete shift from consistent "before" to consistent "after" responding as the delay of the probe was increased by no more than about 40 msec, but the delay at which this shift occurred increased systematically with the angular distance of the probe along the path of the experienced motion. The results for the control condition, in which the stimulus sequences were physically identical but the experienced movement did not pass through the quadrant containing the probe, were in marked contrast. There was no abrupt shift from "before" to "after" responding with increasing delay, and the much smaller and more gradual shift that did occur was not related in a consistent monotonic way to the angular position of the probe.

Comparison with limiting theoretical cases. In the absence of a detailed theory of the internal processes going on in subjects during apparent movement, it is not possible to make precise predictions about the actual probabilities of "before" and "after" responses at particular combinations of position and delay of the probe. Nevertheless, instructive comparisons can be made with theoretical predictions from two limiting extreme sorts of assumptions. One is that subjects respond "before" or "after" entirely randomly with equal probability, regardless of probe delay. In this case, the curves for all four probe positions should fall along the horizontal line labeled "chance performance" in Figure 14.2D. The other extreme sort of assumption is that subjects respond on the basis of a direct comparison between the probe and an internal representation of a bar actually rotating between vertical and horizontal positions. In this case, subjects should always respond "after" or "before," respectively,

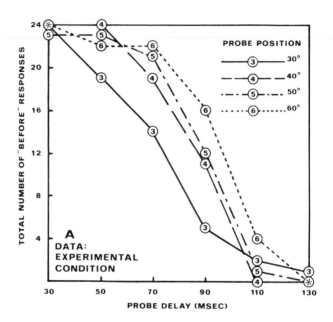

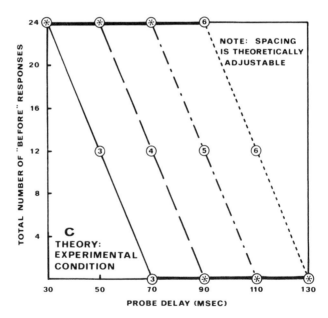

Figure 14.2 Curves, for each of the four probe positions, showing total number of "before" responses as a function of probe delay—as empirically obtained for the experimental condition in which the motion was perceived in the probed

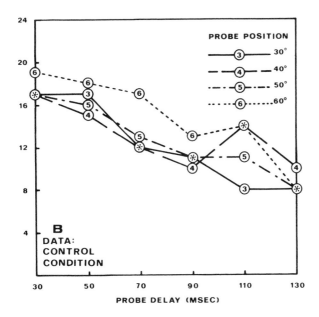

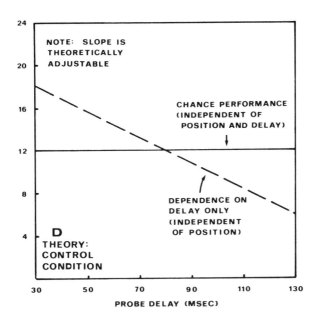

quadrant (A) and for the control condition in which the motion was perceived in the other quadrant (B), and as theoretically derived from alternative limiting assumptions (C and D).

in accordance with whether the internal representation of the rotating bar has or has not yet passed the position of the probe at the moment of its presentation and should give both responses with probability .5 when the probe coincides with the momentarily represented position of the bar. The predicted curves then would take on the shapes illustrated in Figure 14.2C.

The lateral placements of these curves, however, would depend on the particular time course that we assume for the internally represented rotation. The curves displayed in Panel C are based on the quite specific assumption that this rotation proceeds at a constant rate beginning with the vertical orientation precisely at the perceptual offset of the vertical bar and ending with the horizontal orientation precisely at the perceptual onset of the horizontal bar. Although we shall argue below that this assumption is oversimplified and may need modification both on grounds of plausibility and in order to fit the data, the assumption provides a simple and well-defined limiting case for purposes of initial comparison.

Clearly, the data for the experimental condition are much closer to the limiting case in which the subjects are assumed to base their judgments on comparison with an internal representation of a rotating bar, while the data for the control condition are much closer to the limiting case in which the subjects are assumed to make their judgments completely at random. However, the obtained curves also suggest that the subjects were not always operating at the extreme limit represented by one of these theoretically pure cases.

In particular, if, in the control condition, subjects were able to make some crude estimate of the purely temporal position of the probe within the 180-msec interstimulus interval, this could explain the consistent, though much weaker, decline in percent "before" judgments with probe delay shown theoretically by the dashed line in Figure 14.2D and empirically by the four curves for the control condition in Figure 14.2B. The notion that the judgments were thus based primarily on a purely temporal comparison in this condition, rather than on a spatio-temporal comparison with an internally represented moving bar as assumed for the experimental condition, would explain the lack of systematic dependence of the four curves in Figure 14.2B on the spatial position of the probe.

Despite these indications, every subject, when questioned, claimed to have attempted to use the apparent movement as a basis for judgment even (though with much greater difficulty) in the control condition. Most commonly, they described trying simultaneously to focus attention on the timing of the probe and the corresponding position in the opposite quadrant in relation to the moving bar. Indeed, the moderate slope of the functions plotted for the group of subjects in the control condition (Figure 14.2B) heavily reflects the data of 2 of the 12 subjects who reported that, with practice, they were able to develop strategies using the apparent movement in this way that were nearly as effective in the control as in the experimental condition. (These two subjects, incidentally, were the two who had had the most previous experience in making judgments of this kind in our laboratory.)

In fact, judgments of purely temporal order of events within a repeating sequence are remarkably difficult—much more so, apparently, than for two isolated events (Hill & Bliss, 1968; Sternberg & Knoll, 1973, p. 674; Swisher & Hirsh, 1972). In our own pilot work in the visual modality, we substituted homogeneous red and blue fields for the vertical and horizontal bars so that the temporal information was preserved but the spatio-temporal information contained in the motion perceived between the bars was entirely eliminated. The resulting experience was one of the whole background alternately flashing blue and red and, superimposed on this, a small dot flashing yellow with, however, a maddening absence of any determinable temporal relationship between the flashing dot and the flashing background. And, in summarizing the findings of several earlier studies using other modalities, Sternberg and Knoll (p. 674) concluded that "even when onsets of successive stimuli are separated by 100 msec or more in recycling presentation, accuracy is far from perfect." The relatively gradual decline of the curves in Figure 14.2B over a range of probe delays from 30 to 130 msec appears consistent with this conclusion.

Even though we have some reservations about the specific assumptions underlying the theoretical curves exhibited in Figure 14.2C, we attempted a statistical analysis of the degree to which the data from the two conditions departed from these curves. We defined "errors" as responses that were opposite from what would have been correct responses if a bar had actually been rotating at a constant rate between the offset of the vertical and onset of the horizontal bar—that is, as responses of "before" or "after" opposite to what is indicated by the relevant solid curve in Figure 14.2C. By this definition, every subject made more errors in the control condition than in the experimental condition. The mean number of errors (out of 10 possible) were 1.02 and 3.69 for the experimental and control conditions, respectively. Moreover, such a difference between the experimental and control condition was statistically significant for each of the four probe positions ($p < .01$ in every case). The objective results are thus consonant with the subjects' reports that the control condition was always more taxing than the experimental condition, and with the experimenter's informal impression that the judgment latencies, though not recorded, were generally about two to three times longer for the control than for the experimental condition.

Explanations for departures from theoretical curves. Of course, we don't believe the specific assumptions underlying the theoretical curves in Figure 14.2C to be quite correct. In the experimental condition, any fuzziness or variability in the internal representation of the rotating bar would be expected to entail some rounding off of the curves—perhaps as found in Figure 14.2A. (And this would be expected in the perception of real movement as well as in this illusion of apparent movement.) Moreover, there is reason to doubt the assumption that internal rotation commences at the offset of one bar and ends at the onset of the next bar. In accordance with Korte's fourth law, apparent movement has been shown to depend more on onset-onset time than on the interstimulus interval (e.g., see Kahneman, 1967) and, even in the case of apparent rotation, is much the same when this interval is reduced to zero (Shepard & Judd, 1976). In the present case, by assuming that the internal representation of the rotation begins quite a bit later and ends slightly earlier (and, possibly, accelerates and then decelerates), we can predict curves that differ from those in Figure 14.2C in being relatively shifted to the right and compressed together. In this way, the theoretical curves could be brought into a closer approximation to the empirical curves for the experimental condition (Panel A). However, we presently have little basis on which to argue for any particular starting or stopping times for the internally represented rotation (and, in view of the linear functions obtained by Shepard and Judd, we prefer the working assumption that the rate of the represented rotation, once started, is essentially constant). Furthermore, there are other factors that may contribute to the rightward shift and relative compression of the four curves in Figure 14.2A.

In particular, when we ourselves played the role of subject, it appeared to us that, when the probe was close to the vertical bar (i.e., at 30°), the strong afterimage of the bar "above" the probe induced a strong bias to report "before," while, when the probe was close to the horizontal bar (i.e., at 60°), the weaker afterimage of the probe above the bar induced a bias (though probably a weaker one) to report "after." Possibly, the biasing effect of such afterimages could be decreased by reducing the width and brightness contrast of the visual bar.

Spontaneous switches in quadrant of perceived motion. A striking aspect of apparent movement with such inherently ambiguous stimulus displays is the categorically distinct phenomenal appearances of the different ways of perceiving motion under identical stimulus conditions. Seven of the 12 subjects experienced spontaneous switches in the quadrants of the perceived motion during the experiment. Of the 31 such switches reported, 11 occurred on trials in which the probe and bar should, according to the special assumptions underlying the curves in Figure 14.2C, appear simultaneous. This is significantly greater than expected by chance ($\chi^2(1)=7.89$, $p<.01$, two-tailed). Informal observation suggests that the latencies on these trials averaged much longer than on other trials. The reversals might therefore be a consequence of greater cognitive strain or simply of the greater time available for the occurrence of a reversal.

Concluding Remarks

No one experiment can resolve all of the issues concerning the internal representation of apparent movement. We believe, however, that the use of spatiotemporally localized probes during the course of a perceptually related internal transformation shows promise for clarifying the extent to which the internal representations of objects and their transformations are analogical in the sense of having a one-to-one relation to corresponding external objects and events. In the specific case of apparent movement, our results, together with those of Shepard and Judd (1976), appear to furnish some support for the idea that when under identical stimulus conditions a bar is seen to be rocking back and forth either one way or the other way, it is not merely an illusion in which the subject has the retrospective impression that a motion of the one sort or the other has occurred. The precision of the subject's judgments of the relation of the bar to the probe during the course of the perceived motion suggests that a sequence of representations of the bar in successive intermediate orientations may at least schematically have been generated. (Our data do not, however, bear on the question of whether such an intermediate sequence is discrete or continuous.)

Of course, if such an intermediate sequence is internally generated, it may only be generated *after* the presentation of the second stimulus. Logically, this would have to be the case upon the first presentation of the second stimulus since, without knowing what that stimulus was to be, the subject could not know what intermediate sequence to generate. However even "direct" perception takes time, and so it is quite likely in our experiment, as Beck, Elsner, and Silverstein (1977) established in their very recent study of apparent movement, that the internal representation of the movement between two successively presented stimuli (like the internal representation of those stimuli themselves) follows the external events with a time lag comparable to the interstimulus interval.

Finally, our conclusions might seem to be inconsistent with Kolers'

(1963) finding that the apparent movement of a line did not mask a spatiotemporally interposed real line in the way that the corresponding real movement of a similar line did. However, it may be that the internally generated sequence of intermediate representations that we are tentatively postulating is at an abstract representational level too far removed from the peripheral mechanism to produce this kind of sensory masking. The priority of distal relations in three-dimensional space over proximal relations on the two-dimensional retina, noted at the outset, points in this direction. In our own experiment, sensory detectors corresponding to the physical superposition of the yellow dot on the white bar presumably would not themselves ever have been stimulated. It is not surprising, then, that several of our subjects reported that when the dot flashed just as the bar appeared to pass through that position, the dot and bar themselves seemed strangely to elude or to jump around each other without yielding the unmistakable appearance of direct superposition. Nevertheless, the higher level representation of the close encounter between the flashing dot and the moving bar evidently sufficed to permit a remarkably refined temporal judgment.

15 | Shape, Orientation, and Apparent Rotational Motion

Originally authored by Joyce E. Farrell and Roger N. Shepard

Apparent rotational motion was investigated in polygonal shapes ranging in rotational symmetry from random to self-identical under 180° rotation. Observers adjusted the rate of alternation between two computer displayed orientations of any given polygon to determine the point of breakdown of perceived rigid rotation between those two orientations. For asymmetric polygons, the minimum stimulus-onset asynchrony yielding apparent rigid rotation increased approximately linearly with orientational disparity, as anticipated on the basis of the extension of Korte's third law to rotational motion by Shepard and Judd (1976). For nearly symmetric polygons, however, the critical time increased markedly as the disparities approached 180°, owing to the availability of a shorter, nonrigid rotation in the opposite direction. The results demonstrate the existence of competing mental tendencies to preserve the rigid structure of an object and to traverse a minimum transformational path.

There is more to seeing than meets the eye; we often have the perceptual experience of things that aren't physically there. In the illusion of apparent motion, an object that is successively displayed for suitable durations in different locations or orientations is perceived as moving continuously through the intermediate positions in space. Under some circumstances, this automatic filling in or *impletion* of a connecting path can have a perceptual force comparable to that produced by real motion (e.g., Dimmick & Scahill, 1925; DeSilva, 1929; Morinaga, Noguchi, & Yokoi, 1966). Despite the absence of external guidance, this illusory filling in is also remarkably orderly. Hence, as the founders of Gestalt psychology were quick to realize (Koffka, 1935; Wertheimer, 1912/1961), parametric investigations of apparent motion should be revealing of the inherent organizing principles of the brain.

Reprinted by permission from *Journal of Experimental Psychology: Human Perception and Performance*, 1981, 7, 477–486.[1]

Our own work on apparent rotational motion has led us to focus, particularly, on two general principles: (a) Although an object could traverse innumerable paths between any two positions, only one motion is experienced on any one occasion, and that motion tends to be one that is in some sense as short or simple as possible. (b) If the second of two successive presentations of the same object does not follow the first too quickly, the minimization of path evidently is subject to the constraint that the rigid shape of the object be preserved over the interpolated trajectory.

Traversal of minimum path. Following Wertheimer's (1912/1961) original demonstration of the importance of time relations in apparent motion, Korte (1915) established a monotonically increasing, approximately linear relationship between the optimum temporal interval between successive stimuli and their spatial separation, a relationship now generally known as "Korte's third law" (Boring, 1942; Kolers, 1972). More recently, Shepard and Judd (1976) extended this relationship between time and distance to the case of rotational apparent motion, for which distance is specified in terms of the angular disparity between the two successively presented views of an object. Shepard and Judd also obtained more precise, quantitative evidence for a specifically linear increase in critical time with spatial disparity, and found that the critical time for a given rotational difference was the same for rotations in the picture plane as for rotations in depth—just as had been found by Shepard and Metzler (1971) for the very different task of "mental rotation." This last result, together with related earlier results by Ogasawara (1936), Corbin (1942), and Attneave and Block (1973), suggest that the path of motion is constructed at a relatively deep, cognitive level of the perceptual system.

In the case of mental rotation, several kinds of evidence support the idea that the internal process passes through a series of representations corresponding to intermediate orientations in the external world (Cooper, 1976a; Cooper & Shepard, 1973, 1978; Metzler & Shepard, 1974; Shepard, 1975). Likewise, in the case of apparent rotational motion, there are at least two kinds of evidence supportive of the notion that the trajectory of motion is instantiated in a similarly concrete form. First, objects that differ by 180° in orientation can be experienced as rigidly rotating through either of two alternative paths (starting out in the clockwise or counterclockwise direction) and, despite the physical identity of the stimulating conditions, the two experiences are phenomenally distinct (Robins & Shepard, 1977; Shepard & Judd, 1976). Second, the precision of discriminative response concerning the relation of a spatio-temporally localized probe to such an apparently rotating object suggests that the probe is compared against an internal representation of the object as it would appear in successively more and more rotated orientations (Robins & Shepard, 1977).

Preservation of rigid shape. Kolers and Pomerantz (1971) and Shepard and Judd (1976) noted that when the spatial disparity was not too great in relation to a given temporal separation, the apparent motion, was perceived as a rigid motion of the object as a whole. When the spatial disparity became sufficiently large in relation to the temporal separation, however, the perceived motion became nonrigid. Typically, local parts of the object in one display then appeared to deform into similarly shaped parts that were nearby in the other display. Apparently there is an intimate connection between the perception of the identity of an object and the perception of its position in space—a connection that has been insightfully discussed in terms of "what-where connections" (Attneave, 1974a) and "correspondence processes" (Ullman, 1979). (Also see Rock, 1973; Shepard, 1981; and, for differing views on the roles of shape and position, Orlansky, 1940; Kolers, 1972.)

We undertook the present study in order to clarify the relationships between shape, orientation, and apparent motion when preservation of shape is pitted against minimization of transformational path. We chose rotation as the spatial transformation for two reasons: First, we and our associates had already developed techniques and considerable calibrational data for apparent rotation (e.g., Shepard & Judd, 1976). Second, the connection between the shape of an object and its spatial transformations is more intimate for rotational than for other rigid transformations (Shepard, 1979, 1981). Except for the circle in two dimensions and sphere in three (shapes that are unique in being identical to themselves under all rotations), objects have the property that they resemble themselves to different degrees for different angular disparities. For example, while every object is identical to itself under 360° rotation, a rectangle is also identical to itself under 180° rotation and, depending on its length-to-width ratio, it attains some augmented degree of similarity to itself under 90° rotation as well. Indeed, in the spirit of autocorrelational approaches to the representation of form (e.g., Uttal, 1975), shape might be entirely characterized in terms of its self-similarity under all possible rigid transformations in space (Shepard, 1979, 1981, 1982a). Moreover, in the case of compact objects, as opposed to spatially extended patterns (such as textures, tilings, latticeworks, and the like), rotational transformations will be the most important.

The aspect of shape that is of most central concern here, then, is approximation to symmetry under rotation. For simplicity in this first parametric study of the connection between shape and apparent motion, we systematically varied the degree of approximation of otherwise random polygons to a single type of rotational symmetry; namely, self-identity under 180° rotation within the picture plane. Correspondingly, we also restricted the rotational disparities between the two alternately displayed views of such a polygon to disparities of angular orientation within that same picture plane. For each combination of rotational symmetry and angular disparity, we determined the maximum rate of alternation for which observers experienced rigid apparent rotation. We sought in this way to develop a more quantitative characterization of the trade-off in apparent motion between extent of transformation and preservation of shape that had been qualitatively noted by Kolers and Pomerantz (1971) and by Shepard and Judd (1976); and, thus, to take a small step toward a more complete understanding of the mental mechanisms underlying perceptual impletion.

Method

Subjects. Eight Stanford students and members of staff participated, individually, as observers, for three sessions consisting of 60 recorded trials each. Although the trials were self-paced, an average session lasted about one hour.

Stimuli. We first constructed three asymmetric polygons by picking one point on each of 18 equally-spaced radii of polar graph paper and drawing straight line segments between the chosen points on adjacent radii. Two of the points, each chosen to lie 8 units from the origin in opposite directions, determined the vertical axis of the shape. We then determined the distance from the origin of each of the 16 other points by randomly selecting a number between 1 and 17 (excluding 8) without replacement.

To create polygons having 180° rotational symmetry, we cut each of the asymmetric polygons in half along its vertical axis. We then attached each half to a duplicated version of itself that had been rotated 180 degrees. Thus we obtained three rotationally symmetric polygons from the left halves of the asymmetric polygons (called the left-side versions), and three rotationally symmetric polygons from the right halves of the asymmetric polygons (called the right-side versions).

Finally, we constructed polygons of intermediate degrees of symmetry as follows: Placing each symmetric polygon over the asymmetric shapes from which it was derived, so that corresponding halves coincided, we interpolated polygons of intermediate degrees of symmetry by connecting points along radii that fell between a point on the asymmetric polygon and a corresponding point of the symmetric polygon. In the generation of a particular polygon, these interpolated points were all chosen to fall either one-fourth, one-half, or three-fourths the distance from a point on the asymmetric polygon to the corresponding point on the symmetric polygon.

Our final set thus consisted of 27 distinct polygons: the three randomly generated original polygons, with 0% experimentally imposed rotational symmetry; and three left-side and three right-side versions at each of the following four levels of experimentally imposed 180° symmetry: 25%, 50%, 75%, and 100%. However, the qualification "experimentally imposed" should be kept in mind. Even a randomly generated polygon, unlike a perfect circle, must possess some appreciable (though haphazard) increments in self-similarity at certain angular disparities, and it is in fact functional dependence of these self-similarities on angle that characterizes the unique shape of such a polygon. However, these haphazard increments in self-similarity, unlike the experimentally imposed increments, would not be expected to be common to the different polygons within an ensemble (of three or six) at a given level of experimentally imposed 180° symmetry. Representative instances of the polygons are illustrated in Figure 15.1.

We presented each observer with 15 of these distinct polygons: three, based on the original three random polygons, at each of the five levels of symmetry from 0% to 100%. For half the observers the partially symmetric polygons (between 25% and 100% symmetric) were left-side versions and for the other half they were right-side versions. The three asymmetric polygons (0% symmetric) were the same for all observers.

We displayed only one polygon at a time, always centered on the face of a computer-driven cathode ray tube (Tektronix model 604 with P31 phosphor) situated in a dimly illuminated room. At the standard viewing distance, each polygon subtended a visual angle of approximately 4.8°. We presented the polygon, chosen for a given trial, in continuous alternation between two orientations: the arbitrary upright orientation defined by the so-called "vertical axis" used in the generation of the polygon, and an orientation that departed from that "upright" orientation by a fixed angle, throughout that trial, of 30°, 60°, 90°, 120°, 150°, or 180°, clockwise or counterclockwise. On the basis of earlier indications that onset-onset time or *stimulus-onset asynchrony* (SOA) is the most critical temporal determinant of apparent motion (Korte, 1915; Kahneman, 1967; Neuhaus, 1930; Shepard and Judd, 1976, and our own unpublished explorations), we arranged that regardless of the durations of the alternately presented fields, each stationary view immediately replaced the other, without any interstimulus interval.

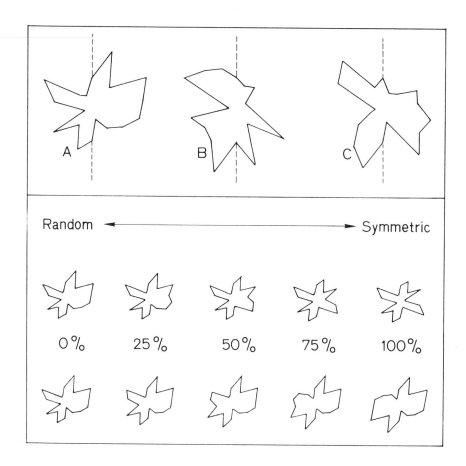

Figure 15.1 The three originally generated random polygons (A, B, C) and, below, the five levels of 180 degree rotational symmetry illustrated for the left-side and right-side versions derived from Polygon A.

Procedure. At the beginning of a trial, the duration of each of the two alternately presented views, that is, the SOA, was always initialized at one second. We asked the observers to "try to imagine the shape rigidly rotating from one orientation into the other, as if the shape were actually physically rotating in the picture plane." In most cases they saw the polygon as thus rigidly rotating either at or soon after the alternation began on each trial. They then tapped a key on one side of the response panel, and in this way decreased the duration of each field by 10%. They continued to tap this key and, hence, to speed up the rate of alternation between the two views until they reached a rate at which the apparently rigid rotation gave way (often rather abruptly) to a qualitatively different, apparently nonrigid motion. They then depressed a key at the center of the response panel whereupon the computer recorded this SOA at which the appearance of rigid rotation had broken down, referred to as SOA 1. Observers then began tapping a key on the other side of the response panel, which increased the SOA each time by the same 10% steps. When rigid motion first reappeared, they once again depressed the center key and, thus, recorded the SOA for the first re-emergence of apparently rigid motion, referred to as SOA 2. This terminated the trial for that polygon at that angular disparity.

Observers were told that if, on a particular trial, they could not succeed in seeing the polygon as rigidly rotating at the initial one-field-per-second rate or no matter how much they slowed the rate of alternation, they should indicate this as well as the nature of the perceived nonrigid motion on a sheet with numbered spaces for comments on individual trials. They then proceeded to the next trial.

Beyond a series of practice trials that followed the initial instructions, and a few warm-up trials at the start of each ensuing session, each observer proceeded in this way through a randomly arranged sequence of 180 recorded trials, one for each polygon in one of the two sets of 15, at each of the 6 clockwise and 6 counterclockwise angular disparities (including the 180° disparities, which were identical for clockwise and counterclockwise rotations). The assignment of the speeding-up and slowing-down functions to the left and right response keys, like the assignment of left-side and right-side versions of the polygons, was counterbalanced over observers.

Results

Mean dependence of critical time on angular disparity. Despite an appreciable hysteresis (to be considered later), plots of the stimulus-onset asynchronies for breakdown (SOA 1) and re-emergence (SOA 2) of rigid apparent motion revealed that these two measures were approximately linearly related to each other and were related in similar ways to the principal independent variables; namely, angular disparity and degree of rotational symmetry. For the purposes of an overall examination of these relations, therefore, we averaged corresponding descending and ascending measures and will refer to each such mean stimulus-onset asynchrony at the transition between rigid and nonrigid apparent motion as the *critical* SOA.

Figure 15.2 shows the dependence of this mean critical SOA on angular disparity, plotted as a separate curve for each of the five levels of 180° rotational symmetry of the polygons. Each point in this figure is averaged over the corresponding shapes derived from the three original polygons, over equivalent clockwise and counterclockwise disparities, and over all eight observers. However, since observers were not always able to see rigid rotation for the more symmetric polygons at the larger angular disparities, some points (particularly for 75% symmetry at 150° and, especially, at 180°) are based on fewer measurements. We believe the patterns of these curves to be quite interpretable.

For the more asymmetric polygons (say 0% and 25% symmetric), critical SOA increased montonically and, indeed, approximately linearly with angular disparity. This general trend, if linearly extrapolated back to 0°, goes from about 150 msec at the point of no angular disparity to about 550 msec at the maximum 180° disparity. Such a dependence of critical time on difference in orientation is broadly consonant with the linear increase reported by Shepard and Judd (1976) for apparent rotation of asymmetric three-dimensional objects; namely, "from about 110 msec at 0° to 300 msec at 180°." Over all, the critical SOAs estimated here do average some 145 msec longer owing to a greater elevation and, especially, a greater slope of the new linear trend. However, the two experiments differ with respect to sample of observers, type of stimuli, and procedural and computational methods for estimating critical SOAs.

Effect of approximation to 180° rotational symmetry. The new information provided by the present experiment concerns the consequences of experimentally imposing rotational symmetry. For the polygons with complete 180° rotational symmetry, the critical SOA increased to 90°, much as it did for asymmetric polygons. Beyond 90°, however, it decreased with a slope of equivalent magnitude to an SOA at 150° that is nearly identical to that at 30°. This is entirely to be expected. For these symmetric polygons, a disparity that exceeds 90° by some amount is exactly equivalent to a disparity in the opposite direction that falls short of 90° by that same amount. Hence the observers experienced a rigid rotation, but through the smaller, supplementary angle in the opposite direction. No point is plotted at 180° for these completely symmetric objects, since the supplementary angle then becomes 0° and no motion of any kind can be seen.

Of particular interest are the polygons that approximate but do not attain complete rotational symmetry. It is for these polygons that we expect a conflict to arise, beyond disparities of 90°, between a strictly rigid rotation through the larger, obtuse angle and a necessarily nonrigid rotation through the oppositely directed supplementary acute angle. This anticipated conflict in fact manifests itself in our data in two ways: First, as we already implied, the fraction of trials on which observers were able to see rigid rotation markedly decreased as the 75% symmetric polygons reached angular disparities of 150° and, especially, 180°. Second, even on those occasions when

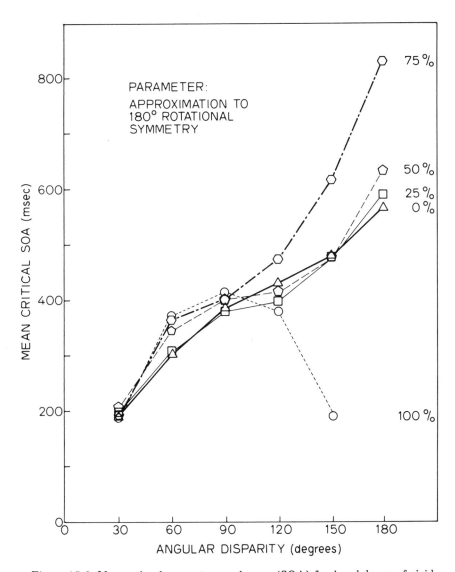

Figure 15.2 Mean stimulus-onset asynchrony (SOA) for breakdown of rigid apparent rotation plotted as a function of angular disparity for each of the five levels of rotational symmetry of the polygons.

they were able to see rigid rotation through these large angles, Figure 15.2 shows that it was only by going to substantially slower rates of alternation than were required for the asymmetric polygons. The observers claimed that it was as if a strong "pull" toward the similarly shaped and rotationally closer alternative impeded their establishment of a connecting path to the identically shaped but rotationally more remote alternative.

A similar consideration seems to explain other, more subtle regularities of the plotted curves. Quite generally, the critical SOA is elevated above the expected linear trend to the extent that there is a relatively short alternative path of transformation. On this hypothesis, the 0% curve for the asymmetric polygons is most linear because there are no strongly competing alternatives. But, even for this curve, the slight upswing at 180° may reflect the existence of an alternative rigid rotation in the opposite direction around the 360° circle and, also, an alternative, nonrigid "flip" in depth to be discussed later.

The more nearly the polygons approach 180° rotational symmetry, at the other extreme, the more nearly would rotations close to 90° in one direction compete with rotations through similar, supplementary angles in the opposite direction. Such a competition between opposite paths might thus explain the elevation of the middle points of the curve for the 100% symmetric polygons (at 60°, 90°, and 120°) above the inverted V-shaped curve that would coincide (to the left of 90°) with the linear curve for the asymmetric polygons. It might also explain the S-shaped deviations from linearity of the curves for intermediate degrees of symmetry: to the extent that the polygons become more symmetric, their critical SOA curves should more closely approximate the middle section of the inverted U curve for completely symmetric polygons. This hypothesized role of competing paths appears to be illustrated especially clearly at 60°. Although the curves for all five levels of similarity are virtually superimposed at 30° disparity, by 60° they have fanned out so that their critical SOAs increase in exactly the predicted order: 0%, 25%, 50%, 75%, and 100% symmetry.

Questions of linear trend and hysteresis. Our interpretation of these systematic departures from an underlying linear trend is necessarily at least as tentative as our conclusion that the underlying trend is linear. For large disparities, close to 180°, the assumed linear trend would be perturbed by the increase in SOA that we conjecture to arise from competition between alternative transformations, whether in the picture plane or in depth (see later discussion of Figure 15.3). And at small angular disparities, there are at least two reasons to suspect departures from a linear trend: (a) the hysteretic difference (SOA 2 - SOA 1), though generally greater than 100 msec for angular departures of 60° or more, dropped to about 70 msec for angular departures of 30° (as well as for the supplementary departures of 150° for the 100% symmetric polygons). (b) Previous work (e.g., by Anstis, 1978; Braddick, 1974; as well as preliminary explorations that we have begun) suggest that different criteria for rigid motion, perhaps depending on more peripheral sensory mechanisms, may come into play for angular disparities much smaller than 30°. Certainly, our observers (like those of DeSilva, 1929, p. 289) reported that the illusion of motion over the longer paths, when achieved, required greater mental effort and was less perceptually compelling than motions experienced over shorter paths. If, as we have assumed, there nevertheless is an underlying linear trend (except, possibly, for very small angular disparities), our current estimate of its slope could fall anywhere between 2.4 msec per degree, as calculated for the whole 30° to 180° range, and 2.0 msec per degree, as calculated after exclusion of the problematic extreme points at 30° and 180°.

Reliability of the pattern of critical SOAs in individual observers. Although the critical SOA for individuals were noticeably more variable than the means for the group plotted in Figure 15.2, they all exhibited the basic trends noted in those means. First, the mean critical SOA, averaged over the five levels of symmetry, not only increased from 30° to 90° but increased monotonically in that range for all eight observers. Second, for all but the completely symmetric polygons, the SOA consistently continued this increase beyond 90° for all eight observers. Third, for completely symmetric polygons, SOA beyond 90° reversed direction and decreased for all eight observers. And fourth, the upswing above the other curves for the 75% symmetric, polygons beyond 90° is consistent. Although the largest angular departures for which rigid apparent motion of the 75% shapes was attainable was 180° for three observers, 150° for three, and 120° for two, in seven out of eight cases the last point of the curve was higher than the corresponding points of all four curves for the other levels of symmetry, and for the eighth observer (for whom rigid motion could be maintained only to 120°) the last point fell above all but one of the other four curves.

Dependence of frequency and type of breakdown on angular disparity and degree of symmetry. Except for the case of the 100% symmetric polygons, for which observers almost always saw rigid rotation, the proportion of trials on which observers experienced rigid motion consistently decreased as angular displacement and amount of symmetry increased. After applying the arc sin transformation to these proportions, we subjected them to an analysis of variance using observers as a repeated measure. The effects of angular disparity, degree of symmetry, and the interaction of these two factors were all significant, with $p < .001$. The interaction between angular disparity and degree of symmetry ($F = 5.86$) describes a trade-off between the preservation of the identity of shape and the tendency to choose the shortest of alternative paths connecting its two successive positions.

On the basis of the observers' reports we divided the trials on which they failed to see rigid motion into two categories: (a) non-rigid motion that appeared to occur largely within the picture plane (usually a deformation together with some rotation in that plane), and (b) nonrigid motion in depth (usually a deformation together with a reflection or "flip" in depth). Figure 15.3 shows that reports of both types of nonrigid motion increased with angular displacements beyond 90°. But, whereas shapes with a high degree of experimentally imposed rotational symmetry were more often seen to deform in the plane, the shapes intended to be asymmetric were more often seen to "flip" in depth. These latter, reflectional deformations appear to have capitalized on some chance approximations to bilateral symmetries in the original random polygons. For example, since Polygon C (at the top right in Figure 15.1) happened to be approximately symmetrical about an axis inclined about 30° clockwise from vertical, when it was alternated with a copy of itself rotated 180° in the picture plane, it tended to be seen as nonrigidly flipping in depth about its orthogonal, long axis. Similar phenomena occurred for the other two random polygons owing to the presence of axes of weak bilateral symmetry. In Polygon A, for example, there are two orthogonal such axes inclined at about 45°.

Theoretical Discussion and Conclusion

Connections between the perception of objects and their transformations. The results of our parametric manipulation of angular disparity and rotational symmetry in apparent motion have confirmed the existence of an intimate relation between the perception of shape, on the one hand, and the perception of orientation and rotational movement, on the other. When an object possesses an approximation to some sort of symmetry, ambiguities arise at certain transformational disparities. An object alternately presented in two different positions may then be seen to move through one or another of the shortest paths that preserve rigid structure, especially if the SOA is sufficiently long, or through a much shorter path that does not preserve rigid structure, particularly if the SOA is short. Moreover, the critical SOA for the transition from rigid to nonrigid motion appears (a) to increase approximately linearly with the extent of the transformation, if there are no alternative paths with a competitive

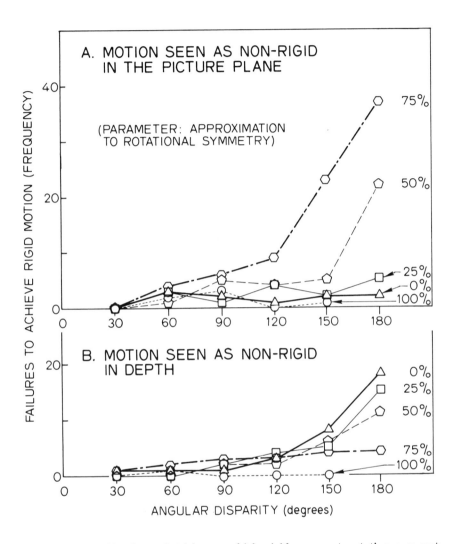

Figure 15.3 Number of trials on which rigid apparent rotation was not achieved, plotted separately for instances in which the nonrigid motion appeared to be in the picture plane (A) or in depth (B), as a function of angular disparity. (Again, each curve is for a different level of rotational symmetry.)

trade-off between directness and rigidity, and (b) to be elevated above this linear trend, if there are. Evidently, the time available between the microgenesis of structural information about each successively presented view, which is determined by the stimulus-onset asynchrony (SOA), is critical for the perceived rigidity of the intervening motion and, hence, of the object itself. This points, again, to the intimate connection between the perception of a shape and the perception of its spatial transformations (cf. Shepard, 1979, 1981).

Our results appear to implicate the operation of internalized rules of object conservation and least action. Having glimpsed two successive visual patterns, the brain attempts to interpret these as manifestations of one enduring object. To the extent that the two patterns differ, the brain strives to represent the intervening existence of the object, concretely, in the form of a spatial transformation (a) that preserves as much as possible of the rigid structure of the external object, and (b) that is the most direct or shortest such transformation. If such a transformation is found, its concrete instantiation satisfies a principle of least action subject to conservation of structural identity. Sometimes, however, a rigid transformation cannot be found—because the external object has in fact undergone a non-rigid deformation, or because insufficient time was available for the brain to construct a rigid transformation. In this case the brain necessarily accepts a weaker criterion of structural identity and, accordingly, instantiates the most direct nonrigid transformation compatible with that weaker criterion. Correspondingly, the object itself, although still perceived as one enduring object, appears as nonrigid, flexible, rubbery, hinged or jointed.

Geometrical aspects of path minimization. Our results are in good agreement with the quantitative predictions of a geometrical model by means of which one of us (Shepard, 1977, 1978a, 1979, 1981) has attempted to represent shortest paths of rigid transformation as geodesic trajectories in a curved "constraint manifold" and of nonrigid deformations as even shorter paths through a higher-dimensional "embedding space" (compare, particularly, the present Figure 15.2 with Figure 10.9 in Shepard, 1981). We hope to undertake a fuller consideration of that geometrical model and its relation to the results of the present and other experiments in a later report.

Here, we remark only that the notion of a shortest transformational path is not completely defined without specifying, further, the metric of the underlying space (or manifold) within which that path is constructed. That this issue is of empirical significance is most clearly illustrated by a study in which Foster (1975) investigated paths of apparent motion between two views of a simple object (a rectangle) differing by a translation as well as a rotation. The path of experienced motion generally was not the path in which the center of the object traversed a straight line while the object rotated about that (moving) center. Rather, the center of the object was generally seen to describe a curved path—in fact, a close approximation to the unique circular path by which the one view could be mapped into the other by a single rigid rotation of the entire two-dimensional plane about some fixed center, without any additional, translational component. Even when a nonrotational, translational component is introduced by the experimenter, then, the perceptual system seems to favor an interpretation in terms of a single rigid rotation (but one in which the center of rotation may have to be at some distance from the object) over an interpretation in terms of a combined translation plus rotation. As Foster (1975) notes, we can still suppose that the path of experienced motion tends to be a minimum path, but the metric with respect to which it is minimum may be the metric of the group of rigid rotations SO(3) rather than the metric of the familiar Euclidean space of the visual objects themselves.

Perhaps the brain has internalized the abstract geometrical principle that any rigid motion of the plane into itself can be described as a rotation about some center—with pure translations corresponding to the limiting case in which the center of rotation moves off to infinity. The same principle presumably underlies the phenomenon reported by Glass (1969), in which two identical random dot patterns when superimposed with a slight random misalignment give rise, in general, to the appearance of a kind of Moiré pattern of concentric circles We conjecture that the brain has also internalized the analogous principle for three-dimensional space; namely, that any rigid transformation can be described as a rotation together with a translation along the axis of rotation—i.e., a "screw displacement" (Coxeter, 1961; cf. Shepard, 1982; and Chapter 16). In agreement with this expectation, in other experiments on apparent motion, we have observed that when the two alternately presented views differ by a size scaling (dilatation) as well as a rotation, observers experience a rigid object advancing and receding in a helical or screw-like motion (see Bundesen, Larsen, & Farrell, 1981b; Shepard, 1981).

Conclusion. We believe that the Gestalt psychologists were correct in regarding the illusory impletion that occurs in apparent motion as particularly revealing of fundamental organizing principles of the perceptual system. We suggest, however, that neither they nor most subsequent investigators of apparent motion have fully appreciated (a) the extent to which these organizing principles represent an internalization of some of the most abstract geometrical constraints governing transformations in three-dimensional Euclidean space, and (b) the extent to which the perception of shape itself is inextricably related to, and perhaps even dependent upon, the representation of its possible transformations in space.

Postscript (added by Shepard, 1981)

Roughly, the geometrical representation of the alternative paths of motion described in this paper can be schematically illustrated as in Figure 15.4. When a partially symmetric object is alternately presented in two orientations differing by a large angle, a rigid motion tends to be experienced over the shortest rotational path (a, in the figure) or, rarely, over the longer rotational path (b). If the rate of alternation is too great, however, the motion "short-circuits" through the space in which the paths of rigid transformation are embedded. The resulting motion, along the more direct path (c), is experienced as a non-rigid rotation through a smaller angle and in the opposite direction from that of the preferred path (a). An accurate representation of this curved structure, which has in fact been recovered by multidimensional scaling (see Chapter 16, p. 318), requires a four-dimensional embedding space (see Shepard, 1979, 1981, 1982a). (Competing paths of apparent motion are now being manipulated more directly—see Shepard & Zare, 1981).

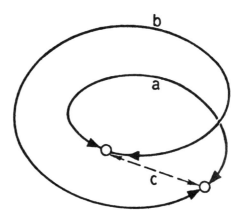

Figure 15.4 Abstract representation of alternative paths of apparent motion between two orientations of a partially symmetric object.

16 | Epilogue to Part III

Apparent Motion

The chapters of Part III have focused on studies of just one kind of apparent motion; namely, rigid rotation about a single axis passing through the object. Here, we consider the relation of this work both to the much earlier work on simple linear apparent motion and to contemporary findings concerning more general classes of transformations. We also outline some theoretical notions concerning the perceptual constraints that govern the selection of a transformational path, and bring the book to a close with a brief discussion of the relevance of such constraints for theories of human perception, thinking, and language.[1]

When two visual displays are presented in temporal alternation, the brain automatically strives to establish a connection between the two displays. If each display features a single object and if the rate of alternation is not too rapid, the brain interprets the two views as manifestations of the same object and instantiates this interpretation in the concrete form of a path of transformation between the views. The type of transformation experienced necessarily depends on the relation between the two views and, as we have seen, on the time available to effect the connection.

Types of Apparent Transformation

If the rate of alternation between the two displays is sufficiently slow, if the two objects displayed do not too closely approximate some symmetry, and if the two objects differ by no more than a shape-preserving similarity transformation in three-dimensional space, then the apparent motion tends to be experienced as a rigid motion. We can nevertheless distinguish cases in which the two views differ by a translation, a rotation, a dilatation (i.e., a uniform expansion or contraction), or some combination of these (as well, under certain conditions, as a reflection). Generally, the transformation is experienced as taking place over just one particular path at any one time. But for some pairs of views (such as those differing by a 180-degree rotation of the object) there are different alternative paths over which the motion may be experienced on different occasions (corresponding, for example, to rotations in opposite directions about the same axis).

If the two alternately displayed objects differ in intrinsic shape, however, and so cannot be mapped into each other by any similarity transformation in three-dimensional space, the two objects still tend to be perceived as a single object undergoing a transformation—but, necessarily, a nonrigid one. Depending on the relation between the two displays, the nonrigid motion may be perceived as a locally rigid, mechanical one in which parts of the object hinge, pivot, or slide with respect to each other; as a plastic deformation in which the object as a whole stretches, contracts, bends, or twists; or as some combination of mechanical motions and plastic deformations. Surprisingly disparate objects will be seen to turn into each other by some such transformation (see Kolers and Pomerantz, 1971). But, for any particular pair of alternately presented objects, if the rate of alternation is not too fast, the motion experienced tends to be one that preserves as much as possible of the structure of the object (Shepard, 1981).

Also, as we have seen (Chapters 13 and 15), even if the two objects differ by a rigid transformation, if the rate of alternation is increased, there may no longer be sufficient time for the brain to model that rigid transformation. In this case, a smaller but nonrigid transformation will tend to be experienced. Correspondingly, the object, which appeared rigid under slower rates of alternation, will appear rubbery, hinged, or jointed. At intermediate rates, the same alternating display may sometimes be seen as a large rigid motion or a smaller nonrigid one. Here too, then, the same physical stimulus can lead to perceptual experiences of quite distinct transformational paths.

Before turning to a consideration of the principles governing the selection among such alternative paths and, hence, the preservation of different kinds of structure in the object transformed, we consider the general relation between time and distance that seems to underlie such principles.

Relation Between Time and Distance

Korte's third law. The study of apparent motion began with the simplest case of translational motion between two successively presented visual spots differing only in spatial position (Exner, 1875). Wertheimer (1912/1961), who later carried out some of the earliest systematic studies, found that as the two successively presented spots were separated by larger spatial distances, the temporal separation had to be increased as well in order to maintain an optimum illusion of apparent motion of one spot between the two locations. Korte (1915), on the basis of more extensive parametric investigations of such phenomena of simple apparent motion, later formalized this principle in his "third law" of apparent motion, according to which the increase in optimum difference in time is essentially proportional to any increase in separation in space or, equivalently, that the critical time increases linearly with distance. Figure 16.1 presents in graphic form a replotting of the results reported by Corbin (1942) for such translational apparent motion. A linear function does indeed appear to offer a good approximation.

Nevertheless, there is not complete agreement, even today, concerning the general validity of Korte's law and/or the appropriate procedures for estimating the optimum difference in time corresponding to a given separation in space. Those approaching the phenomena of apparent motion from the tradition of sensory psychophysics, tend (a) to focus on proximal physical variables, such as the retinal separation, brightness, and duration of the two stimuli, and the brightness and duration of the interstimulus background, that most directly affect the peripheral neurophysiological response; (b) to study cases in which either the distance of separation or the amount of structure to be preserved is quite small and, hence, the corresponding times are relatively short; and, under these conditions, (c) to question the applicability of Korte's law. By contrast, we and our associates, in approaching the phenomena of apparent motion from the orientation of cognitive science, tend (a) to focus on informational variables concerning the structure and relations of the distal objects in three-dimensional space and the delays between onsets of the two presentations of visual information; (b) to study cases in which both the distance (or angle) between the objects and their structural complexities are quite large and, hence, the corresponding times are relatively long; and, under these circumstances, (c) to find a generally linear dependence of time on distance.

Phenomenal versus retinal measures of transformational distance. As was just implied, we find the most consistent linear relation when we define the separation between two alternately presented views in terms of the corresponding distance (or angle) between the distal objects as they exist (or are portrayed to exist) in three-dimensional space—not when we define this separation in terms of any distance (or angle) between two-dimensional retinal projections of those objects. Our demonstration of nearly equal critical times for pairs of objects differing by a rigid rotation in the picture plane or in depth (Chapter 13) established this for apparent rotational motion, just as Ogasawara's (1936), Corbin's (1942), and Attneave and

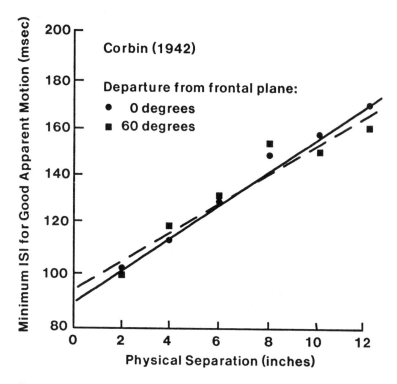

Figure 16.1 Minimum interstimulus interval for good apparent motion between two dots as a function of their physical separation on the frontal plane or on a plane tipped 60° back in depth (plotted from data reported by Corbin, 1942).

Block's (1973) earlier demonstrations of similar critical times for rectilinear motions in the picture plane and in depth established it for apparent translational motion.

Figure 16.1 is representative of these earlier results. The plotted circles and fitted solid line are based on Corbin's data for visual spots separated in the picture plane (i.e., along a line normal to the line of sight), while the plotted triangles and fitted dashed line are based on Corbin's data for visual spots separated along a line tipped 60° out of the picture plane. The critical times appear to be determined by physical distance in three-dimensional space in both cases, and not by projected distance on the two-dimensional retina. For the same physical separation, retinal distance would be only half as large for spots separated along the line inclined at 60° to the picture plane. Again, this result may hold only for the higher-level impletion of rigid motion (so-called "beta" movement), and not for impletion over very short paths (so-called "phi" movement), which is evidently mediated by more local sensory mechanisms (see Boring, 1942; Braddick, 1974; Larsen, Farrell, & Bundesen, 1981).

Global versus local measures of transformational distance. The evidence that apparent motion is generated at a relatively deep level of the perceptual system—i.e., a level in which the internal representations have a closer relation to the external objects that they represent than to the retinal images from which they most directly derive—comes not only from the comparison between motion in the picture plane and motion in depth. Such evidence comes also from a comparison of rotational and translational motion, even when both types of motion are confined to the picture plane. Whereas any relatively peripheral analysis of motion in the visual input would be expected to depend on disparities of time and distance at the retinal level, we consistently find that in the case of alternately presented objects differing by a rotation (even a rotation confined to the picture plane), it is the angular disparity between the two views of the object as a whole that is the critical variable rather than the corresponding linear disparities in each local region of the retinal projection. (For a somewhat different view, see Ullman, 1979).

As part of her Stanford doctoral dissertation, Joyce Farrell (1981) undertook a direct comparision of the relative roles of the angular difference in the orientations of two views of an object as a whole and the linear differences in the positions of corresponding local parts of the two views. She determined how the minimum stimulus-onset asynchrony (SOA) for apparent rigid motion between two alternately presented asymmetric geometrical figures differing only in planar orientation depended on both (a) the angular difference between those figures and (b) the visual angle subtended by each. The two figures presented in alternation were always both of the same size on any one trial but, on different trials, varied together by an overall linear scale-size factor of 1, 2, 3, or 4. Independently, on any one trial the two planar stimuli differed in picture-plane orientation by an angle of 30, 60, 90, or 120 degrees.

In agreement with the earlier results on apparent rotational motion, described in Chapters 13 and 15, the minimum SOA yielding rigid apparent motion increased linearly with angular difference (by about 125 msec over the 90-degree range), and did so for all four sizes of stimuli. Best-fitting linear functions accounted for 99% of the variance of the mean critical SOAs, and the residual deviations from linearity were not statistically significant. The intercepts of the linear functions did systematically increase with size of the figures (by about 50 msec over the four-fold range of size). But there was no significant difference between these four linear functions in slope. Perhaps more time was needed to form an internal representation of each larger figure. But, once such a representation was formed, the time needed to implete the rigid transformation evidently depended only on the angular difference in orientations of the two objects treated globally—not on the linear distance that any one local part of the object must traverse in such a transformation, which would be four times greater for the largest than for the smallest figures.

Extension to other rigid transformations. Recent studies of apparent motion carried out by our associates Bundesen, Farrell, and Larsen have verified that the linear dependence of critical time (SOA) on the extent of the transformation (Korte's third law)—in addition to holding for translations and rotations, as just discussed—holds for size scalings and combinations of size scalings and rotations (Bundesen, Larsen, & Farrell, 1981b) as well as for combinations of translations and rotations (Farrell, 1981). Size scalings, incidentally, are generally perceived as rigid translations in depth, and size scalings combined with rotation as rigid helical or screw-like motions in depth (a twisting advance and recession). The evidence so far suggests that the critical SOA for such a combined motion is an additive combination of the critical SOA's of the two component motions, such as expansion and rotation (Bundesen, et al., 1981b). We return to a consideration of such combined motions in discussing "minimization of transformational path" in a subsequent section.

Basis of the linear dependence of critical time on transformational distance. There is reason to believe that the rates of mental transformation inferred from the slopes of the functions relating critical times to angular differences in our studies both of mental rotation (Part I) and of apparent motion (Part III) reflect limiting rates of the underlying informational flow rather than on acquired knowledge of the rates at which physical objects actually rotate in the three-dimensional world. Although there is evidence that observers can extrapolate a presented motion, whether linear (Michotte, 1955; Rosenbaum, 1975) or rotational (Cooper & Vallone, 1979), during a short period of occultation, the experiments that we have been describing in this book have measured the *minimum* time needed to implete or to traverse the path corresponding to a rigid transformation. They have not been concerned with the ability of observers to extrapolate a motion presented at some experimentally fixed, slower rate. Of course, the minimum times that we have reported here depend on the particular path that the internally represented transformation takes and, accordingly, on whether the object is represented as rigid or nonrigid during its transformation. But, over any one such path, the critical time seems to be determined by something like a limiting rate of propagation, computation, or iterative adjustment in a complex neural network (see Shepard, 1981).

It also appears that this limiting rate is much greater in the more perceptual and automatic case of apparent motion, in which the internal process is being externally driven (and in which the observer is not required to discriminate matching from non-matching end states), than in the more intellectual and effortful case of mental rotation, in which the transformational process must be internally generated (and must preserve the detailed structure of the object all along the way in order to permit an ensuing judgment of match or mismatch). Despite the marked differences in overall level of critical times estimated from the more automatic apparent motion and the more effortful imaginal transformation, the striking similarity in the patterns of critical times seems to us to support our intro-spections that the same transformational paths are traversed in the two cases.

It would probably be a mistake to think of the mental processes in either type of task as concrete simulations of physical processes in which such inertial concepts as mass and momentum play a major role. In none of the studies of mental rotation or apparent motion have we seen evidence of the kind of acceleration, deceleration, or overshoot that would be expected if an internal analogue of angular momentum were operative. The marked linearity of the obtained functions points, instead, to a constant limiting rate on an essentially inertialess process.

Indeed, in the case of apparent motion, the alternating presenta-tion of a vertical and horizontal bar (Chapter 14) almost always yields the perception of a bar that rotates from vertical to horizontal and then back, in the reverse direction, to vertical. Only with great effort can one sometimes experience the bar as continuing to rotate in the same direction back to vertical. It is as if the transit through one quadrant has potentiated the path through that particular quadrant—even for a passage over that path in the reverse direction—in preference to a passage in the name direction over a new path through a different quadrant. As we indicate in a following section on "minimization of path," the empirical results suggest that the limiting constraints on apparent and imagined transformations reflect an internalization of very abstract, geometrical constraints governing objects in three-dimensional Euclidean space more than the concrete physical constraints governing some particular physical object with its particular mass, moment of inertia, and so on.

Connection Between the Representation of Objects and of Their Transformations

Influence of the representation of an object's transformations on the representation of the object itself. The phenomenon of apparent motion reveals an intimate connection between the transformational path that is mentally traversed and the representation of the object transformed. Thus, when the rate of alternation is increased until a rigid transformation can no longer be impleted, the object itself comes to appear flexible, rubbery, hinged, or jointed.

The perceived structure of an object similarly depends on the perception of its motion in the phenomenon of kinetic depth, in which a rotating three-dimensional configuration of random points is experienced as a rigid system even when only its nonrigid two-dimensional projection is presented (Braunstein, 1976; Green, 1961; Wallach & O'Connell, 1953). Indeed, such a system of moving points, when presented against a background of other (e.g., stationary) points, maintains its status as a distinct visual object only by virtue of the "common fate" of its coherent motion; upon cessation of that motion, the subset of previously moving points loses its identity as figure and rapidly fades back into the ground of remaining points.

It may even be that the perception of a stationary object depends on the representation of its self-similarity under its various possible rigid transformations (Shepard, 1981). Thus a rectangle might be recognized as such in part on the basis of its self-identity under 180° rotation, and its appreciable self-similarity under 90° rotation and under rectilinear translation along two orthogonal directions. The possible importance of transformations in the perception of visual objects has in fact long been suggested, for example, by Cassirer's (1944) early discussions of the role of transformational groups in perception; Garner's (1974b) definition of the goodness of a figure in terms of the size of the class of figures that are equivalent to it under rigid spatial transformations such as reflections and rotations; and Gibson's (1966) emphasis on the free mobility of the perceiver and on the correlated transformations induced in the optic array (Gibson, 1977). The idea receives support, also, from Franks and Bransford's (1971) demonstrations of the psychological effectiveness of transformationally defined distance between stimuli; from the already noted demonstrations of kinetic depth; and from such more or less related demonstrations of "event perception" as those of Johansson (1950, 1976), Cutting, Proffitt, and Kozlowski (1978), and Shaw and Pittenger (1977).

Evolutionary considerations also support such a view (Shepard,

1981). For, whereas an object possesses virtually unlimited degrees of freedom of shape (as well as of texture and coloration), its global movements are restricted to just three degrees of freedom of location and three of orientation. Moreover, although the objects relevant to organisms at different levels of the evolutionary tree differ widely in shape and other properties, their global movements are, and always have been, describable in terms of the same six dimensions of position. If the most ubiquitous and simply described (that is, low-dimensional) constraints in the world are the ones that have been most deeply internalized during evolutionary history, then the representation of spatial transformations may have come to serve as the basis for representing the complexities of the intrinsic shapes of objects, rather than the other way around.

Certainly, an essential part of the experience of any object seems to be a clear, if unarticulated, recognition of the possible spatial perturbations of that object—precisely the three degrees of freedom of location (movements left or right, up or down, nearer or farther) and three of orientation (attitude, pitch, and yaw). Moreover, these seem to be immediately and fully given as part of the experience of an object in space, even when the identity of the object and the representation of its shape are not fully established. We may know how to avoid an object, brush it aside, grasp it, or save it from tipping over, before we even know what the object is (Shepard, 1981).

Influence of the representation of an object on the representation of its transformations. The influence between the representation of objects and of their transformations evidently operates in both directions. As part of an as yet unpublished experiment on apparent motion, Shepard and Koto alternately exposed the two patterns in Figure 16.2A. Observers often reported seeing the black square at the top as stationary and the two black squares at the bottom as sliding back and forth as a rectangular unit. When, however, a single connecting square was also blackened as shown in Figure 16.2B, observers invariably reported seeing the resulting set of four black squares as a rigid L-shaped unit. Preservation of the rigidity of this object required that the two black squares at the bottom no longer be seen as sliding back and forth. Instead, the entire structure was now seen as rigidly rotating 180° out into depth about the axis defined by the common vertical column of three black squares.

Similarly in another as yet unpublished experiment, when Shepard and Judd alternately presented one of Cooper's (1975) random polygons (such as the one shown in Figure 16.3A) and the mirror image of that polygon (B), observers reported seeing the polygon flip 180° around a vertical axis, in depth. Moreover, when the original polygon was alternated with the same polygon compressed by 50% in

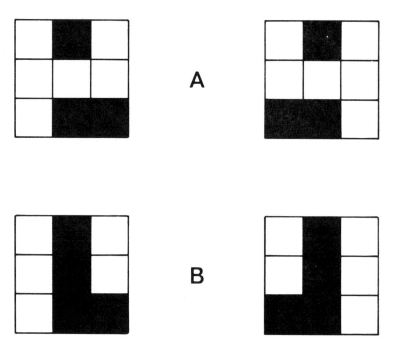

Figure 16.2 Two pairs of alternately presented grid patterns from an experiment on apparent motion by Shepard and Koto (reproduced from Shepard, 1981).

the horizontal direction (C), observers reported seeing the polygon undergo a rigid (presumably 60°) rotation into depth rather than seeing it undergo a nonrigid compression within the picture plane. Most dramatic was the limiting case: When the polygon was alternated with nothing more than a vertical line segment of the same vertical extent (D), observers reported seeing the polygon as rigidly rotating 90° in depth between the completely flat and directly edge-on orientation. In all these cases, moreover, the critical onset-onset times were in approximate agreement with times for apparent rotation of the same polygon through corresponding angles confined to the picture plane.

The angularity of these random polygons, as well as those described in Chapter 15, evidently favored the interpretation of the figures as rigid objects and, thence, the perceptual experience of their rigid rotation. Curved free forms are more apt to appear three-dimensional (see Shepard & Cermak, 1973). In exploratory experiments, subjects were more likely to see such curved forms as moving in depth; hence they were less able to achieve or to maintain the illusion of a strictly rigid rotation over large angles in the picture plane. Furthermore, much as some figures can be seen as two- or three-dimensional objects, some can be interpreted as either rigid or deformable objects. An ellipse, for example, can be seen as a foreshortened circle or as a deformable rubber band or three-dimensional balloon.

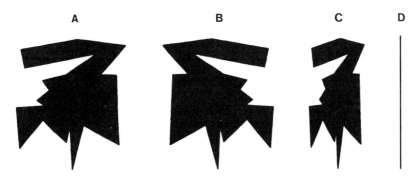

Figure 16.3 One of Cooper's (1973) random polygons (A), and three other stimuli (B, C, D) presented in alternation with it in exploratory experiments by Shepard and Judd.

Conservation of Object Structure

Preference for maintenance of rigid shape. The evidence suggests that under suitable conditions, the perceptual system will represent the shape of an object as rigid by the impletion of a trajectory of rigid transformation between two successive views. This one principle will explain (a) why a change in size of a two-dimensional projection tends to be perceived, instead, as a change in the distance of the object, (b) why a mirror reversal or a compression tends to be perceived as a rotation in depth, and (c) why a large rigid rotation of a nearly symmetric object (Chapter 15) may still be experienced in preference to a much smaller but nonrigid transformation.

Hierarchy of criteria of object identity. When the rate of alternation between the two views is sufficiently increased, however, the brain does not have time during each cycle to complete the connecting path corresponding to the required rigid transformation. In this case, the identity of the two successively displayed objects can no longer be concretely instantiated in the strongest, and therefore most preferred, form of a complete identity of structure. Instead, because most objects that do not conserve strictly rigid structure conserve semirigid structure, because most objects that do not conserve even semirigid structure at least conserve volume, number, or some other general property, the brain takes recourse to successively weaker stations in a hierarchy of criteria of object identity. It relinquishes only in extremity the root hypothesis that the two objects, however transmogrified, are nevertheless the same object. More stringent criteria of object identity thus correspond both to the preservation of more structure in the object and, hence, to the greater restriction on the paths of possible transformation.

The parametric investigation of apparent motion seems capable of providing information about the formation as well as the transformation of internal representations. The slower rate of alternation needed to produce the illusion of a rigid transformation stems from two sources: (1) The impletion of path for a rigid transformation is longer than the path for a nonrigid one because it is subject to more constraints. (2) The microgenesis of the perception of an object as rigid requires the elaboration of the deep structure of the object at a more exacting level in the hierarchy of criteria of object identity. At basis, however, these two sources may be the same (see Shepard, 1981).

Minimization of Transformational Path

Multistability of path impletion. Apparent motion, like the perception of a static object such as the reversible Necker cube (Attneave, 1971), is often multistable. The identical stimulus display can be very differently experienced, for example, as an object rigidly rotating 180° clockwise, rigidly rotating 180° counterclockwise, or (if the object has an approximation to some symmetry) nonrigidly rotating through some smaller angle or flipping in depth. Only one of such alternative transformational paths is experienced on any one occasion, and each is too distinct, phenomenally, to be confused with another.

The multistability reveals the operation of alternative interpretive processes. Moreover, these interpretive processes evidently go on at a level that is far removed from the two-dimensional sensory array and at a level that is concerned, rather, with the internal modeling of distal objects in the external world. This is indicated by the fact that the relevant variables are those pertaining to distances and angles in three-dimensional space more than to distances and angles on the retina. It is also indicated by some of the highly constructive transformational paths that are sometimes unexpectedly experienced.

An instructive example arose in the course of exploratory work leading to the experiment by Robins and Shepard (Chapter 14). On one occasion one of us (RNS) was experiencing the bar as rotating back and forth between the north-east and south-west quadrants, as illustrated in Figure 16.4A. Failing in a voluntary effort to achieve a shift in perceived motion to the other two quadrants (north-west and south-east), the observer covered the lower right half of the field with a blank card on the assumption that when all that remained visible was a half of the former bar alternately projecting upwards and then to the left, those two half-bars would be perceptually identified with each other and hence the motion would be seen in the desired quadrant, as indicated in B. To our astonishment, however, the motion continued to be experienced as before with one end of the complete bar apparently going behind the card as the previously obscured other end of the complete bar apparently emerged from behind the card—as diagrammed in C. Phenomena of this sort point to the important role of high level interpretive processes and seem to be difficult to explain on the basis of currently available sensory-neural models for apparent motion.

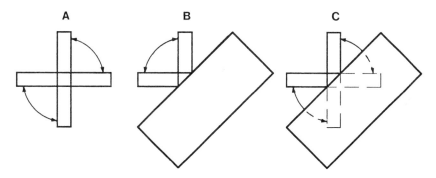

Figure 16.4 Alternating vertical and horizontal bars used by Robins and Shepard (A), and two possible kinds of apparent motion between them following occlusion of part of the display (B and C).

Towards a principle of least action. The existence of alternative transformational paths raises the question of the principles governing the likelihood that any one particular path will be impleted. Although different paths may be traversed on different occasions, the experiments we have been reporting suggest that when there is time to traverse a path that preserves rigid structure, the path of this sort that is in some sense the shortest, simplest, or most direct will generally be preferred. Thus, if two alternately presented objects differ by an angle of 140° in the picture plane, the apparent rotation will generally be seen to take place through that angle rather than through the 220° angle in the opposite direction. The same tendency to traverse the shortest structure-preserving path also emerged in our studies of mental rotation (Part I and, especially, Chapter 3).

The already noted fact that a combination of a change in scale and a rotation is experienced as a rigid helical motion of twisting advance and recession provides further support for a least-path impletion. In fact, according to a theorem in geometry (see Coxeter, 1961, pp. 101, 321) any two positions of a rigid object in three-dimensional Euclidean

space can be regarded as differing by such a "screw displacement"—
that is, by a combination of a rotation together with a translation
along the axis of the rotation. In order to formulate a principle of
least action or minimum path, however, we have first to specify the
metric with respect to which the path is minimized.

An experiment by Foster (1975) on the apparent motion that is
experienced between two successively presented positions of a
rectangular bar differing by a combined translation and rotation in
the picture plane illustrates this point with particular clarity. One
might at first guess that the experienced motion between two such
positions of the bar as shown in Figure 16.5 would correspond to
one in which the center of gravity of the bar moves along a straight
line between the two positions while the bar itself rotates (through
the necessary angle) around this rectilinearly moving center, as
illustrated in A. However, an adjustable probe bar that observers
positioned to coincide with the position of the bar during its apparent
flight generally fell, instead, on a curved path, as illustrated in B.
This curved path seemed in fact to approximate the unique circular
trajectory whereby the one rectangle could be mapped into the
other by a single rigid rotation about some fixed point in the plane,
without any additional translation.

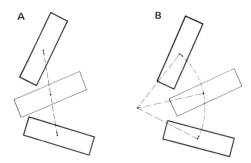

Figure 16.5 Two possible paths of apparent motion (A and B) between
presentations of a rectangle in two positions (shown in heavy outline)
differing in location and orientation (as in the experiment by Foster,
1975).

Here, again, is evidence that the internalized constraints revealed
by the brain's perceptual impletions reflect rather abstract and
general geometrical constraints governing motions in Euclidean
space rather than the more concrete and specific constraints characterizing particular physical or inertial events. The perceptually
completed motion is not the one in which the center of gravity of the
object traverses a shortest path in terms of the metric of physical
space itself, and in which a second, rotational transformation must
therefore be superimposed on that translational displacement. Rather,

the perceptually impleted motion is the simpler single rigid rotation about some center in the underlying (two-dimensional) space—even though the center of the object will therefore be seen to traverse a curved path.

That such a center of rigid rotation always exists follows from the two-dimensional specialization of the geometrical theorem noted before. Just as any rigid displacement in three-dimensional Euclidean space can be regarded as a helical motion (Coxeter, 1961), any rigid displacement in the plane can be regarded as circular motion, with the limiting case of a pure translation approached as the center of rotation moves off to a point at infinity. This is why the superimposition on itself of a displaced random dot pattern generally yields a Moiré pattern of concentric circles (Glass, 1969). In both the case of the static display described by Glass (1969) and the case of the dynamic display investigated by Foster (1975) the brain seems to be quick to pick up the fixed point of the implied simple rigid rotation that relates the two simultaneously or successively displayed visual configurations. We conjecture that the brain would similarly pick up the fixed axis of the implied screw displacement in the corresponding three-dimensional analogues.

In more abstract and general terms, the metric with respect to which the path of impleted motion is minimized is not the metric of distances between positions of objects (e.g., in the case considered, of rectangular bars), which is the standard Riemannian metric on the sphere S^2 (Foster, 1975; Shepard, 1977, 1979, 1981). Instead, evidently, it is a bi-invariant Riemannian metric on the group of rigid motions of S^2, that is, the group SO(3) (see Foster, 1975, 1978).

Trade-off between translation and rotation. Unfortunately, the notion that the perceptual system always reduces a rigid planar motion of an object to a simple rotation becomes implausible as the required center of rotation becomes far removed from the object. This implausibility does not arise in the task, used by Foster (1975), in which the dependent variable is the path of experienced motion as indicated by the observer's positioning of a movable marker or probe. Rather, it arises in the task, used by Farrell and Shepard (Chapter 15), in which the dependent variable is the minimum time required for the observer to experience the traversal of that path. For, whereas the results of Farrell and Shepard (1981), Shepard and Judd, and, particularly, Farrell (1981) have indicated that the critical independent variable in the case of a rotation is angular difference rather than linear distance, a purely translational disparity does entail an increase in critical time (see, again, Figure 16.1) even though the angular difference (with the center of rotation at infinity in this case) is always zero.

Farrell has been investigating how the critical time in apparent motion changes as both angle of rotation and distance of the center of rotation from the object are varied independently. So far, the chronometric results indicate that the rotational and translational components combine additively. Hence, the perceptual system evidently treats the transformation as a pure rotation only when the center of rotation is sufficiently close to the object transformed. Presumably, as the center of rotation becomes sufficiently distant, the critical times must approach what would be obtained for a pure translation. As of this writing, a metric capable of specifying length of transformational path for the purposes both of determining the shortest path and the time to traverse that path has yet to be fully characterized.

Trade-off between path minimization and conservation of structure. As the experiment by Farrell and Shepard demonstrates (Chapter 15), the abstract principle that a minimum path is impleted subject to conservation of the rigid structure of the object can hold, anyway, only when sufficient time is allowed to implete that path and when there is not a competing path that is both (a) much shorter and (b) still preserves most (though not all) of the structure of the object. It may still prove possible to account for the selection of transformational paths in general by introducing a generalized metric in which distances are decomposable into two parts: a distance corresponding to a rigid transformation (e.g., a rotation), and a distance corresponding to a nonrigid transformation (e.g., a deformation).

One attempt in this direction shows some promise (Shepard, 1981). The space of possible orientations of a rigid object is represented by a closed, unbounded manifold that is topologically equivalent to projective space. And the various symmetries and approximations to symmetry of the object are represented by deformations of this manifold in a higher-dimensional embedding space. Rigid rotations correspond to least-path (geodesic) trajectories within the manifold while nonrigid transformations correspond to paths cutting directly through the embedding space. A general transformation, then, can be analyzed into a rigid component (its projection onto the lower-dimensional manifold) and a nonrigid component (orthogonal to that manifold).

As noted by Farrell and Shepard (Chapter 15), their chronometric results were consistent with the pattern anticipated on the basis of this geometrical model. Moreover, for the representations of the planar orientations of partially symmetric polygons (Figure 1 of Chapter 15), additional (as yet unpublished) chronometric data, subsequently collected by Farrell and Shepard, when analyzed by a variety of multidimensional scaling (INDSCAL of Carroll & Chang, 1970), yielded exactly the double-wound closed curve on the surface of a torus in four dimensions required by that model.

It may yet be that the principle of least action, which has evolved from its early formulation by Maupertuis into a possible foundation for the whole of modern physics (as in the formalisms of Schwinger and Tomanaga—see Dyson, 1980) will offer a unifying principle for perception as well.

Apparent Motion in Auditory Pitch

Types of transformations in the auditory domain. In the interest of generality, it is perhaps worth noting that there are close parallels between the kinds of transformations that we have been considering in the visual domain and transformations that can be mentally carried out or perceptually experienced in the auditory domain. On first consideration, the closest auditory analogue of the visual phenomena of mental rotation and apparent motion might seem to be those in which the auditory stimuli to be compared or to be alternately presented differ in their positions in three-dimensional physical space.

For example, one of the two stimuli might consist of a "spatial chord" (Julesz & Levitt, 1966) in which two distinct components (e.g., a whistle and a buzz) originate at 90° from each other in the horizontal plane (with, say, the whistle directly ahead and the buzz to the right), while the other might consist of that same spatial chord rotated through some angle in the horizontal plane (with, for example, the whistle now to the right and the buzz directly behind). In experiments quite analogous to the visual experiments on mental rotation by Cooper and Shepard (e.g., Chapters 4 and 5), we might determine the time to prepare for or to identify normal versus reflected spatial chords as a function of their angular departure from each other or from an originally learned orientation. And, in experiments quite analogous to the visual experiments on apparent motion (e.g., Chapters 13 and 15), we might determine the fastest rate of alternation between two such relatively rotated chords for which the experience is of a single such chord undergoing a structure-preserving shift in orientation.

More interesting, though, might be a further extension in which the space in which the transformation takes place, rather than being this three-dimensional physical space, is the more abstract space of pitch. Indeed, there are reasons to believe that for the auditory modality, the continuum of pitch rather than the continuum of position in physical space may afford the closer analogue of position in visual space. For, in the case of audition, pitch space, more than physical space, is in a well-defined sense "indispensable" (Kubovy, 1981) and form-bearing or "morphophoric" (Attneave & Olson, 1971)—particularly when interpreted musically (Attneave & Olson, 1971; Shepard, 1981, 1982b; Krumhansl & Shepard, 1979). One might nevertheless object that pitch space is less interesting because it is merely one-dimensional and so precludes many important transformations such as rotations. The premise on which this objection is based turns out, however, to be incorrect (see Balzano, 1981; Shepard, 1964, in press; and the following section).

Multistability of path impletion. The phenomenon of apparent motion in auditory pitch might at first seem much weaker than the phenomenon of apparent motion in visual space or, indeed, it might seem nonexistent. Certainly, an alternation between two tones differing in pitch is not mistaken for a continuous up-and-down glissando. However, we suggest that the essential characteristic of an apparent motion be that it demonstrably takes place over a well-defined path—not that it cannot be discriminated from a real motion over that path (though such a failure of discrimination may also occur under some circumstances). Thus we experience the visual alternation between a vertical and horizontal bar as a motion either through the northeast and southwest or through the northwest and southeast quadrants, and the two experiences are distinctly different (Chapter 14). It is the discriminability of the motions over these two paths from each other and the clear identification of each with the corresponding real motion that forces us to recognize the occurrence of an apparent motion over one path or the other. An apparent motion can be experienced as corresponding to a particular real motion in this way without being indiscriminable from that real motion.

But, because we think of pitch as being a unidimensional continuum, we take it for granted that an alternation between two tones differing in pitch is just an alternation between lower and higher on that one dimension. Because there seems to be no alternative to the path of this shift, perhaps, we tend to be unaware that a motion was actually impleted over this path. That there was nevertheless such a motion becomes clear as soon as we provide an alternative path, as when the tones are the computer-generated "circular" tones described by Shepard (1964). When two such tones a half octave apart are sounded in succession, the second tone is heard as shifting through the musical interval of a tritone—but sometimes upward and sometimes downward in pitch. Because the two experienced shifts are subjectively distinct, each such shift clearly occurs over a definite path (one way or the other around the "chroma circle").

Auditory analogue of Korte's third law. Additional evidence for a passage over such a connecting path can be found in a dependence between time and distance that is analogous to Korte's third law for visual apparent motion. If two tones separated by a particular musical interval (of less than a half octave, say) are played in slow alternation, one hears a melody consisting of a single tone going up and down in pitch. When the rate of alternation is sufficiently increased, however, there comes a point at which the "illusion" of a single tone going up and down is suddenly replaced by the experience of two separate tones (one higher and one lower) going on and off independently. Moreover the further apart the two tones are in pitch, the sooner does the illusion of motion (or melody) break down with increase in rate of alternation (cf. Bregman, 1981; Jones, 1976; Shepard, 1981). The transition from the experience of a single stimulus moving back and forth along a path to the experience of two stimuli going on and off independently appears to be governed by the relation between time and distance in essentially the same way for tones separated in pitch as for visual spots separated in physical space.

In the auditory case, moreover, the governing relation between time and distance evidently underlies a variety of phenomena, including "melodic fission and fusion" or "auditory stream segregation" (see Bregman & Campbell, 1971; Dowling, 1973; McAdams & Bregman, 1979; van Noorden, 1975) and the "trill threshold" (Miller & Heise, 1950) in the perception of music, and related phenomena in the perception of speech (Cole & Scott, 1973; Dorman, Cutting, & Raphael, 1975; Lackner & Goldstein, 1974).

The implied structure of pitch space. Because pitch, when interpreted musically, is not a simple rectilinear dimension of "pitch height" but contains demonstrable circular components of tone chroma and the cycle of fifths (Shepard, 1982b), musical objects such as melodies and chords, just as visual objects, are subject to rigid transformations of rotation as well as rectilinear translation (or transposition) in pitch. Indeed, a multidimensional analysis of Krumhansl and Shepard's (1979) data on relationships among tones in a musical context (using, again, the INDSCAL method of Carroll and Chang, 1970) has yielded a representation of musical tones as a double (helical) curve wrapped around the same four-dimensional torus underlying the double curve obtained from a similar analysis (already described) of chronometric data for Farrell and Shepard's (1981) visual objects differing in planar orientation. That similar abstract geometrical structures are implicitly contained in data on the perception of visual shapes and the perception of musical tones is a consequence of the rotational transformations and symmetries that we presume to underlie the perceived relations among the objects in both domains alike.

Path Impletion in Thinking and Language

Thinking and problem solving. In closing, we return to the possibility, raised in the introduction (Chapter 1), that the constraints that have evolved in the perceptual system as an internal reflection of the most pervasive, enduring, and (often) abstract constraints in the external world have subsequently become to some extent liberated from the preemptive control of sensory input. The wisdom about the world and, particularly, about space and spatial transformations that is embodied in these constraints may thus have become available for the internal modelling of hypothetical situations, responses to these, and probable outcomes. If so, the hypothesized principles of conservation of structure and minimization of path would generally serve to ensure two desirable qualities of problem solving and thought; respectively, realism and efficiency.

Language and comprehension. According to this viewpoint, the purely linguistic apparatus, though in some ways still more abstract and versatile, if forced to operate without the benefit of the powerful constraints incorporated in the perceptual system, would fail to deal effectively with the physical realities of this particular world. The language system is of course of enormous value—particularly, in the present context, for the establishment of abstract goals and for translating the results of the analog simulation of possible paths to such goals into an externalizable and communicable form. However, the conceptual-linguistic system may itself have evolved as an abstract extension of the spatial-perceptual system, and may at some deep level reveal the perceptual-spatial character of its origin (cf. Clark, 1973; Miller & Johnson-Laird, 1976; Shepard, 1981). In the words of the linguist Jackendoff (1976, p. 149), insight into the semantics of natural language is to be found "in the study of the innate conceptions of the physical world and in the way in which conceptual structures generalize to ever wider, more abstract domains."

So, some consideration should perhaps be devoted to the psycholinguistic ramifications of the notion that the mental construction of connecting paths that we have so much emphasized here may play a fundamental role in thinking and comprehension, as well as in perception (Shepard, 1981). The linguists Bennett (1974), Gruber (1967), and Jackendoff (1978) have explicitly suggested that the comprehension of sentences may sometimes require the implicit impletion of a mental path. Thus, in a comparison of the two verbs "look" and "see", Gruber found compelling linguistic reasons to take "a sentence such as 'John sees a cat' to be a metaphorical extension of 'John goes to a cat'." And Bennett explicitly argued that a mental path must be constructed in order to understand such a sentence as "The post office is over the hill". For, here, the preposition "over" is not understood as a relation in which one of the two objects mentioned is literally above the other in a physical space (as it might be in "The helicopter is over the hill"); it is strictly only the implied connecting path between the interlocutors and the post office that has a spatially superior relationship to the hill.

Perhaps the most ambitious and promising attempt to explain the entire range of linguistic phenomena on the basis of spatial ideas including, particularly, mental paths is to be found in the recent development by Langacker and his followers of what they call "space grammar" (Langacker, 1979a, 1980, 1981). This system, in which such spatial notions as "landmarks," "trajectors," and "images" play a central role, appears to account for an impressive variety of phenomena in a number of languages, including English (Brugman, 1981; Langacker, 1979b, 1980; Lindner, 1981), Spanish (Tuggy, 1981), Cora (Casad, 1981), and other, Uto-Aztecan languages (Langacker, 1981).

Close in spirit to these various linguistic observations are experiments in which the comprehension of sentences appears to require an implicit spatial transformation. The following example is taken from Black, Turner, and Bower's (1977) study of spatial reference points in comprehension. For each of the initial statements labeled A, the continuation B1 is given from a spatially consistent point of view and, so, is more easily and accurately comprehended or remembered than the continuation B2, which is given from a spatially shifted point of view:

A.   Terry finished working in the yard
B1. and *went* into the house.
B2. and *came* into the house.

A.   Fred was just sitting down
B1. when his dog *brought* him his slippers.
B2. when his dog *took* him his slippers.

This sort of paradigm could readily be extended to cases involving other spatial transformations. And comprehension time, as well as accuracy, might be found to reflect the extent or complexity of the implicit transformations. One of us (RNS), has begun to look at comprehension times for sequences (A-B) constructed from such sentences as the following:

A1. The dog chased the goat.
A2. The dog faced the goat.
B1. The goat kicked the dog.
B2. The goat butted the dog.

The sequences A1-B1 and A2-B2 are consistent and do not require a spatial transformation for comprehension, while the sequences A1-B2 and A2-B1 appear to require an additional 180° rotation.

Mental rotation may also play a role in the comprehension of other types of sentences. To elaborate on an example suggested by

Clark (1973), the statement "There is a fly above her knee" can be ambiguous if the person referred to is not in the canonical upright position but, say, is lying flat upon the beach. The fly can then be interpreted as hovering in the air "above" the knee with respect to the global coordinate framework of the external world (as in the example of the helicopter above the hill), or it can be interpreted as crawling on the leg "above" the knee with respect to the very different local coordinate framework of the recumbent person or even of her possibly upraised leg. The latter interpretation may, however, require a mental rotation between the canonical and the currently appropriate coordinate systems.

Concluding remark. The view of the nature and origin of the human mind that seems to be emerging from the work presented in this book resembles that of the empiricist philosophers mentioned in the introduction in this one respect: It looks to what comes into the mind from outside (i.e., from the world) as the ultimate source of knowledge and wisdom. However, the view to which we are led differs from the traditional empiricist view in two fundamental respects: First, it sees that a major part of this knowledge has been internalized through biological evolution and so, for each individual, is pre-wired rather than acquired. And, second, it sees that this innate portion of each individual's wisdom about the world—unlike the knowledge about concrete, specific objects and events, which presumably has to be learned through individual experience—reflects very abstract and general constraints governing, for example, the conservation, projection, and transformation of objects in three-dimensional Euclidean space.

It is of course possible that the internal constraints underlying some mental capacities, such as that for language, do not derive from anything outside the mind itself—and not, in particular, from anything in the external world. Such rules, it seems, would be essentially arbitrary. Faced with this alternative, we prefer to continue our search for the ways in which the mind has internalized structure that pre-existed in the world. The study of mental images and their transformations seems to us to have provided a reasonable starting point.

References

Anderson, J. R. 1978. Arguments concerning representations for mental imagery. *Psychological Review*, 1978, *85*, 249-277.

Anstis, S. M. 1978. Apparent movement. In R. Held, H. W. Leibowitz, & H-L Teuber, eds., *Handbook of sensory physiology*, Vol. VIII, pp. 655-673. Berlin: Springer-Verlag, 1978.

Attneave, F. 1957. Physical determinants of the judged complexity of shapes. *Journal of Experimental Psychology*, 1957, *53*, 221-227.

Attneave, F. 1971. Multistability in perception. *Scientific American*, 1971, *225*, 62-71.

Attneave, F. 1974a. Apparent movement and the what-where connection. *Psychologia*, 1974, *17*, 108-120.

Attneave, F. 1974b. How do you know? *American Psychologist*, 1974, *29*, 493-499.

Attneave, F. & Arnoult, M. D. 1956. The quantitative study of shape and pattern perception. *Psychological Bulletin*, 1956, *53*, 452-471.

Attneave, F., & Block, G. 1973. Apparent movement in tridimensional space. *Perception & Psychophysics*, 1973, *13*, 301-307.

Attneave, F., & Olson, R. K. 1967. Discriminability of stimuli varying in physical and retinal orientation. *Journal of Experimental Psychology*, 1967, *74*, 149-157.

Attneave, F., & Olson, R. K. 1971. Pitch as a medium: A new approach to psychophysical scaling. *American Journal of Psychology*, 1971, *84*, 147-165.

Balzano, G. J. 1980. The group-theoretic description of twelve-fold and microtonal pitch systems. *Computer Music Journal*, 1980, *4*, 66-84.

Bamber, D. 1969. Reaction times and error rates for "same"-"different" judgments of multidimensional stimuli. *Perception & Psychophysics*, 1969, *6*, 169-174.

Bartlett, F. C. 1932. *Remembering.* Cambridge: Cambridge University Press, 1932.

Bassman, E. S. 1978. Cognitive processes in imagined and perceived cube-folding. Unpublished doctoral dissertation, Stanford University, 1978.

Baylor, G. W. 1972. A treatise on the mind's eye: An empirical investigation of visual mental imagery. Doctoral dissertation, Carnegie-Mellon University. Ann Arbor, Michigan: University Microfilms, 1972, No. 72-12, 699.

Beck, J., Elsner, A., & Silverstein, C. 1977. Position uncertainty and the perception of apparent movement. *Perception & Psychophysics,* 1977, *21,* 33–38.

Beech, J. R., & Allport, D. A. 1978. Visualization of compound scenes. *Perception,* 1978, *7,* 129–138.

Bennett, D. C. 1974. *Spatial and temporal uses of English prepositions.* New York: Longmans, 1974.

Besner, D. 1978. Pattern recognition: Are size and orientation additive factors? *Perception & Psychophysics,* 1978, *23,* 93.

Besner, D., & Coltheart, M. 1976. Mental size scaling examined. *Memory & Cognition,* 1976, *4,* 525–531.

Besner, D., & Colheart, M. in press. Visual pattern recognition: Size preprocessing re-examined. *Quarterly Journal of Experimental Psychology,* in press.

Black, J. B., Turner, T. J., & Bower, G. H. 1979. Point of view in narrative comprehension memory and production. *Journal of Verbal Learning and Verbal Behavior,* 1979, *18,* 187–199.

Bobrow, D. G. 1975. Dimensions of representation. In D. G. Bobrow & A. M. Collins, eds., *Representation and understanding: Studies in cognitive science.* New York: Academic Press, 1975.

Boring, E. G. 1942. *Sensation and perception in the history of experimental psychology.* New York: Appleton-Century-Crofts, 1942.

Boring, E. G. 1950. *A history of experimental psychology,* 2nd ed. New York: Appleton-Century-Crofts, 1950.

Bower, G. H. 1972. Mental imagery and associative learning. In L. Gregg, ed., *Cognition in learning and memory.* New York: Wiley, 1972.

Braddick, O. 1974. A short-range process in apparent motion. *Vision Research,* 1974, *14,* 519–528.

Braunstein, M. L. 1976. *Depth perception through motion.* New York: Academic Press, 1976.

Bregman, A. S. 1981. Asking the "what for" question in auditory perception. In M. Kubovy & J. R. Pomerantz, eds., *Perceptual organization.* Hillsdale, N.J.: Lawrence Erlbaum Associates, 1981.

Bregman, A. S. & Campbell, J. 1971. Primary auditory stream segregation and the perception of order in rapid sequences to tones. *Journal of Experimental Psychology,* 1971, *89,* 244–249.

Brooks, L. R. 1967. The supression of visualization by reading. *Quarterly Journal of Experimental Psychology,* 1967, *19,* 289–299.

Brooks, L. R. 1968. Spatial and verbal components of the act of recall. *Canadian Journal of Psychology,* 1968, *22,* 349–368.

Brugman, C. 1981. Story of *over.* Paper presented at the conference *Language and imagery.* University of California at Berkeley, May 8–10, 1981.

Bundesen, C., & Larsen, A. 1975. Visual transformation of size. *Journal of Experimental Psychology: Human Perception and Performance*, 1975, *1*, 214-220.

Bundesen, C., Larsen, A., & Farrell, J. E. 1981a. Visual transformations of size and orientation: Spatial imagery and perceptual processes. In J. Long & A. Baddeley, eds., *Attention and performance IX*. Hillsdale, N.J.: Lawrence Erlbaum Associates, 1981.

Bundesen, C., Larsen, A., & Farrell, J. E. 1981b. Visual apparent movement: Transformations of size and orientation. Unpublished manuscript, 1981.

Caelli, T., Hoffman, W. C., & Lindman, H. 1978. Subjective Lorentz transformations and the perception of motion. *Journal of the Optical Society of America*, 1978, *68*, 402-411.

Carpenter, P. A., & Eisenberg, P. 1978. Mental rotation and frames of reference in blind and sighted individuals. *Perception & Psychophysics*, 1978, *23*, 117-124.

Carpenter, P.A., & Just, M. A. 1975. Sentence comprehension: A psycholinguistic processing model of verification. *Psychological Review*, 1975, *82*, 45-73.

Carpenter, P. A., & Just, M. A. 1978. Eye fixations during mental rotation. In J. W. Senders, D. F. Fisher, & R. A. Monty, eds., *Eye movements and the higher psychological functions*. Hillsdale, N.J.: Lawrence Erlbaum Associates, 1978.

Carpenter, P.A., & Just, M.A. 1981. Spatial ability: An information-processing approach to psychometrics. Unpublished manuscript, Carnegie-Mellon University, 1981.

Carroll, J. D., & Chang, J.-J. 1970. Analysis of individual differences in multidimensional scaling via an N-way generalization of "Eckart-Young" decomposition. *Psychometrika*, 1970, *35*, 283-319.

Casad, E. H. 1981. Cora images. Paper presented at the conference *Language and imagery*, University of California at Berkeley, May 8-10, 1981.

Cassirer, E. 1944. The concept of group and the theory of perception. *Philosophy & Phenomenological Research*, 1944, *5*, 1-35.

Church, R. M. 1974. Strategies of pattern transformation. Paper presented at the annual meeting of the Psychonomic Society, Boston, 1974.

Church, R. M., & Church, K. W. 1977. In P. W. Frey, ed., *Chess skill in man and machine*. New York: Springer-Verlag, 1977.

Clark, H. H. 1969. Linguistic processes in deductive reasoning. *Psychological Review*, 1969, *74*, 387-404.

Clark, H. H. 1973. The language-as-fixed-effect fallacy: A critique of language statistics in psychological research. *Journal of Verbal Learning and Verbal Behavior*, 1973, *12*, 335-359.

Clark, H. H. 1973. Space, time, semantics, and the child. In T. E. Moore, ed., *Cognitive development and the acquisition of language*. New York: Academic Press, 1973.

Clark. H. H., Carpenter, P. A., & Just, M. A. 1973. On the meeting of semantics and perception. In W. G. Chase, ed., *Visual information processing*. New York: Academic Press, 1973.

Clark, H. H., & Chase, W. G. 1972. On the process of comparing sentences against pictures. *Cognitive Psychology*, 1972, *3*, 472-517.

Clark, H. H., & Chase, W. G. 1974. Perceptual coding strategies in the formation and verification of descriptions. *Memory and Cognition*, 1974, *2*, 101-111.

Cohen, G. 1969. Pattern recognition: Differences between matching patterns to patterns and matching descriptions to patterns. *Journal of Experimental Psychology*, 1969, *82*, 427-434.

Cole, R. A., & Scott, B. 1973. Perception of temporal order in speech: The role of vowel transition. *Canadian Journal of Psychology*, 1973, *27*, 441-449.

Cooper, L. A. 1973. Internal representation and transformation of random shapes: A chronometric analysis. Unpublished doctoral dissertation, Stanford University, 1973.

Cooper, L. A. 1975. Mental rotation of random two-dimensional shapes. *Cognitive Psychology*, 1975, *7*, 20-43.

Cooper, L. A. 1976a. Demonstration of a mental analog of an external rotation. *Perception & Psychophysics*, 1976, *19*, 296-302.

Cooper, L. A. 1976b. Individual differences in visual comparison processes. *Perception & Psychophysics*, 1976, *19*, 433-444.

Cooper, L. A. 1980. Spatial information processing: Strategies for research. In R. Snow, P-A. Federico, & W. E. Montague, eds., *Aptitude, learning, and instruction: Cognitive process analyses*. Hillsdale, N.J.: Lawrence Erlbaum Associates, 1980.

Cooper, L. A. 1982. Strategies for visual representation and processing: Individual differences. In R. Sternberg, ed., *Advances in the psychology of human intelligence*. Hillsdale, N.J.: Lawrence Erlbaum Associates, 1982.

Cooper, L. A., & Farrell, J. E. Effects of stimulus structure on rate of mental rotation. Paper in preparation.

Cooper, L. A., & Podgorny, P. 1976. Mental transformations and visual comparison processes: Effects of complexity and similarity. *Journal of Experimental Psychology: Human Perception and Performance*, 1976, *2*, 503-514.

Cooper, L. A., & Shepard, R. N. 1973. Chronometric studies of the rotation of mental images. In W. G. Chase, ed., *Visual information processing*. New York: Academic Press, 1973.

Cooper, L. A., & Shepard, R. N. 1973. The time required to prepare for a rotated stimulus. *Memory & Cognition*, 1973, *1*, 246-250.

Cooper, L. A., & Shepard, R. N. 1975. Mental transformations in the identification of left and right hands. *Journal of Experimental Psychology: Human Perception and Performance*, 1975, *104*, 48-56.

Cooper, L. A., & Shepard, R. N. 1978. Transformations on representations of objects in space. In E. C. Carterette & M. P. Friedman, eds., *Handbook of perception* (Vol. VIII: *Space and object perception*). New York: Academic Press, 1978.

Cooper, L. A., & Vallone, R. 1979. Mental extrapolation of a perceived transformation. Unpublished data, 1979.

Corballis, M. C., & Beale, I. L. 1970. Bilateral symmetry and behavior. *Psychological Review*, 1970, *77*, 451-464.

Corballis, M. C., & Roldan, C. E. 1975. Detection of symmetry as a function of angular orientation. *Journal of Experimental Psychology: Human Perception and Performance*, 1975, *1*, 221-230.

Corballis, M. C., Zbrodoff, J., & Roldan, C. E. 1976. What's up in mental rotation? *Perception and Psychophysics*, 1976, *19*, 525-530.

Corbin, H. H. 1942. The perception of grouping and apparent movement in visual depth. *Archives of Psychology*, 1942, No. 273.

Courant, R., & Robbins, H. 1948. *What is mathematics?* London: Oxford University Press, 1948.

Coxeter, H. S. M. 1961. *Introduction to geometry*. New York: Wiley, 1961.

Cunningham, J. P., Cooper, L. A., & Reaves, C. C. 1980. *Visual comparison processes: Identity versus similarity decisions*. Unpublished paper, presented in part at the annual meeting of the Psychonomic Society, St. Louis, Missouri, November 15, 1980.

Cutting, J. E., Proffitt, D. R., & Kozlowski, L. T. 1978. A biomechanical invariant for gait perception. *Journal of Experimental Psychology: Human Perception and Performance*, 1978, *4*, 357-372.

DeSilva, H. R. 1929. An experimental investigation of the determinants of apparent visual movement. *British Journal of Psychology*, 1929, *19*, 268-305.

Dimmick, F. L., & Scahill, H. G. 1925. Visual perception of movement. *American Journal of Psychology*, 1925, *36*, 412-417.

Dixon, P. Numerical comparison processes. 1978. *Memory & Cognition*, 1978, *6*, 454-461.

Dixon, P., & Just, M. A. 1978. Normalization of irrelevant dimensions in stimulus comparisons. *Journal of Experimental Psychology: Human Perception and Performance*, 1978, *4*, 36-46.

Dorman, M. F., Cutting, J. E., & Raphael, L. J. 1975. Perception of temporal order in vowel sequences with and without format transitions. *Journal of Experimental Psychology: Human Perception and Performance*, 1975, *4*, 121-129.

Dowling, W. J. 1973. The perception of interleaved melodies. *Cognitive Psychology*, 1973, *5*, 322-337.

Dyson, F. 1980. *Disturbing the universe*. New York: Harper & Row, 1980.

Egeth, H. 1966. Parallel versus serial processes in multidimensional stimulus discrimination. *Perception & Psychophysics*, 1966, *1*, 245-252.

Egeth, H., & Blecker, D. 1971. Differential effects of familiarity on judgments of sameness and difference. *Perception & Psychophysics*, 1971, *9*, 321-326.

Einstein, A. 1949. Autobiographical notes. In P. A. Schlipp, ed., *Albert Einstein: Philosopher-scientist*. Evanston, Ill.: Library of Living Philosophers, 1949.

Emlen, S. T. 1975. Migration: Orientation and navigation. In D. S. Farner & J. R. King, eds., *Avion biology* (Volume V). New York: Academic Press, 1975.

Exner, S. 1875. Ueber das Sehen von Beuregungen und die Theorie des zusammengesetzen Auges. *Sitzungsberichte Akademie Wissenschaft Wien*, 1875, *72*, 156-190.

Farrell, J. E. 1979. What goes where in apparent motion of forms. Paper presented at the annual meeting of the American Psychological Association, New York, September 1, 1979.

Farrell, J. E. 1981. Visual transformations underlying apparent movement. Unpublished doctoral dissertation, Stanford University, 1981.

Farrell, J. E., & Shepard, R. N. 1979. The effect of form on apparent motion. Paper presented at the European conference on visual perception, Noodwijkerhout, The Netherlands, October 15-18, 1979.

Farrell, J. E., & Shepard, R. N. 1981. Shape, orientation, and apparent rotational motion. *Journal of Experimental Psychology: Human Perception and Performance*, 1981, 7, 477-486.

Festinger, L., Ono, H., Burnham, C. A., & Bamber, D. 1967. Efference and the conscious experience of perception. *Journal of Experimental Psychology Monographs*, 1967, 74, (4, Whole No. 637).

Findlay, A. 1948. *A hundred years of chemsitry*, 2nd ed. London: Duckworth, 1948.

Finke, R. A., & Pinker, S. 1981. Spontaneous imagery scanning in mental extrapolation. Manuscript submitted for publication, 1981.

Foster, D. H. 1975. Visual apparent motion and some preferred paths in the rotation group SO(3). *Biological Cybernetics*, 1975, 18, 81-89.

Foster, D. H. 1978. Visual apparent motion and the calculus of variations. In E. L. J. Leeuwenberg & H. F. J. M. Buffart, eds., *Formal theories of visual perception*. New York: Wiley, 1978.

Franks, J. J., & Bransford, J. D. 1971. Abstraction of visual patterns. *Journal of Experimental Psychology*, 1971, 90, 65-74.

French, J. W., Ekstrom, R. B., & Price, L. A. 1963. *Manual for a kit of reference tests of cognitive factors*. Princeton, N.J.: Educational Testing Service, 1963.

Gardner, M. *The ambidextrous universe*. 1969. New York: New American Library, 1969.

Garner, W. R. 1974. *The processing of information and structure*. Hillsdale, N.J.: Lawrence Erlbaum Associates, 1974.

Gaylord, S. A., & Marsh, G. R. 1975. Age differences in the speed of a spatial cognitive process. *Journal of Gerontology*, 1975, 30, 674-678.

Gibson, E. J., Owsley, C. J., & Johnston, J. 1978. Perception of invariants by five-month-old infants: Differentiation of two types of motion. *Developmental Psychology*, 1978, 14, 407-415.

Gibson, J. J. 1950. *The perception of the visual world*. Boston: Houghton Mifflin, 1950.

Gibson, J. J. 1966. *The senses considered as perceptual systems*. Boston: Houghton Mifflin, 1966.

Gibson, J. J. 1977. The theory of affordances. In R. E. Shaw & J. Bransford, eds., *Perceiving, acting, and knowing*. Hillsdale, N.J.: Lawrence Erlbaum Associates, 1977.

Glass, L. 1969. Moiré effect from random dots. *Nature*, 1969, 223, 578-580.

Glushko, R. J., & Cooper, L. A. 1978. Spatial comprehension and comparison processes in verification tasks. *Cognitive Psychology*, 1978, 10, 391-421.

Green, B. F., Jr. 1961. Figure coherence in the kinetic depth effect. *Journal of Experimental Psychology*, 1961, 62, 272-282.

Gregory, R. L., Wallace, J. G., & Campbell, F. W. 1959. Change in size and shape of visual after-images observed in complete darkness during changes of position in space. *Quarterly Journal of Experimental Psychology*, 1959, *11*, 54–56.

Gruber, J. S. 1967. Look and see. *Language*, 1967, *43*, 937–947.

Hadamard, J. 1945. *The psychology of invention in the mathematical field.* Princeton, New Jersey: Princeton University Press, 1945.

Hartley, A. A. 1977. Mental measurement in the magnitude estimation of length. *Journal of Experimental Psychology: Human Perception and Performance*, 1977, *3*, 622–628.

Hartley, A. A. 1981. Mental measurement of line length: The role of the standard. *Journal of Experimental Psychology: Human Perception and Performance*, 1981, *7*, 309–317.

Hawkins, H. L. 1969. Parallel processing in complex visual discrimination. *Perception & Psychophysics*, 1969, *5*, 56–64.

Helmholtz, H. von. 1894. Über den Ursprung der richtigen Deutung unserer Sinneseindrücke. *Zeitschrift für Psychologie und Physiologie der Sinnesorgane*, 1894, *7*, 81–96.

Herschel, Sir J. F. W. 1867. *Familiar lectures on scientific subjects.* London: Strahan, 1867.

Hill, J. W., & Bliss, J. C. 1968. Perception of sequentially presented tactile point stimuli. *Perception & Psychophysics*, 1968, *4*, 289–295.

Hinton, G. 1979. Some demonstrations of the effects of structural descriptions in mental imagery. *Cognitive Science*, 1979, *3*, 231–250.

Hintzman, D. L, O'Dell, C. S., & Arndt, D. R. 1981. Orientation in cognitive maps. *Cognitive Psychology*, 1981, *13*, 149–206.

Hochberg, J., & Gellman, L. 1977. The effect of landmark features "mental rotation" times. *Memory and Cognition*, 1977, *5*, 23–26.

Hock, H. S., & Tromley, C. L. 1978. Mental rotation and perceptual uprightness. *Perception & Psychophysics*, 1978, *24*, 529–533.

Hölldobler, B. 1980. Canopy orientation: A new kind of orientation in ants. *Science*, 1980, *210*, 86–88.

Holton, G. 1972. On trying to understand scientific genius. *American Scholar*, 1972, *41*, 95–110.

Hubel, D. H., & Wiesel, T. N. 1962. Receptive fields, binocular interaction and functional architecture in the cat's visual cortex. *Journal of Physiology*, 1962, *160*, 106–154.

Hubel, D. H., & Wiesel, T. N. 1963. Receptive fields of cells in striate cortex of very young, visually inexperienced kittens. *Journal of Neurophysiology*, 1963, *26*, 994–1002.

Hubel, D. H., & Wiesel, T. N. 1968. Receptive fields and functional architecture of monkey striate cortex. *Journal of Physiology*, 1968, *195*, 215–243.

Hume D. 1907. *An enquiry concerning human understanding.* Chicago: Open Court, 1907. Originally published 1748.

Hunt, I., Draper, W. W. 1964. *Lightning in his hand: The life story of Nikola Tesla.* Denver, Colorado: Sage, 1964.

Hutchinson, J. W. & Lockhead, G. R. 1977. Similarity as distance: A structural principle for semantic memory. *Journal of Experimental Psychology: Human Learning and Memory*, 1977, *3*, 660–678.

Huttenlocher, J. 1968. Constructing spatial images: A strategy in reasoning. *Psychological Review*, 1968, *75*, 550-560.

Huttenlocher, J., & Presson, C. C. 1973. Mental rotation and the perspective problem. *Cognitive Psychology*, 1973, *4*, 277-299.

Huttenlocher, J., & Presson, C. C. 1979. The coding and transformation of spatial information. *Cognitive Psychology*, 1979, *11*, 375-394.

Jackendoff, R. 1976. Toward an explanatory semantic representation. *Linguistic Inquiry*, 1976, *1*, 89-150.

Jackendoff, R. 1978. Grammar as evidence for conceptual structure. In M. Halle, J. Bresnan, & G. A. Miller, eds., *Linguistic competence and psychological reality*. Cambridge, Mass.: M.I.T. Press, 1978.

Johansson, G. 1950. *Configuration in event perception*. Uppsala, Sweden: Almqvist and Wiksell, 1950.

Johansson, G. 1976. Spatio-temporal differentiation and integration in visual motion perception. *Psychological Research*, 1976, *38*, 379-393.

Jones, M. R. 1976. Time, our lost dimension: Toward a new theory of perception, attention, and memory. *Psychological Review*, 1976, *83*, 323-355.

Julesz, B., & Levitt, H. Spatial chords. 1966. *Journal of the Acoustical Society America*, 1966, *40*, 1253.

Just, M. A., & Carpenter, P. A. 1975. The semantics of locative information in pictures and mental images. *British Journal of Psychology*, 1975, *66*, 427-441.

Just, M. A., & Carpenter, P. A. 1976. Eye fixations and cognitive processes. *Cognitive Psychology*, 1976, *8*, 441-480.

Kahneman, D. 1976. An onset-onset law for one case of apparent motion and metacontrast. *Perception & Psychophysics*, 1976, *2*, 577-584.

Kant, I. 1781. *Critique of pure reason*, trans. F. M. Muller. New York: Macmillan, 1881. Original publication in German, 1781.

Klatzky, R. L., & Thompson, A. L. 1975. Integration of features in comparing multifeature stimuli. *Perception & Psychophysics*, 1975, *18*, 428-432.

Koffka, K. 1935. *Principles of Gestalt Psychology*. New York: Harcourt Brace, 1935.

Kohler, I. 1964. The formation and transformation of the perceptual world, trans. H. Fiss. *Psychological Issues*, 1964, *3*, No. 4, 1-173.

Kolers, P. A. 1963. Some differences between real and apparent visual movement. *Vision Research*, 1963, *3*, 191-206.

Kolers, P. A. 1972. *Aspects of motion perception*. Oxford: Pergamon Press, 1972.

Kolers, P. A., & Perkins, D. N. 1969. Orientation of letters and their speed of recognition. *Perception & Psychophysics*, 1969, *5*, 275-280.

Kolers, P. A., & Pomerantz, J. R. 1971. Figural Change in apparent motion. *Journal of Experimental Psychology*, 1971, *87*, 99-108.

Korte, A. 1915. Kinematoskopische Untersuchungen. *Zeitschrift für Psychologie*, 1915, *72*, 193-296.

Kosslyn, S. M. 1973. Scanning visual images: Some structural implications. *Perception & Psychophysics*, 1973, *14*, 90-94.

Kosslyn, S. M. 1974. Constructing Visual Images: An Exercise in Neo-Mentalism. Unpublished doctoral dissertation, Stanford University, 1974.

Kosslyn, S. M. 1975. Information representation in visual images. *Cognitive Psychology*, 1975, 7, 341-370.

Kosslyn, S. M. 1980. *Image and mind.* Cambridge, Mass.: Harvard University Press, 1980.

Kosslyn, S. M. 1981. The medium and the message in mental imagery: A theory. *Psychological Review*, 1981, 88, 46-66.

Kosslyn S. M., Ball, T. M., & Reiser, B. J. 1978. Visual images preserve metric spatial information: Evidence from studies of image scanning. *Journal of Experimental Psychology: Human Perception and Performance*, 1978, 4, 47-60.

Kosslyn, S. M., Pinker, S., Smith, G., & Shwartz, S. P. 1979. On the demystification of mental imagery. *The Behavioral and Brain Sciences*, 1979, 2, 535-581.

Kosslyn, S. M., & Pomerantz, J. R. 1977. Imagery, propositions, and the form of internal representations. *Cognitive Psychology*, 1977, 9, 52-76.

Krumhansl, C. L., & Shepard, R. N. 1979. Quantification of the hierarchy of tonal functions within a diatonic context. *Journal of Experimental Psychology: Human Perception and Performance*, 1979, 5, 579-594.

Kubovy, M. 1981. Concurrent-pitch segregation and the theory of indispensable attributes. In M. Kubovy & J. R. Pomerantz, eds., *Perceptual organization*. Hillsdale, New Jersey: Lawrence Erlbaum Associates, 1981.

Kubovy, M., & Podgorny, P. 1981. Does pattern matching require the normalization of size and orientation? *Perception & Psychophysics*, 1981, 30, 24-28.

Lackner, F. R., & Goldstein, L. M. 1974. Primary auditory stream segregation of repeated consonant-vowel sequences. *Journal of the Acoustical Society of America*, 1974, 56, 1651-1652.

Langacker, R. W. 1979a. Grammar as image. Paper presented at the conference *Neurolinguistics and cognition*, University of California at San Diego, March 23-25, 1979.

Langacker, R. W. 1979b. Remarks on English aspect. Paper presented at the conference *Tense and aspect: Between semantics and pragmatics*, University of California at Los Angeles, May 4-6, 1979.

Langacker, R. W. 1980. Space grammar, analyzability, and the English passive. Unpublished manuscript, University of California at San Diego, 1980.

Langacker, R. W. 1981. The nature of grammatical valence. Paper presented at the conference *Language and imagery*, University of California at Berkeley, May 8-10, 1981.

Lansman, M. 1981. Ability factors and the speed of information processing. In M. P. Friedman, J. P. Das, & N. O'Connor, eds., *Intelligence and learning*. New York: Plenum, 1981.

Larsen, A., & Bundesen, C. 1978. Size scaling in visual pattern recognition. *Journal of Experimental Psychology: Human Perception and Performance*, 1978, 4, 1-20.

Larsen, A., Farrell, J. E., & Bundesen, C. 1981. Visual apparent movement: Evidence for separate short- and long-range processes. Unpublished manuscript, 1981.

Lea, G. 1975. Chronometric analysis of the method of loci. *Journal of Experimental Psychology: Human Perception and Performance*, 1975, 1, 95-104.

Levin, J. A. 1973. *Network representation and rotation of letters.* Unpublished manuscript, University of California, San Diego, September, 1973.

Lindner, S. 1981. A lexico-semantic analysis of verb-particle construction with *out* Paper presented at the conference *Language and imagery*, University of California at Berkeley, May 8–10, 1981.

Lockhead, G. R., Gaylord, S. A., & Evans, N. J. 1977. Priming with non-prototypical colors. Paper presented at the annual meeting of the Psychonomic Society, Washington, D. C., November 11, 1977.

Mach, E. 1959. *The analysis of sensation* (C. M. Williams, trans.). New York: Dover, 1959. Originally published, 1886.

MacKenzie, N. 1965. *Dreams and dreaming.* London: Aldus Books, 1965.

Mackworth, N. H. 1967. A stand-mounted eye-marker camera for line-of-sight recording. *Perception & Psychophysics*, 1967, *2*, 119–127.

Maier, N. R. F. 1929. Reasoning in white rats. Comparative Psychology Monographs, 1929, *6*, (No. 29).

Marmor, G. S. 1975. Development of kinetic images: When does the child first represent movement in mental images? *Cognitive Psychology*, 1975, *7*, 548–559.

Marmor, G. S., & Zaback, L. A. 1976. Mental rotation by the blind: Does mental rotation depend on visual imagery? *Journal of Experimental Psychology: Human Perception and Performance*, 1976, *2*, 515–521.

Max, N. L., & Clifford, W. H., Jr. 1975. Computer animation of the sphere eversion. *Computer Graphics*, 1975, *9*, 32–39.

McAdams, S., & Bregman, A. 1979. Hearing musical streams. *Computer Music Journal*, 1979, *3*, 26–44.

McGee, M. G. 1979. *Human spatial abilities: Sources of sex differences.* New York: Praeger, 1979.

Metzler, J. 1973. Cognitive analogues of the rotation of three-dimensional objects. Unpublished doctoral dissertation, Stanford University, 1973.

Metzler, J., & Shepard, R. N. 1971. Mental correlates of the rotation of three-dimensional objects. Paper presented at the annual meeting of the Western Psychological Association, San Francisco, April, 1971.

Metzler, J. & Shepard, R. N. 1974. Transformational studies of the internal representation of three-dimensional objects. In R. L. Solso, ed., *Theories of Cognitive Psychology: The Loyola Symposium.* Potomac, Md.: Lawrence Erlbaum Associates, 1974.

Michotte, A. 1955. Perception and cognition. *Acta Psychologica*, 1955, *11*, 69–91.

Miller, G. A., & Heise, G. A. 1950. The trill threshold. *Journal of the Acoustical Society of America*, 1950, *22*, 637–638.

Miller, G. A., & Johnson-Laird, P. N. 1976. *Language and perception.* Cambridge, Massachusetts: Harvard University Press, 1976.

Milojkovic, J. D. 1980. Chess imagery in novice and master. Unpublished manuscript, Stanford University, 1980.

Minsky, M. 1961. Steps toward artificial intelligence. *Proceedings of the Institute of Radio Engineering*, 1961, *49*, 8–30.

Mitchell, D. B., & Richman, C. L. 1980. Confirmed reservations: mental travel. *Journal of Experimental Psychology: Human Perception and Performance*, 1980, *6*, 58–66.

Morinaga, S., Noguchi, K., & Yokoi, K. 1966. Direct comparison of real and apparent visual movement. *Perceptual and Motor Skills*, 1966, *22*, 346.

Moyer, R. S., & Landauer, T. K. 1967. Time required for judgments of numerical inequality. *Nature*, 1967, *215*, 1519-1520.

Neisser, U. 1976. *Cognition and reality*. San Francisco: W. H. Freeman, 1976.

Nerlich, G. 1973. Hands, knees, and absolute space. *Journal of Philosophy*, 1973, *70*, 337-351.

Neuhaus, W. 1930. Experimentelle Untersuchung der Scheinbewegung. *Archiv für gesamte Psychologie*, 1930, *75*, 315-348.

Nickerson, R. S. 1967. "Same"-"different" response times with multi-attribute stimulus differences. *Perceptual and Motor Skills*, 1967, *24*, 543-554.

Nielsen, G., & Smith, E. 1973. Imaginal and verbal representations in short-term recognition of visual forms. *Journal of Experimental Psychology*, 1973, *101*, 375-378.

Noll, A. M. 1965. Computer-generated three-dimensional movies. *Computers & Automation*, 1965, *14*, 20-23.

van Noorden, L. P. A. S. 1975. *Temporal coherence in the perception of tone sequences*. Eindhoven, The Netherlands: Institute for Perception Research, 1975.

Norman, D. A., & Rumelhart, D. E., eds., 1975. *Explorations in cognition*. San Francisco: W. H. Freeman, 1975.

Ogasawara, J. 1936. Effect of apparent separation on apparent movement. *Japanese Journal of Psychology*, 1936, *11*, 109-122.

Olson, G., & Laxar, K., 1973. Asymmetries in processing the terms "right" and "left." *Journal of Experimental Psychology*, 1973, *100*, 284-290.

Orlansky, J. 1940. The effect of similarity and difference in form on apparent visual movement. *Archives of Psychology*, 1940, *246*, 85.

Paivio, A. 1970. *Imagery and verbal processes*. New York: Holt, Rinehart & Winston, 1970.

Palmer, S. E. 1974. Structural aspects of perceptual organization. Unpublished doctoral dissertation, University of California, San Diego, 1974.

Palmer, S. E. 1975. Visual perception and world knowledge: Notes on a model of sensory-cognitive interaction. In D. A. Norman and D. E. Rumelhart, eds., *Explorations in cognition*. San Francisco: W. H. Freeman, 1975.

Palmer, S. E. 1978. Fundamental aspects of cognitive representation. In E. Rosch & B. B. Lloyd, eds., *Cognition and categorization*. Hillsdale, N.J.: Lawrence Erlbaum Associates, 1978.

Pellegrino, J. W., Mumaw, R. J., Kail, R. V., & Carter, P. 1979. Different slopes for different folks: Analyses of spatial ability. Paper presented at the annual meeting of the Psychonomic Society, Phoenix, November 1979.

Phillips, A. 1966. Turning a surface inside out. *Scientific American*, 1966, *214 (5)*, 112-120.

Pinker, S. 1980. Mental imagery and the third dimension. *Journal of Experimental Psychology: General*, 1980, *109*, 354-371.

Pinker, S., & Finke, R. A. 1980. Emergent two-dimensional patterns in images rotated in depth. *Journal of Experimental Psychology: Human Perception and Performance*, 1980, *6*, 244-264.

Pinker, S., & Kosslyn, S. M. 1978. The representation and manipulation of three-dimensional space in mental images. *Journal of Mental Imagery*, 1978, *2*, 69-84. 69-84.

Place, U. T. 1956. Is consciousness a brain process? *British Journal of Psychology*, 1956, *47*, 44-50.

Podgorny, P. 1975. Mental rotation and the third dimension. Unpublished senior honors thesis, Stanford University, 1975.

Posner, M. I. 1969. Abstraction and the process of recognition. In G. H. Bower & J. T. Spence, eds., *The psychology of learning and motivation.* (Volume V.) New York: Academic Press, 1969, pp. 44-100.

Posner, M. I. 1973. Coordination of internal codes. In W. G. Chase, ed., *Visual information processing.* New York: Academic Press, 1973.

Posner, M. I., Boies, S. J., Eichelman, W. H., & Taylor, R. L. 1969. Retention of visual and name codes of single letters. *Journal of Experimental Psychology*, 1969, *79* (1, Pt. 2).

Posner, M. I., & Mitchell, R. F. 1967. Chronometric analysis of classification. *Psychological Review*, 1967, *74*, 392-409.

Pylyshyn, Z. W. 1973. What the mind's eye tells the mind's brain: A critique of mental imagery. *Psychological Bulletin*, 1973, *80*, 1-24.

Pylyshyn, Z. W. 1979. The rate of "mental rotation" of images: A test of a holistic analogue hypothesis. *Memory & Cognition*, 1979, *7*, 19-28.

Pylyshyn, Z. W. 1981. The imagery debate: Analogue media versus tactic knowledge. *Psychological Review*, 1981, *87*, 16-45.

Rawlings, E. I., Rawlings, I. L., Chen, S. S., & Yilk, M. D. 1972. The facilitating effects of mental rehearsal in the acquisition of rotary pursuit tracking. *Psychomonic Science*, 1972, *26*, 71-73.

Reed, S. K. 1974. Structural descriptions and the limitations of visual images. *Memory & Cognition*, 1974, *2*, 329-336.

Reed, S. K., & Johnsen, J. A. 1975. Detection of parts in patterns and images. *Memory & Cognition*, 1975, *3*, 569-575.

Richardson, A. 1969. *Mental Imagery.* New York: Springer, 1969.

Robins, C., & Shepard, R. N. 1977. Spatio-temporal probing of apparent rotational movement. *Perception & Psychophysics*, 1977, *22*, 12-18.

Rock, I. 1973. *Orientation and form.* New York: Academic Press, 1973.

Rock, I., & Heimer, W. 1957. The effect of retinal and phenomenal orientation on the perception of form. *American Journal of Psychology*, 1957, *70*, 493-511.

Rosenbaum, D. A. 1975. Perception and extrapolation of velocity and acceleration. *Journal of Experimental Psychology: Human Perception and Performance*, 1975, *1*, 395-403.

Samuels, M., & Samuels, N. 1975. *Seeing with the mind's eye.* New York: Random House, 1975.

Santa, J. L. 1977. Spatial transformations of words and pictures. *Journal of Experimental Psychology: Human Learning and Memory*, 1977, *3*, 418-427.

Sauer, E. G. F. 1958. Celestial navigation by birds. *Scientific American*, 1958, *199* (2), 42-47.

Segal, S. J., ed. 1971. *Imagery*, New York: Academic Press, 1971.

Segal, S. J. & Fusella, V. 1970. Influence of imaged pictures and sounds on detection of visual and auditory signals. *Journal of Experimental Psychology*, 1970, *83*, 458-464.

Segal, S. J., & Gordon, P. E. 1969. The Perky effect revisited: Paradoxical thresholds or signal detection error? *Perceptual and Motor Skills*, 1969, *28*, 791-797.

Sekuler, R., & Abrams, M. 1968. Visual sameness: A choice time analysis of pattern recognition processes. *Journal of Experimental Psychology*, 1968, *77*, 232-238.

Sekuler, R., & Nash, D. 1972. Speed of size scaling in human vision. *Psychonomic Science*, 1972, *27*, 93-94.

Selfridge, O. G. 1959. Pandemonium: A paradigm for learning. In *The mechanisation of thought processes*. London: H. M. Stationery Office, 1959.

Seymour, P. 1969. Response latencies in judgments of spatial location. *British Journal of Psychology*, 1969, *60*, 31-39.

Seymour, P. 1973a. Judgments of verticality and response availability. *Bulletin of the Psychonomic Society*, 1973, *1*, 196-198.

Seymour, P. 1973b. Semantic representation of shape names. *Quarterly Journal of Experimental Psychology*, 1973, *25*, 265-277.

Seymour, P. 1974a. Asymmetries in judgments of vertically. *Journal of Experimental Psychology*, 1974, *102*, 447-455.

Seymour, P. 1974b. Generation of a pictorial code. *Memory and Cognition*, 1974, *2*, 224-232.

Seymour, P. 1974c. Pictorial coding of verbal descriptions. *Quarterly Journal of Experimental Psychology*, 1974, *26*, 39-51.

Seymour, P. 1974d. Stroop interference with response, comparison, and encoding stages in a sentence-picture comparison task. *Memory and Cognition*, 1974, *2*, 19-26.

Seymour, P. 1975. Semantic equivalence of verbal and pictorial displays. In R. A. Kennedy & A. W. Wilkes, eds., *Studies in long-term memory*. London: Wiley, 1975.

Shaw, R. E., & Pittenger, J. 1977. Perceiving the face of change in changing faces: Implications for a theory of object perception. In R. E. Shaw & J. Bransford, eds., *Perceiving, acting, and knowing*. Hillsdale, N.J.: Lawrence Erlbaum Associates, 1977.

Shepard, R. N. 1964. Circularity in judgments of relative pitch. *Journal of the Acoustical Society of America*, 1964, *36*, 2346-2353.

Shepard, R. N. 1975. Form, formation, and transformation of internal representations. In R. Solso, ed., *Information processing and cognition: The Loyola Symposium*. Hillsdale, N.J.: Lawrence Erlbaum Associates, 1975.

Shepard, R. N. 1977. *Trajectories of apparent transformations*. Paper presented at the annual meeting of the Psychonomic Society, Washington, D.C., November 10, 1977.

Shepard, R. N. 1978a. The circumplex and related topological manifolds in the study of perception. In S. Shye, ed., *Theory construction and data analysis in the behavioral sciences*. San Francisco: Jossey-Bass, 1978.

Shepard, R. N. 1978b. Externalization of mental images and the act of creation. In B. S. Randhawa & W. E. Coffman, eds., *Visual learning, thinking, and communication*. New York: Academic Press, 1978.

Shepard, R. N. 1978c. The mental image. *American Psychologist*, 1978, *33*, 125-137.

Shepard, R. N. 1978d. On the status of "direct" psychophysical measurement. In C. W. Savage, ed., *Minnesota studies in the philosophy of science.* (Volume IX.) Minneapolis: University of Minnesota Press, 1978.

Shepard, R. N. 1979. Connections between the representation of shapes and their spatial transformations. In R. Bajcsy & N. Badler, eds., *Representation of three-dimensional objects.* Proceedings of a workshop held at the University of Pennsylvania in May, 1979. (To be published by Springer-Verlag.)

Shepard, R. N. 1981. Psychophysical complementarity. In M. Kubovy & J. R. Pomerantz, eds., *Perceptual organization.* Hillsdale, N.J.: Lawrence Erlbaum Associates, 1981.

Shepard, R. N. 1982a. Perceptual and analogical bases of cognition. In J. Mehler, M. Garrett, & E. Walker, eds., *Perspectives in mental representation.* Hillsdale, N.J.: Lawrence Erlbaum Associates, in press.

Shepard, R. N. 1982b. Structural representations of musical pitch. In D. Deutsch, ed., *Psychology of music.* New York: Academic Press, in press.

Shepard, R. N. & Cermak, G. W. 1973. Perceptual-cognitive explorations of a toroidal set of free-form stimuli. *Cognitive Psychology,* 1973, *4,* 351-377.

Shepard, R. N., & Chipman, S. 1970. Second-order isomorphism of internal representations: Shapes of states. *Cognitive Psychology,* 1970, *1,* 1-17.

Shepard, R. N., & Feng, C. 1972. A chronometric study of mental paper folding. *Cognitive Psychology,* 1972, *3,* 228-243.

Shepard, R. N., & Hurwitz, S. 1981. Mental rotation in map reading: Discrimination of right and left turns. Unpublished manuscript, 1981.

Shepard, R. N., & Judd, S. A. 1976. Perceptual illusion of rotation of three-dimensional objects. *Science,* 1976, *191,* 952-954.

Shepard, R. N., & Metzler, J. 1971. Mental rotation of three-dimensional objects. *Science,* 1971, *171,* 701-703.

Shepard, R. N., & Podgorny, P. 1978. Cognitive processes that resemble perceptual processes. In W. K. Estes, ed., *Handbook of learning and cognitive processes* (Vol V). Hillsdale, N.J.: Lawrence Erlbaum, 1978.

Shepard, R. N., & Zare, S. 1981. *Path-guided apparent motion.* Paper presented at the annual meeting of the Psychonomic Society, Philadelphia, Pennsylvania, November 1981. *Bulletin of the Psychonomic Society,* 1981, *18,* 67. (abstract)

Shulman, G. L., Remington, R. W., & McLean, J. P. 1979. Moving attention through visual space. *Journal of Experimental Psychology: Human Perception and Performance,* 1979, *5,* 522-526.

Silverman, W. P. 1973. The perception of identity in simultaneously presented complex visual displays. *Memory and Cognition,* 1973, *1,* 459-466.

Smart, J. J. C. 1959. Sensations and brain processes. *Philosophical Review,* 1959, *68,* 141-156.

Smith, E. E., & Nielson, G. 1970. Representation and retrieval processes in short-term memory: Recognition and recall of faces. *Journal of Experimental Psychology,* 1970, *85,* 397-405.

Smith, I. McFarlane. 1964. *Spatial ability.* London: University of London Press, 1964.

Spelke, E. S., & Born, W. S. 1980. Perceiving the unity of detached visible objects in infancy. Unpublished manuscript, University of Pennsylvania, 1980.

Sperry, R. W., & Levy, J. 1970. Mental capacities of the disconnected minor hemisphere. Paper presented at the meeting of the American Psychological Association, Miami, September 4, 1970.

Sternberg, S. 1966. High-speed scanning in human memory. *Science*, 1966, *153*, 652-654.

Sternberg, S., & Knoll, R. L. 1973. The perception of temporal order: Fundamental issues and a general model. In S. Kornblum, ed., *Attention and performance IV*. New York: Academic Press, 1973.

Stratton, G. M. 1897. Vision without inversion of the retinal image. *Psychological Review*, 1897, *4*, 341-360, 463-481.

Sutherland, N. S. 1969. Shape discrimination in rat, octopus, and goldfish: A comparative study. *Journal of Comparative and Physiological Psychology*, 1969, *67*, 160-176.

Swisher, L., & Hirsh, I. 1972. Brain damage and the ordering of two temporally successive stimuli. *Neuropsychologia*, 1972, *10*, 137-152.

Taylor, R. L. 1972. Reading spatially transformed digits. *Journal of Experimental Psychology*, 1972, *96*, 396-399.

Tesla, N. 1956. *Lectures, patents, articles*. Beograd: Nikola Tesla Museum, 1956.

Thompson, A. L., & Klatzky, R. L. 1978. Studies of visual synthesis: Integration of fragments into forms. *Journal of Experimental Psychology: Human Perception and Performance*, 1978, *4*, 244-263.

Thorpe, W. H. 1950. A note on detour behaviour with *Ammophila pubescens* Curt. *Behaviour*, 1950, *2*, 257-264.

Trabasso, T., Rollins, H., & Shaughnessy, E. 1971. Storage and verification stages in processing concepts. *Cognitive Psychology*, 1971, *2*, 239-289.

Tsal, Y. 1981. *Movements of attention across the visual field*. Paper presented at the annual meeting of the American Psychological Association, Los Angeles, August 27, 1981.

Tuggy, D. 1981. Imagic meaning and dative possessors in Spanish. Paper presented at the conference *Language and imagery*. University of California at Berkeley, May 8-10, 1981.

Tversky, B. 1969. Pictorial and verbal encoding in a short-term memory task. *Perception and Psychophysics*, 1969, *6*, 225-233.

Tversky, B. 1975. Pictorial encoding of sentence-picture comparison. *Quarterly Journal of Experimental Psychology*, 1975, *27*, 405-410.

Ullman, S. 1979. *The interpretation of visual motion*. Cambridge, Massachusetts: MIT Press, 1979.

Uttal, W. R. 1975. *An autocorrelation theory of form detection*. Hillsdale, N.J.: Lawrence Erlbaum Associates, 1975.

Uttley, A. M. 1956. A theory of the mechanism of learning based on the computation of conditioned probabilities. *Proceedings of the 1st International Congress on Cybernetics*, Namur, 1956, 830-856.

Vandenberg, S. G. 1971. A test of three-dimensional spatial visualization (based on the Shepard-Metzler "mental rotation" study). University of Colorado, July 15, 1971.

Vandenberg, S. G. 1975. Sources of variance in performance on spatial tests. In J. Eliot & N. J. Salkind, eds., *Children's spatial development*. Springfield, Illinois: Charles C. Thomas, 1975.

Vanderplas, J. M. & Garvin, E. A. 1959. The association value of random shapes. *Journal of Experimental Psychology*, 1959, *57*, 147-154.

Verplank, W. 1979. Imagined transformations in solving string puzzles. Personal communication, 1979.

Wallach, H., & O'Connell, D. N. 1953. The kinetic depth effect. *Journal of Experimental Psychology*, 1953, *45*, 205-217.

Warren, R. M., & Warren, R. P. 1968. *Helmholtz on perception: Its physiology and development*. New York: Wiley, 1968.

Watson, J. D. 1968. *The double helix*. New York: New American Library, 1968.

Weber, R. J., & Castleman, J. 1970. The time it takes to imagine. *Perception & Psychophysics*, 1970, *8*, 165-168.

Wertheimer, M. 1961. Experimentalle Studien über das Sehen von Bewegung. *Zeitschrift für Psychologie*, 1912, *61*, 161-265. Translated in part in T. Shipley, ed., *Classics in psychology*. New York: Philosophical Library, 1961.

Wertheimer, M. 1945. *Productive thinking*. New York: Harper, 1945.

Zusne, L. 1970. *Visual perception of form*. New York: Academic Press, 1970.

Notes

CHAPTER 1 (INTRODUCTION)

1. Concerning the four newly written chapters, primary responsibility for preparing an initial draft was assumed by Cooper for the epilogue to the major section, Part I (Chapter 8), and by Shepard for the present introduction (Chapter 1) and the two remaining epilogues (Chapters 12 and 16).

CHAPTER 2 (MENTAL ROTATION)

1. In the interest of brevity, some of the less central material appearing in the original memorandum has been omitted from the version printed here.

CHAPTER 3 (ROTATION OF 3-D OBJECTS)

1. For the purposes of the present volume, an abstract has been added, and some of the less essential material (which can be found in the original publication—Metzler & Shepard, 1974) has been deleted, as specifically noted in the following notes. The following acknowledgment accompanied the original publication:

> The work reported in this paper was supported by National Science Foundation research grants GB-31971X and GS-2283 to Roger Shepard. During this work Jacqueline Metzler was supported by a National Institutes of Mental Health predoctoral fellowship. We are indebted to the Bell Telephone Laboratories and, particularly, to Jih-Jie Chang of those laboratories for essential assistance in the computer generation of the perspective views used in Experiments I and II. We also wish to thank Janet Elashoff for her helpful advice concerning the statistical analyses. Finally, important programming help in connection with the statistical analyses and the computer plotting of the reaction-time distributions was provided by Phipps Arabie and Paul Goldstein.

2. A more complete description of how the pairs of perspective views were selected, illustrated by means of an additional figure and table, can be found in the original paper (Metzler & Shepard, 1974). A complete set of all seven views of all ten objects can be obtained by writing to Roger N. Shepard, Department of Psychology, Stanford University, Stanford, California 94305.

3. Experiment II was first presented, orally, in a paper by Metzler and Shepard (1971). For a complete description of the experimental method, somewhat abbreviated here, see the published version (Metzler & Shepard, 1974).

4. To save space, we have eliminated some material here—including (a) a discussion of the relatively inconclusive evidence concerning differences between individuals, sexes, and left- and right-handed subjects, which immediately preceded this theoretical section in the original paper (Metzler & Shepard, 1974), and (b) several portions of the rather lengthy discussion included in the theoretical section itself.

5. Subsequent analyses of patterns of eye fixations during mental rotation, reported by Carpenter and Just (1978), have been quite informative. (See the Epilogue to Part I—especially pp. 171-176.)

CHAPTER 4 (ROTATION OF LETTERS/NUMBERS)

1. For the purpose of the present volume, an abstract has been added and some of the less essential material (which can be found in the original publication—Cooper & Shepard, 1973) has been deleted, as specifically noted in the following notes. The following acknowledgments accompanied the original publication:

> This work was supported by the National Science foundation through research grants GS-2283 and GB-31971X to Roger Shepard. The present report was jointly prepared by the two authors while Cooper was on a National Science Foundation Predoctoral Fellowship and while Shepard was a John Simon Guggenheim Fellow at the Center for Advanced Study in the Behavioral Sciences, Stanford. We are indebted to many colleagues for a variety of important contributions to this work. Joseph Klun's earlier work (in collaboration with Shepard) provided much parametric information that was extremely useful to us in designing the present Experiment I. Ernest Hilgard generously permitted us to use an Iconix three-field tachistoscope provided by his NIMH grant No. 03859. Lincoln Moses offered valuable advice concerning the half-replicated design and the statistical analyses. Elizabeth Smith and James Cunningham assisted extensively in the running of the experiments. Finally, we owe a special debt of gratitude to Christine Feng for her unstinting and indispensable assistance throughout all phases of the work, from the preparation of the stimuli to the plotting of the data.

2. The idea that mental images are "perceptual anticipations" that can somehow be "manipulated" has subsequently been elaborated upon by Neisser (1976, pp. 130-138, 147-149).

3. In the original paper we conjectured that the rates of mental rotation that we estimated here exceeded the 60 degree per second estimated from the earlier results of Shepard and Metzler (1971; see the preceding Chapter 3) because alphanumeric characters are simpler and more familiar than the three-dimensional objects used earlier. The difference may also (or even instead) be attributable to the change in task, from a comparison of two external objects to a comparison of a single external object with an already established internal representation.

4. For a more complete account of the statistical analyses, see the original paper (Cooper & Shepard, 1973b).

5. Hock and Tromley (1978) have since reported evidence supporting the first of these four explanations for the nonlinearity: For letters having a narrow range of tilts within which the letter appears upright (e.g., the letters "e" and "G") the reaction-time function became nearly linear.

6. See acknowledgment of Klun's contribution under Note 1, above.

7. As before, a more complete account of the statistical analyses can be found in the original paper (Cooper & Shepard, 1973b).

CHAPTER 5 (ROTATION OF 2-D SHAPES)

1. Part of the original paper, already covered in Chapters 3 and 4, is omitted. A more complete account of the statistical analyses (which have been slightly abridged here) can be found in that paper (Cooper, 1975) and, even more fully (along with the complete results for individual subjects), in the dissertation on which that paper was based (Cooper, 1973). The following acknowledgments accompanied the original publication:

This report is based on a thesis submitted in partial fulfillment for the Ph.D. degree at Stanford University. The author thanks, especially, her thesis advisor, Roger Shepard, for his advice, encouragement, and inspiration. Thanks are also due to the other members of the dissertation committee— Herbert Clark, Leo Ganz, and Edward Smith. This research was supported by National Science Foundation Grant GB-31971X to Roger Shepard.

2. See Cooper (1973, 1975) for a more complete account of the statistical analyses, which were based on F-ratios, quasi F-ratios, and estimates of degrees of freedom as recommended by Clark (1973).

3. These data do not distinguish between a rotation of the test form into the trained orientation and a rotation of the memory representation of the standard version into the orientation of the test form. Either alternative is both theoretically and empirically acceptable; however, the introspective reports of the subjects suggest that the test form was rotated into congruence with a memory representation of the standard in the trained orientation.

4. The mean difference between the slopes and a confidence interval of one SD was .505 ± .229.

5. Again, see Cooper (1973, 1975) for more complete accounts of the statistical analyses.

CHAPTER 6 (ROTATION AND COMPARISON)

1. A more complete account of the statistical analyses (slightly abridged here) can be found in that paper (Cooper & Podgorny, 1976). The following acknowledgments accompanied the original publication:

This research was supported primarily by National Science Foundation Grant GB-31971X to Roger Shepard and also in part by National Institute of Mental Health Small Grant MH 25722-01 to Lynn Cooper and National Institutes of Health Grant MH 15828-06 to the Center for Human Information Processing, University of California, San Diego. Roger Shepard provided financial support and invaluable discussion and advice. James Cunningham was involved in all stages of this research, from suggestions concerning the generation of the stimuli to comments on the final version of the manuscript.

2. This fast-slow distinction is based only on overall RT_2. In terms of the slope of the RT_1 functions, one of the fast subjects had the smallest slope value, but two of the slow subjects had smaller slope values than the other fast subject. Thus, discriminative response speed is not necessarily related to speed of mental rotation.

CHAPTER 7 (ANALOG NATURE OF ROTATION)

1. A more complete account of the statistical analyses (slightly abridged here)

can be found in that paper (Cooper, 1976a). The following acknowledgments accompanied the original publication:

This research was supported primarily by National Science Foundation Grant GB-31971X to Roger Shepard and also in part by National Institute of Mental Health Small Grant MH 25722-01 to Lynn Cooper. Roger Shepard provided extremely helpful discussion and advice during all stages of this research. Jim Cunningham and Jay McClelland provided valuable comments on the manuscript. Special thanks go to Peter Podgorny for his indispensable and enthusiastic assistance in running the subjects and analyzing the data and also for fruitful discussions concerning all aspects of this research.

2. It could be argued that the equivalence of reaction times to familiar and unfamiliar expected probes resulted from the fact that during the course of the experiment, subjects became "familiar" with probes presented in "unfamiliar" orientations. While it is difficult to evaluate this objection, three features of the present experiment render it unlikely. First, unfamiliar probes were presented on a small proportion of the trials (only 36 of the 252 experimental trials). Second, order of presentation of trials of all three types ("probe-expected, familiar," "probe-expected, unfamiliar," and "probe-unexpected") was random. Third, on each of the 36 "probe-expected, unfamiliar" trials, a unique combination of standard shape, test-form version, and probe orientation was presented.

CHAPTER 8 (EPILOGUE TO PART I)

1. We thank Randall Mumaw for his comments on a preliminary draft of this chapter.

CHAPTER 9 (MENTAL PAPER FOLDING)

1. The following acknowledgment accompanied the original publication:

This research was supported by National Science Foundation Grant GS-2283 to Roger Shepard.

CHAPTER 10 (IDENTIFICATION OF HANDS)

1. A more complete account of the statistical analyses (which have been slightly abridged here) can be found in that paper (Cooper & Shepard, 1975). The following acknowledgments accompanied the original publication:

This research was supported by National Science Foundation Grant GB-31971X to Roger Shepard and was conducted while Lynn Cooper was a predoctoral NSF Fellow at Stanford. We wish to thank Christine Feng for her invaluable assistance in running the subjects and preparing the stimulus materials. Ernest Hilgard generously permitted us to use his Iconix tachistoscope provided by National Institutes of Mental Health Grant 03859.

2. Details are given in the original paper (Cooper & Shepard, 1975).
3. Factors contributing to the nonlinearity of the dependence of reaction time on orientation in the case of familiar stimuli with a preferred "upright" orientation are discussed in Chapter 4 and, more fully, in the original article on which that chapter is based (Cooper & Shepard, 1973a).

CHAPTER 11 (MENTAL ASSEMBLY)

1. A more detailed account of the results and their statistical analyses can be found in that paper (Glushko and Cooper, 1978). The following acknowledgments accompanied the original publication:

This research was funded primarily by National Science Foundation Grant BMS 75-15773 and National Institutes of Mental Health Small Grant MH 25722-01 to the second author. Experiment 2 was supported by National Science Foundation Grant BMS 76-15024 to David E. Rumelhart. Some pilot work by the first author was funded by National Science Foundation Grant GB-31971X to Roger Shepard at Stanford University. The first author held a National Science Foundation Graduate Fellowship while this paper was written. We acknowledge the help of Jack Catlin, Jim Cunningham, Colin MacLeod, Jay McClelland, Jeff Miller, Allen Munro, Don Norman, Steve Palmer, Peter Podgorny, Dave Rumelhart, Arty Samuel, Roger Shepard, and Al Stevens.

CHAPTER 12 (EPILOGUE TO PART II)

1. Small portions of this chapter are based on sections of previously published papers (*viz.*, Cooper & Shepard, 1978; Shepard, 1981).

CHAPTER 13 (APPARENT ROTATION OF 3-D OBJECTS)

1. The original work was supported by National Science Foundation Grant BNS 75-02806 to Roger Shepard.

CHAPTER 14 (PROBING OF APPARENT ROTATION)

1. A more detailed account of the statistical analyses (slightly abridged here) can be found in that paper (Robins & Shepard, 1977). The following acknowledgment accompanied the original publication:

This work was supported by National Science Foundation Grant BNS 75-02806 to Roger Shepard. The authors are indebted to Merrill Carlsmith for helpful suggestions concerning the statistical analyses.

CHAPTER 15 (SHAPE AND APPARENT ROTATION)

1. The following acknowledgment accompanied the original publication:

This work was supported by National Science Foundation Grant BNS 75-02806 to Roger Shepard. Portions of the work have previously been described in oral presentations by Shepard (1977, 1979) and by Farrell (1979; Farrell & Shepard, 1979).

CHAPTER 16 (EPILOGUE TO PART III)

1. Small portions of this chapter are based on sections of previously written papers (Shepard, 1981, 1982a).

Name Index

Pages on which complete references can be found are set in italics.

Subject Index